D1860518

THE GAME ANIMALS OF INDIA, BURMA, MALAYA AND TIBET

THE GAME ANIMALS

OF

INDIA, BURMA, MALAYA, AND TIBET

BEING A NEW AND REVISED EDITION OF 'THE GREAT AND SMALL GAME OF INDIA, BURMA, AND TIBET'

BY

R. LYDEKKER

WITH NINE PLATES AND FIFTY-NINE OTHER ILLUSTRATIONS

GYAN

© **Author**
All rights reserved. No part of this work may be reproduced, stored, adapted, or transmitted in any form or by any means, electronic, mechanical, photocopying, micro-filming, recording or otherwise, or translated in any language, without the prior written permission of the copyright owner and the publisher. The book is sold subject to the condition that it shall not, by way of trade or otherwise, be lent, resold, hired out, or otherwise circulated without the prior publisher's written consent in any form of binding or cover other than that in which it is published.

The views and opinions expressed in this book are author(s) own and the facts reported by them have been verified to the extent possible, and the publishers are not in any way liable for the same.

ISBN : 978-81-212-1525-1(HB)

First Published, 1907

Published, 2018

Published by

Gyan Publishing House
5, Ansari Road
Daryaganj, New Delhi-110002
Phone: 011-47034999, 9811692060
www.gyanbooks.com
E-mail: books@gyanbooks.com

Printed at: G. Print Process, Delhi.

PREFACE

SEVEN years have elapsed since the publication of the original quarto edition of this work, which is now out of print. During that interval considerable progress has been made in the recognition of local races of many of the animals described therein ; some of these races, such as the Shan brown bear and the Tibetan bruan, adding very largely to the geographical range of the species. Another important addition to our knowledge is the occurrence of a goral in Burma.

Descriptions of these newly recognised forms, together with much other important information, have been incorporated in the present edition, which has thus been brought thoroughly up to date.

Another innovation is the inclusion of the Malay Peninsula, which is now an integral portion of the British Empire, in the area coming within the purview of the volume.

In its present smaller and cheaper form the work will be found more convenient to the sportsman in the field than the original edition.

Since the text was in type I have had an opportunity of seeing the head and neck of the red serow, an animal which has never previously come under my notice.

This serow was described by Blyth under the name of *Capricornis rubida*, from a specimen obtained in the hill-ranges of Aracan, on the sea-board of Upper Burma. It was subsequently regarded by Dr. Blanford as inseparable from the ordinary Burmese serow (*Nemorhædus sumatrensis*), of which I suggested that it might be a local race. The new specimen, which is almost entirely of a foxy-red colour, with a little brownish on the backs of the ears, and becoming rather paler on the throat, was obtained by Mr. A. Sinclair Thomson, of the Essex Regiment, near Mogaung, nearly due north of Bhamo, on the eastern border of the Singpho country. The occurrence of the red serow in localities so distant as Aracan and Mogaung indicates that its range extends right across that of the ordinary serow, and suggests a colour-phase rather than a local race. Indeed, in view of recent observations as to the red phase of the African tiger-cat being merely the early stage of the dusky form of that species, the suspicion arises that a similar change may take place in the case of the serow. Accordingly, any observations bearing on this point from sportsmen in Burma will be of interest.

R. LYDEKKER.

HARPENDEN, *July* 1907.

CONTENTS

Contents

LIST OF ILLUSTRATIONS

Plates

Text-Figures

List of Illustrations

CORRIGENDUM

Page 75, line 17 from top, *for* H. L. Butler *read* A. L. Butler.

ADDENDA ET CORRIGENDA

Pages 101 and 103.—*Dele* "the late" from before the name of Major F. H. Taylor, and *add* that the specimen figured came from Waziristan.

Page 139 *et seq.*—Mr. R. I. Pocock (*Abstr. Proc. Zool. Soc.* 1908, p. 12), who employs the name *Capricornis* for the serows and transfers *Nemorhædus* to the gorals, has described four new races of the former, which, with the retention of the generic name usually employed, are briefly characterised as follows:—(1) The Kashmiri race (*N. sumatrensis humei*), with a rufous brown head. (2) The Chamba race (*N. s. rodoni*), with a patch on the throat and the area between the two branches of the lower jaw, as well as the under-parts and lower portions of the limbs, white, and the coat long, thick, and provided with under-fur. (3) The Darjiling race (*N. s. jamrachi*), with a short black coat, blackish under-parts, and the lower portions of the limbs partially rufous. (4) The Selangor race (*N. s. robinsoni*), which is black, with a scarcely appreciable amount of red in the mane.

Page 142, line 19 from top, for *Nemorhædus bubalinus typicus* read *Nemorhædus sumatrensis typicus*.

Page 148 *et seq.*—Mr. Pocock (*op. cit.*) regards the grey goral as the original species, and accordingly proposes the name *hodgsoni* for the *Urotragus goral* of this volume, and transfers the designation *goral* to *U. bedfordi*. Confusion will, however, be avoided by allowing matters to remain *in statu quo* as regards nomenclature.

Page 157 *et seq.*—The Bhutan takin has been described by myself (*Field*, vol. cx. p. 887) as a distinct race, characterised by its relatively small horns, under the name of *Budorcas taxicolor whitei*.

Page 192 *et seq.*—The Yarkand, or Saikik, gazelle has been raised by myself (*op. cit.* vol. cxi. p. 499, 1908) to the rank of a species, *Gazella yarcandensis*, with a local race, *G. y. kennioni*, in Eastern Persia and Baluchistan.

Page 241 *et seq.*—The hog-deer is represented in Siam by a large unspotted race to which (*Field*, vol. cxi. p. 583, 1908) I have given the name *Cervus porcinus hecki*. The stag figured on page 244 is a specimen of the Siamese Schomburgk's deer (*C. schomburgki*).

Page 263.—The Chinese muntjac is probably a distinct species, *Cervulus sclateri* (see *Field*, vol. cx. p. 667, 1907).

R. L.

April 1908.

THE GAME ANIMALS OF INDIA, BURMA, MALAYA, AND TIBET

INTRODUCTION

THE area of which the game animals (or rather mammals) are described in the present volume may be designated in popular language "the Sportsman's India." Roughly speaking, it comprises the drainage-basins of the Indus, Bramaputra, and Irawadi Rivers, or the greater portion thereof, together with the whole of India, Ceylon, the province of Tenasserim, and the Malay Peninsula. Including a large part of Baluchistan and Afghanistan, the area is well defined towards the north-west by the barrier of the Hindu-Kush and Karakoram ranges. Eastwards of the latter the boundary is fixed by the Tangla Mountains, to the north of Lhasa, whence an arbitrary line may be drawn to the eastern frontier of Burma, which may be taken as the boundary in this direction. The whole of Tibet and the Himalaya consequently fall within the area treated of; but, on the other hand, Eastern Turkestan and China, as well as Siam and Cochin-China, are excluded.

It has to be acknowledged that, in fixing these limits, a somewhat arbitrary division has been made. It has indeed been suggested to the author that it would have been better to include the whole of Asia, as it seems rather illogical to describe certain of the wild sheep and deer of Central Asia to the exclusion of others, and undoubtedly there is much to be said for this view. On the other hand, the fauna of Western Asia passes imperceptibly into that of Eastern Europe, so that if Asia were taken as the limits of the area to be included, the boundary would be fully as arbitrary, from the point of view of the fauna, as is at present the case, if, indeed, it were not more so.

The area, as thus limited, contains an assemblage of game animals belonging to two great zoological provinces; those of the cis-Indus and cis-Himalayan portion of the area, together with Burma, Tenasserim, and the Malay Peninsula, pertaining to what is called the Oriental region, while those beyond these limits are included in the Eastern Holarctic or Palæarctic region. The northern frontiers of India and Burma are, in fact, the meeting-place of two great faunas. In Burma and India themselves minor zoological subdivisions are indicated by the distribution of the game and other animals. In Tenasserim, for example, the animals are distinctly of a Malay type, as is instanced by the presence of the tapir, the Malay bear, the bantin, and the binturong. And these Malay types, with an intermingling of peculiar species, like the thamin deer, are traceable into Assam and the Eastern Himalaya; the Malay forms being perhaps even more pronounced in the latter area than they are in Burma. Other Malay types are the two smaller species of Asiatic rhinoceros, one of which has penetrated into Lower Bengal.

Of the game animals of Burma itself, some, like the gaur, are specifically identical with those of India; others, like the bantin, are Malay; while others again may be regarded as Eastern representatives of Indian species. As an instance of the latter class may be cited the thamin deer and the Malay sambar, which are respectively the Burmese representatives of the Indian swamp-deer and Indian sambar. Assam forms the meeting-ground of the Indian and the Burmese faunas.

Peninsular India, properly restricted to the area south of the great plain formed by the alluvium of the Indus and Ganges, although often considered to extend to the foot of the Himalaya, is the home of the true Indian fauna, examples of which are the chital, or spotted deer, the hog-deer, the swamp-deer, the Indian sambar, the nilgai, and the sloth-bear. Even apart from minor divisions due to varying conditions of climate, soil, vegetation, etc., Peninsular India is by no means uniform as regards its animals. The Malabar coast, for instance, is very distinct in this respect from the whole of the remainder of the area, although showing considerable resemblances to Ceylon, except the north of the latter, which is more akin in its animals to Peninsular India generally. Many characteristic Indian animals, such as the tiger, the Indian wolf, and the swamp-deer, are, however, absent from Ceylon.

In the trans-Indus districts of the Punjab, and still more markedly in Western Sind, Baluchistan, and Afghanistan, we gradually take leave of the fauna of Peninsular India (and with it that of the Oriental region generally), and find it replaced by a Persian element ; these Persian types belonging to the Holarctic fauna of Western Asia and Europe. Examples of such western types are met with in the form of the European wolf, the Persian leopard, the wild ass, and the Persian gazelle. The lion, too, belongs to this Persian fauna, although it has succeeded in penetrating farther into India than some of the other members. All traces of the Malay fauna, such as tapirs, the two smaller species of rhinoceros, and the Malay bear, are wanting from the area occupied by the Persian fauna.

In the cis-Indus Salt Range of the Punjab we meet with an outlier of the Persian fauna in the form of the

Salt Range urial. This sheep, together with the straight-horned markhor goat of the trans-Indus Suleman Range, likewise serves to connect the Punjab-Persian fauna with that of Central Asia, which also forms a part of the Holarctic region.

It has been already mentioned that the animals of the Eastern Himalaya display a marked resemblance to the Malay type. Passing westwards along the chain, this Malay element practically disappears west of Nepal; and from thence the Himalayan fauna as far north as the forests reach is to a great extent transitional between that of Peninsular India on the one hand and that of Central Asia on the other. Kashmir, which comes within the limits of this intermediate zone, exhibits the transition between the Oriental and Central Asian faunas very markedly, with some indications of a Persian element. The Himalayan black bear is a very characteristic animal of this zone, as are also the tahr and the goral.

With the high Himalaya and the arid districts of Gilgit, Ladak, etc., we enter the area inhabited by the Tibetan fauna, which is more or less markedly distinct from that of the rest of Central Asia. Among these peculiar Tibetan types may be cited the yak, the chiru antelope, the goa gazelle, and the Tibetan wild ass or kiang, together with various wild sheep, all of which are inhabitants of dry and elevated country. Farther eastwards, in the Lhasa district, we enter the limits of a subdivision of this fauna adapted to live at a lower elevation in a more humid climate; among the members of this group being the short-tailed panda, the takin, Thorold's deer, and the Tibetan blue bear.

Passing on to Turkestan and the Altai country, the home of Marco Polo's sheep, the true argali, the Eastern Asiatic wapitis, and the Siberian roebuck, we reach the tract inhabited by the typical Central Asian fauna, lying beyond the limits to which this volume is restricted. The tiger is probably to be regarded as a wanderer from the Central Asian fauna into India and the Malay countries.

With these few preliminary remarks on an interesting subject, the descriptions and histories of the various species may be commenced.

THE INDIAN OR ASIATIC ELEPHANT

(*Elephas maximus*)

NATIVE NAMES.—*Hathi*, *Hathni* (female), HINDUSTANI; *Hasti* AND *Gaja*, SANSCRIT; *Fil*, PERSIAN; *Haust*, KASHMIRI; *Gaj*, BENGALI; *Ane*, TELEGU, TAMIL, CANARESE, etc.; *Yani* OF THE GONDS; *Hattanga*, *Khonda*, AND *Eniga*, TELEGU; *Yanei*, *Kunjaram*, AND *Veranum*, MALABARI; *Ata* AND *Allia*, CINGALESE; *Tengmu* OF THE LEPCHAS; *Langcheu* AND *Lambochi* OF THE BHOTIAS; *Mongma* AND *Naplo* AMONG THE GARO HILL TRIBES; *Migung*, KACHARI; *Atche* OF THE AKAS; *Sotso*, *Supo*, *Chu*, AND *Tsu* OF THE NAGAS; *Sitte* AT ABOR; *Tsang* IN KHAMTI; *Magui*, SINGPHO; *Saipi* OF THE KUKIS; *Amieng* AND *Manyong* IN THE MISHMI HILLS; *Samu* OF THE MANIPURIS; *Tsheng*, BURMESE; *Tsing*, TALAIN; *Tsan* IN THE SHAN STATES; *Kahsa* OF THE KARENS; *Gaja*, MALAY.

(PLATE i, fig. 1)

In all works of sport and in the majority of those on natural history the Indian elephant, if it be not called *Elephas asiaticus*, is termed *E. indicus*; but at the present day it is the fashion to follow priority in nomenclature, and according to this the proper name is *E. maximus.* It may be objected that the Indian elephant is a smaller animal than its African relation, and that the latter name is thus invalid; but objections of this class are disregarded by naturalists.

As the largest and most strange in appearance of all

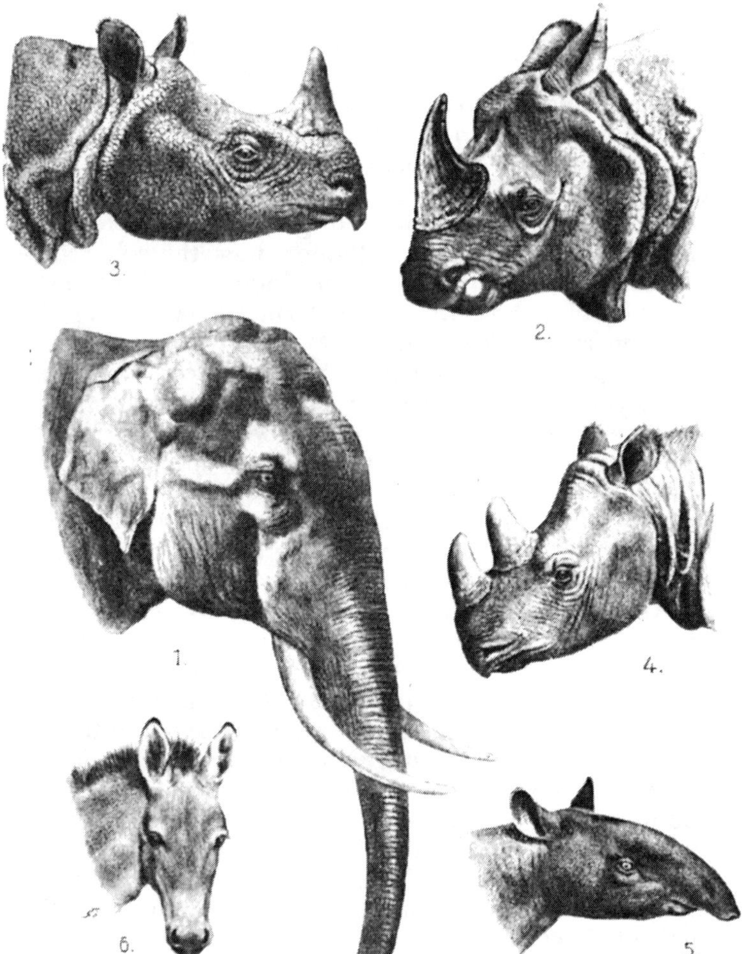

Plate I

1. Indian Elephant.
2. Great Indian Rhinoceros.
3. Javan Rhinoceros.
4. Sumatran Rhinoceros.
5. Malay Tapir.
6. Kiang.

the animals of India, the elephant looms large in the ancient traditions and religions of the country, figuring in the Hindu mythology as Ganesa—the elephant-headed god. From its ancient Sanscrit names Hasti and Gaja are derived most of its titles among the Aryan tribes of India ; while even the Malays, who speak a tongue of totally different origin, have adopted the latter of these names. Although now the sole representative of its tribe in Asia, the Indian elephant is the survivor of a host of species formerly inhabiting the country from which it takes its name ; some of these extinct species coming close to their descendant, while others (mastodons) had teeth of a totally distinct type, some even carrying tusks in the lower as well as in the upper jaw. From the number of fossil species, coupled with the fact that it is here alone that a complete transition is to be found between the mastodons and the true elephants, it is probable that South-Eastern Asia was the original home of the latter.

As everybody knows an elephant by sight, while many persons are acquainted with the leading external differences between the Asiatic and the African species, it will be unnecessary to point out the characteristics of elephants in general, or to enter in detail into the consideration of the features by which the two living representatives of the group are distinguished from one another. An exception in regard to one particular feature of elephant anatomy may, however, be made, seeing that comparatively few persons understand the mode of development and replacement obtaining in the teeth of these animals.

As regards the tusks (which do not correspond to the tusks of a wild boar, but to one of the pairs of incisor or front teeth of that animal), these arise from the upper jaw, and grow throughout the life of their owner, after they have once made their appearance. In very young elephants they are preceded by a pair of milk-tusks, which are soon shed.

As regards the molar or cheek-teeth, there are six pairs developed in each jaw, but only portions of two of these are in use at one time, and in an aged animal

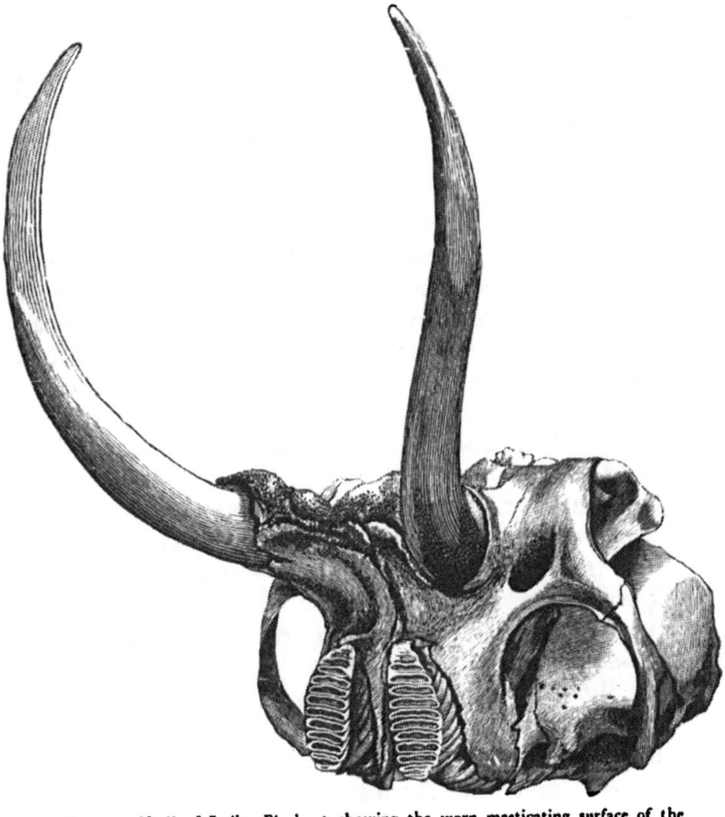

FIG. 1.—Skull of Indian Elephant, showing the worn masticating surface of the fifth pair of molars, behind which are the unworn sixth pair, whose summits during life were still in the gum.

there is but one on each side of both the upper and the lower jaw. These teeth are composed of a number of vertical transverse plates closely packed together; the number of such plates gradually increasing from the first tooth, in which there are four, to the last, which may have as many as twenty-four. The teeth are pushed up in the jaws in an arc of a circle, and as each tooth in the front of the series becomes worn down, it is gradually thrust out from behind by its successor, which at the same time takes its place. The end of this process is, of course, that the animal is eventually left with but a single pair of grinding teeth in each jaw; and when these are completely worn away, a term is put to the life of their owner.

Compared with those of its African relative, the molars of the Indian elephant have their component plates narrower and more numerous, with the layers of enamel thrown into a number of fine puckers or pleats. Consequently, on the worn surface of the crown, the disks formed by the abraded plates are more numerous and narrower in the Indian species, while their enamel-borders are thin and pleated instead of comparatively thick and plain.

The females of the Indian elephant carry, as a rule, only very small tusks, which do not project beyond the lips, and in some cases the males show an equally poor development of these weapons. Such tuskless males are known in India as *makhna*, in contradistinction to the *dauntela*, or tuskers.

Usually the Indian elephant has five polished hoof-like nails on the fore, and four on the hind feet; but the most striking external point of distinction between it and the African species is to be found in the comparatively small size of the ears. Next to this comes the presence of a finger-like process on the front edge only of the tip of the trunk, the African species having such a process on both the front and hind margins. The trunk, too, of the Indian species differs markedly from that of the African elephant, being comparable to a tapering india-rubber tube, whereas in the African elephant this appendage consists of a series of segments of varying calibre, and may be likened to the joints of a telescope. The skin is comparatively smooth, and the coarse bristles on the tail are confined to the front and back edges for some distance above the tip. Other noticeable features in the present species are the comparative flatness of the forehead and the regularly convex profile of the back.

Much discussion has taken place with regard to the height attained by the Indian elephant, but since the subject has been thoroughly threshed out, it will be treated very briefly on the present occasion. Roughly speaking, about 9 feet may be given as the ordinary height for large males, and 8 feet for females, but in Ceylon the average is from 7 feet 6 inches to 8 feet 6 inches. An elephant of about 9 feet 9 inches has, however, been killed in Ceylon,[1] and one of 9 feet 7 inches in Mysore; while two are known to have attained the height of 10 feet 1 inch, a third of 10 feet 4 inches, and a fourth (killed by the late Viscount Powerscourt in Gurhwal) of 11 feet. A very large elephant was also recorded some time ago in one of the Indian papers. These dimensions appear to be dwarfed by a skeleton in the Indian Museum, Calcutta, which seems to indicate an animal of nearly a dozen feet high.

Of tusks, the three longest specimens on record respectively measure 8 feet 9 inches, 8 feet 2 inches, and 8 feet; their respective weights being 81, 80, and 90 lbs; but these are by no means the heaviest—one, whose length is 7 feet 3⅜ inches, weighing 102 lbs., while a second, of which the length is 7 feet 3¼ inches, scaled 97½ lbs., both the two latter being from Ceylon. Of the largest pair in the British Museum, belonging to an elephant killed in 1866 by the late Colonel G. M. Payne in Madura, one tusk measures 6 feet 8 inches in length, and weighs 77¾ lbs., while the other is somewhat smaller. As regards the circumference of the base of the foot, the following dimensions,

[1] Storey, *Hunting and Shooting in Ceylon*, p. 110.

namely, 67½, 62½, 61, 60½, and 60 inches have been recorded.

Within the area treated of in this volume, the elephant inhabits the forest-districts of India, Ceylon, Assam, and Burma, although now exterminated in several parts of the country where it formerly flourished. Indeed, were it not for the protective laws established both in India and Ceylon this noble beast would have long since disappeared from most of its haunts, even if it had not ceased to exist. Eastwards and southwards of Burma the elephant is to be met with in the Malay Peninsula, Siam, and Cochin-China, as well as in the great islands of Sumatra and Borneo, although in the last of these its presence may be originally due to human agency.

There has long been a difference of opinion as to whether the Sumatran and the Ceylon elephants, which were at one time grouped together, are distinct from the continental animal. So long ago as the year 1834 Mr. Brian Hodgson, writing in the *Proceedings of the Zoological Society of London*, suggested that the elephant of Ceylon was distinct from that of the mainland, as typified by the sal-forest animal. Whether, however, the two were to be regarded as species or races was left an open question. According to this communication, the Cingalese elephant has a smaller and lighter head, and is taller at the withers than the mainland animal; while the latter sometimes has five nails on the hind-foot. Nothing was, however, stated with regard to the presence or absence of tusks or the relative sizes of the two races. A dozen years later Temminck, who apparently based his conclusions on information afforded by his colleague Schlegel, announced that the elephants of Sumatra and Ceylon indicated a species distinct from the continental *E. maximus* (*indicus*), which it was proposed to call *E. sumatranus*; the typical form being, of course, the Sumatran elephant.

Schlegel subsequently formulated the characters by

which the Sumatran and Cingalese animal might be distinguished from the continental elephant. Both, he writes, have, as compared with the African elephant, the same general form and small ears, but the Sumatran species is a more slender and more finely built animal with a longer and more slender trunk, and the tip of the tail more expanded and carrying longer and stronger bristles. He then goes on to say that the Sumatran elephant is more docile and intelligent than its Indian brother, from which it is further distinguished by certain differences in the skeleton and teeth, detailed in the original paper.

The subject was again taken up by Dr. Hugh Falconer in a memoir communicated to the *Natural History Review* for January 1863, in which it was shown that many of the dental and osteological characters (notably an alleged difference in the number of vertebræ) were untrustworthy; and he came to the conclusion that there was but a single living Asiatic species of elephant. In this he is no doubt correct; but it is important to note that in a later portion of the memoir he makes the admission that this species is "modified, doubtless, according to his more northern or southern habitat, but not to an extent exceeding that of a slight geographical variety." This is equivalent to saying that there may be local "races," as now understood, of the Asiatic species. It should, moreover, be mentioned that in De Blainville's *Ostéographie*, published from 1839 to 1864, the Ceylon elephant had been designated *Elephas indicus zeylanicus*.

Although nothing is said as to any local varieties of the elephant in Blanford's *Mammals of India*, it is mentioned that the Ceylon elephant is reported to be generally tuskless; and it is evident that if this form be distinguished from the continental Indian elephant, it must, on distributional grounds, be also distinct from the Sumatran representative of the species. It may be added that Schlegel makes no mention of the rarity or absence of large tusks as a distinctive characteristic of Temminck's *Elephas sumatranus.*

The distinctness of the Ceylon elephant has been taken up by Mr. Alfred Clark, of the Ceylon Forest Department, in a little work called *Sport in the Low-Country of Ceylon*, published in 1901 at Colombo. The more important of these observations are as follows :—

"As is well known, the majority of male elephants in Ceylon have no tusks, but only small tushes set vertically in the upper jaw. Females also have tushes, but they are very small. Tuskers are sometimes met with, but are extremely scarce. It is probable that there are not now more than fifty of all ages in the whole island. That they were numerous in former days is shown by the fact that, when Kandy was conquered in 1815, among the loot were 289 tusks, weighing 5915½ lbs. Tuskers are usually not so big as the tuskless bulls, but are broader across the forehead and have bigger frontal bumps, while the hollow between the ear and eye is not so marked. . . . Very fine tusks, quite as big as the average size of Indian ones, have been got from tuskers shot in Ceylon.

"One reason which has been given for the rarity of tuskers in Ceylon is the 'scarcity of phosphates in the soil,' which sounds learned, but is nonsense. Such a theory would account for the absence of tusks, or for their universal imperfect development, but not for the fact that some elephants have perfectly developed tusks and others none at all, but tushes instead. There can be little doubt *that tuskers and tuskless elephants are two distinct varieties*, the latter being the one indigenous to the island. The tuskers found in our forests are probably the descendants of imported Indian elephants which ran wild. It is reasonable to suppose that if there are two breeds of elephants in Ceylon, cross-breeding would, in the course of time, produce a species of hybrid animal. Native elephant-catchers and traders assert the existence of such creatures and call them 'makanians.' There was an elephant belonging to the Rameswaram Temple a few years ago which was said to be one of this class. It had tusks, but they were set vertically, almost touching the ground, and the whole shape of the animal was abnormal."

The evidence adduced in these extracts as to the marked distinction of the great majority of Cingalese elephants from those of the mainland, and the suggestion made to account for the presence of a certain number of tuskers in the island, are certainly worthy the consideration of naturalists. Unfortunately there is no evidence that Indian elephants were at any time imported into Ceylon, and as the introduction (assuming it to have taken place) must have occurred at a date comparatively remote, it is unlikely that such evidence will ever be forthcoming. Whether elephants could have been carried across the Palk Straits in native craft, or whether they could have crossed by swimming *via* the so-called Adam's Bridge, it is not easy to say; but Mr. Clark's suggestion certainly offers an explanation of the facts which does not appear to present insuperable difficulties. Provisionally accepting this explanation, there seems evidence in favour of regarding the Cingalese elephant as a distinct local race, of which the proper name is *Elephas maximus zeylanicus.* This presumed race will be characterised by the absence of large tusks in the males, and the peculiarities in the form of the head referred to by Mr. Clark.

The statement as to the Cingalese tuskless elephants being larger than the tuskers seems to require a little modification; for, according to Mr. H. Storey, it is only in the Tawankaduwa district of the island that there exists a large herd of tuskless elephants, some of which reach, it is said, a height of nearly ten feet, whereas elsewhere a height of nine feet is uncommon. Whether these Tawankaduwa giants indicate a second Ceylon race, has yet to be determined.

It should be added that the name *Elephas maximus* appears to have been originally bestowed on Ceylon animals; since, however, these were almost certainly tuskers, they would seem, on Mr. Clark's hypothesis, to be identical with the mainland race.

Whether the "makhnas," "kumariahs," and "dauntelas" of the mainland also indicate as many distinct races inhabiting continental India, there is not sufficient material at hand to determine. It is noteworthy, however, that according to Falconer "the experienced mahouts attached to the Government Commissariat in Bengal will tell at a glance the district where a recently caught elephant has been bred; whether the sal-forests of the North-West Provinces, Assam, Sylhet, Chittagong, Tipperah, or Cuttack." Should it be eventually possible to distinguish two or more continental Indian races, the difficulty would arise as to which was to be regarded as the typical *Elephas maximus* of Linnæus, which, as already indicated, may, after all, be the Ceylon animal.

With regard to the Sumatran elephant, geographical considerations are probably of themselves sufficient to indicate its right to stand as a local race (*E. maximus sumatranus*) of the Asiatic species, distinguished by the external characters recorded by Temminck and Schlegel. Comparison would, however, probably indicate other points of distinction between this and the Indian and Cingalese races. If, as is suggested, the elephants now found wild in Borneo have been introduced by human agency, they are perhaps identical with the Sumatran race. It may be added that if the natives have been able to introduce these animals into Borneo, there is no reason why they should not have done the same in Ceylon.

Whether the elephants of Cochin-China, Siam, the Malay States, and Burma are or are not identical with the Sumatran or the Indian race, there are at present no means of determining. It is noteworthy, however, that so-called white elephants appear to be less uncommon in these eastern states than in either India or Ceylon ; and there is also the circumstance that Burmese elephants breed more readily in confinement than is the case with Indian elephants. So far as they go, these are points in favour of the racial distinctness of the elephants of the mainland on the eastern side of the Bay of Bengal from their Indian and Cingalese relatives.

The Malay elephant differs from the Ceylon race in that practically all the males are tuskers. These animals are to be met with all over the Federated Malay States, but are less numerous in Selangor and Perak than elsewhere.

As regards their present distribution in India, elephants are found along the foot of the Himalaya as far west as the valley of Dehra Dun, where the winter temperature falls to a comparatively low point. A favourite haunt used to be the swamp of Azufghur, lying among the sal-forests to the northward of the station of Meerut. In the great tract of forest between the Ganges and Kistna rivers they occur locally as far west as Bilaspur and Mandla ; they are met with in the Western Ghats as far north as between latitude 17° and 18°, and are likewise found in the hill-forests of Mysore (the hunting district of G. P. Sanderson in his earlier days) as well as still farther south. In this part of the peninsula they ascend the hills to a considerable height, as they do in the Newera Ellia district of Ceylon, where they have been encountered at an elevation of over 7000 feet above the sea. There is evidence to prove that about three centuries ago elephants wandered in the forests of Malwa and Nimar, while they survived to a much later date in the Chanda district of the Central Provinces. At the comparatively remote epoch when the Deccan was a forest tract, they were probably also to be met with there, but the swamps of the Bengal Sandarbans appear to be unsuited to their habits.

So many excellent accounts of the mode of life of the wild Indian elephant are extant (those by Sir J. E. Emerson Tennent, Sir S. Baker, and Mr. G. P. Sanderson being among the best), that a short notice will here suffice. The structure of the teeth is sufficient to indicate that the food consists chiefly of grass, leaves, succulent shoots, and fruits ; and this has been found by observation to be actually the case. In this respect the Asiatic species differs widely from its African relative, whose nutriment is largely composed of boughs and roots. Another difference between the two is to be found in the intolerance of the direct rays of the sun displayed by the Asiatic species, which never voluntarily exposes itself to their influence. Consequently, during the hot season in Upper India, and at all times except during the rains in the more southern districts, elephants keep much to the denser parts of the forests. In Southern India they delight in hill-forest, where the undergrowth is largely formed of bamboo, the shoots of which form a favourite delicacy ; but during the rains they venture out to feed on the open grass-tracts. Water is essential to their well-being ; and no animals delight more in a bath. Nor are they afraid to venture out of their depth, being excellent swimmers, and able, by means of their trunks, to breathe without difficulty when the body is submerged. The herds, which are led by females, appear in general to be family parties ; and although commonly restricted to from thirty to fifty, may include as many as one hundred head. The old bulls are generally solitary for a considerable portion of the year, but return to the herds during the pairing season. Some "rogue" elephants—*gunda* of the natives—remain, however, permanently separated from the rest of their kind. All such solitary bulls, as their colloquial name indicates, are of a spiteful disposition ; and it appears that with the majority the inducement to live apart is due to their partiality for cultivated crops, into which the more timid females are afraid to venture. "Mast" elephants are males in a condition of—probably sexual—excitement, when an abundant discharge of dark oily matter exudes from two pores in the forehead. In addition to various sounds produced at other times, an elephant when about to charge gives vent to a shrill loud "trumpet"; and on such occasions rushes on its adversary with its trunk rolled up out of danger, endeavouring either to pin him to the ground with its tusks (if a male tusker) or to trample him to death beneath its ponderous knees or feet.

Exact information in regard to the period of gestation of the female elephant is still a desideratum; this being largely due to the fact that in India elephants rarely breed in captivity, although they do so much more commonly in Burma and Siam. From observations on elephants in a menagerie in Philadelphia, Mr. H. C. Chapman estimated the duration of pregnancy at as much as twenty-two months; but other observers have put it at nineteen, while by some it has been reduced to eighteen months. Possibly the native explanation, that the period is twenty-two months in the case of bull calves, and eighteen in that of females, may prove to be correct. The newly-born calf almost immediately stands on its feet, and soon after sucks, effecting the latter operation by raising its trunk and applying its mouth to the maternal teats, which are two in number and situated between the fore-legs. Very rarely two calves are produced at a birth.

Here it may be mentioned that an elephant drinks by sucking up water with its trunk and then pouring it into its mouth; all food being likewise conveyed to the mouth by the same organ.

Elephant-shooting, which is practised on foot, is perhaps the most dangerous of all Indian field-sports; and a charging elephant needs all the nerve and coolness of the sportsman. Describing the charge of an elephant, Mr. Sanderson observes that "the cocked ears and broad forehead present an immense frontage; the head is held high, with the trunk curled between the tusks, to be uncoiled in the moment of attack; the massive fore-legs come down with the force and regularity of ponderous machinery; and the whole figure is rapidly foreshortened, and appears to double in size with each advancing stride. The trunk being curled and unable to emit any sound, the attack is made in silence, after the usual premonitory shriek."

With modern weapons of precision and great penetrating power, and the accurate knowledge possessed of the vital points of their anatomy by the majority of sportsmen, elephants are now generally despatched with comparative speed and certainty. Not so, however, in the old days, as the following account of an old "rogue," whose skull is now in the British Museum, sufficiently attests. This elephant, writes Dr. Falconer, "was killed in the jungles on the banks of the Ganges, at no great distance from Meerut, in May 1833, by a party of five experienced sportsmen, who went out for the express purpose of killing it. The savage animal made no fewer than twenty-three desperate and gallant charges against a battery of at least sixteen double-barrelled guns, to which it was exposed on each occasion, and fell, after several hours, with its skull literally riddled with bullets. Besides the shot-holes of its last engagement, the frontal plateau alone bears, above the nasals, the healed canals of at least sixteen bullet-holes received in previous encounters, exclusive of those effaced by the confluent fissures of its latest wounds."

The battered skull shows that not a single bullet had penetrated the comparatively small brain-chamber; all having traversed merely the surrounding mass of honeycomb-like bone, where they could do little damage. To reach the vital brain-cavity, the sportsman selects one of three shots. In the case of the front shot, the point at which to aim varies according to the position of the elephant at the moment of pulling the trigger.

When, for instance, the animal is standing facing the sportsman in the ordinary position the point at which to aim is situated in the middle line of the forehead about three inches above the plane of the eyes. On the other hand, if the elephant is in the act of charging, the front shot must be planted lower down, near the base of the trunk; and since the bullet has then to traverse a much greater thickness before entering the brain-chamber, high penetrative power on the part of the projectile is of the utmost importance; moreover, a very slight error in the aim will render this shot ineffectual. When the sportsman is on one side of the elephant, the temple-shot is the most effective; the rifle being aimed so that the bullet should strike the aperture of the ear, or the immediate neighbourhood of the same, in such a manner as to pass out on the opposite side of the skull in the same region. The rear, or ear-shot, should be planted in the hollow just above the conspicuous bump or swelling at the junction of the jaw and the neck, and taken so as to form an angle of about 45° with the elephant's course from behind. In addition to these three head-shots, there is one behind the shoulder, although this does not find much favour among sportsmen.

With the aid of the diagrams given in Mr. Sanderson's *Thirteen Years among the Wild Beasts of India*, the sportsman who essays elephant-shooting for the first time should make a careful study of the vertical section of the skull of one of these animals, so as to render himself acquainted with the locality and relations of the brain-chamber. With regard to the best methods of tracking and approaching elephants in the jungle, he cannot possibly do better than consult the work last named.

Allusion has already been made to the fits of passion which occur in elephants when *mast*; but the following instance of a wild elephant trying conclusions with a railway train which occurred at Perak, in the Malay

Peninsula, on August 18, 1899, is worthy of special mention. According to an article in the *Asian* newspaper, it seems that "the duel occurred in broad daylight, and the elephant was the deliberate aggressor. It appears that the engine-driver, seeing a big tusker ahead on the permanent way, brought his train to a standstill; whereupon the tusker, encouraged by his enemy's unwillingness to attack, took the offensive and charged bravely, so bravely that he knocked his tusks to pieces and injured his head, doing, as may be supposed, commensurate damage to the engine. For over an hour, says the story, the elephant held the position, charging repeatedly; when the driver backed his engine the elephant stood aside, but the moment it advanced he renewed the attack. A truly resolute elephant this, for when he had battered his head sore upon the engine, he turned his hind-quarters to it and endeavoured thus to overcome it!"

Later on in the same article it is stated that "on the night of September 16, 1892, an elephant, described as 'not a very old one,' forced his way through the fence near Okturn station on the Rangoon-Mandalay Railway, and strolling up the embankment got upon the metals just as the Mandalay mail came at full speed round a curve. Probably he was utterly bewildered by the rush and roar, with its accompaniment of blazing lamp and spark-showers. At all events he stood his ground and received the attack on his head, with the result that his skull was literally shattered and his carcase thrown over the embankment, the train passing on its way without injury. The fact that the line ran on the top of an embankment at the spot where this encounter took place was probably an important factor in securing the safety of the train. If the collision had occurred in a narrow cutting the elephant's carcase must have derailed the train, and caused a serious accident. This recalls the railway accident on the night of September 28, 1882. The Bengal-Nagpur up-mail, while travelling at speed about half-past nine through the jungles which flank the line between Gaikara and Monarpur, came suddenly in collision with an elephant. It was a pitch-dark night, the engine appears to have struck the beast on the flank, for the cowcatcher swept him off his legs, and he rested partially on the foot-plate until the driver reduced speed and his body slid down in front of the engine, which now pushed him along the metals, mangling him in a terrible fashion before his remains fell over the embankment. The train was travelling at a rate of 30 miles an hour, and the elephant was a big bull with tusks 6 feet long; and although his weight before the engine helped the brake to stop the train, it was derailed before it could be brought to a standstill. As this collision took place on an embankment, it was sheer good luck that the engine took the elephant fair and square as it did. The remains of the elephant were found dead at the foot of the embankment next morning; the engine lost both its head lights in the encounter, the brake-gear was injured, and the smoke-box door partially battered in."

In a letter to the *Malay Mail* of May 9, 1905, Mr. T. R. Hubback describes certain peculiarities in the tusks of an elephant shot by himself near the Triang River, Malay Peninsula, in April. These tusks diverged from one another at an unusually wide angle, so that, while on leaving the gum the axes of the two were only a foot apart, their points were separated by an interval of 3 feet 3 inches, and this despite the fact that the longer tusk projected only 1 foot 9 inches from the head. More remarkable still is the backward extension of the roots of the tusks into the skull, these, according to the author's description, reaching upwards to a point considerably behind the eye, instead of ending above the level of the root of the trunk; that is to say, just below the nasal chamber. In fact, the longer tusk had a length of no less than 2 feet 8 inches within the skull, and is stated to have ended (or rather commenced) in the cavity situated between the eye and the ear. Such an unusual backward extension of the tusks would, the writer points out, interfere with the ordinary "eye-shot," as the bullet, on its way to the brain, would have had to pass through the root of the tusk. It is to be hoped that Mr. Hubback will either publish a figure of this skull or send the specimen to a London museum, where it may be examined by anatomists, as the abnormality is certainly one of considerable interest. According to the author's description, it would appear that the roots of the tusks, in place of being confined to the sheaths in the maxillary bones (which, as already mentioned, terminate at the base of the nasal chamber), extend upward, so as to penetrate the sinuses of the frontal, and perhaps also of the parietal, bones, this being effected by a marked outward divergence from the normal course.

Before concluding the subject, it may be mentioned that elephants are peculiar among existing warm-blooded quadrupeds for the almost vertical position occupied by the bones of the limbs. The motions and positions of the elephant's limb, as shown by instantaneous photography, are so peculiar that it is safe to say the study of the skeleton alone would have given a false conception of the animal. The two most striking features are the great play of the wrist-joint and the straightness of the limbs; the bones of the fore-limb, when in a standing posture, forming a nearly vertical line from the shoulder-blade downwards. The elbow-joint is, in fact, much straighter in extreme extension than could have been inferred by fitting the bones of the arm and fore-arm together.

Still more remarkable is the fact that the Indian elephant (together probably with its African cousin) differs from all other mammals in the absence of a distinct bag (pleuron) enclosing the lungs, which are thus in direct contact with the walls of the chest.

The Indian or Asiatic Elephant

Young Indian elephants, as shown by a specimen in the British Museum, have hairy coats.

As already mentioned, the elephant figures largely in Hindu mythology ; the goddess Lakshmi being represented surrounded by elephants, while the god Ganesh who sprang from an elephant-incarnation of Parvathi, holds a position higher than other gods in religious ceremonies. The story of his origin is as follows : Parvathi was accused by her husband Shiva of infidelity, whereupon her son Ganesh intervened to protect her. His father, seizing a sword, cut off Ganesh's head at a blow. Parvathi was disconsolate and would not speak to her husband till he had given life to the slain son. Shiva, solicitous to humour his wife and yielding to the entreaties of all the gods, sent his army to find a creature which slept with its head to the north ; and when found to kill it and bring back its head to replace that of the murdered Ganesh. The soldiers returned with the head of an elephant, and placing it on the trunk of Ganesh, there sprang into existence a creature with the face of an elephant and the body of a man. Little wonder that the elephant is credited with remarkable intelligence. It is believed, for instance, to be conscious of its dignity and importance the moment its trappings are put on ; feeling that it is the centre of attraction, and that without its presence the procession would be a poor show. Peculiar forms of worship or "puja," are performed in honour of the elephant-god ; and at each of the eight cardinal points of the compass there are believed to be a pair of elephants and a divinity, who support the earth in its place. According, however, to another version, the globe is supported by a single elephant, which stands on a tortoise.

THE GREAT INDIAN RHINOCEROS

(*Rhinoceros unicornis*)

NATIVE NAMES.—*Gainda* AND *Gargadan*, HINDUSTANI ; *Karkadan*, PUNJABI ; *Gonda*, BENGALI

(PLATE i, fig. 2)

No one is likely to confound a "rhino" with a giraffe, and yet these are the only two groups of living land animals furnished with a horn situated in the middle line of the skull. The horn of a giraffe is, however, very unlike the horn (or horns) of a rhinoceros, being composed of a boss of bone, covered with skin, and situated on the forehead of the skull, to which in adult age it is immovably attached. In all living rhinoceroses, on the other hand, the horn (or horns) is composed of agglutinated hairs, and has no firm attachment to the bones of the skull, which are merely roughened and somewhat elevated so as to fit into the concave base of the solid horn. As Sir Samuel Baker has well remarked, the attachment of the horn of a rhinoceros to the skull is very like that of the leaves of an artichoke to the "choke." In those species of living rhinoceros in which there is a single horn, this is placed immediately above the nose, and it is only in the two-horned species that there is a horn on the forehead, comparable in position with the giraffe's median horn. There is, however, an extinct Siberian rhinoceros with a single horn having the same situation as the latter. An equally marked structural difference obtains between the solid hair-like horn of a rhinoceros and the hollow horn of an ox, sheep, or antelope on the one hand, and the entirely bony antler of a deer, so that these appendages are absolutely distinctive of the former animals. It happens, however, that the female of the Javan rhinoceros is frequently more or less completely hornless, and since the same condition obtained in both sexes of certain extinct species (some of which are found in India), it is obvious that other characters must be sought in order to properly define these animals.

Rhinoceroses are huge, clumsily-built animals, with long bodies, large heads surmounted by the aforesaid horn or horns, short and thick legs, and sparsely-haired or naked skins of great thickness. In all the living species there are three toes to each foot, each encased in a small hoof-like nail at its termination; the middle one being larger than either of the others, and symmetrical in itself. The long and low head presents a markedly concave profile, rising posteriorly into an abrupt ridge or crest, on which are situated the medium-sized and more or less tube-like ears, whose margins are fringed with bristly hairs. Although there is no trunk, the upper lip is frequently produced into a pointed and semi-prehensile tip; and the eyes, which are situated on the sides of the head, are small and pig-like. The cylindrical tail does not reach within some distance of the hocks; and the cows have a pair of teats, situated in the groin.

Very characteristic of rhinoceroses are their teeth, although the number of these varies considerably in the different species, the African members of the group having none in the front of the jaws. In spite of showing minor specific modifications, the cheek-teeth are characterised by a distinct pattern of grinding surface; the essential elements in those of the upper jaw being a continuous vertical outer wall, from which proceed two transverse crests, separated by a deep open cleft, towards the inner margin of the crown. In some cases the plane of the grinding surface is nearly horizontal, while in others it is ridged; and the transverse crests and inner surface of the outer wall may be complicated by projections jutting into the intervening channel.

Although now confined to Africa and the warmer parts of Asia, rhinoceroses were formerly distributed over the whole of the Old World (with the exception of Australasia), where they ranged as far north as Siberia, and were likewise represented by hornless species in North America. The living species may therefore be regarded as survivors of an ancient type. The three species found in Asia are broadly distinguished from their African allies by the possession of teeth in the front of the jaws, and by their skins being thrown into a number of loose folds, instead of forming a tight-fitting jacket. Their extinct relatives appear to have been of the same general type.

The great Indian rhinoceros is the largest of the three named Asiatic species, and specially characterised by the possession of a single horn, coupled with the fact that the fold of skin in front of the shoulder is not continued across the back of the neck, and likewise by the skin of the sides of the body being thickly studded with large rounded tubercles, which have been aptly compared to the heads of the rivets in an iron boiler. Very characteristic, too, are the great folds of skin which surround the back of the head like a coif; the head itself being larger and more elevated at the ears than in either of the other Asiatic species.

With the exception of a fringe on the margins of the ears, and some bristly hairs on the tail, the coarse and massive skin is completely nude; the tubercles attaining their maximum development on the shoulders, thighs, and hind-quarters, where they not unfrequently measure an inch in diameter. On the limbs the place of these tubercles is taken by a number of small many-sided scales. The main folds in the skin of the body are three, namely, one in front of the shoulder, a second behind the same, and a third in front of the thighs and hind-quarters; the second and third are alone continued across the back, the first inclining backwards towards the second and dying out on the shoulder. In addition to the coif-like folds around the head, a deep horizontal pleat separates the shoulder-shield from the fore-leg, while a similar fold divides the rump-shield from the hind-limb. Folds also occur on the hind border of the rump-shield, so that the tail is enclosed in a deep groove, in such a manner that only its terminal portion is visible in a side view. The horn, although never attaining dimensions approaching those of the front horn of the African species, is well developed in both sexes; and the colour of the skin is blackish grey, showing more or less of pink on the margins of the folds.

A male measured by General A. A. Kinloch stood 5 feet 9 inches at the shoulder, and was 10½ feet in length from the tip of the nose to the root of the tail; the tail itself being 2 feet 5 inches in length. Larger dimensions are, however, recorded, by Mr. Rowland Ward in *Records of Big Game*, in the case of specimens shot by the Maharaja of Kuch-Behar; the height in three of these being respectively 6 feet 4 inches, 6 feet 1 inch, and 6 feet ½ inch; the length of the head and body 11 feet 11 inches, 11 feet 2 inches, and 11 feet 8 inches; and the total length 14 feet 1 inch, 13 feet 2 inches, and 13 feet 10 inches.

As a rule, the length of the horn does not exceed about a foot. A length of 24 inches is, however, recorded in a specimen formerly in the possession of Dr. Jerdon, and assigned to the present species; and 19½ inches is the length of the horn of a mounted specimen in the Ipswich Museum. Three specimens of 16 inches, or over, are recorded from Assam and Kuch-Behar; and the Maharaja of Kuch-Behar has obtained the horn of a female measuring 16¼ inches in length, which is the record for that sex.

The Indian rhinoceros usually has one pair of upper and two of lower incisors; the outermost pair of the latter being large, tusk-like, and projecting from the angles of the lower jaw, so as to make formidable weapons of offence. The cheek-teeth are characterised by their flat plane of wear and complex pattern, the former feature being indicative of grass-eating habits. Teeth of this type have been discovered in Madras and at Bunda, in the North-West Provinces, as well as in the river-gravels of the Narbada valley, and may be taken to indicate that the range of the species included these parts of India. There is historical evidence to prove that during the early part of the sixteenth century the great Indian rhinoceros was common in the Punjab, where it extended across the Indus as far as Peshawur ; and down to the middle of the last century, or even later, it was to be met with along the foot of the Himalaya as far west as Rohilcund and Nepal, and it survived longer still in the Terai of Sikhim. Not improbably the rhinoceroses found till about the year 1850 in the grass-jungles of the Rajmahal Hills, in Bengal, belonged to the present species. Now, however, this animal has retreated almost, if not entirely, to the eastward of the Tista valley, on the borders of Kuch-Behar ; its main strongholds being the great grass-jungles of that province and of Assam.

In the jungles of Assam the Indian rhinoceros not only dwells, but is as completely concealed as is a rabbit in a cornfield. To those who have never seen Indian grass-jungles, it may seem incredible that such a huge animal should be hidden by such covert, but when it is realised that the grass of which they are formed grows to a height of between 10 and 20 feet, the difficulty vanishes. As a matter of fact, the rhinoceros, like the Indian buffalo, makes regular tunnels, or "runs," among this gigantic grass ; and from these retreats it may be driven out by beating with a line of elephants, or by tracking on foot. When driven into the open, the animal will often stand for a few minutes, shaking its ears, before it makes up its mind in which direction to flee. A calf and its mother always issue forth together, but the old bulls and cows keep mostly apart, although both may have their home in the same patch of jungle. Those who have seen an Indian rhinoceros careering round its enclosure in the Zoological Gardens after a mud-bath, with its heavy, lumbering gallop, will not fail to realise that a charge from such a monster must be a serious matter. Fortunately, in spite of stories to the contrary, the creature in its wild state appears to be of a mild and harmless disposition, seeking rather to escape from its enemies by flight than to rout them by attack. When badly wounded, or so hustled about by elephants and beaters as to become bewildered, a rhinoceros will, however, occasionally charge home. In such onslaughts it is the common belief that the animal, like its African cousins, uses its horn as its weapon of offence; but this is an error; the real weapons being the triangular, sharp-pointed lower tusks. With these a sweeping cut can be made in the leg of an elephant, in much the same way as a boar rips up a horse. Probably all the Asiatic members of the group attack in the same fashion.

Like all its kindred, the great Indian rhinoceros loves a mud-bath, and when plastered over with the mud of some swamp or pool, looks a more than ordinarily unprepossessing creature. Its favourite haunts are generally in the neighbourhood of swamps; and hilly districts are avoided. Morning and evening are the chief feeding-times, the heat of the day being generally passed in slumber. As already stated, the structure of the teeth indicates that its food is chiefly grass; and such observations as have been made confirm the truth of this inference. Individuals have lived for over twenty years in the London Zoological Gardens, and it is stated that others have been kept in confinement for fully fifty years. Consequently, there is no doubt that the animal is long-lived, and it has been suggested that its term of life may reach as much as a century. The cow gives birth to a single young one at a time, but information is required in regard to the duration of the period of gestation and the frequency with which births take place.

It was an old idea that the hide of the Indian rhinoceros was bullet-proof; but this was erroneous even in regard to such weapons as the military "brown Bess." As trophies, sportsmen may preserve either the entire head or the horn alone; in addition to which a shield-shaped piece of skin is frequently cut from the under surface of the body, where it is thinner than elsewhere, and kept as a memento of a successful "shikar." Kuch-Behar is now one of the centres for rhinoceros-shooting. Fine examples have been obtained by the Maharaja himself; and it was in this territory that the Duke of Portland obtained specimens in 1882. To shoot females is prohibited.

THE SINGPHO RHINOCEROS

In this place reference may be made to the occurrence of an unknown rhinoceros in the Singpho country, concerning which the following notice by the present writer appeared in the *Field* newspaper of July 23, 1905. According to native reports, there exists in the Singpho country a rhinoceros of larger size than either the two-horned *Rhinoceros sumatrensis* or the single-horned *R. sondaicus*. For this animal the natives have a name distinct from those which they apply respectively to the two species just named, and they further describe it as being of huge size, comparing it in this respect with an elephant. Now the Singpho country, which is the area marked in the *Times Atlas* as the district inhabited by the Kachins or Singphos (Kakhyens), is the tract lying on the headwaters of the Chindwin River, this being separated from the north-eastern extremity of the Assam Valley only by the Naga Hills and the Patkai Range. Consequently, the suggestion naturally arises that the Singpho rhinoceros may be a representative of the great Indian *Rhinoceros unicornis*, whose chief habitat at the present day is the Assam Valley. That the Singpho animal is not absolutely identical with the Assam rhinoceros is practically certain when it is borne in mind that the latter is a plain-dwelling species, and that the mountain barrier between the Assam and Chindwin Valleys is of very considerable height.

I have endeavoured to ascertain whether there are any traces of the Singpho rhinoceros in public or private collections, and have succeeded in finding one specimen which affords decisive evidence of the existence of such an animal. In the third (1899) edition of Mr. Rowland Ward's invaluable *Records of Big Game*, there occurs under the heading of the great Indian rhinoceros, the entry of a horn from "Singpo," Burma, belonging to Sir C. A. Elliott, K.C.S.I., the specimen measuring 19 inches in length and 18 inches in girth. From the fourth edition of Mr. Ward's book the entry has been omitted, probably for the reason that the editor thought there must be an error in recording the great Indian rhinoceros from Burma. The Singpho horn, it may be added, accords much better in dimensions with that of the great Indian species than with those of either of the other Asiatic rhinoceroses, and indicates a large animal.

Upon obtaining this information I wrote to Sir Charles Elliott, who, in reply, informed me that when in Sadiya, the extreme north-eastern station of Assam, in the winter of 1882-83, or thereabouts, he heard that a fine rhinoceros horn had been brought down to the bazaar by some Singphos for sale. This specimen, together with a smaller horn, was purchased by Sir Charles, the former being mounted as a trophy, and the latter being made into an inkstand. The owner informs me that there is every reason for believing the two horns to have been derived from one and the same animal. If this be so, it is practically certain that the Singpho rhinoceros cannot be identical with the great Indian species, despite the story current in Assam that the latter, when very old, will sometimes grow a second horn.

Nevertheless, it seems within the bounds of probability, judging from the native reports as to the great size of the animal and also from the large dimensions of the horn in Sir Charles Elliott's possession, that the Singpho rhinoceros may turn out to be more or less closely related to *Rhinoceros unicornis*, although provided with two horns. The definite addition of such an animal to the Asiatic fauna would be a matter of great interest, and sportsmen and officials connected with Upper Burma should use every effort to obtain at least the skull and head-skin of the Singpho rhinoceros, in order that its real affinities may be determined. It may be added that, in view of the comparatively recent date at which we became definitely acquainted with the tsaine, or Burmese bantin, there is nothing improbable in a rhinoceros which inhabits a still more remote, and consequently less known district, proving to be at least subspecifically distinct from any of the named representatives of the group.

THE JAVAN RHINOCEROS

(*Rhinoceros sondaicus*)

NATIVE NAMES.—*Gainda*, HINDUSTANI ; *Gonda*, BENGALI ; *Kunda*, *Kedi*, AND *Kweda* OF THE NAGAS ; *Kyeng* AND *Kyan-tsheng*, BURMESE ; *Badak*, MALAY.

(PLATE i, fig. 3)

Although possessing only a single horn, the Javan rhinoceros is a very different beast, both externally and in its internal anatomy, from the preceding species. In the first place, although measurements of adult males are still required, it is a somewhat smaller and lighter-built animal, with a relatively less bulky and less elevated head. The folds of skin round the neck are also much less developed, and the body-fold on the shoulders is continued right across the back in the same manner as are the other two great folds. Moreover, owing to the absence of the deep groove on the rump, the tail stands out quite distinct from the hind-quarters, so that its whole extent is exposed in a side view. Very characteristic also is the structure of the skin, which lacks the "boiler-rivets" of the great Indian species, and is marked all over with a kind of mosaic-like pattern, caused by the presence of a network of fine cracks in the superficial layer. A piece of skin cut from any part of the body is therefore amply sufficient to determine to which of the two species it pertained.

Yet another peculiarity of the Javan rhinoceros is to be found in the frequent, if not invariable, absence of the horn in the female. Male horns of between 10 and 11 inches in length are recorded.

As regards the height of the animal, the most authentic measurement of a wild specimen is that of a female, which stood $5\frac{1}{2}$ feet at the shoulder ; but males must almost certainly attain larger dimensions.

The present species is of the same dusky-grey colour as the last, and its hide is equally devoid of hair. The cheek-teeth, however, although numerically the same as in the Indian rhinoceros, show a simpler pattern, while their crowns wear into ridges instead of a uniformly flat plane. This may be taken to indicate that the present species feeds chiefly upon twigs and leaves.

Typically an inhabitant of Java, this rhinoceros is also found in the islands of Borneo and Sumatra, as well as in the Malay Peninsula, whence it extends northwards through Burma into Assam, and so into

Eastern Bengal and the Sandarbans; while a specimen has been killed as far west as the Sikhim Terai. So far as present information goes, the mainland form cannot be distinguished from those inhabiting the Malay islands, so that separate local races cannot yet be differentiated. It is, however, quite likely that this is due to the want of a good series of specimens, the British Museum having, in addition to skulls and skeletons, only the skin of a young calf in a condition fit for public exhibition.

Although found in the swampy Sandarbans of Lower Bengal, within a day's journey of Calcutta, the Javan rhinoceros prefers forest tracts to grass-jungles, and is generally met with in hilly districts, where it apparently ascends in some parts of its habitat several thousand feet above sea-level. In most other respects the mode of life of this species is probably very similar to that of its larger relative; its disposition is, however, stated to be more gentle, and in Java tame individuals are frequently to be seen wandering about the villages of the natives. Mr. T. R. Hubback,[1] on the evidence of native testimony, affirms that either this or the next species uses its lower tusks for fighting in the same way as the great Indian rhinoceros.

THE SUMATRAN RHINOCEROS

(*Rhinoceros sumatrensis*)

NATIVE NAMES.—*Kyan* AND *Kyan-shaw*, BURMESE; *Badak*, MALAY

(PLATE i, fig. 4)

Although possessed of two horns, the Sumatran rhinoceros resembles its Asiatic brethren in having

[1] *Elephant and Seladang Hunting in the Federated Malay States*, 1905, p. 24.

teeth in the front of the jaw, as well as by its folded skin, and has therefore nothing to do with the African representatives of the family. As compared with the other Asiatic species (exclusive of the still unknown Singpho rhinoceros), the presence of an additional horn, coupled with the fact that it has only a single pair of lower front teeth (the small central pair occurring between the tusks in the other two species being absent), afford ample grounds for regarding this rhinoceros as the representative of a group by itself; and it is noteworthy that an extinct rhinoceros (*R. hundsheimensis*) from the continent of Europe appears to be another member of the same group of the genus.

To distinguish the present species from all its relatives, it is sufficient to state that it is the only named living rhinoceros with two horns and a folded skin ; but since it is an animal by no means familiar to most sportsmen, it is advisable to enter somewhat into details. In the first place, this species is the smallest of living rhinoceroses, as it is also the most hairy, its usual height at the shoulder not being more than 4 to 4½ feet, and the length from the tip of the muzzle to the root of the tail only about 8 feet. Some female specimens even fall short of the foregoing dimensions, an old individual from the Malay Peninsula being only 3 feet 8 inches at the withers. The weight has been estimated at a couple of thousand pounds.

As though suggestive of a transition towards the smooth-skinned rhinoceroses of Africa, the folds in the skin of the present species are much less pronounced than in the other Asiatic kinds ; and of the three main folds, only one, namely, that situated behind the shoulder, is continued across the back. In structure, the outer surface of the skin is finely granular ; and its colour, which varies from earthy-brown to almost black, is likewise different from that of either of the one-horned species. Hair grows sparsely all over the head and body, but attains its maximum development on the ears and the tail; its colour varying from brown to black. At their bases the two horns are separated from one another by a considerable interval; and although in captive individuals they are generally much worn down, when fully developed they are slender for the greater part of their length, the front one curving backwards in an elegant sweep, and attaining very considerable size. The longest known specimen of the front horn is in the British Museum, and has a length of 32½ inches, with a basal girth of 17⅜ inches; a second specimen in the same collection measuring 27⅛ inches in length, and 17⅞ in circumference.

As regards the cheek-teeth, those of the upper jaw are practically indistinguishable from the corresponding molars of the Javan rhinoceros, and may accordingly be taken as indicative of the leaf- and twig-eating propensities of this species.

The Sumatran rhinoceros inhabits the islands of Sumatra and Borneo, and is also met with in the Malay Peninsula, whence it extends northwards through Burma and Tenasserim to Chittagong and Assam, and it also occurs in Siam. Compared with the typical Sumatran animal (*R. sumatrensis typicus*), a specimen from Chittagong formerly living in the London Zoological Gardens was distinguishable by its superior dimensions, paler and browner hair, shorter and more fully tufted tail, and the strongly developed fringe on the margins of the ears, the interior of which was bare. The skull was proportionately broader; but this seems a feature of minor import. Although originally regarded as a separate species, the Chittagong rhinoceros is best classed as a local race of the Sumatran animal, with the name *Rhinoceros sumatrensis lasiotis*. Other specimens of the hairy-eared race have been subsequently obtained in Assam, where the species is rare; and one example has been killed in Tippera, and a second in the Bhutan Duars. In Tenasserim and the Malay Peninsula it is replaced by a smaller, blacker, and less hairy form, which if distinct from the typical Sumatran animal (as is probably the case) should be known as *R. sumatrensis niger*.

In habits the Sumatran rhinoceros appears to be very similar to the Javan species; both affecting forested hill-country, which may be at a considerable altitude above the sea. In the Mergui Archipelago a rhinoceros, which may be this species, is stated to have been seen swimming from island to island; and it is probable that all the Asiatic representatives of the family will take readily to the water, although in Somaliland the African rhinoceros is found in absolutely arid districts, where it cannot even drink for long periods.

The type specimen of the hairy race of the Sumatran rhinoceros was a female, captured at Chittagong in the year 1868. When discovered by native hunters she was embedded in a quicksand, and well-nigh exhausted by her struggles to reach *terra firma*. By attaching ropes to her neck she was safely extricated from her perilous position, and fastened to a tree, where next morning she was found so refreshed and so violent that her captors were afraid to approach. Accordingly, a report of the capture was sent to Chittagong, and soon after a couple of English officials arrived with elephants, to one of which the rhinoceros was made fast, and, after some trouble, marched into the station, where she soon became tame. Eventually she was secured for the London Zoological Society, in whose *Proceedings* for 1872 her coloured portrait appeared. By a lucky coincidence a specimen of the typical representative of the species was procured by the Society at the close of 1872, so that the two forms were exhibited side by side. While in the docks the Chittagong animal gave birth to a young one; and from certain facts that came to his knowledge, the late Mr. A. D. Bartlett was led to conclude that the period of gestation in the species was only a little over seven months. According to an article by Mr. L. Wray in the *Journal* of the Federated Malay States Museums, the Sumatran rhinoceros is becoming extremely scarce in the Dindings district of the Malay Peninsula, owing to persistent trapping on the part of the natives. The rhinoceroses are caught in deep concealed pitfalls made in their runs ; and the Malays state that fifty individuals have been taken in this way in and near the Dindings alone. Catching and exporting these animals has, indeed, become a regular trade in the district for some years past, with the result that, whereas they were formerly quite common, they are now very scarce and difficult to trap.

THE MALAY TAPIR

(*Tapirus indicus*)

NATIVE NAMES.—*Tara-shu*, BURMESE ; *Kuda-ayer* AND *Tennu*, MALAY

(PLATE i, fig. 5)

Tapirs (so called by an abbreviation of the native name of one of the South American species) offer little attraction to the sportsman, since they yield nothing in the way of trophies except their skulls and skins, and the latter are valuable only as leather. Nevertheless, they are animals by no means lacking in interest, if only from the point of view of their remarkable geographical distribution. Although the typical South American tapir was known by repute to the Swiss naturalist Linnæus, who at first described it as a terrestrial species of hippopotamus, but afterwards had doubts as to its very existence, it was not till 1816 that naturalists were made aware that another species inhabits the jungles of the Malay Peninsula. For this information they were indebted to a Major Farquar, who described an individual then living in the menagerie of the Governor-General of India at Barrackpur, although he omitted to assign to the Oriental species a distinctive name.

This discovery revealed the fact that while tapirs are common to the Malay countries and South and Central America, they are found at the present day in no other part of the world. Were it not for the investigations into the past history of our globe, we should have been at a loss to explain such a remarkable instance of discontinuous distribution; but we now know that in past epochs these animals were distributed over a considerable portion of the northern hemisphere, whence they wandered southwards to their present widely sundered dwelling-places.

Although in Asia, at any rate, animals that seldom come under the ken of the sportsman in their wild condition, tapirs have been made familiar to the public from specimens exhibited in menageries and museums. In size they may be compared to heavily-built and short-limbed donkeys, but from their comparatively bare skins, general shape, and long flexible snouts, they present a superficial resemblance to large swine, with which group many persons are inclined to associate them. An examination of their feet, in which one toe is much larger than either of the others, and symmetrical in itself, is, however, sufficient to show the incorrectness of this idea, and to indicate that their relationship is with rhinoceroses.

Unlike the latter animals, tapirs have, however, four toes on the front feet, although on the hind-feet the number is three in both groups. From rhinoceroses they are likewise distinguished by the production of the nose and upper lip into a short, mobile proboscis, or trunk. The teeth, too, are very different, both in number and form, from those of rhinoceroses; the total number being forty-two. Both jaws are furnished with a full set of incisors, or "nippers," and tusks;

while the cheek-teeth present a pattern totally distinct from that found in rhinoceroses. Tapirs have the tail short, the ears of medium size and oval shape, small, pig-like eyes, and short, sparse hair.

The Malay species, which is the largest of the group, is readily distinguished from all its South American cousins by the parti-coloured hide of the adult; the head, limbs, and front part of the body being dark brown or black, while all that portion of the body situated behind the shoulders, including the rump and the upper part of the thighs, together with the tips of the ears, is greyish white or white in the adult. In very young animals, on the other hand, that is to say, those not exceeding from four to six months in age, the ground-colour is blackish brown or black, marked (as in the young of the American species) with longitudinal streaks of yellow on the head and sides and of white on the under-parts. The hair, too, is markedly denser than in the full-grown animal. In height an adult Malay tapir stands from 3 to 3½ feet at the withers and about 4 inches more at the rump; the length from the tip of the snout to the root of the tail, measured along the curves of the body, being about 8 feet.

The geographical distribution of this animal includes the island of Sumatra and the Malay Peninsula, and thence northwards into the Tenasserim province about as far as the fifteenth parallel of north latitude.

In its wild state, little or nothing authentic has been ascertained with regard to the mode of life of the Malay tapir; and the writer is unacquainted with any account of the chase of this animal by European sportsmen. Its habits, are, however, in all probability very similar to those of the American representatives of the genus. These latter are shy and retiring animals, dwelling amid thick jungle in the neighbourhood of water, to which they take readily. Between the years 1840 and 1896 seven examples of the Malay tapir were exhibited in the Menagerie of the

London Zoological Society. The majority, however, survived but a short period, at least two of them dying within a year of their acquisition.

THE KIANG, OR TIBETAN WILD ASS

(*Equus hemionus kiang*)

NATIVE NAME.—*Kiang*, TIBETAN

(PLATE i, fig. 6)

Although the designation wild ass is commonly applied to the Asiatic members of the horse family, locally known by the names of chigetai, kiang, onager, and ghor-khar, these animals are really more nearly allied to the horse, especially the wild Mongolian *Equus caballus przewalskii*, and differ very markedly from the true wild asses of North Africa. In common with the latter they have short, upright manes, and no warts, or callosities, on the hind-legs; but the dark marking on the upper-parts is restricted to a stripe down the back.

The chigetai (*Equus hemionus*) of Mongolia and Turkestan is the typical representative of a species which includes the kiang as a local race, and whose range extends northwards to Transbaikalia and westwards to Transcaspia. The species, inclusive of both the chigetai and the kiang, may be characterised as follows:—

Size large, the height at the shoulder reaching to 4 feet 3 inches. Ears (in comparison with those of the African wild ass, *E. asinus*) relatively small and horse-like. Hoofs large and broad, the width of the front pair markedly exceeding that of the hind ones. Tail-tuft large, and a slight rudiment of a forelock present. Dark dorsal stripe relatively narrow, reaching the tail-tuft, and (in most cases at any rate) not bordered with white. No shoulder-stripe, or dark barrings on the limbs; a dark ring immediately above the hoofs. General colour of upper-parts in summer coat varying from bright rufous chestnut (with a more or less marked tinge of greyish fawn on the neck) to reddish sandy; muzzle, inside of ear, throat, under-parts, inner side of legs, and a streak on the buttocks, pure white or buffish white. In the long winter coat the general colour apparently not distinctly grey, although greyish in the typical form. Cry, a "shrieking bray."

The skull of the kiang differs markedly from that of the onager, but from lack of specimens of that of the chigetai, I am unable to give the cranial characters of the species as a whole.

The kiang is characterised by the great width of the hoofs, more especially the front pair. In this respect it approaches the horse, *Equus caballus* (as it does in its relatively small ears and its colour), and differs widely from *E. asinus*. The ghor-khar and onagers, on the other hand, have small and narrow hoofs, like those of the last-named species.

As regards colour, the kiang is by far the reddest of all the Asiatic wild asses, and apparently becomes but little greyer in winter. On the other hand, some of the ghor-khar and onager group are quite grey in winter.

In addition to its small ears, broad hoofs, narrow dorsal stripe, and general colour, the kiang appears to be affiliated to the horse (inclusive of the wild horse of Mongolia, *Equus caballus przewalskii*) by the nature of its cry, which there is little doubt is to a great extent intermediate between that of the horse and the ass. It is true that there is a certain amount of discrepancy between the accounts of the kiang's cry given by different observers. General Cunningham, for instance, in his work on Ladak, calls it a neigh, and other observers have described it as being as much like neighing as braying. On the other hand, Moorcroft, and subsequently General Strachey, described it as more like braying than neighing ; the latter traveller

FIG. 2.—The Kiang, from a specimen at Woburn Abbey, photographed by the Duchess of Bedford.

observing that "my impression of the voice of the kiang is that it is a shrieking bray, not like that of the common ass, but still a real bray, and not a neigh." Evidently it is perfectly distinct from the bray of *E. asinus*, while it also differs from the cry of one of the races of *E. onager*.

The characteristics of the kiang, as distinct from the chigetai, are as follows :—

Profile sinuous, being concave below the eyes, and above the nose distinctly convex. Dorsal stripe always narrow, chocolate in colour, without trace of white borders. Tips of ears, mane (which is rather long), a narrow ring just above each hoof, and tail-tuft dark brown or blackish. General colour of upper-parts full rufous chestnut, sometimes with a tinge of greyish fawn on the neck, and tending to sandy on the rump and legs ; muzzle, inside of ear, side of neck, throat, chest, under-parts, inner surface of legs, and a streak on the hind border of the thigh, pure white, sharply defined from the rufous and fawn areas. The light area of the under-parts may run behind the shoulder so as to partially insulate the rufous of the latter. The winter coat does not differ markedly in colour from the summer one.

In a mounted specimen in the British Museum the height at the withers is 4 feet $3\frac{1}{4}$ inches, the length of the ear $7\frac{3}{4}$ inches, the width of the front hoof $3\frac{1}{3}$ inches, and that of the hind hoof $3\frac{1}{8}$ inches.

The kiang inhabits the higher desert tracts of Ladak and Tibet, from about 13,000 to 18,000 feet above the sea, or even more ; and is found commonly in the Chang-chenmo valley, as well as on the Indus itself, some few days' march above the town of Leh. Here it is generally met with in small troops, but sometimes singly ; and in districts where it has not been much disturbed displays but little fear, galloping in circles round the mounted traveller as he approaches its haunts. Young individuals sometimes display a curiosity which overcomes all sense of fear ; one (of which the skull is now in the Museum of the Royal College of Surgeons) having on a certain occasion rashly ventured into the writer's camp in Chang-chenmo. Across their rough native country these animals are wonderful goers, their hoofs being as hard as iron ; and could they only be properly domesticated, they would be invaluable as beasts of transport across these dreary elevated regions, where ponies often succumb to the climate and want of proper food. Being able to subsist on the scrubby herbage, they would be far more useful than yak, which cannot do without grass. But, although the individual at Woburn Abbey whose portrait is here given is fairly amenable to discipline, kiang, as a rule, refuse to submit themselves to the hardships of servitude ; the writer having a vivid recollection of the malignant disposition of one kept in captivity by the Governor of Ladak about 1876.

As an animal of sport, little can be said in favour of the kiang, as it yields no trophies, and can be easily approached within 150 yards, or even less, when a well-placed bullet should drop it dead in its tracks, or at all events after a short run. Many sportsmen shoot a specimen or two, and bring back the hide or skull, or both ; but this generally suffices for most men. In addition to yielding nothing worth having to the sportsmen, kiang are frequently positively detrimental to those in quest of nobler game, such as argali, as by careering wildly about in the neighbourhood of the stalker, they render all the animals within sight suspicious of danger, even although their human foe may be concealed from their view. In such cases an apparently favourable stalk may frequently be brought to an abrupt conclusion by the sudden disappearance of all the game, which have taken alarm from the movements of the kiang.

Whether, in the rarefied atmosphere of the elevated regions in which it dwells, the kiang is as fleet an animal as the wild ass of Baluchistan and Kutch, has not yet been determined. Neither have we, apparently, any definite information as to the season when the foals are dropped, and the length of the period of gestation. The latter is, however, probably much the same as in the mare and the domestic ass, and the young are almost certainly born during the summer. Both the wiry grass of Ladak and various dwarf scrubby plants serve as the chief food of the kiang.

THE GHOR-KHAR, OR BALUCHI WILD ASS

(*Equus onager indicus*)

NATIVE NAMES.—*Ghor-khar*, PERSIAN AND HINDUSTANI; *Ghur* AND *Ghurdu*, BALUCHI

The ghor-khar, or wild ass of Baluchistan and the deserts of Western India, is a local race of the Persian onager (*Equus onager*).

The range of the species (inclusive of all its local races) embraces the desert districts of Western and (?) W. Central Asia and North-Western India; while its distinctive features are as follows:—

Size considerably less than in *E. hemionus*, the minimum recorded height being 3 feet 8 inches and the maximum 3 feet 10 inches. Ears apparently much the same as in the latter. Hoofs narrow and ass-like; the front pair little wider than the hind pair. Profile of face nearly straight or markedly sinuous. Tail-tuft moderate. Dark dorsal stripe very broad, in some cases stopping short of the tail-tuft, and bordered, at least posteriorly, by a band of white or whitish, which joins the white on the buttocks and the back of the thighs. Colour of upper-parts, in the summer coat, usually some shade of pale reddish fawn or sandy (isabelline); the light areas, which vary from pure white to whitey-brown, much the same as in *E. hemionus*, but extending more on to the buttocks, and thence along the sides of the dorsal stripe, and in some cases occupying more of the body and head. In winter, the long and rough coat more or less decidedly grey; in one instance distinctly mouse-grey with sharply defined white areas.

The cry of the Indian ghor-khar is described as being a "shrieking bray," and therefore perhaps not unlike that of the kiang; but in the case of the Syrian onager, and probably also in that of the true onager, it is stated by the late Mr. E. Blyth to be more like that of the common ass, to the wild forms of which animal the present species approximates not only in its narrow hoofs, broad dorsal stripe, and small tail-tuft, but likewise in the distinctly grey colour of the winter coat in at least one of the local races.

The ghor-khar, or Indian race of the species, inhabits the Indian desert (Bickanir, Jeysulmere, and the Rann of Kutch), thence apparently ranging eastwards into Baluchistan, Afghanistan, and Southern Persia to the north of the Khorasan Desert.

Height at shoulder (from a wild specimen) 3 feet 10 inches. Profile of face straight. General colour of upper-parts sandy in summer, with the light band on each side of the dorsal stripe narrow, ill-defined, and whitey-brown in colour; and the white on the rump not pure. The coloration—presumably in the summer coat—is described by Dr. P. Matschie as follows: Upper-parts bright sandy; throat, under-parts, etc., white, the white extending to the flanks; the broad dark dorsal stripe bordered with white posteriorly, and stopping short of the tail-tuft; but in the specimens I have seen the under-parts are dirty white.

The Baluchi wild ass appears to be a much more gregarious animal than its Tibetan relative, thirty or forty head being frequently seen in a troop; and Dr. J. Aitchison, when on the Afghan Delimitation Commission, states that in North-Western Afghanistan, during the month of April, he encountered a troop estimated to include about a thousand individuals.

In the trans-Indus districts the mares give birth to their foals during the summer, from June to August.

The horsemen of the Rann of Kutch take advantage of the mares when in foal by riding them down and spearing them ; this feat (which is certainly practised) being probably impracticable under any other circumstances, on account of the extreme fleetness of these animals. Baluchis, mounted on their swift mares, capture young ghor-khar by riding after them in relays, sometimes with the aid of greyhounds, until they succumb from sheer exhaustion. Probably in certain parts of their habitat, such as the Rann of Kutch, where, at certain seasons, there is no water but such as is salt, ghor-khar must go for considerable periods without drinking. Like the kiang, these wild asses, in spite of their fleetness of foot, are by no means well-bred-looking animals, the head being disproportionately large and heavy, as well as ungracefully carried.

THE GAUR, OR INDIAN BISON

(*Bos* [*Bibos*] *gaurus*)

NATIVE NAMES.—*Gaur* AND *Gauri-gai*, HINDUSTANI ; *Gayal* IN ORISSA ; *Gaor* (male) AND *Gaib* (female) IN CHUTIA NAGPUR ; *Sainal*, HO-KOL ; *Gaviya*, MAHRATHI ; *Pera-mao* OF THE SOUTHERN GONDS ; *Katuerimai*, TAMIL ; *Karkona*, *Karti*, *Kard-yemme*, *Kard-korna* AND *Doddu*, CANARESE ; *Karthu* AND *Paothu*, MALABARI ; *Mithan*, ASSAMESE ; *Selori* IN CHITTAGONG ; *Pyoung*, BURMESE ; *Seladang*, MALAY.

(PLATE ii, figs. 1, 1*a*)

In addition to the foregoing list of designations, the great wild ox of India is frequently called in various parts of the peninsula by several names meaning wild buffalo. By English sportsmen, on the other hand,

Plate II

1, 1*a*. Gaur. 3. Burmese Bantin, or Tsain.
2, 2*a*. Gayal. 4, 4*a*. Yak.
5, 5*a*. Indian Buffalo.

this magnificent animal is almost invariably called bison —a title properly belonging to *Bos bonasus* of Lithuania and the Caucasus. Questions are sometimes asked in sporting newspapers whether the application of the term bison to the gaur is legitimate. The answer is very simple, namely, that it is not. Domesticated oxen (together with their extinct wild progenitors), gaur and gayal, bison, yak, and buffaloes collectively constitute the ox tribe ; and since the domesticated ox is the type of the whole group, they may all, in a general sense, be classed as oxen. Had the bison of Europe been made the typical representative of the group, then that term might likewise have been employed in the same general sense, and the gaur termed a bison as it now is an ox ; but as matters stand, such a usage is indefensible. The true domesticated oxen form one division of the group. Next to this comes a second and nearly allied section of the group comprising the gaur, the gayal, and the bantin ; all the members of which are characterised by their elevated withers, short hair, and "white-stockinged" limbs. The third section includes the European and American bisons, with which the yak may perhaps be included ; all these having long hair on some part of the body, uniformly dark limbs, and lacking the ridge-like hump of the second section. Lastly, there are the buffaloes, differing from all the others by the peculiar form of their horns. Each sectional group is perfectly well defined, and it would be just as logical to call the gaur a buffalo as to dub it a bison ; but since there are few things more difficult to amend than popular misapplications of names, a bison it will probably remain among sportsmen.

Of the general characteristics of the ox tribe, little need be stated. With the exception of a few stunted island forms, the members of the group are large and heavily-built animals, with a short and deep neck, a massive head, carried somewhat low, and frequently a large dewlap on the throat and chest. The broad

Fig. 3.—A Bull Gaur killed by the Maharaja of Kuch-Behar.

muzzle is devoid of hair, with a moist skin ; there are no glands on the face, on the legs, or between the hoofs ; and the cows have four teats. The horns (which, in common with those of all the members of the *Bovidæ*, form a transversely situated pair, and consist of hollow sheaths of horn surmounting conical bony cores arising from the skull) are present in both sexes, and not very much smaller in the cows than in the bulls. They are placed on or near the vertex of the skull, and are usually widely separated at the base. Their direction is at first more or less outwards, after which they curve upwards, and generally more or less inwards towards the tips. Although cylindrical in the more typical members of the group, in the buffaloes they are distinctly triangular in cross-section ; and while in the former they are almost completely smooth externally, in the latter they are marked with irregular transverse groovings and ridges. In colour the horns may be of any shade between olive-green and black. The ears are of medium size and bluntly pointed ; and the long cylindrical tail is generally tufted at the tip, although in some cases long-haired throughout. In regard to the length and abundance of the coat, there is every gradation from the sparsely-haired hide of the buffaloes to the long-haired skin of the yak ; there is little or no seasonal difference in the colour of the coat, which, with the occasional exception of the lower portion of the legs, and very rarely of the buttocks, is uniform. Lastly, it is important to mention that oxen are specially characterised by the square prismatic form of their tall-crowned cheek-teeth.

The group of wild oxen of which the gaur is the typical representative is confined to the Indo-Malay countries, and includes two wild species, with local races, and a third form which apparently only exists in a semi-domesticated condition. Compared with the ancient wild ox of Europe, these Oriental oxen are distinguished by the shorter forehead, the nearer approximation of the eyes to the base of the horns, a more or less marked compression of the horns, especially near the base, and the relatively shorter tail, the tufted tip of which hangs but little below the level of the hocks. More important is an elevated ridge extending from the neck and shoulders to the middle of the back, where, in its most developed condition, it forms a sudden step-like descent towards the loins. In old bulls the colour is generally blackish brown, but in cows and young bulls either a paler shade of the same or red or fawn; the legs, from above the knees and hocks downwards, being, in both sexes and at all ages, white or yellowish. All the species have short sleek coats, without a mane or long hair on the withers; the hoofs in all are narrow and game-like; and the number of pairs of ribs in the skeleton is thirteen.

The bull gaur is one of the boldest and handsomest members of the ox tribe, and in the opinion of the late Mr. G. P. Sanderson "undoubtedly the finest species of the genus *Bos* in the world." Standing occasionally as much as 6 feet or even 6 feet 4 inches (19 hands)[1] at the withers, although frequently not exceeding 5½ feet, the bull gaur is distinguished by the great arched and forwardly curving crest, communicating a marked concavity to the profile of the forehead, of which there is no trace in other species. The massive horns, much flattened from back to front at the base, where they are marked by exfoliating rings, spread outwards from each side of this broad crest in a bold sweep, the curve continuing throughout their length, with the tips, when perfect, inclining inwards and slightly backwards. Frequently, however, one or both tips are broken off during the combats for supremacy in which the bulls engage. In colour the horns are pale greenish or yellowish for the greater portion of their length,

[1] Mr. Stuart Baker (*Asian*, February 27, 1900) says that gaur may stand 21 hands (7 feet) in Kachar. A similar statement is made by Colonel Pollok with regard to the Burmese representative of the species.

gradually passing into black at the tips. Horns of 35 inches and over along the curve may be regarded as fine; the "record" specimen having a length of 46 inches along the outer curve, with a basal circumference of 20½ and a tip-to-tip interval of 33 inches. This specimen came from the Malay States, and is therefore referable to the race locally known as Seladang. The next best, with a length of 44¼ inches, belongs to the Burmese race; while the third, with a length of 43½ inches, is a typical Indian gaur from Travancore.

Regarding other features of the bull gaur, it may be mentioned that while ears are relatively large and spreading, the tail is comparatively short, only just reaching the hocks; and the dewlap in most Indian specimens is but slightly developed, although larger in some from Travancore, and always more distinct in the Burmese race. A marked character is the strong development of the dorsal ridge, and its sudden termination in a step about midway between the shoulders and the root of the tail. The general colour of the short and sleek hair, which becomes very sparse on the back of aged bulls, is olive-brown, tending almost to black; on the under-parts it becomes paler, but is golden brown at the points of origin of the legs; the forehead, from between the eyes across the horn-crest, and so on to the nape of the neck, is ashy grey, in some instances passing into whitey brown or dirty white; the muzzle is pale slate-coloured; and the lower portions of the limbs, from above the knees and hocks downwards, are typically pure white. The iris of the eye is, in both sexes, light blue. In cows and young bulls the general hue is rather paler, in some cases, especially during winter and in dry and open districts, tending to rufous. Calves are stated to show a dark dorsal streak. The horns of cows (fig. 4) are smaller, thinner, and less expanded than those of bulls. The longest pair of gaur horns definitely recorded as those of a cow are from Travancore, and are represented in the annexed text-figure. They measured 24 inches in length along the outer curve, 13¼ in basal circumference, and 13 between the tips.

Being essentially forest-dwelling animals, gaur are

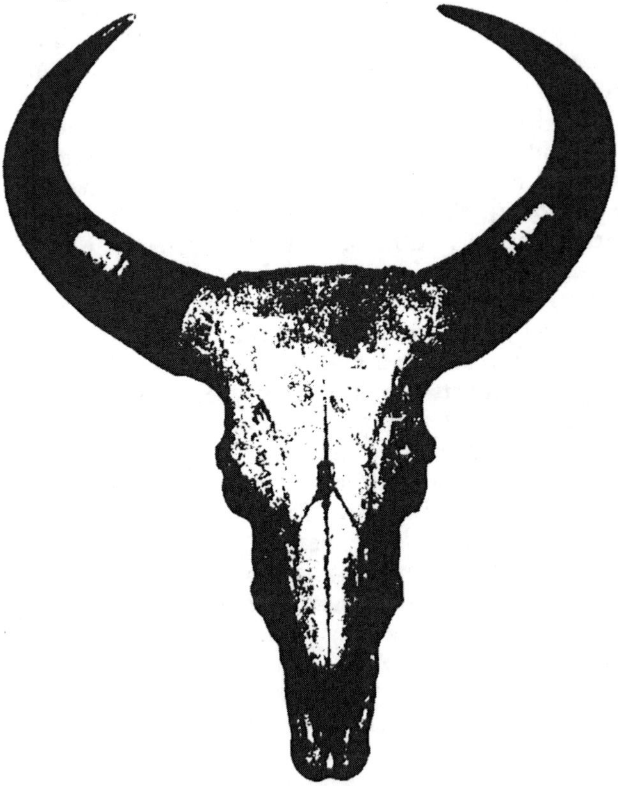

FIG. 4.—Skull and Horns of a Cow Gaur, from a specimen in the possession of Mr. A. O Hume.

not, for the most part, found in the tall grass-jungles of the Ganges plain, which form the home of the Indian buffalo and rhinoceros, although to a certain extent they enter this tract along the foot of the Himalaya. Their ordinary resorts are the tracts of hill-forests occurring in many parts of India, Burma, the Malay Peninsula, and probably also of Cochin-China and Siam. These cattle are unknown in any of the Indo-Malay islands ; but there is a tradition that they formerly existed in Ceylon, although if this were really the case, it is probable they were introduced. The north-western range of the species in India is probably limited by the Rajpipla Hills, in the neighbourhood of Broach ; while to the west of the eightieth parallel of latitude the northern limit is nearly coincident with the line of the Narbada valley. Along the foot of the Himalaya gaur are found in the forest-tracts as far westward as Nepal ; while to the southward of the Ganges valley they survive in many of the forests of Chutia Nagpur, Orissa, the Northern Circars, the Central Provinces, Hyderabad, Mysore, and the Western Ghats, although from some districts they have already disappeared, and are becoming scarcer in others.

The fact that cows and young bulls inhabiting dry and open districts are less darkly coloured than those from dense and damp forests is an example of a common feature among animals.

In spite of its bulk and heavy build, the gaur is very active in getting over rocky country (which is the ordinary resort of the species) ; and the manner in which a herd will make their way up an impossible-looking hill-side is little short of marvellous. Although, as already said, generally found on forest-clad hills, gaur are sometimes to be met with on the plains ; and in Mysore and the Wynad district they frequent rocky hills whose flattened, open summits afford excellent grazing-grounds, the herds ascending to elevations of from 2500 to 6000 feet above sea-level.

In the Narbada district the habits and *shikar* of gaur have been admirably described by Captain Forsyth in his *Highlands of Central India*, while Mr. G. P. Sanderson, in *Thirteen Years among the Wild Beasts of India*, has done the same for the Mysore country. Gaur are seldom seen in herds exceeding twenty head, and more frequently in small parties of from five to ten. In the Western Ghats, and doubtless in other districts, they are generally to be found on the open grass-tracts for some hours after the early morning feed, but as the sun increases in power they one by one rise to their feet and seek shelter in the surrounding forest. When driving is resorted to, the beaters should not be allowed to commence their work till the herd has in this manner betaken itself to covert, as if it is attempted while the animals are in the open, failure will most certainly ensue; and it is important to ascertain that no stragglers have been left lying down in the open. The alternative to beating is by following up the animals with the aid of native trackers, such as the Bhils and Gonds.

Although the finest bulls are solitary, a certain number of this sex keep with the herds. In writing of the herds, Mr. Sanderson says that their members "are shy and retiring in their habits, and retreat at once if intruded upon by man. They avoid the vicinity of his dwellings, and never visit the patches of cultivation in the jungle, as do wild elephants, deer, and wild hog. . . . The food of the gaur,[1] as of the wild elephant, consists chiefly of grasses, and only in a secondary degree of bamboo leaves and twigs, the thick and succulent tuberous shoots of the bamboo which appear during the rains, and of the bark of some trees. . . . Gaur feed till about nine in the morning, or later in cloudy and rainy weather; they then rest, lying down in bamboo-covert or light forest till the afternoon, when they rise to graze and drink; they also invariably lie down for some hours during the night. Although certainly quick in detecting an intruder, gaur can scarcely be considered naturally wary animals, as they seldom encounter alarms. Unsophisticated herds will frequently allow several shots to be fired at them before making off, and even then

[1] In these extracts "Gaur" is substituted for "Bison."

probably will not go far. But if subjected to frequent disturbance, they quickly become as shy as deer. . . . I have never known a case of herd-gaur attacking man, except such individuals as were wounded, and, being pursued, found themselves unable to escape."

The narrator then proceeds to state that in many of their habits gaur resemble elephants, and that herds of both may not infrequently be seen feeding together. Solitary bulls, which often show their age by the number of scars they bear on their nearly hairless hides, have a bad reputation for ferocity, being reported to charge without provocation. While admitting that this is to a certain degree the case, Mr. Sanderson accounts for it by their greater liability to being suddenly surprised while reposing than are the members of a herd, some of whom are always on the watch. And when thus surprised, like other animals, they not uncommonly attack the disturber of their slumbers.

It has long been a question whether the gaur inhabiting the countries to the eastward of the Bay of Bengal could be subspecifically distinguished from the typical Indian animal. The head of a bull obtained from Myitekyina, in Upper Burma, by Mr. Joseph Reade seems, however, to leave little doubt that the question should be answered in the affirmative, so far as regards the pyoung, or Burmese representative of the species. The result of numerous comparisons tends to show that the skulls of gaur from the countries on the eastern side of the Bay of Bengal differ from those of the Indian animal by the greater breadth across the forehead. The Burmese gaur is also stated to be taller than the Indian animal, with the ridge on the shoulder extending farther along the back, the concavity of the forehead more pronounced, and the horns larger, heavier, and shorter, with the tips seldom worn. It used to be stated that the gaur is characterised by the absence of a dewlap, and of many specimens this appears to be true. On the other hand, it appears, as stated above, that in Travancore some of the old bulls display a strongly developed dewlap, although this character is not constant in the district. More important still is a statement by Mr. C. W. A. Bruce, to the effect that Burmese gaur are always distinguished by the presence of a large dewlap in the old bulls, as well as by their very dark colour.

FIG. 5.—Head of Burmese Gaur, or Pyoung, from Mr. Reade's specimen.

Unfortunately, Mr. Reade's specimen does not exhibit the whole of the throat, but sufficient remains to show not only that there was a well-marked dewlap, but that the upper portion of this, at any rate, carries a tuft of long black hair. Such a throat-fringe is unknown in Indian gaur, and its occurrence in the Burmese form seems sufficient to indicate the racial distinctness of the latter. In the type specimen (fig. 5) the hair of the face is marked by a number of small light-coloured spots, very similar in hue to the light area on the forehead; whether, however, this is anything more than an individual peculiarity, I am unable to say. Very noticeable is a band of tawny hair immediately above the naked portion of the muzzle, which is always light-coloured in gaur. A trace of this tawny band is observable in the plate accompanying a notice by Dr. W. T. Blanford of a young bull from the Malay Peninsula;[1] but it is wanting in the two mounted Indian gaur in the British Museum, in which the whole of the hairy part of the muzzle is dark-coloured, with the exception of a small streak on each lip.

It may also be mentioned that the general colour of the hair of the Burmese head (both in the dark and light areas) apparently differs somewhat from that of Indian examples, although I have not had an opportunity of making an exact comparison in this respect. The horns, too, are distinctly different in appearance from those of Indian gaur, being decidedly peculiar. In old Indian bull gaur it is generally, if not invariably, the right horn that has its tip worn away by the animal constantly using this horn more than its fellow. In the Burmese specimen, on the other hand, it is the left horn that is thus worn; what value to attach to this difference it is difficult to determine.

The name *Bos gaurus readei* was suggested by myself for the Burmese gaur in the *Zoologist* for 1903, on the evidence of the head shown in fig. 5. This race is characterised by its tall stature, dark colour (nearly black), the more thickly haired and fringed ears, the presence of a well-developed dewlap carrying a tuft or fringe of long hair in the adult, the greater downward extension of the tawny colour on the forehead, and sometimes by a tawny band round the lower part of the jaw immediately above the muzzle.

If the pyoung, or Burmese gaur, is separated from the Indian animal, there can be no reasonable doubt

[1] *Proc. Zool. Soc. London*, 1890.

that the seladang, or Malay representative of the species, is likewise entitled to similar rank. This probability is converted to a certainty by the distinctive features presented by three adult bull seladang heads recently sent to London by Mr. T. R. Hubback, author of *Elephant and Seladang Hunting in Malaya*, London, 1904. In that work Mr. Hubback himself states that in adult seladang there is no dewlap, and the colour of

FIG. 6.—Head of Seladang, sent home by Mr. T. R. Hubback.

the "stockings" is dirty yellow. The heads just referred to show that the seladang has a much smaller development of the ridge between the horns than the Indian gaur, a greater extent of tawny on the forehead, and also a distinct whitish band above the muzzle. In one of the heads there is a fair development of the intercornual ridge, but in the other two the line between the horns is quite straight; in fact, if it were not for the horns, which are of the characteristic gaur type, their two heads might almost be referred to gayal.

They render it practically certain that the latter is not specifically distinct from the gaur; and it is significant in this connection that the one supposed specimen of a wild gaur was killed in Tenasserim.

In the young seladang referred to above, figured in plate xlix. of the Zoological Society's *Proceedings* for 1890, the development of the intercornual ridge appears to be slight in the front view, but is more marked in the profile sketch; possibly the latter may have been drawn from an Indian gaur.

The seladang may be named *Bos gaurus hubbacki*; a specimen presented by Mr. Hubback to the British Museum being taken as the type.

THE GAYAL, OR MITHAN

(*Bos* [*Bibos*] *frontalis*)

NATIVE NAMES.—*Gayal*, or perhaps preferably *Gaial*, HINDUSTANI; *Mithan*, *Bunerea-goru*, AND *Gavi* OR *Gabi*, ASSAMESE AND IN CHITTAGONG; *Sandung*, MANIPURI; *Shel* OR *Shio* OF THE KUKIS; *Jhongnua* OF THE MUGHIS; *Bui-sang* AND *Hui* OF THE NAGA TRIBES; *Phu* OF THE AKAS; *Siba* OF THE DAPHLA HILL TRIBES; *Nuni* AND *Tsaine*, BURMESE.

(PLATE ii, figs. 2, 2*a*)

There has been much discussion as to whether the gayal, or mithan, is a truly wild animal, or only a domesticated breed. If it be the former, there can be no question as to its right to be regarded as a distinct species, or race. If, as seems more likely, it is nothing more than a domesticated breed, then it is probably an artificial derivative from the gaur.

Although a magnificently built animal, the bull gayal never attains the same dimensions as the gaur, from which it differs by the shorter limbs, the somewhat less elevation of the dorsal ridge, the great development of the dewlap, and the form of the skull and horns. In place of the arched ridge between the horns and the concave profile of the typical gaur, we have in the gayal a straight line on the vertex of the skull between the widely separated horns, while the entire forehead is

FIG. 7.—Skull and Horns of a Bull Gayal from Tenasserim, in the collection of Mr. A. O. Hume.

flat and of great relative width and shortness. The horns, too, which are blackish, more or less mingled with yellowish, show only a slight curvature, inclining outwards and somewhat upwards, without trace of a terminal inward sweep. In the skull (fig. 7), the marked shortness of the nasal bones forms a notable point of distinction from the gaur. As regards colour, the gayal is distinctly darker than its relative, the whole of the upper-parts, with the exception of the forehead, which is frequently tawny, being in both sexes blackish brown ; the legs, from above the knees and hocks downwards, showing the usual white or yellowish "stockings." Parti-coloured, or even wholly white, gayal are stated to be by no means uncommon.

Mr. E. C. Stuart Baker of Kachar, who studied the two animals for upwards of thirteen years, has written as follows concerning the relationship between the gaur and the gayal in the *Asian* newspaper of February 20 and 27, 1900. "During the first two or three years of this period," he observes, "I held the opinion that they were identical. After this I veered round a good deal, and began to think that the reasons for considering them distinct might be right ; this because I quite failed to obtain certain necessary links between the two forms. The last two or three years, however, have produced specimens which have shown every one of these same links, and I am now forced to the conclusion that there is no difference of specific value between the two animals, such differences as do exist being principally, if not entirely, the result of domestication."

Although several of the gaur skulls figured in Mr. Baker's article are those of immature animals, yet they show evidence of a transition between the typical forms of the two animals ; this evidence being strongly supplemented by the Malay form of the gaur described above.

Such a transition does not, however, by any means invalidate the points given above as characteristic of the two animals—such features being those of their typical representatives. It may be added that, so far as the present writer's knowledge goes, it is only in the Kachar and Assam districts and Malaya that skulls intermediate between the typical gaur and the typical gayal are met with ; the Madras gaur preserving, when fully adult, the distinctive peculiarities of that animal in all cases.

There is no evidence that the gayal exists in a truly

wild condition in Northern India, and until further information is forthcoming with regard to its alleged occurrence in this state in Tenasserim, it seems advisable to accept Mr. Baker's view.

Horns of pure-bred gayal measuring 15, $14\frac{1}{2}$, 14, and $12\frac{5}{8}$ inches in length are on record; the respective basal circumference of these being $11\frac{1}{2}$, $13\frac{1}{2}$, 14, and $13\frac{1}{4}$ inches, and the tip-to-tip interval of the first, second, and fourth of these specimens being $26\frac{3}{8}$, 28, and $27\frac{3}{4}$ inches.

Gayal, in a domesticated or semi-domesticated condition, are met with among certain tribes both to the north and south of the Assam valley, in the neighbourhood of Manipur and Kachar, as well as in hill Tippera, Chittagong, and the Lushai hills as far south as Chittagong itself. Many, or all, of these domesticated gayal are allowed to run by themselves through the forest, returning to the villages of their owners at nightfall.

Horns of cow gayal (plate ii, fig. 2*a*) are much more slender than those of the bulls.

THE BANTIN, OR TSAINE

(*Bos* [*Bibos*] *sondaicus*)

NATIVE NAMES.—*Tsaine* OR *Hsaine*, BURMESE; *Bantin* AND *Sapi-utan*, MALAY

(PLATE ii, fig. 3)

The tsaine, or bantin (for the name sapi-utan, meaning forest-ox, is applied by the Malays alike to this species and the little anoa of Celebes), is the characteristic wild ox of the Malay countries; and although belonging to the same group as the gaur and the gayal, displays some of the distinctive characters of the group in a less marked degree, and thus departs less widely from the common ox. It has, for example, the ridge on the withers much less developed, and not terminating posteriorly in a distinct step; while the cows, and in the Burmese race the bulls also, are reddish-fawn coloured. Perhaps the two most distinctive features of the species are the horny callous shield on the vertex of the head between the bases of the horns, and the large white patch on the buttocks, which surrounds, although it does not include, the root of the tail. Standing from about 5 feet to at least 5 feet 9 inches in height at the withers, the bantin is a rather lighter-built animal than the gaur, with a less massive and more elongated form of head. The dewlap is imperfectly developed, the well-tufted tail descends somewhat below the level of the hocks, and the ears are proportionately smaller than in either the gaur or the gayal. Compared with those of the former animal, the horns of the bull bantin are comparatively slender and more nearly cylindrical; the only compression being found at the base of those of fully adult individuals. They are more or less rugged near their origin from the head, but are smooth for the remainder of their length. At first the direction of their sweep is outwards and somewhat upwards, but towards the tips they take an inward and slightly backward curvature. In the dried skull their bases are seen to flange out in a characteristic manner. In cows and young bulls the general colour of the short and sleek hair of the upper-parts is reddish brown, approaching chestnut: the under-parts being much lighter-coloured, sometimes even whitish or white, as are the inner surfaces of the ears, the lips, the inner side of the legs, and the rump-patch. The legs in adult cows are white from above the knees and hocks downwards to the hoofs; although in calves their outer sides are chestnut, like the body, a dark streak also running down the middle of the back. Except in the case when the rump-patch is wanting, the general distribution of colour is the same in adult bulls as in full-grown cows, but the tint of the upper-parts may be of almost any shade between dark reddish brown and blackish brown.

The typical bantin (*Bos sondaicus typicus*) is an inhabitant of Java, but an identical or nearly allied

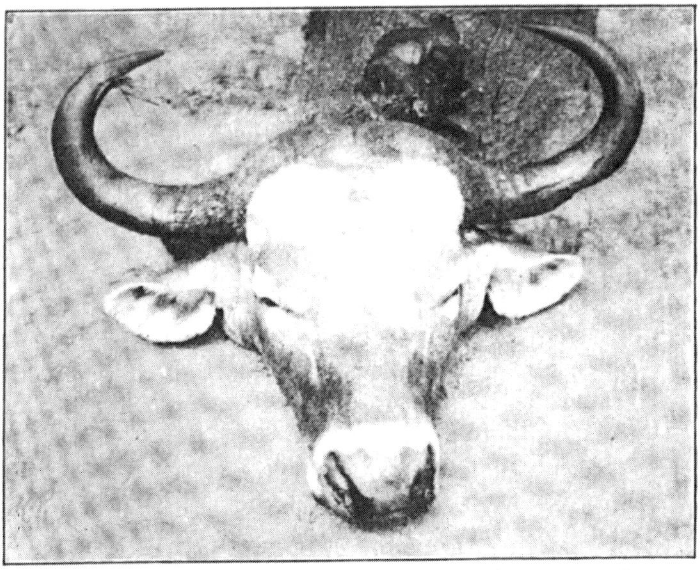

Fig. 8.—Freshly killed Head of Burmese Bantin, or Tsaine, from a specimen shot by Mr. R. McD. Hawker.

form is met with in Borneo, and probably Sumatra; the adult bulls of this typical race having the dark area of the upper-parts blackish brown or even black, and the forehead and face coloured like the back. Tame bantin are bred in the island of Bali and exported to Singapore for food. The Burmese and Malay bantins form distinct races.

In the tsaine, or Burmese bantin (*Bos sondaicus birmanicus*), the general colour of the upper-parts in adult bulls is dark chestnut, appearing darker in some lights than in others, and shading off into light brown below. The face, as exemplified by one mounted head in the British Museum, is tawny grey, with a light chestnut patch some distance above the muzzle; the margin of the lips and the inner surface of the ears being whitish, and the muzzle blackish. The head of a bull shot by the late Mr. C. W. A. Bruce in Upper Burma is very similar, but more uniformly tawny. Very old bulls may apparently become darker. With the exception that the upper part of the fore-legs is darkish grey, the rest of the coloration is similar to that of the typical race. Young bulls, in which the white markings are less distinct, are lighter and brighter in colour. At all ages the cows are bright reddish chestnut, with the face somewhat paler than the back, especially on the forehead, round the eyes, and near the muzzle, where, like the under-parts and the lower portion of the legs, it becomes dirty white. The specimens of which the height has been recorded do not run so large as the typical Javan race, a bull standing 5 feet 4½ inches, and a cow 5 feet 1 inch at the withers. In the notes quoted below it will be seen that there are considerable variations from the above type of coloration.

The Burmese race of the bantin is found in Burma, Pegu, and Arakan, whence it may perhaps extend northwards to the hill ranges east of Chittagong. Bantin also occur in Manipur, but these, as mentioned below, may belong to another race. For accounts of the Burmese bantin I am indebted to Major Evans, and Mr. C. W. A. Bruce, the latter of whom wrote in the *Asian* newspaper of October 10, 1899, under the initials C. W. A. B. as follows:—

The Burmese distinguish three varieties of tsaine, viz.—(*a*) The common light-red bulls and chestnut cows called by them Tsaine Bya. (*b*) Dark chocolate bulls and cows darker chestnut than in variety (*a*);

Tsaine Nyo of the Burmans; sometimes this variety is spoken of as Tsaine Mwe. (*c*) Dark-faced bulls with red bodies, Tsaine Ni of the Burmans. I have shot bulls of all three varieties, and the differences are well marked, especially so in the case of the tsaine nyo, which, except in shape and in the position of the white markings, might be another species altogether.

All three varieties inhabit the same kind of jungle and may be found in the same forest, but I have never seen herds containing two of the above varieties in the same herd. All herds I have seen have consisted of individuals of one variety only.

Since all these varieties occur in the same area they cannot be regarded as local races, although the alleged differences in the colour of the different herds is remarkable.

In all parts of their habitat bantin frequent less hilly ground than gaur, and are more often found in grass-jungles, or grass-jungles with scattered trees, than in thick forest.

The following notes on the habits of the Burmese bantin are abbreviated from Mr. Bruce's account. During the hot weather these animals wander about the plains of engdain forest, consisting mainly of the in-tree (*Dipterocarpus tuberculatus*). This tree is gregarious and usually has an undergrowth of coarse grass, thekai (*Imperata cylindrica*), or "kain" (*Saccharum* sp.). All engdain forests are broken up by open expanses devoid of tree-growth, but covered with thekai grass. Such places are known to the Burmese as kwins; depressions between plateaux in the engdain devoid of tree-growth also occur. These are usually covered with kain grass. In April the grass, as a rule, gets burnt off by forest-fires, and it is to eat the tender young shoots of the new growth of the two varieties of grasses that the tsaine frequent the plains, though they are also found in these places at other times of the year, particularly in the cold weather. They also eat leaves, shoots of bamboos, and fruits of trees, but prefer grass. In the hot weather the engdain forest is a sure find for tsaine. They occasionally go into the foot-hills, if there are any adjoining, to sleep during the day, descending again about 4.30 P.M., and returning at about 9 A.M.; but I have found tsaine feeding in the middle of the day in the height of the hot weather, and have also seen them sleeping in the engdain, under the sparse shade of a big in-tree. I have never found tsaine high up in the hills, and doubt if they go much over 2000 feet above sea-level. In the rains, when the new bamboo-shoots are sprouting, they leave the engdain entirely, and frequent bamboo-forest to feed, like many other animals in Burma, on these shoots. They feed mostly at night, but also at intervals throughout the day, and do not seem to mind heat at all. They are fond of frequenting salt-licks; as well as licks of a peculiar light-grey earth (*myehnan*), the "smelling-earth" of the Burmese, usually found in the banks of dry nalas in the engdain, into which the tsaine scrape holes with their tongues. Bulls, especially solitary ones, are very fond of butting down young trees along the path they may be travelling, and the strength exerted to break some of these must be considerable. I have never heard a tsaine calling like a gaur, and the Burmese say they make no sound, except the snort of alarm or warning. This is very similar to that of the gaur, but more prolonged and only a single instead of a double snort. On alarming a herd more than one snort may be noticed, but these are probably made by different individuals. I once came across a young tsaine asleep in a patch of unburnt grass in engdain-jungle; which bolted in the direction numerous footsteps indicated a herd had travelled. This was in May, and the animal was probably very young, and had been hidden by its mother while the herd was grazing. As all, or nearly all, the herds seen in April and May had young calves with them, the young are probably born at the beginning of the hot season. The sense of smell in tsaine is very keen; but hearing and sight seem badly developed, as I have often watched tsaine, which, if I remained perfectly still, have either gone on grazing or moved slowly away if the wind was favourable. Solitary bulls are more wary than herds, and on being disturbed usually dash straight off and travel considerable distances. The members of a herd snort, however, on being alarmed, dash off for 100 yards or so, and then stop for a few seconds to look round. They are not particularly dangerous; I have never been charged by one, and the Burmese show less fear of tsaine, wounded or unwounded, than they do of gaur. Only twice have I seen a tsaine bull prepare to charge, and each time, as the ground was open, I was able to stop his intention.

The Burmese say that if you lie down flat, you are safe from a charging gaur, as he cannot pierce you with his horns and will not tread on you, but that you are not safe in the same position from a tsaine. The horns of a tsaine bull diverge at right angles to the face, whereas those of a gaur are nearly in the same line as the face.

As regards the number of tsaine in a herd there is considerable variation. I have met two females and one calf alone, as well as solitary bulls; but it is usual to find a herd of, say, seven to twelve cows and a few calves with one bull. The smallest herd I have seen consisted of a bull, two cows, and a calf; while the biggest comprised about twenty cows, numerous calves, and one magnificent bull, although there may have been more. I never got a shot, as the animals saw me before I saw them, and dashed off, and as it was evening, there was no hope of coming up with them before dark. The track is more heart-shaped and pointed than that of the gaur, and also differs in size.

As already mentioned, bantin occur in the Manipur district, especially in the Kubbu valley between Manipur and Northern Burma; and there is considerable probability that these are subspecifically distinct from the Burmese animal.

For information with regard to the Manipur bantin I am indebted to Captain H. S. Wood, who states that the bulls stand about 5 feet at the shoulder, and are red at all ages, while they show no white patch on the buttocks, although this is fully developed in the cows. The bulls have comparatively small ears ; and their general colour is dark red, passing into greyish white on the face, the under surface of the body, and the inside of the legs. They have no dark streak running down the back ; the front of the fore-legs above the knee is reddish black ; the tip and front margin of the ears are deep velvety black ; the eye is encircled with a greyish white ring ; while the front and sides of the upper part of the head are tawny white, the naked muzzle being greyish black. In the cows the ears are larger, and the general colour of the upper-parts light red, with a dark streak running down the middle of the back, but no black on the ears or the front of the fore-legs. The under surface of the body, the legs from the knees and hocks to the hoofs, and the rump-patch are pure white. A cow measured by Captain Wood stood 4 feet 10 inches at the withers.

If the absence of the white rump-patch be a constant feature in the bulls, and the presence of a dark dorsal streak an equally distinctive feature of the cows, there would seem little doubt as to the racial distinctness of the Manipur bantin. Skins of both sexes of the Burmese and the Manipuri bantin are much needed ; and until these are available the distinctive features and the range of colour-variation in either cannot be properly determined.

Although the bantin is represented in parts of the Malay Peninsula, it appears to be very scarce and local ; and there are no skins available for comparison. According to the late Mr. W. Davison (*Proc. Zool. Soc.* 1889, p. 448), a bull from the Malay Peninsula, apparently referable to *B. sondaicus*, had the lower part of the legs reddish instead of white.

In 1905 I received from Mr. H. C. Robinson, curator of the Selangor State Museum, the skull of a reputed wild ox from the Malay Peninsula, characterised by very small horns (some 6 inches in length). It belonged to an animal shot by Capt. J. C. Lamprey, of the Malay States Guides, in Perak ; and is figured in the *Journal* of the Bombay Natural History Society, vol. xiii. p. 192 (1900). The animal was lost when fired at (in the evening), but the carcase was found two days later partially devoured by a tiger. Capt. Lamprey described its colour as rich reddish chestnut, with no white rump-patch, but with blackish "stockings" and muzzle.

When describing this specimen in the journal cited Mr. H. L. Butler, then curator of the Selangor Museum, expressed the opinion that it could not belong to any known race of bantin, and also quoted an extract from a work published in 1858 to the effect that the Malay bantin has no rump-patch and very small horns, although not unlike in other respects to the domesticated bantin of Bali. A young cow, stated to be 6 feet 2 inches at the shoulder (!), is described as brown in colour with dirty white feet.

If, as seems probable, Captain Lamprey's specimen is a female both the above descriptions refer to cows. In Davison's description of the bull the general colour is said to be blackish, with reddish stockings ; the horns are stated to be large, and no mention is made of a white rump-patch.

The available evidence thus points to the conclusion that the Malay bantin has no white rump-patch, and "stockings" varying in colour from dirty white to blackish or reddish, while the females have very small horns. In that the old bulls are stated to be dark-coloured, and the young and cows rufous, the description accords with the Javan and Bornean rather than with the tsaine or Burmese race of the bantin, in which both sexes are fawn-coloured.

If the foregoing data are trustworthy there seems to be decisive evidence that the Malay sapi-utan is a distinct form, although apparently a race of the bantin rather than a distinct species. The skull from Perak referred to above was presented by Mr. Robinson to the British Museum, and has been made by myself[1] the type of the Malay race, with the name of *Bos sondaicus butleri*.

Assuming the specimens mentioned above to be rightly identified, the most interesting feature about the Malay bantin is the extremely small size of the horns of the cows, for in this respect it appears to connect the typical bantin with the extinct *Bos etruscus* of the Upper Tertiary deposits of the Val d'Arno, in which the cows are hornless. *Bos etruscus* was long ago regarded by the late Professor Rütimeyer as nearly related to *B. sondaicus*, and the relationship now seems to be made still closer. In fact, if the data are trustworthy, the Malay sapi-utan seem to be the primitive type of bantin, connecting those races in which the cows have long horns with *B. etruscus*. This is in harmony with the fact that the Malay fauna includes several survivors of ancient types.

THE YAK

(*Bos* [*Poëphagus*] *grunniens*)

NATIVE NAMES.—*Dong*, *Brong-dong* (wild race), *Pegu* (domesticated breed), TIBETAN; *Yak*, LADAKI AND IN NORTH KUMAON; *Ban-choar*, HINDUSTANI; *Kuch-gau*, PUNJABI; *Boku* (old bull) and *Kotass*, KIRGHIZ.

(PLATE ii, figs. 4, 4*a*)

By the older naturalists the yak, or wild ox of Tibet, was almost invariably spoken of as the grunting

[1] *The Field*, vol. cv. p. 151, 1905.

ox; and so far as the domesticated breeds (from which the original description was taken) are concerned, the attribute in question is distinctive of the species. It appears, however, that the "grunting" is confined to these domesticated breeds; and it has, therefore, been proposed to regard the latter as a distinct species,

Fig. 9.—Parti-coloured and White Domesticated Yak at Woburn Abbey, from a photograph by the Duchess of Bedford.

under the name of *mutus*. This seems an unnecessary refinement, and the most that would be justifiable in this direction would be to designate the wild race as *Bos grunniens mutus*; it is true that such a combination of names would involve a contradiction, but such inconsistencies are not regarded as important by naturalists.

Structurally the yak appears to be closely allied to the bisons, of which group it may be regarded as an aberrant member specially modified by long isolation and the high elevation at which it lives.

How great is the elevation above the sea-level at which this animal ordinarily dwells in the wild state is probably not realised by most persons; and it may perhaps assist the imagination to state that if the Tibetan plateau were at the summit of a cliff rising sheer up from the sea-shore, a yak looking over the edge would be about four miles above the level of the sea!

In addition to certain features in the skull and the setting-on of the horns, as well as in the form of the latter, the yak approximates to the bisons in the long hair with which portions of its body are clothed, and also in possessing fourteen pairs of ribs, instead of the thirteen found in the gaur and its allies; the bisons having fifteen pairs. The long hair is, however, more elongated than in the bisons, and differently disposed on the body; while the mass of bushy hair clothing the lower half of the tail serves to differentiate the yak from all its kindred.

In general build the wild bull yak is a massive, not to say clumsy-looking, animal; attaining a height of at least 5½ feet at the withers, and, according to some reports of sportsmen, falling little, if at all, below 6 feet in exceptionally fine examples. The head is generally carried low, thus tending to accentuate the elevation of the withers, which form a more or less conspicuous hump, behind which the back is fairly level, without any decided falling away at the rump. The muzzle and ears are comparatively small, there is no dewlap, and the short and stout limbs terminate in large and massive hoofs. Very characteristic of the bull yak are the long, massive, and gracefully curved black horns (fig. 10) which form some of the finest trophies of which the Indian sportsman can boast. Although slightly compressed at the base in aged bulls, yak-horns are nearly cylindrical in section and smooth throughout their length ; their curvature being at first upwards and outwards, then forwards, and finally inwards and upwards, with a slightly backward inclination in some examples. The horns of the cows (plate ii, fig. 4*a*) are much more slender than those of the

FIG. 10.—Skull and Horns of Yak, from a specimen in the British Museum.

bulls. The longest horns on record are a pair in the Museum at Lucknow, stated to measure 39 inches along the curve. Next to these is a pair measuring 38¾ inches in length, 17 in girth, and 19 between the tips.

As regards general characters, the hair on the head, back, and upper portion of the sides is comparatively short and smooth, but on the lower part of the flanks becomes elongated to form a pendent fringe extending across the shoulders and thighs; there is likewise a tuft of elongated hair on the front of the chest, and the lower half of the tail is enveloped in a huge bunch of still longer hair, reaching somewhat below the hocks. In wild yak the coat is uniformly blackish brown throughout, although showing a little white in the region of the muzzle, with a sprinkling of grey on the head and face in old animals, and tending to rusty on the back in aged bulls. The semi-domesticated yak of the elevated plateau of Rupshu are very large, and generally, if not always, as dark-coloured as their wild kindred; but in most parts of Ladak and the Tibetan districts of the Himalaya the domesticated breed is much smaller, and may be of any colour from black to white. In such breeds, which may have a strain of the Indian humped cattle in their blood, the cows (as shown in fig. 9) may be hornless. It is from the tails of such parti-coloured or white yak that the fly-whisks, or *chaories*, so much in vogue in the plains of India, are made. Pure-bred domesticated yak have two great disabilities—they will neither eat corn nor cross a bridge.

Wild yak are restricted to the plateau of Tibet, ranging from the eastern part of Ladak as far as Kansu, in North-West China, and extending northwards to the chain of the Kuen-Lun. In summer they are found at elevations between about 14,000 and 15,000 feet, and even in winter it is probable that, in Ladak at least, they seldom, if ever, descend much below 13,000 feet. So far as the writer is aware, wild yak have never been brought into Leh (11,500 feet), and it is probable that they could not exist at levels much below this. The parti-coloured domesticated breeds, as well as the small black yak frequently seen at Darjiling, will, however, thrive, under suitable conditions, at the sea-level.

In Ladak the great district for yak is the Chang-chenmo valley, and the dreary regions between this and the Upper Indus; but these animals are yearly becoming scarcer within the territories under the rule of the Maharaja of Kashmir, although reported to be numerous in Tibet proper. One of the earliest British sportsmen in the Chang-chenmo district was General A. A. Kinloch, who has given an excellent account of the habits of wild yak. A remarkably fine head belonged to an animal shot in the Kuen-Lun range by the late Mr. A. Dalgleish, who about the year 1875 was in the employ

FIG. 11.—Black Domesticated Yak at Woburn Abbey, from a photograph by the Duchess of Bedford.

of the Central Asian Trading Company. More recently yak have been shot by Mr. St. George Littledale, by Mr. H. Z. Darrah and Major P. H. G. Powell-Cotton, and others. An interesting account of yak-shooting by Mr. Edgar Phelps will be found in vol. xiii. of the *Journal* of the Bombay Natural History Society (1900).

Yak feed chiefly upon the tufts of wiry grass dotted over the arid soil of the Tibetan plateau, and grow fat upon such apparently insufficient fodder. In search of food, or merely from a roving disposition, they are in the habit of traversing long distances, and feed mostly during the early morning and evening, reposing in the daytime on some bleak hillside, where they can receive timely warning of the approach of danger. As in the case of other cattle, the old bulls are either solitary or associate in small parties of three or four ; while the herds, which in undisturbed districts may include from about half-a-score to a hundred head, are formed by the cows, young bulls, and calves. Yak will eat snow during the winter, or at very high altitudes at all seasons, when no other means of obtaining drink is available. Smell seems to be their most acute sense, hearing and sight being apparently less keenly developed.

Mr. Darrah has given the following account of a stalk after yak :—" Lying flat down, and pushing the Lee-Metford in front of me, I got behind a stone on the summit, and saw a large number of yaks in front of me, most of them some 250 to 350 yards off. It was easy enough to make out the principal bull of the herd, he was so much larger than the rest, but I could not distinguish any others of a decent size, though I saw two or three small ones. I lay where I was for some ten minutes, trying to make out which to fire at after the first shot at the big bull, but could not come to any satisfactory conclusion. The animals were entirely unconscious of danger ; some were lying down chewing the cud, and some feeding quietly. The big bull was sometimes grazing, sometimes looking about him, but all the time moving more or less to the west, that is, to my right and up the nalla. I did not like risking a shot at the distance he was off, and examined the ground to my right to see if there was any chance of getting nearer."

An opportunity for gaining a more favourable situation presenting itself, the big bull was crippled at the first shot, and soon afterwards dispatched. From the fact of his being with the herd it would seem that this stalk, which took place in August, was during the pairing-season.

THE ARNA, OR INDIAN BUFFALO

(*Bos* [*Bubalus*] *bubalis*)

NATIVE NAMES.—*Arna* (bull), *Arni* (cow), OR, MORE COMMONLY, *Arna bhainsa* AND *Jangli bhains* (*bhains* being the name of the domesticated buffalo), HINDUSTANI; *Mang* IN BHAGALPUR; *Mains*, BENGALI; *Birbiar* OF THE HO-KOLS; *Gera erumi* OF THE GONDS; *Mi Harak*, CINGALESE; *Moh*, ASSAMESE; *Siloi* OF THE KUKIS; *Gubui*, *Rili*, *Ziz*, AND *Le* OF THE NAGAS; *Misip*, KACHARI; *Iroi*, MANIPURI; *Kywai*, BURMESE; *Pana* OF THE KARENS; *Karbo* OR *Karabu*, MALAY

(PLATE ii, figs. 5, 5*a*)

Those who have seen the domesticated buffalo of Italy, Egypt, and India are acquainted with a degenerate descendant of the magnificent Indian wild buffalo, whose spread of horn exceeds that of any existing member of the *Bovidæ*. The wild animal itself is, however, known to few besides sportsmen, since only two examples have been exhibited in the London Zoological Gardens, one of which was lent in 1870, while the second (a cow) was presented by the Maharaja of Bhaonagar in 1893; but whether the former was a truly wild animal, the writer has no means of knowing.

All buffaloes differ from the other members of the genus *Bos* by the distinctly triangular section of their horns, as well as by the rounded form of the hinder part of the skull, and likewise by the sparsely haired skin, which may indeed be well-nigh naked in aged individuals. Such points of distinction are here regarded as only of subgeneric value, so that the full name of the Indian species is *Bos* (*Bubalus*) *bubalis*, but many naturalists regard *Bubalus* (as also *Bison*) in the light of a genus by itself.

From its distant cousin the African buffalo, the Indian, or, as it might perhaps be better termed, the Asiatic buffalo is distinguished by the form of the horns and the wide space by which these are separated at their bases from one another on the forehead in both sexes, as well as by the much greater length of the head, and the narrower and less densely haired ears. The profile of the head is nearly straight, and the convexity of the forehead moderate. The horns, of which male and female specimens are shown in the plate, are entirely black in colour, and curve almost in the same plane; those of bulls are much more massive than those of cows. As regards curvature, two distinct and well-marked types are recognisable. In the one, the horns curve regularly upwards from each side of the head in a semicircular manner, so as to be separated by a comparatively small interval at the tips (plate ii, fig. 5). In the other type (of which the pair represented in fig. 5*a* of the plate is a medium example) they spread almost directly outwards for the greater portion of their length, after which they curve somewhat upwards and inwards, the interval between their tips being consequently much greater than in the first type. Specimens belonging to the two sexes of each type are now exhibited in the British (Natural History) Museum.

The circular form of horn may be regarded as the typical race of the species (*Bos bubalis typicus*); while the straight type was distinguished by Brian Hodgson in the first half of last century as a distinct race or variety, under the name of *Bos bubalis macroceros.* Whether these two types constitute subspecies, or local races, in the modern acceptation of that term, or whether they are rather to be looked upon in the light of phases, is not at present evident; but in any case it is convenient to retain distinct names for them. The largest horns known are a detached pair in the British Museum, given to Sir Hans Sloane (whose collection formed the nucleus of that institution) as a fee. One of these horns measures no less than 77⅜ inches in length. The British Museum possesses the complete skull and horns of another very large bull of this type shot in Assam, and presented by Colonel Mathie; the horn-length being 65¾ inches. No such bulls appear now to be met with; and it is possible that the straight-horned type is nearly, if not completely, exterminated as a wild animal in Assam.

Apart from the above-mentioned specimens, the longest horns entered in Mr. Rowland Ward's *Records of Big Game* (5th ed.) are those of a cow measuring 70½ inches, next to which come those of a bull with a length of 70 inches.

As already mentioned, the ears of the Indian buffalo are relatively small and of somewhat tubular form, with only a few long hairs on their margins, although with a larger quantity in the interior. The tail, which terminates in a small tuft, reaches down about to the level of the hocks. Although aged animals are well-nigh nude, younger individuals have a certain amount of coarse, bristly hair all over the head and body; and it is noteworthy that, unlike the African buffalo, this hair is directed forwards from the haunches to the back of the head; a whorl on the hind-quarters marking the point at which the hair of this region commences to be directed backwards. In the typical race, and apparently also in the long-horned type, the colour of the skin and hair is ashy or blackish grey, although there may be a more or less pronounced tendency to the development of dirty white on the lower part of the legs; this being especially noticeable in domesticated breeds. In height it is probable that the largest adult bulls do not fall much, if at all, short of 6½ feet at the withers; although the maximum recorded measurement appears to be 6 feet 2½ inches (18½ hands).

The dense grass-jungles covering the alluvial flats of the Ganges and Bramaputra, from Eastern Assam to

Tirhut, form some of the favourite haunts of the wild Indian buffalo ; but the animal is also to be met with in many other parts of the peninsula, as, for instance, on the maritime plains of Orissa and Midnapur, as well as on the grass-lands of the eastern portions of the Central Provinces, especially in Mandla, Raipur, Sambulpur, and Bastar, whence it extends at least as far south as the Godaveri and Pranhita valleys. Wild buffaloes are also found in the northern districts of Ceylon, and in Burma and the Malay countries ; but whether the latter are aboriginally wild is not easy to determine. Both are referred to in the sequel.

The arna (to use a term properly restricted to the male as applicable to both sexes) is very similar in its mode of life to the Indian rhinoceros, being a grazing animal, inhabiting by preference tall grass-jungles, or reed-brakes, in which it is completely concealed, avoiding hills and rocks, and always seeking the neighbourhood of marshy swamps, in the warm mud of which it delights to wallow. Buffaloes are indeed the most water-loving of all cattle, frequently immersing their whole bodies and leaving only their heads exposed, instead of standing midleg-deep after the fashion of European cattle. Never (save for its magnificent horns) a handsome creature, the Indian buffalo looks positively hideous when a thick coat of brown mud has dried on its hide after a bath in a *jhil*, or swamp. Associating in large herds, buffaloes feed during the early morning and again at evening, while they pass the greater portion of the day in repose, either quietly chewing the cud or sleeping. When disturbed during the midday siesta, an old bull is much more likely to prove an awkward customer than is one stalked during its feeding hours. In place of their usual haunts, buffaloes may occasionally be encountered amid low scrub-jungle, but are seldom if ever seen in tree-forest. The pairing-season is in the autumn, and the calves (of which there are not unfrequently two at a birth) are

A series of skulls and horns of Indian Buffalc
Shot by H.H. the N

ıle and female (together with other trophies).
ıraja of Kuch Behar.

born in the summer; the period of gestation being ten months.

Buffalo may be hunted either by beating with a line of elephants, by tracking on a single elephant, or by walking them up on foot; the hot season, in April and June, being the best for the latter description of sport, as the long grass is then dried and broken, or burnt down, while, as water is scarce, the animals are obliged to resort to such pools as remain. Buffaloes have been known to charge even before being wounded; and when they do charge, wounded or unwounded, they generally press the attack home. The way in which a buffalo charges an elephant is described in V. Ball's *Jungle Life in India.* "Having fired or dropped all my 'express' cartridges," writes the narrator, "I fell back upon my old muzzle-loading 12-bore rifle, and then advanced; whereupon the calf ran out, being soon followed by the cow, in full charge at the elephant. Anarkalli [the elephant], not liking the aspect of things, trumpeted and turned tail, and put on a pace which fairly astonished me. All this time I had no little difficulty in keeping myself and four guns on the pad. However, as the buffalo came on I fired the heavy rifle at her with one hand, while I held on with the other. The bullet hit on the horn just as she was making a vigorous butt at Anarkalli's stern quarters. She then returned to her lair, and quite disappeared from sight by lying down. With some difficulty the mahout got the elephant back again; but as she was very nervous, I got off the pad into the branches of a tree. Presently the cow stood up, and I then gave her a shot behind the ear which immediately dropped her dead. In all she had received seven bullets, one of the 'express' balls having, strange to say, broken one of her hind-legs high up near its insertion with the pelvis. In spite of this she had run a long distance, and made the gallant charge I have described."

The head of a wild buffalo from Upper Assam in

the Indian Museum in Calcutta differs from the ordinary form by the uniformly dun-coloured hair; the skull being also distinguished by the relative shortness of the face. On account of these differences this buffalo has been made the type of a distinct race of the species, with the name of *Bos bubalis fulvus*.

The observations of Mr. H. Storey[1] seem to indicate that the wild buffalo of the northern districts of Ceylon is entitled to rank as a separate race, although it has not received a distinctive name. After stating that the horns are smaller and less regular in form than those of the buffalo of the Indian mainland, Mr. Storey observes that, "In India they seem almost all to curve boldly outward and upwards, finally curving in towards each other at the points. In Ceylon they are very irregular, and usually much shorter, though occasionally they may be more massive than Indian horns. The commonest form are those curving outwards and upwards [in] crescent form, but not with the bold, almost half-circular, sweep of the Indian heads."

Information is still required concerning the buffaloes of the Malay Peninsula. The late Dr. Blanford in the *Fauna of British India* stated that "some buffaloes are also found in the wild state in Burma and the Malay Peninsula, but it is uncertain whether they are not descended from herds escaped from captivity." In 1907 the author had the opportunity of seeing a photograph of two skulls, with the horns, brought by a missionary from Singapore, which strongly suggest that the Malay buffalo is a truly wild animal. Although measurements are not available, in both skulls, which appear to be those of cows, the size and spread of the horns are as great as in good Assam specimens. More remarkable still is the fact that while the horns of one specimen are of the strongly curved form regarded as the typical *Bos bubalis*, those

[1] *Hunting and Shooting in Ceylon*, 1907.

of the other are of the straight type, to which Hodgson applied the name *macroceros*. The occurrence of these two types of horns both in Assam and the Malay Peninsula seems to indicate the advisability of regarding them as dimorphic phases rather than geographical races. As it is, nevertheless, a matter of convenience to have distinctive names for two such diverse types, there appears, as already mentioned, no good reason for ceasing to use the term *Bos bubalis macroceros* as the designation of the straight-horned type. Any authentic information that sportsmen can furnish with regard to wild buffaloes in Burma and the Malay States will be of value and interest.

MARCO POLO'S SHEEP

(*Ovis poli*)

NATIVE NAMES.—*Kuchkar* (male), *Mesh* (female), WAKHAN ; *Kulja* OR *Gulja* (male), *Arkar* (female), TURKI OF EASTERN TURKESTAN

(PLATE iii, figs. 1, 1*a*)

Although exceeded in massiveness by those of the argali, the horns of Marco Polo's sheep are longer than those of any other species of the genus *Ovis*, and thus form perhaps the most magnificent trophies yielded by the wild sheep. Since every sportsman knows the distinctive features of sheep, it will be unnecessary to consider them in detail. Apart from their horns, sheep differ markedly from the oxen in the form and structure of the muzzle, which is narrow and pointed, with the skin covered with fine velvety hairs, except for a small naked area immediately above the nostrils, and a narrow groove or cleft extending downwards from the same to divide the upper lip. In place of the two pairs found in the ox-tribe, the ewes possess a single pair of teats ; and glands are developed on the face below the eyes in most, as well as others between the hoofs in all species ; all such glands being wanting in the oxen. In all the Asiatic members of the group the tail is short ; and in none of the species is there a dewlap or a beard on the chin ; while in none do the males exhale a strong, unpleasant odour. All the species inhabiting India and Central Asia have horns in both sexes ; but while those of the rams are large and spreading, in the ewes these appendages are small, slender, and more upright. The horns of the rams, at first starting, are directed obliquely outwards from the sides of the head, and then usually form a circular or spiral curve, with the upper border at first convex, and the tips pointing outwards. In section, the horns are generally more or less triangular, while the surface is usually marked by fine parallel transverse wrinkles, separated by grooves ; and at intervals there occur lines of division marking the annual growths. Except in the bharal, the colour of the horns in the Eastern Asiatic species is some shade of yellowish olive or brown. In all wild species the hair is short, dense, stiff, and upright, unlike the wool of the European domesticated breeds, and is frequently elongated into a ruff on the throat. An important point of distinction from oxen is to be found in the characters of the upper cheek-teeth, which have tall and narrow (instead of broad) crowns.

Marco Polo's sheep is probably slightly inferior in height to the argali and of somewhat slighter build, while the horns of the rams are thinner and frequently longer. In fully adult rams the latter are long, slender, and form more than one complete circle ; typically with the front angle prominently developed, and the wrinkles on the front surface placed relatively far apart, but those on the lateral surfaces often indistinct. In the summer coat, which appears to be rather longer than in the argali, the general colour of

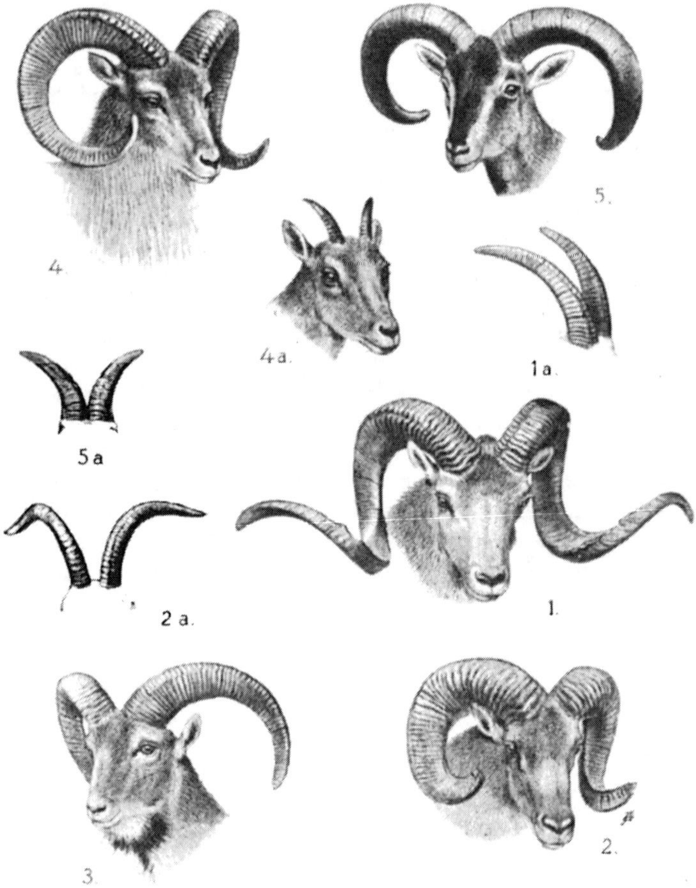

Plate III

1, 1*a*. Marco Polo's Sheep.
2, 2*a*. Tibetan Argali.
3. Shapo.
4, 4*a*. Urial.
5, 5*a*. Bharal.

the upper-parts of old rams is light speckled brown; the greater portion or the whole of the face, as well as the throat, the chest, the under-parts, the buttocks, and the legs are white; the white also extending on to the outer surface of the thighs. A black streak runs from the nape of the neck to the withers. No distinct ruff of long hairs is developed on the throat in the summer coat; but in winter, when the whole coat is considerably longer, such a ruff—pure white in colour—makes its appearance on the throat and chest. At this season, too, the fur on the back shows a more decided rufescent tinge, especially towards the boundary dividing the dark from the light areas. In the ewes during winter the neck is brown in front, and there may be a dark line extending from the head to the root of the tail, this streak being absent in summer. The horns of ewes (plate iii, fig. 1*a*) appear to be more upright, deeper, and more sharply keeled in front than in the argali; although there may be an individual variation in this respect.

A mounted male specimen of *Ovis poli* in the British Museum stands 3 feet 5 inches at the shoulder; and the weight of an adult ram is estimated at 22 stone. The four finest pairs of horns on record respectively measure 75, 73, 71, and 70 inches along the front angle; their respective basal girths being 16, 15, 15½, and 17 inches, and the tip-to-tip intervals 54½, 48, 53¾, and 52 inches.

This magnificent wild sheep has an extensive range in Central Asia, the details of which are given in *Wild Oxen, Sheep, and Goats of All Lands*. It only enters the area treated of in the present volume in the plateau north of Hunza, a district on the southern flanks of the Karakorum or Mastag range, north-west of Gilgit. It is commonly found at elevations between 10,000 and 18,000 feet above the sea-level.

If not inconvenienced by living at such a height, the sportsman will find *Ovis poli* stalking less fatiguing

Fig. 12.—Head of Marco Polo's Sheep, with horns measuring 59 inches along the curve, in the possession of Mr. David T. Hanbury.

than is the pursuit of markhor and ibex in the middle Himalaya; the reason being that the great sheep dwells on the top of the Central Asian plateau, where the country has not been cut up by the action of rivers and glaciers into the deep gorges and precipitous cliffs characteristic of the middle ranges of the Himalaya. The ground may, in fact, be described as partaking more of the nature of a rolling plain than of precipitous mountains, and difficult places are seldom encountered. Nevertheless, although the sheep themselves are not excessively wary, stalking is by no means easy, owing to the open nature of the country, so that it is seldom that the sportsman can get to closer quarters with his quarry than a distance of between two and three hundred yards. Moreover, it must not be supposed that *Ovis poli* invariably restricts itself to open country, any more than does the argali, both species crossing rugged hills in wandering from one feeding-ground to another, or in retiring to places of safety. An example of the precipitous country to which *O. poli* will sometimes betake itself is afforded by the photograph of a living specimen in Mr. R. P. Cobbold's *Innermost Asia*, where the animal is shown standing on the face of a cliff which would try the powers of an ibex.

The general habits of this species appear similar to those of other wild sheep; the large flocks being composed of ewes of all ages and young males, while the old rams go by themselves in small parties of from two or three to eight or ten, and occasionally more. In summer the parties of old males keep to the highest accessible ground; but in winter, when many perish from starvation, they seek lower levels. It is not, however, from shortness of food alone that their numbers are diminished, for in the winter of 1897-98 rinderpest raged among the flocks on the Pamirs to such an extent that in certain districts an almost clean sweep was made of them.

The enormous weight of their horns causes the old rams when galloping to keep their heads nearly erect, instead of stretched out ; and from their length the old rams cannot touch the ground with any part of the head except the muzzle.

When running at top speed at high elevations, these sheep frequently show signs of shortness of wind by opening their mouths ; up-hill they never go at a great pace, being compelled to halt from time to time to take breath. As a rule, they avoid snow-fields, and display great care in steering clear of drifts and snow-filled gullies. After grazing during the early morning, they spend most of the day in repose, feeding again about three or four in the afternoon. This, however, is in summer, and in the short winter day their midday hours of repose are probably shortened. On the way to and from their grazing-grounds the old rams frequently butt at one another after the manner of domesticated sheep, when the sound of their clashing horns is audible at a great distance ; a low kind of grunt being uttered during these combats. When danger threatens, these sheep stare at the intruder and stamp with their fore-feet before taking to flight in precisely the same manner as the domesticated breeds.

THE TIBETAN ARGALI, OR HODGSON'S SHEEP

(*Ovis ammon hodgsoni*)

NATIVE NAMES.—*Nyan* (male), *Nyanmo* (female), LADAKI ; *Nyang*, *Nyand*, AND *Hyan*, TIBETAN

(PLATE iii, figs. 2, 2*a*)

Although often regarded as a species by itself, the nyan of Ladak comes so close to the typical *Ovis ammon* of the Altai, that it is best classed as a local race of the latter. The males of the argali appear to be the largest of all wild sheep, and are characterised by their massive horns, in which the basal girth is very large, and both the front and lateral surfaces are very broad. In most cases both the inner and outer front angles of the horns are rounded off in the basal portion of their length, and the transverse wrinkles are numerous and closely approximated, with the intervening grooves deep, and strongly developed on both the front and lateral surfaces. As regards curvature, the horns form a spiral varying from somewhat less to considerably more than a complete circle. In the ewes (plate iii, fig. 2*a*) the horns are much smaller and more erect, with a backwards and outwards curvature, becoming thin and strap-like towards the extremities. In winter the hair is comparatively short, close, and coarse; but in summer, and more especially in aged rams, it is short and thin, recalling that of a closely-clipped horse. There may be an abundant ruff of long white hair on the throat. On the upper-parts the general colour in the rams varies from wood-brown in winter to a kind of speckled whitey brown in summer, at least in aged individuals. There is a more or less distinct white disk on the buttocks (most developed in winter); the face and front of the legs vary from whitey brown to brown, according to season and race; the inner side of the limbs and most of the under-parts are whitish; but the thighs are always dark like the back. Ewes apparently show less white on the face, legs, and rump, and may have a tuft of longish hair on the nape of the neck.

The general characters of the horns of adult rams of the typical *O. ammon* are so different from those of *O. poli* that there is no difficulty in distinguishing between the two animals, which are further differentiated by colour, the former having the outer surface of the thighs coloured like the back, while in the latter it is white. In the Tibetan race, where they are often more angulated, the horns are much more massive than those of *poli*, as well as considerably shorter.

In the Tibetan, or Hodgson's, argali the height at the shoulder ranges from about 3½ feet to 3 feet 10 inches. The horns of the rams are less massive than in the typical race, and form a less open spiral, which does not exceed, and often falls short of, a complete circle. In nearly all instances their tips are broken, the wrinkles are but moderately prominent, and the outer front angle is, even in adult examples, frequently distinct. Adult rams have a ruff of long whitish hair on the sides of the neck and the throat, believed to be present at all seasons; and there is a crest of dark hair running from the nape of the neck to the withers. In the ewes there is a shorter ruff of dark hair on the throat.

Apart from the throat-ruff, the colour is very similar to that of the typical race, but old rams seem to be darker. Greyish brown is the general colour of the upper-parts, the throat, chest, under-parts, and inner side of the limbs being white or whitish. The whole of the upper portion of the face is brown, at least in the winter dress, but the lower part is generally somewhat lighter. There is also a dark streak down the front of the legs below the knees and hocks in the winter dress; but whether in summer these parts become lighter is not ascertained, specimens in the short summer coat being lacking.

In a ram killed by Major Greenway the length from the nose to the tip of the tail was 76 inches, and the weight about 212 lbs. In one shot by Major Powell-Cotton, of which the age was estimated at ten years, the shoulder-height was 3 feet 9 inches, the girth 4 feet 2 inches, and the weight 205 lbs. The largest pair of horns on record, obtained by Mr. Arnold Pike in Ladak, measures 57 inches along the front curve, and has a girth of 18¾ inches, and a tip-to-tip interval of 29 inches. The four next largest specimens recorded by Mr. Rowland Ward respectively measure 50½, 50, 49¾, and 48½ inches in length; their basal girths being 18¼, 17, 18, and 19 inches.

The range of this sheep includes the plateau of Tibet, extending from Northern Ladak at least as far east as the districts north of Sikhim, and northwards to the Kuen-lun and perhaps beyond the Mustag range, while farther east it may embrace the southern confines of the Gobi Desert. Unknown to the southward of the main Himalayan axis, and not even entering Zanskar, the argali is seldom found in Ladak, where Chang-chenmo is one of its favourite resorts, below 15,000 feet, although descending to 12,000 feet during winter.

Although the large flocks of ewes and young rams met with in Chang-chenmo may be approached within a short distance, the case is different with the old rams, which in summer keep apart from the flocks and resort to the highest grounds on which subsistence is procurable. Even when in broken country, stalking is difficult enough, but when in the open, it requires all the skill of the sportsman to get within range. Younger rams may be seen with two or three ewes even in the summer. As the general habits of the nyan are practically the same as those of Marco Polo's sheep, it will suffice to say that the pairing-season occurs in the middle of the winter, and that the lambs are born five months later—in May or June.

THE SHAPO, OR URIAL

(*Ovis vignei*)

NATIVE NAMES.—*Sha*, *Shapo* (male), *Shamo* (female), LADAKI ; *Urin*, IN ASTOR ; *Guch* (male), *Mish* (female), PERSIAN ; *Koh-i-dumba* (mountain sheep), PUSHTU ; *Koch*, *Gad* (male), *Garand* (female), BALUCHI AND SINDI ; *Kar* (male), *Gad* (female), BRAHUI ; *Urial*, PUNJABI

(PLATE iii, figs. 3, 4, 4*a*)

The sha or shapo of Astor and Ladak and the urial (oorial) of the Punjab Salt Range are local races of a species distinguishable at a glance from both of the preceding kinds of wild sheep by its greatly inferior size and lighter horns. And since there is no possibility of mistaking the present animal for either of the latter, its description may be brief.

The species is closely allied to *Ovis orientalis*, the wild sheep of Armenia and North-Eastern Persia, of which the so-called *O. ophion* of the Troodos Mountains of Cyprus is nothing more than a local race. In both species the colour of the coat tends more or less markedly to rufous chestnut, the rams have a large ruff of long hair on the throat, and the ewes develop small horns. The urial, or shapo, is distinguished by the colour tending very generally to fawn, but more especially by the forward curvature of the horns, which sweep along the sides of the face, and show more or less pronounced angles bordering the flattened front surface. The old rams do not show the light saddle-mark so conspicuous in the Armenian wild sheep. So far as can at present be determined, four local forms, or races, of urial may be recognised, their distinctness from one another being based partly on actual physical differences and partly on geographical distribution.

From this it will be inferred that it will not be possible in all cases to refer a given specimen to its respective race without knowing its place of origin.

Firstly, we have the typical urin (*Ovis vignei typica*) of Astor, from which the shapo of Ladak appears to be inseparable. This Ladak urial, as it may be conveniently called, is a comparatively large sheep in which the coat is fawn-coloured rather than foxy rufous. As a rule, the horns of the old rams turn markedly inwards at their tips, and have their front angles moderately prominent.

Secondly, there is the Baluchi urial (*O. vignei blanfordi*), in which the horns tend to turn outwards at the tips, forming a more open spiral, and have the front angles prominent and occasionally showing a beaded structure. This race (at first regarded as a distinct species) was described by Mr. A. O. Hume in the *Journal* of the Asiatic Society of Bengal for 1877, on the evidence of the skull of a ram from the Kelat district of Baluchistan, in which the tips of the horns curve outwards, so as to form a very open spiral. So open, indeed, is the spiral that a portion of the inner surface (which in other urial is completely concealed) is visible in a front view. In a skull from Kelat in the British Museum the spiral is, however, much less open, and there is no marked outward divergence of the tips. Still it must evidently belong to the same race. Moreover, the presumption is that the urial from the rest of Baluchistan and Afghanistan, and, in fact, from the Trans-Indus districts in general, likewise belong to *O. v. blanfordi*, as the Indus must almost certainly form an impassable barrier to these sheep. In confirmation of this view, it may be mentioned that the horns of a very fine male urial obtained by Dr. Aitchison, when on the Delimitation Commission in Afghanistan, show a tendency to form an open spiral, and have very prominent front angles. In another head in the British Museum, from the hills north of Peshawar, the front angles are more prominent than in any Salt Range urial in the collection, and are also raised into a number of knobs, but there is no decided tendency to an out-turning of the tips, although the spiral is rather open. It is practically certain that the specimen is racially distinct from the true urial of the Cis-Indus districts. On the other hand, the urial head shown in fig. 13 has a decided outward turn of the tips of the horns, and, in fact, appears to be very similar in this and other respects to the type of *O. blanfordi*. The specimen, which belonged to the late Major F. H. Taylor, is stated to be from "the Punjab," and there is accordingly nothing to prevent its having come from the Trans-Indus districts. This race probably enters Southern Persia.

As regards the third race of the species, namely, the true urial (*O. v. cycloceros*) of the Salt Range and other hills of the Cis-Indus districts of the Punjab, this appears to be a smaller and redder animal than either of the preceding, with the horns forming a very close spiral, and showing no tendency to turn out at the tips, while their front angles are not prominent, and the anterior one is often more or less rounded off.

Finally, we have the Kopet-Dagh urial (*O. v. arkal*), from the range dividing Persia and Turkestan and the Ust-Urt plateau to the west of Lake Aral,[1] in which, as exemplified by a skull presented by Mr. St. George Littledale to the British Museum, the front surface of the horns is very broad and nearly flat, with few transverse wrinkles, but very prominent front angles. Sheep apparently referable to this race have been obtained by Major R. L. Kennion on the north side of the Elburz Range.

In the shapo or urin of Ladak and Astor the height reaches to as much as 36 inches at the withers; while the horns of old rams are massive at the base and

[1] Dr. Satunin, *Mitteil. Kaukas. Mus.*, vol. ii. p. 375, 1906, restricts *O. v. arkal* to the Ust-Urt sheep, and proposes the name *O. v. varentsowi* for the Kopet-Dagh sheep.

form a wide circle, with more or less markedly divergent tips. Their front angles are rounded to a greater or less degree, so that they do not ever appear to form distinct beads or keels, and the transverse ridges on their front edge are never very coarse. The general tone of the summer coat tends rather to brown than to red; and the ruff on the throat seems to be always smaller and mainly blackish brown.

In the thirteen largest horns of this race recorded by Mr. Rowland Ward in his book on horn-measurements the length along the front curve varies between 32¼ and 39 inches, while the basal girth ranges between 10 and 12¼ inches, although three examples fall below 11 inches.

The head shown in plate iii, fig. 3 is taken from a specimen in the British Museum shot in Ladak by Major Powell-Cotton. Although the horns are not large, the animal is fully adult, so that the characters of the ruff may apparently be taken as distinctive of the race. It will be seen that this ruff is restricted to the upper part of the throat, and is mainly formed of black or blackish brown hairs, although in front these are partially over-lain by white hairs; and it is these latter which become more developed to form the long white ruff distinctive of the Punjab and Kelat races.

The geographical range of this race of wild sheep extends from Astor, where it is known as urin, to Zanskar, Ladak, and other districts in Tibet, where it is known as sha. Eastwards the habitat extends through Gilgit to the confines of Afghanistan. In Ladak and Zanskar these sheep are found at high elevations, in comparatively open country, where the herbage is scanty and forests do not exist. In Astor and Gilgit, on the other hand, they inhabit lower levels, where there are extensive grassy tracts below the forest-belt. Their habits, allowing for the difference in the nature of the country, are probably very similar to those of the Punjab and Kelat urial.

The Shapo, or Urial

The true Salt Range urial which, as already stated, is a rather small and brightly coloured local race of *Ovis vignei*, is the only wild sheep inhabiting India proper; and since it is to be met with in localities comparatively close to civilisation, where stalking is by no means difficult, its pursuit does not entail the time and hardships inseparable from sheep-stalking in Tibet

Fig 13.—Head of Baluchi (?) Urial, from the "record" specimen formerly owned by the late Major F. H. Taylor.

and other parts of Central Asia. To the north it passes into the above-mentioned Baluchi urial.

In height the rams seldom appear to exceed about 32 inches. The summer coat is a bright rufous brown, or foxy red; and the ruff on the throat and chest attains a great development, the long hairs on the front of its upper portion being pure white in old rams. Compared with those of the shapo the horns form a less open and more compact spiral, with their tips convergent and approximating to the eyes.

In the thirteen largest specimens of Salt Range and Baluchi urial horns catalogued by Mr. Rowland Ward, the length along the front curves ranges between 32½ and 39½ inches, while the basal girth varies between 8¼ and 11 inches, six of the specimens measuring less than 10 inches. It is true that there is one specimen with a basal circumference of 11¾ inches (the length being 30¾ inches); but, speaking generally, it may be affirmed that urial horns are of inferior girth to those of shapo.

The typical urial occurs in the Salt Range of the Punjab, whence it extends into the Cis-Indus ranges of the Western Punjab and Sind.

Urial in the Punjab are met with in low hills or on undulating ground deeply intersected with narrow gullies and ravines, usually preferring the scarped hill-sides to bush or jungle. In the Jhelam district much of the ground they frequent consists of reddish coloured rocks, against which their foxy red coats are almost invisible except at very close quarters. Both sexes are commonly seen together, although during summer the old rams separate themselves to a certain extent from the flocks, which may vary in number from as few as three or four to as many as twenty or thirty. In the Punjab the pairing-season takes place in September, and the young, of which there may be either one or two at a birth, are produced about six months later. In many of their habits urial are very like ordinary domesticated sheep, their usual cry being a bleat, while when frightened they utter a shrill whistle and stamp vigorously on the ground with their fore-feet. When the sun shines with its full power on the hill-sides and ravines where they dwell, the heat in summer becomes excessive, and the urial then seek shelter under shady rocks or among the jungle, feeding only in the comparative coolness of the mornings and evenings. In the cold season, especially when the sky is cloudy, and probably also during the rains, they may be seen on the move at all hours. They are better than argali at getting over rough and rocky ground, although decidedly inferior in this respect to bharal. In undisturbed districts they seldom wander far from their feeding-grounds, and often descend into the open fields to graze on young wheat and other crops. On the other hand, when much shot at, they retire to a distance from the grazing-grounds before reposing for the midday hours. The steep ridges and ravines among which they dwell afford excellent stalking-ground, if the sportsman can walk over the loose stones and shingle without alarming his game; but even if thus disturbed, the flock will frequently be found in an adjoining ravine.

THE BHARAL, OR BLUE SHEEP

(*Ovis* [*Pseudois*] *nahura*)

NATIVE NAMES.—*Bharal*, *Bharar*, AND *Bharut*, HINDUSTANI; *Na* OR *Sna*, LADAKI; *Wa* OR *War* IN THE SUTLEJ VALLEY; *Nervati*, NEPALI; *Nao* OR *Gnao* OF THE BHOTIAS

(PLATE iii, figs. 5, 5*a*)

The bharal or blue sheep of Tibet is markedly distinct from all other wild sheep, and makes a step in the direction of the goats. One of its most striking features is to be found in the horns, which in rams show a peculiar S-like curvature, and are rounded or sub-quadrangular at the base, with the whole surface (except for the annual rings of growth) nearly smooth, without the transverse wrinkles and grooves so characteristic of those of other Asiatic wild sheep. The horns of the ewes (plate iii, fig. 5*a*) are also unlike those of other sheep, being short, approximated at their bases, much compressed, and curving upwards and outwards in a somewhat scimitar-like fashion. Then, too, there are no traces of the glands below the eyes found in all the species of the genus hitherto noticed. Neither is the coloration less distinctive; there being a distinct black stripe running along the flanks to divide the fawn of the back from the white of the belly, as well as similar stripes down the front of all four legs, and a dark streak down the face.

In this latter respect, as well as in the absence of face-glands, the bharal is indeed more like a goat than an ordinary wild sheep, and it may consequently be asked why the species is classed among the latter rather than among the former animals, especially as the tail is longer than in other Asiatic wild sheep. The bharal lacks, however, the beard found in the males of all species of goats, as well as the unpleasant odour of the latter. Moreover, there are glands between the hoofs in all the feet, whereas in goats such glands are absent in the hind-limbs. Still the distinction between sheep and goats is slight, and the bharal forms one of the connecting links between the two groups.

In size the bharal stands about 36 inches at the withers; the build is rather heavy, the head long and narrow, the ears short, and the coat, which is thick and close, without a mane on the neck or a ruff on the throat. The general colour of the hair on the rest of the upper-parts is brownish grey with a tinge of slaty blue, tending more to brown in summer and more to slaty grey in winter; but the under-parts, the inner and hind surfaces of the legs, and the buttocks as far as the root of the tail are white. In full-grown rams the face and chest, a stripe running down the front of the legs (interrupted by a white patch at the knees), a band along the lower part of the flanks bordering the white below, as well as the terminal two-thirds of the tail, are black; these black markings being wanting in ewes at all ages. The horns are blackish olive. A full-grown bharal weighs about one hundred and thirty pounds.

The longest pair of bharal horns on record belongs to Captain W. de L. Williams, and measures 32½ inches along the curve. The two next largest are respectively 32 and 31½ inches in length, the latter having a basal circumference of 13½ inches, and a tip-to-tip interval of 22½ inches. Several other specimens have a length of 30 inches or over.

Bharal inhabit Tibet and the adjacent districts at high elevations, being seldom found in winter below 10,000 feet, and in summer ascending to between 14,000 and 16,000 feet, or even higher. Their range extends from the main axis of the Himalaya in the south to the Kuen-lun and Altyn-tag in the north. Eastwards they are known to extend as far as Moupin, in Eastern Tibet, while westwards they range to Shigar, in Baltistan, and to the neighbourhood of Gujhal, in the upper Hunza valley near Passu.

As bharal approximate to goats in structure and coloration, so they show certain resemblances to the latter in the matter of habits; for, although displaying an ovine habit in dwelling on open undulating country and resting at midday on or near their feeding-grounds, they are more active mountaineers than other Asiatic wild sheep, ascending steep cliffs with comparative ease, and taking to difficult places when disturbed. In the more remote valleys in the neighbourhood of Leh the traveller may occasionally stumble on a flock of bharal feeding or reposing on his line of route, as once happened to the present writer, when, with luck, two or more rams may be obtained without difficulty, since, after being fired at, the members of the flock run but a short distance before turning round to gaze at the intruder after the manner of sheep in general. Many of the valleys they frequent are strewn with boulders or masses of rock projecting through the turf, so that at a distance it is difficult to distinguish between boulders and bharal. The number of individuals in a flock commonly varies from ten or less to forty or fifty, but occasionally there may be as many as a hundred. In some districts on the upper Indus the old rams are stated to betake themselves to feeding-grounds apart from the rest of the flock; but in certain places, at any rate, both sexes may be seen together during at least a portion of the summer. It does not appear that bharal and shapo are found together, but bharal and ibex have been observed on the same ground, and bharal and tahr grazing in company.

THE SIND WILD GOAT

(*Capra hircus blythi*)

NATIVE NAMES.—*Pasang* (male), *Boz* (female), AND, COMMONLY, *Bozpasang*, PERSIAN; *Borz*, PUSHTU; *Sair*, *Phashin*, *Pachin*, AND *Borzkuhi* (female), BALUCHI; *Chank* (male), *Hit*, AND *Haraf* (female), BRAHUI; *Ter* AND *Sarah*, SINDI

(PLATE iv, figs. 1, 1*a*)

As already mentioned, goats (which include ibex) are so closely connected by means of the bharal and other aberrant species with sheep that it is difficult to draw up a definition for either group. No goat has, however, glands either on the face or between the hoofs of the hind-feet, while the bucks are furnished with a more or less conspicuous beard on the chin, and likewise exhale the well-known "goaty" odour. In the typical genus *Capra* the horns of the full-grown males, which are of great relative length, arise close together on the forehead, and are more or less compressed or angulated, springing above the plane of the forehead either in a scimitar-like curve or in a spiral. In the does the horns are much shorter and placed further apart at their bases.

The Sind wild goat—the Sind ibex of sportsmen—is a near relative of the Persian wild goat (*Capra hircus agagrus*), which is itself the wild representative of the

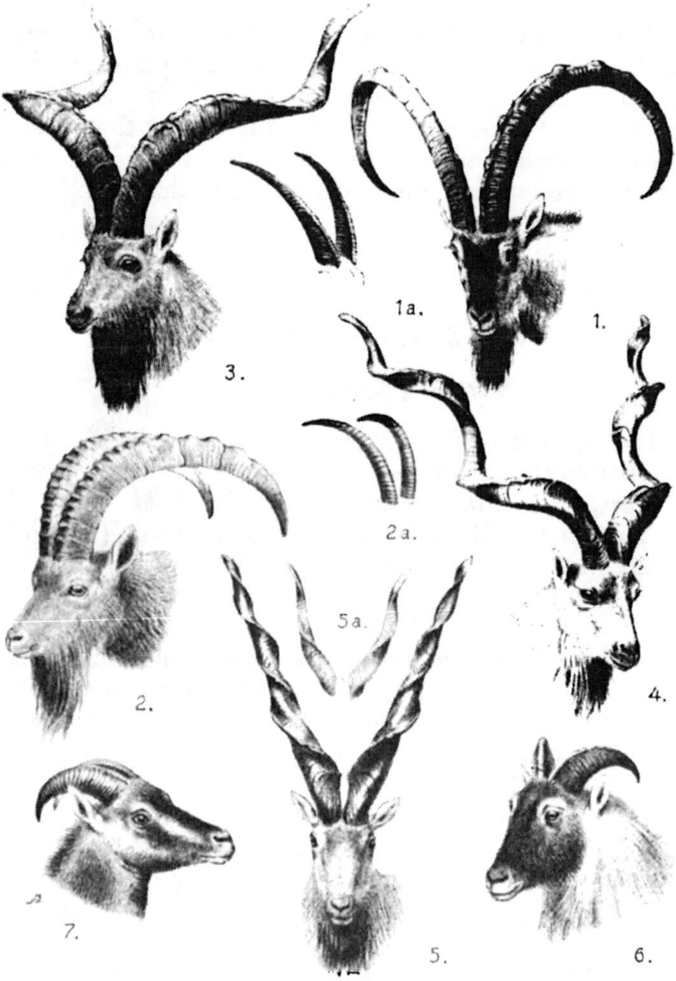

Plate IV

1, 1*a*. Sind Wild Goat.
2, 2*a*. Asiatic Ibex.
3. Astor Markhor.
4. Pir Panjal Markhor.
5, 5*a*. Suleman Markhor.
6. Tahr.
7. Nilgiri Tahr.

domesticated goat. The Persian wild goat is of comparatively slender build, standing about 37 inches at the withers. In old males the long scimitar-shaped backwardly-curving horns are compressed, with the front edge sharp and keeled for some distance above its base, after which it carries several bold and widely

Fig. 14.—A Sind Wild Goat, killed in the Lora Haman Hills, north-west of Kelat, by Sir Robert Harvey.

separated knobs. On their inner side the horns are nearly flat, externally they are convex, and posteriorly rounded off. Although occasionally directed outwards, their tips are usually inclined inwards; throughout their length they are marked by faint transverse striations, and in colour they are nearly black. In the does (plate iv, fig 1*a*) the horns are less compressed, not longer than the head, and devoid of knobs. The beard of old bucks is long, especially in winter, and occupies the whole width of the chin, but in younger ones is restricted to the middle portion. During the winter the hair on the neck and shoulders becomes markedly longer than in summer; and in the colder

FIG. 15.—Skull and Horns of Sind Wild Goat, from a specimen in the collection of Mr. A. O. Hume.

portions of its habitat the animal develops a coat of woolly under-fur, or pashm, at the base of the hairs. In winter the general colour of the under-parts may be described as some shade of brownish grey, and in summer as reddish brown; but at all seasons very old bucks tend to become paler. On the under surface, as well as on the inner sides of the buttocks and thighs, the hair is white or whitish. Although some degree of individual variation is observable in the extent and form of the black and white markings, it may be stated, speaking generally, that in the full-grown and sub-adult bucks the face, a broad streak from the nape of the neck to the root of the tail, the whole of the latter, a collar on the neck expanding below into a breastplate, the throat, the chin, the beard, the front surface of the legs, with the exception of the knees, and a stripe along the flanks defining the brown of the back from the white of the under-parts and joining the dark streak on the front of the thighs, are dark blackish brown, passing in some examples almost into black on the beard, face, and certain other parts. The knees, the hind and inner surfaces of the fore-legs immediately below, together with the hocks and the corresponding surfaces of the lower portion of the hind-legs, are white.

Compared with the Persian animal, the Sind wild goat appears to be slightly inferior in size, with the horns of the bucks either without knobs or carrying only a few small ones. The ground-colour of the coat is likewise decidedly paler. Sometimes the neck and the fore part of the body behind the dark collar are much lighter than the rest of the animal, the bucks often showing a large patch of dirty white on each side of the neck, and having the greater part of the body behind the shoulder-collar (which is dark mahogany brown) nearly pure white. Sir Robert Harvey describes them as very different-looking animals to the specimen figured in *Wild Oxen, etc., of All Lands*. Another feature is that, in proportion to their length, the horns may be more approximated at their tips than in the Persian wild goat. The three finest pairs of horns on record respectively measure 52⅜, 48, and 46¾ inches in length, with basal girths of 7⅞, 8, and 7⅝ inches, and tip-to-tip intervals of 8¾, 20½, and 14 inches. The second specimen is an exception to the general rule in respect to the interval between the horn-tips being comparatively small.

The Sind race of the wild goat is an inhabitant of the mountains of the country from which it takes its name, as well as those of Baluchistan. In the eastern districts of the last-named country it probably passes imperceptibly into the Persian race. Whether the wild goat of Afghanistan is identical with the Persian or the Sind representative of the species is not determined.

In connection with the names of the Sind wild goat in its own country, it is interesting to note that one of its titles is *Ter*, which suggests affinity with the term *Tur*, applied to the wild goats of the Caucasus, and likewise with *Tahr*, the appellation of the Himalayan representative of the short-horned goats.

In Sind the wild goat inhabits more barren and less wooded country than does its Persian representative, and it appears to be found at no very great elevation above the sea-level. Allowing for this difference, its habits are probably very similar.

THE SAKIN, OR ASIATIC IBEX

(*Capra sibirica*)

NATIVE NAMES.—*Skin* or *Sakin* (male), *Dabmo* or *Danmo* (female), LADAKI; *Kel*, KASHMIRI; *Tangrol* IN KULA; *Buz* IN KUNAWAR; *Skin*, BALTI.

(PLATE iv, figs. 2, 2*a*)

The Asiatic or Siberian ibex is one of the handsomest of all wild goats, its long, sweeping, and boldly knotted horns being much thicker and more massive than those of the Arabian ibex, while they greatly exceed in length the horns of the Alpine ibex. Apart from the special characters of its several local races, the Asiatic ibex presents the following distinctive features. The height at the withers is between 40 and 42 inches, the general build is heavy, with the legs coarse and clumsy, and the long pointed beard occupies the middle of the chin. In the scimitar-shaped horns of the males the front surface is broad, with no bevelling-away of the outer edge, and bears a number of prominent and thick knots or knobs, of which the outer is almost as much developed as the inner side. In section these horns form a complete triangle, with the hinder angle compressed. Female horns are much smaller, more widely separated at their bases, and coarsely rugose or ringed, without knots; their transverse section being oval at the base but compressed above: they curve slightly backwards. The fur is coarse, dense, and somewhat brittle; along the back of the old bucks it is elongated to form a kind of crest, and in winter, at any rate, it is underlain by a thick coat of under-fur, or pashm, which may be visible at the surface during the season when the coat is shed.

The colour varies so much according to sex, age, and locality, that it is difficult to give a description applicable to all the varieties. In summer the prevailing colour of the upper-parts is, however, some shade of brown, varying from whitey brown to chocolate (in old males), and in some instances with a large buffish-white saddle on the hind part of the back, and a smaller patch of the same on the withers. The under-parts may be nearly the same colour as the back, or markedly lighter. In winter the coat is generally paler, being often yellowish or dirty white; but especially in old males in the early part of the season, it may be chocolate, with the light saddle. At all times a chocolate streak generally runs down the middle of the back; and the beard, tail, and legs are usually dark chocolate-brown, although the latter may be white on the hind surface. The females, which are smaller than their mates, are generally more uniformly coloured, being greyish brown with dark legs; but in one race they are lighter-coloured, with the under-parts pure white. The winter coat appears to become lighter as the season advances, owing to bleaching by exposure to the weather.

Although only three or four of them occur within the area covered by the present volume, it will be convenient to give a brief account of the various local races or phases of the Asiatic ibex which have received distinct scientific names.

In 1900 the present writer proposed the name *Capra sibirica wardi* for the dark-coloured ibex from Baltistan, while in the same year the Hon. Walter Rothschild bestowed the title of *C. sibirica lydekkeri* on the ibex of the Katutay range of the Irtish Altai. Subsequently the author defined and figured the Himalayan ibex as *C. sibirica sacin*, while other writers have named additional races. Still later Dr. Lorenz von Liburnau, who visited the principal museums of Europe with the object of studying Central Asian ibex, published a review of all that is known on the subject, with the description of yet other races.

As is usual when we have to deal with a large number of local races, a difficulty crops up with regard to English names. For the species in general the proper title is the Asiatic or Siberian ibex; and the various sub-species ought to be known as such-and-such races of that species. *Capra sibirica wardi* should, for instance, be called the Balti race of the Asiatic ibex. This is, however, somewhat cumbersome, and it is generally known as the Balti ibex. On the other hand, this makes it appear as a distinct species. A way out of the difficulty would be to call the Asiatic ibex the skin (= skeen), or sakin, and we should then have the Balti sakin, the Katutay sakin, etc., which would make matters simpler.

The typical *Capra sibirica*, according to Dr. von Lorenz, is from the northern slope of the Sayansk range, in the neighbourhood of Munku Sardyk to the eastward of Lake Baikal. This Sayansk ibex, or sakin, is therefore *Capra sibirica typica.* In colour the whole of the upper-parts is dirty yellowish white tending to a purer white on the middle of the back ; on the belly the hairs are brown, with bluish tips ; but the forehead, a ring round each eye, the occiput, the ears, and the sides of the neck are darker. There is a small white line on the upper and a larger one on the lower lip : a narrow dark dorsal stripe and also an indistinct shoulder-stripe are present. The hind-legs are brown in front and whitish on the outer side inferiorly, and there is some white on the hind side of the fore-foot near the lateral hoofs. Old bucks sometimes become almost wholly white. The absence of a distinct white saddle is characteristic of this race.

The ibex from the district known to Germans as the Bia Altai, in the neighbourhood of Lake Telezko (neither marked in the *Times Atlas*) has been named *C. sibirica fasciata.* It is yellowish brown above, with a dark spot on the lower lip at the angle of the mouth, and a broad horizontal black band on the lower part of the fore-leg ; there is a light patch on the back surface of the lower portion of the hind-leg, and a distinct whorl of hair on the outer side of the same ; the ears are large and rounded—lighter inside than out—and the eyes brownish red, instead of yellowish grey, as in the next race.

The Irtish ibex, or sakin, *C. sibirica altaica*, is wholly greyish brown in the summer coat, without a white saddle or neck-patch. In the latter respect it seems to agree with the typical race, from which it differs somewhat in bodily form, the shape of the horns, and colour. *Café-au-lait* brown is said to be its general colour, with a dark dorsal stripe. The horns are light-coloured, and strongly curved at the tips. This ibex occurs at Tarbagatai. In the Katutay ibex, or sakin, *C. sibirica lydekkeri* of the Katutay range of the Irtish Altai, the general colour is umber-brown, slightly lighter than that of the Thian Shan race in winter, with the face, forehead, neck-patch, a dorsal saddle, and the

Fig. 16.—The Balti Race of the Asiatic Ibex, from a specimen in the British Museum.

hind side of the lower part of the legs dirty or creamy white. The light saddle is intermediate in size between that of the Thian Shan and that of the Balti race, and much expanded in the middle over the flanks. The horns are extraordinarily massive, with very large knots.

The Kobdo ibex, *C. sibirica hagenbecki*, appears to be widely distributed in Northern Mongolia, and is of a pale breadcrust-brown colour, without a light saddle, and specially characterised by the presence of a callosity on the knee-joint. The horns have a curvature similar to those of the typical race, but the knots in the middle are larger and more approximated; while there are also differences in their contour.

The Thian Shan ibex, which ranges southward to Lake Issik Kul and Kuldja, is named *C. sibirica almasyi*; it is represented in the British Museum by specimens killed at Kuldja by Messrs. Vander-Byl and Littledale. It is lighter-coloured than *C. sibirica lydekkeri*, with a broader white saddle and much larger horns, which display several peculiarities.

The ibex of the Central Thian Shan, in the neighbourhood of Naryn, which has been separated as *C. sibirica merzbackeri*, is stated to differ from the last by the lighter colour of the dark areas, the more distinctly defined dorsal saddle, and the much shorter, more divergent, and more heavily knotted horns.

More information is required with regard to the ibex of Tashkent and the Kara-kul, for the former of which the name of *C. sibirica alaiana* and for the latter that of *C. sibirica transaliana* have been proposed. The former is said to be rufous in winter, and in summer to lack the white saddle; but both these features are probably based on error, as rufous is the summer and grey the winter tint of all these ibex. Probably the two are identical; but if they indicate a distinct race, the former name stands.

The Balti ibex, *C. sibirica wardi* (fig. 16), is a well-defined race, characterised by its dark colour, and the large white saddle, separated only by a narrow dark band from the white neck-patch. In point of size the saddle is intermediate between the relatively small one of *C. sibirica lydekkeri* and the large one of *C. sibirica sacin*. The horns are not unlike those of the Thian Shan race, but stouter, shorter, and narrower in transverse section.

As to *C. sibirica dauvergnei* from an unknown locality near or in Kashmir, it is impossible to say anything definite at present. The horns are dark-coloured.

The Himalayan ibex, *C. sibirica sacin*, as represented by a male in winter coat from the Zoji-la (between Kashmir and Dras), is characterised by the whole back and the hind part of the back of the neck being light brownish white, with only a narrow light brown dorsal stripe, becoming darker and broader near the tail. There is a narrow light greyish brown band along each flank ; the shoulders and thighs are a darker brown, the under-parts deep golden brown with a brown spot on the hinder side of the hind-foot above the hoof, and the head brownish. The horns are relatively slender.

The Ladak ibex cannot, for want of sufficient material, at present be determined.

For the Gilgit ibex, which has very slender horns, Dr. von Lorenz proposes the provisional name of *C. sibirica pedri*, after Prince Pedro of Orleans, but it cannot yet be defined.

The Afghan and Chitral ibex, which (as represented by a male from Chitral in the summer coat) has no distinct light saddle, and small and slender light-coloured horns, Dr. von Lorenz considers will probably be found to represent yet another race. It may be suggested, however, that (at all events so far as the Chitral animal is concerned) it is not really distinct from the Gilgit race.

Of the ibex found in Northern Sikhim and to the north of Lhasa nothing definite is known.

The longest horns of the Asiatic ibex (including all its races) recorded in Mr. Rowland Ward's book measure 57⅜ inches along the curve, and were obtained from the Thian Shan, while a pair of 56 inches came from the Tagdumbash district. Horns from the neighbourhood of Gilgit and Baltistan are known of which the respective lengths are 54¾, 53¼, and 52 inches, while the basal girth ranges from 10 to 11½ inches. In the Himalayan race the maximum recorded length is 51½ inches.

So much has been written with regard to the habits of the Asiatic ibex, that a short notice will suffice on this occasion. Mr. Darrah, whose specimens were obtained in the Gilgit district, has given, in *Sport in the Highlands of Kashmir*, the following excellent account. "Ibex and markhor seem only to move morning and evening. During the day they lie in covert, or under rocks, or on snow, usually in some inaccessible spot, far up on the ranges amongst which they are found. They go downwards in the evening for the sake of such grazing as the barren mountains they frequent produce, which is naturally best at the lowest elevations. In the mornings they graze their way upwards again to the places they occupy during the day. Here, while the others sleep, one or two of the herd carefully watch the hill-sides below them, ready to give the alarm at the first appearance of danger. Consequently they cannot be approached from below at all. And from above they are almost equally hard to reach, though for different reasons. Ibex delight in snow, and usually get up as far as possible—so far, indeed, that it is generally a practical impossibility to get above them. . . . Such being the habits of these two species of goat, the midday halt became a necessity, and the morning and evening were alone devoted to searching the hillsides."

The same writer, like all those who have described ibex-stalking, was much struck with the marvellous vitality of these animals, which when hard hit will frequently go a considerable distance as if nothing were amiss. One which Mr. Darrah eventually secured travelled a long way without showing much signs of suffering, when it had received five bullets.

Exclusive of the Pir Panjal, and apparently the Kaj-nag range, the Asiatic ibex inhabits the higher elevations of the Himalaya from the neighbourhood of Kashmir at least as far eastwards as the source of the Ganges ; while, as already mentioned, it extends to Mongolia, Lhasa, and Shigatze.

THE MARKHOR

(*Capra falconeri*)

NATIVE NAMES.—*Markhor*, PUSHTU, PUNJABI, AND SOUTH KASHMIRI ; *Rache*, *Raphoche* (male), AND *Rawache* (female), LADAKI ; *Rezkuh*, *Matt* (male), AND *Hit* OR *Haraf* (female), BRAHUI ; *Pachin* AND *Sara* (male), *Buzkuhi* (female), BALUCHI.

(PLATE iv, figs. 3, 4, 5, 5*a*)

Although ibex are represented by several species and have a comparatively wide geographical distribution, the magnificent goat generally known by its Pushtu name of markhor (snake-eater) is restricted to the mountains of Afghanistan, Kashmir, Baltistan, and the neighbouring districts, where it is represented by a single species. This species varies, however, locally to such a degree in the shape of its horns that were only the extreme modifications known they would be entitled to rank as separate species ; but the intermediate forms serve to connect these types so closely as to indicate that they are really phases or races of a single variable species. In other words, the extreme types may be regarded as incipient species, requiring only the extinction of the intermediate ones to permit their being regarded in the light of full-blown species. Natives for the most part fail to distinguish by name between such local modifications; so that the native titles quoted above refer to the markhor generally.

From all other wild goats the markhor differs so decidedly that by no possibility can it be mistaken for any of its relatives; the spiral twist formed by the magnificent horns of the old bucks being unlike those of all other species of the genus *Capra*, the nearest approach being made by those of the Spanish ibex (*Capra pyrenaica*).

Inclusive of its local varieties, the markhor may be described as a heavily-built goat, standing from about 35 to 41 inches in height at the withers, with the hair of the body long and silky in the winter coat, and under-fur, or pashm, wanting. At all times of the year the old bucks are furnished with a flowing beard of long hair, extending downwards from the middle of the chin to the throat and chest, whence it spreads upwards to the base of the ears and the nape of the neck. In young bucks, on the other hand, there is none of this excessive hirsute development, the beard being confined to the chin, as in other goats. It is a peculiarity of the species that the does are provided with a beard like that of young bucks. In males the horns, which attain an enormous length and weight, and arise close together, are much compressed laterally, and twisted into a spiral, of which the front keel or ridge[1] has at first an outward direction; the form of the spiral presenting a gradation from that of an open corkscrew to that of an ordinary screw, of which the keels in front and behind form the threads. In young animals the front and back keels of the horns are sharp and distinct throughout their length, but with advancing age the keel on the front of the base

[1] In all these wild goats this ridge begins at the back of the horn and sweeps forwards, whereas in all tame goats, except the Circassian breed, the ridge begins in front and sweeps backwards.

disappears, so that the horn is here rounded. Females have much smaller horns, of the same general spiral form.

The general colour of the winter coat is some shade of grey, and that of the summer coat reddish brown, but old males tend to become more or less whitish. The under-parts, which may be whitish, are ordinarily lighter than the back ; a dark stripe runs from the

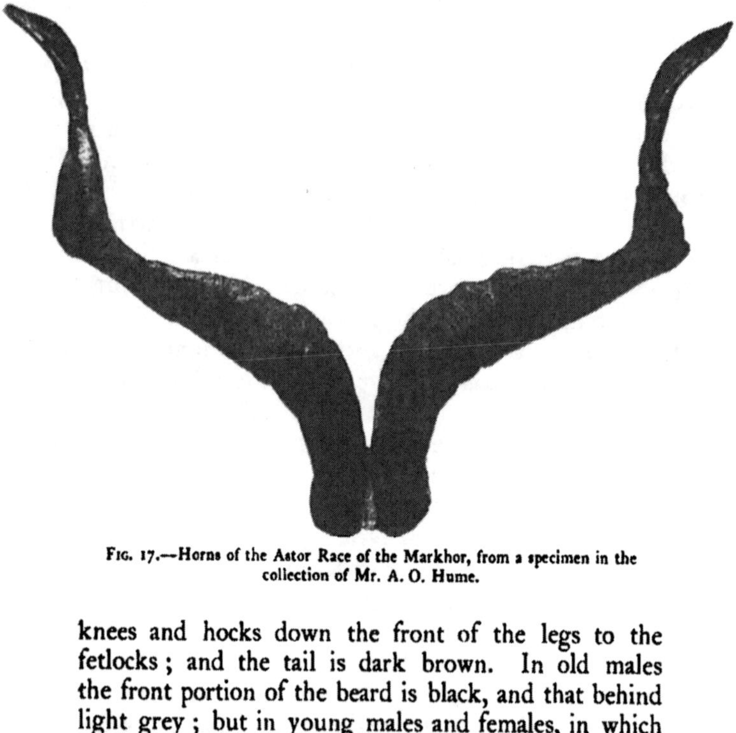

FIG. 17.—Horns of the Astor Race of the Markhor, from a specimen in the collection of Mr. A. O. Hume.

knees and hocks down the front of the legs to the fetlocks ; and the tail is dark brown. In old males the front portion of the beard is black, and that behind light grey ; but in young males and females, in which only the front portion is represented, it is wholly black. Young animals are greyish brown in colour, with a dark dorsal streak. The horns are black.

The race with the most widely spread and most openly twisted horns is the Astor markhor, in which the spiral apparently never forms more than one and a half turns: it is the typical representative of the species, so that its full title is *Capra falconeri typica.* It is found on the ranges of Astor and Baltistan; and on the confines of Hazara and Gilgit apparently passes into the Pir Panjal race. Horns from Astor are known respectively measuring 60 and 56 inches along the outside curve.

Although inhabiting a country where there are considerable patches of forest at a medium elevation, this race of the markhor is stated to resort to these only for the sake of protection from insects in summer, keeping at other times to the open. In winter it descends to comparatively low levels. Markhor are sometimes seen grazing in company with ibex. Mr. Darrah, who shot these animals to the north of the great bend of the Indus above Gilgit, in the Haramosh district, writes as follows of their general habits:—"Markhor do not like snow, and seldom go higher than the snow-line, looking for crags and rocks at that elevation. It is therefore possible sometimes to get above them, but the ground they select is usually so precipitous that nothing can be done, and they are practically as safe as ibex when lying up for the day."

Although horns of the Pir Panjal race of the markhor (*Capra falconeri cashmiriensis*), plate iv, fig. 4, are readily distinguishable from those of typical representatives of the Astor race, there are specimens so nearly intermediate between them that it is frequently difficult to decide to which they should be assigned. It is probable that such intermediate examples occur on the confines of the respective habitats of the two races. In typical Pir Panjal heads, such as the one shown in the annexed figure, the horns are less divergent and have a somewhat less open spiral, which forms from one to two complete turns. In size the animal is fully the equal of its Astor relative, standing from 40 to 41 inches at the shoulder. From the Pir Panjal range which forms the southern barrier of the vale of Kashmir, this markhor

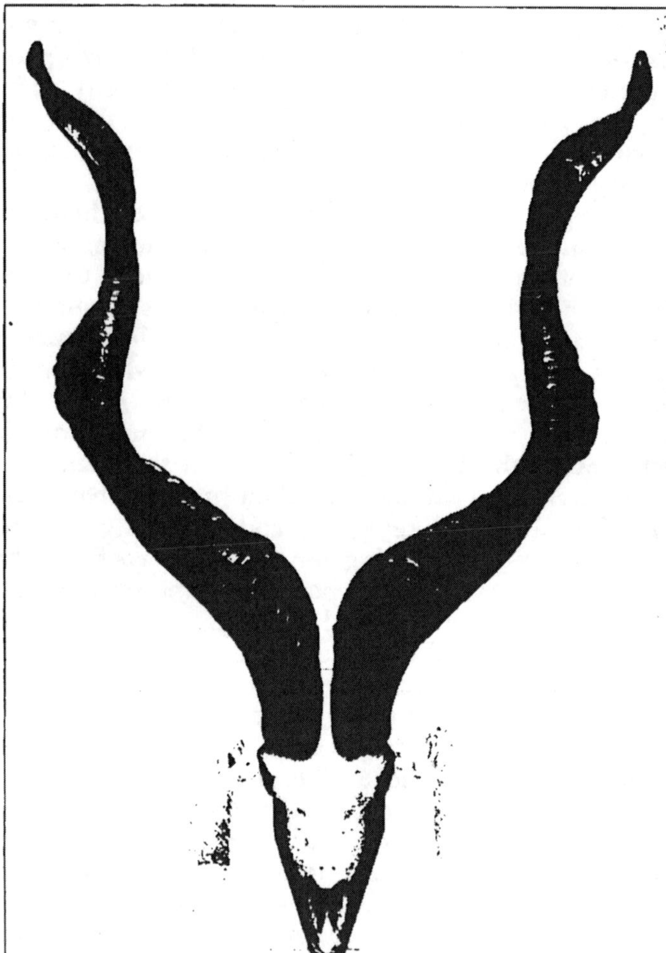

Fig. 18.—Skull and Horns of the Pir Panjal Markhor, from a specimen in the possession of Mr. A. O. Hume.

crosses the Jhelam into the Kaj-nag, which is really the north-western continuation of the Pir Panjal. Thence it appears to extend northwards into Hazara and Chilas and then towards Gilgit; but the markhor of Gilgit may be a distinct race. The longest markhor horns on record are a pair picked up on the Pir Panjal or Kaj-nag range, the length being 63 inches; other specimens from the same ranges respectively measure 59 and 56½ inches, while a pair from Gilgit reaches 58½ inches.

By the Pir Panjal shikaris it is only to the old bucks that the name markhor is assigned, the younger bucks being termed rind, and the does bakri (she-goat). In both the Pir Panjal and the Kaj-nag ranges this goat is an inhabitant of the dense forests of pine and birch clothing the scarped hillsides; its feeding-grounds being formed by the intervening grassy glades. Although generally difficult to find, the old bucks are almost sure to show themselves at the first gleam of sunshine after one of the storms which at certain seasons rage on these mountains. The late summer is the season when the old bucks keep most to dense covert. In former days markhor-shooting was one of the finest of Kashmir sports, but the numbers of old bucks with fine horns have been much reduced in recent years. A favourite starting-point to the ground is the nala joining the Jhelam valley at its bend below Naushahra.

The horns represented in fig. 19 differ to a certain extent from those of the typical Pir Panjal markhor, and perhaps indicate a distinct race. In regard to these horns Mr. Hume communicated the following note:—"The horns of this form, hitherto never seen on the entire skull, but usually on the frontal bone only, are brought down occasionally to Peshawar from Cabul, and again find their way sometimes into the Srinagar bazaar. They come from the west, and from a long way off, and that is all that can usually be learned about them. They belong to the cork-screw group, but differ from those of the two preceding races in being much slenderer, and also in the greater number of turns put in by their main ridge in any given length of horn measured straight from base to tip. In this respect they are to the Pir Panjal and Astor races what the Suleman Range ones are to those

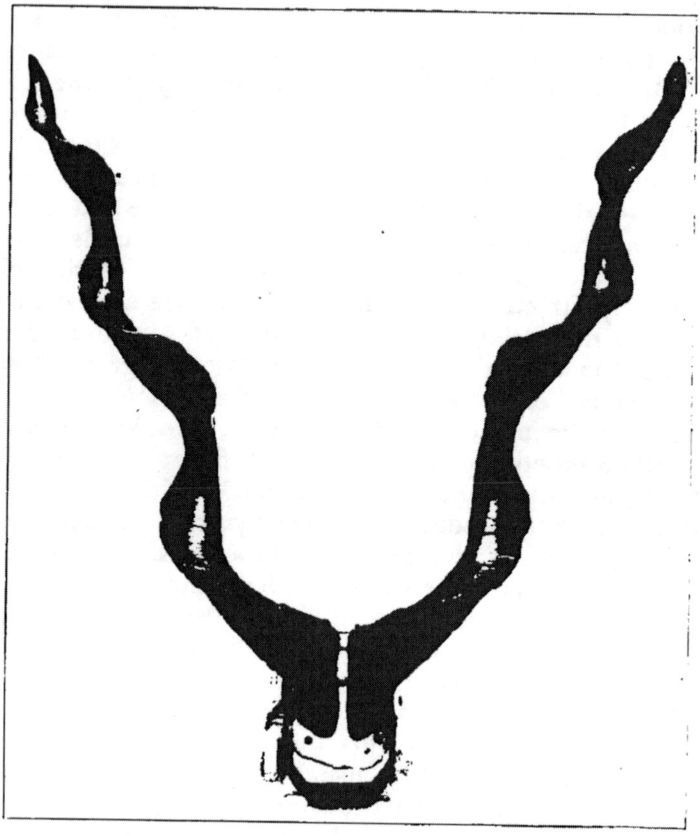

FIG. 19.—Horns of Gilgit (?) Markhor, from a specimen in the collection of Mr. A. O. Hume.

of the Cabul mountains. The horns make a regular V, broader or narrower, but the tip-to-tip measurement never, I believe, exceeds the length straight, and usually, I think, falls at least one-sixth short of this. The

Cabuli from whom the specimen figured was purchased said he believed that they came from Hazara—at the time I thought that he meant British Hazara, but I now believe he meant Afghan Hazara. I have often thought that perhaps they come from Kafiristan, and that they form a connecting link between the Pir Panjal and Cabul races."

On the other hand the intermediate character of the horns is suggestive of the Gilgit district.

The markhor (*Capra falconeri megaceros*) inhabiting the mountain ranges of Northern Afghanistan forms another stage in the gradation from the Astor to the Suleman race, its horns (fig. 20) being intermediate between those of the latter and those of the Pir Panjal race. In full-grown bucks, although nearly straight, they form a slightly open spiral, or, in other words, show a tendency towards the cork-screw type so conspicuous in the preceding races. It is probable, indeed, that a complete gradation may be found from the Pir Panjal to the Suleman type by means of the present form.

Indications of such a gradation are afforded by two heads the writer had an opportunity of seeing in 1906. They were from animals shot by a British officer in Chitral; both being fully adult males, and members of the same flock. Indeed, as regards colour and markings they were so exactly alike that they might be brothers; but there is a most remarkable difference in their horns, which in both cases are fine. In one specimen the horns diverge in the form of a V and have a comparatively close twist, being, in fact, precisely similar to those of the male from the same district figured by the present writer in plate xxvi of the Zoological Society's *Proceedings* for 1902, which undoubtedly belongs to the Cabul race of the species. In the second specimen, on the other hand, the horns are more divergent, with a more open twist, and a tendency to be U-shaped. They are, in fact, inseparable from the Pir Panjal race, as represented by the head shown in fig. 18. If it is the Pir Panjal race which occurs in the Chilas district, Chitral is just the locality where we should

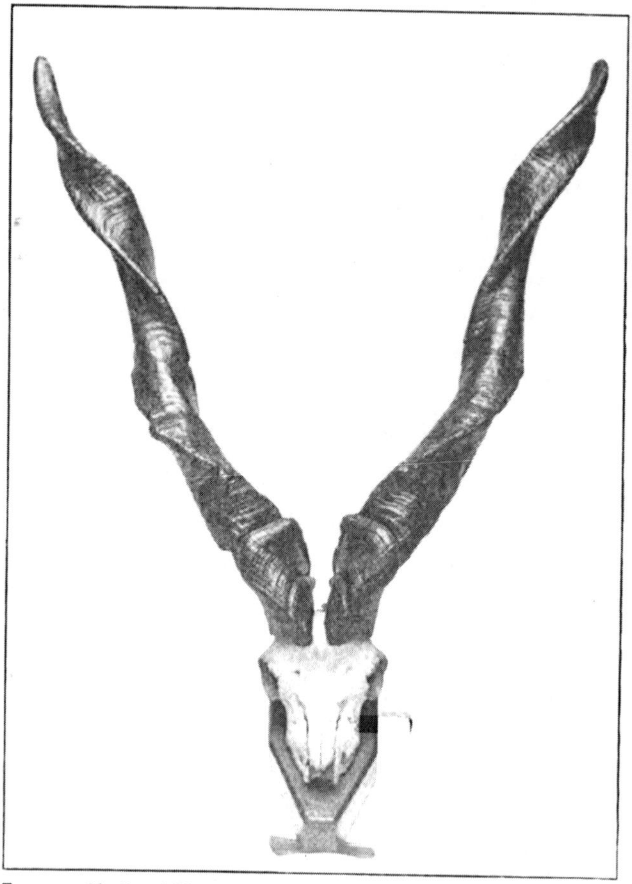

FIG. 20.—Skull and Horns of the Cabul Markhor, from a specimen in the possession of Mr. A. O. Hume.

expect that and the Cabul race to intergrade. The two specimens now under consideration are alone sufficient to demonstrate the propriety of regarding all the local forms of the markhor as races rather than species; the essential idea of races being that they should intergrade with one another, although in many instances the connecting links have died out. It may be added that information is still required with regard to the Chilas markhor. The habitat of the Cabul markhor includes the Trans-Indus mountains in the neighbourhood of Cabul, and perhaps some of those farther to the southward: thus forming the north-westerly limits of the geographical range of the species. The longest horns assigned to the present race are a pair from Chitral which measure 56 inches along the spiral.

Mr. Hume has written as follows in reference to this race:—"The Cabul horns are rare, but every specimen which I have been able to localise accurately belonged to this type. Hutton's figure of his Cabul specimen shows that it belonged to this type. Vigne's vignette, in his personal narrative, of the specimen killed for him in the Lughman Hills by Akhbar Khan shows that this too belonged to this type. Two specimens sent to me from Cabul (fig. 20) are of the same type, and so too was the one huge horn which Hutton had in his possession in 1852, and of which I noted the length at 50 inches. In reference to this he said, 'They say in Cabul that if you stand a good pair on the tips a big man can pass through them on hands and knees,' which must refer to horns at least 4 feet straight measurement. This race extends throughout the northern portions of Afghanistan which lie adjacent to Cabul—how much farther it extends in any direction is uncertain."

The markhor (*Capra falconeri jerdoni*) of the Suleman range, on the eastern frontier of Afghanistan, has been aptly designated the straight-horned race; the horns of the bucks, which never attain the dimensions of those of the Astor race, forming a perfectly straight cone (plate iv, figs. 5, 5*a*), upon which the front and back keels are wound in a sharp spiral, like the threads of a double-threaded screw. In fine examples, such as the one shown in fig. 21, two or three

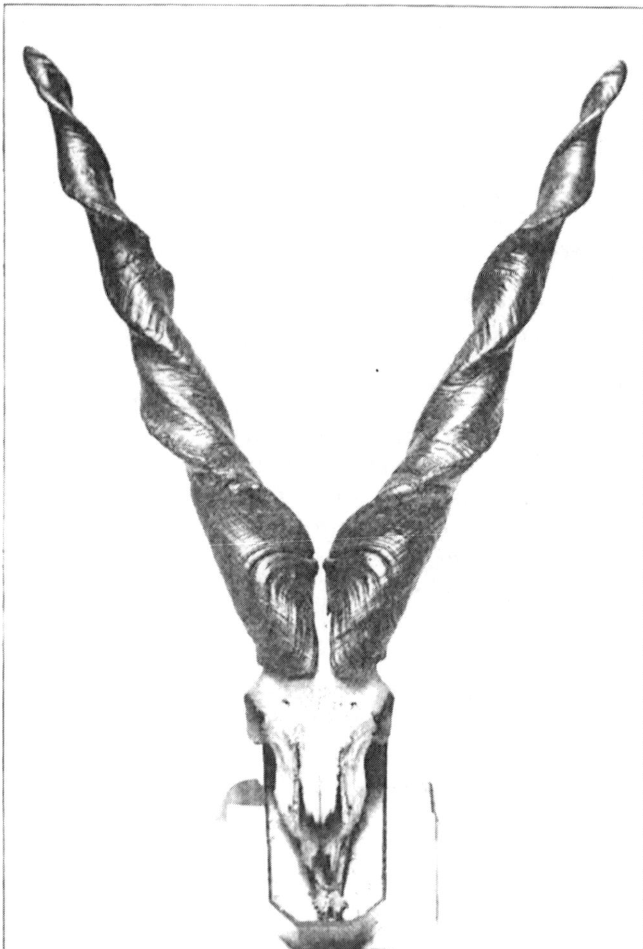

FIG. 21.—Skull and Horns of the Suleman Markhor, from a specimen in the possession of Mr. A. O. Hume.

complete turns are formed. As regards size, this markhor is a smaller animal than the typical race, its shoulder-height apparently not exceeding about 35 inches; but specimens are needed in order to test this statement. The habitat of the straight-horned markhor includes the Trans-Indus hill-ranges of the Punjab frontier, together with those of south and eastern Afghanistan and Baluchistan. In the Suleman range this markhor is found as far south as the neighbourhood of Mithankot, and it also occurs in the Quetta district, where, however, the horns are stated to show a tendency towards the assumption of a less compact spiral. The longest horn on record is a single one picked up on the Suleman range, of which the length is 48½ inches. Next to this is a pair in the British Museum from Afghanistan, measuring 39⅜ inches, while the third in point of size is the head shown in fig. 22, in which the horns are 39¼ inches in length.

The hill-ranges frequented by this race of the markhor are comparatively barren and bare, and in summer subject to a heat equalled in few parts of India. Consequently the habits of the animal must be different from those of its forest-dwelling relative on the snow-clad scarps of the Pir Panjal; but the life-history of this goat still remains to be told, and all that can be said at present is that, compared with the Astor race, the Suleman markhor is the counterpart, so far as habitat is concerned, of the urial of the Salt Range, as contrasted with the urin or shapo of Astor and Ladak.

Mr. Hume observes that "the horns of females, though smaller and slenderer, are of the same general character as those of males, but differ in two noteworthy points. First, the back or main ridge seems more rounded and never so sharply pinched-up as in the male. Second, the secondary ridge, which never, I believe, shows itself in the male lower than the end of the first half-turn of the horn, in the female runs right down on to the frontal point, and is there as prominent as the main ridge behind. In this respect female horns are half-way between those of the males of the wild and tame goats respectively of this general type.

"This race occurs right down the Suleman range

FIG. 22.—Head of the Suleman Markhor, from a specimen shot by Mr. A. J. Grant in Waziristan.

from Kohat to opposite Mithankot. It also occurs on certain high hills not far from Quetta, but not farther south in Baluchistan proper, nor, according to the

Afghans, north of Kandahar in Afghanistan, though Sir O. B. St. John considered that it extended through the higher eastern hills inland from the Suleman."

THE TAHR

(*Hemitragus jemlaicus*)

NATIVE NAMES.—*Tehr* OR *Jehr* IN THE WESTERN HIMALAYA ; *Kras* AND *Jagla*, KASHMIRI ; *Jhula* (male) AND *Tahrni* (female) IN KUNAWAR ; *Esbu* IN THE UPPER SUTLEJ VALLEY ; *Kart* IN KULU AND CHAMBA ; *Jharal*, NEPALI.

(PLATE iv, fig. 6)

In spite of the circumstance that its distinctness was pointed out and a generic name proposed for it by Brian Hodgson so far back as 1841, the Himalayan tahr was for many years included in the genus *Capra*, although it is now regarded as representing a genus apart. The short-horned goats, as the various species of tahr may be termed, are distinguished from other goats by the absence of the beard in the bucks, and the comparative shortness of the horns, which are placed close together at the base, and do not greatly exceed the length of the head. A further distinctive feature is that the horns of females are but little smaller than those of males, thus indicating a transition from other goats towards serows and gorals. The bucks exhale the same strong odour as those of other goats. The muzzle bears a small naked area ; but glands are wanting on the face and in the feet. A remarkable difference between the females of the two Indian representatives of the genus is that while one has four teats, the other bears but two. The black horns, which spring from the skull in the plane of the forehead and curve sharply backwards, are much compressed, with the front edge angulated.

The Tahr

The Himalayan tahr is a long-haired and shaggy animal; so shaggy, indeed, that stuffed specimens, in which the hair has been combed during preparation, scarcely ever exhibit this characteristic feature in perfection. In height the tahr stands from 36 to 40 inches at the withers; and it is of somewhat heavy and clumsy build, with a long, narrow, and straight face. The horns of the bucks, which are almost, if not completely, in contact at their bases, are much compressed, and for some distance flattened on both sides; the lateral surfaces being distinctly marked with transverse striæ, and the front angle forming a sharp keel, bearing at intervals small knob-like elevations. After diverging from their bases and curving sharply backwards, the horns become slightly convergent towards the tips. Although the hair on the head and face is mostly short, elsewhere it is long and soft, attaining its maximum length and shagginess on the neck, shoulders, and chest of the old bucks, where it forms a huge mane, extending at least to the knees. Darker in old males than in younger bucks and females, the general colour of the hair is reddish or dark brown; but some individuals are paler than others, and in old bucks the fore part of the mane tends to assume a whitish or hoary tinge. The hairs are pale-coloured at the root and dark brown at the tip. The face, as well as the front surfaces of the legs, are of such a dark shade of brown as to appear almost black in some examples; and a dark streak runs down the back, although in old males this becomes indistinct. In bucks the hind surface of the legs is pale or rusty red. Immature tahr of both sexes are greyish brown, while kids are very pale-coloured. The short, flattened tail is devoid of hair on its under surface; as are the hard pads, or callosities, on the knees. The female has two pairs of teats. About 200 lbs. is the approximate weight of a full-grown male. The lengths of the four largest recorded pairs of tahr-horns are $15\frac{1}{2}$, 15, $14\frac{13}{16}$, and

$14\frac{7}{8}$ inches; the basal girths of the two first examples being respectively $8\frac{1}{4}$ and $9\frac{3}{4}$ inches. Two of these specimens were obtained in Chamba; while a third came from Gahrwal, but the locality of the first is unknown.

The tahr retains its long coat at all seasons, the same being to a great extent the case with the Astor and Pir Panjal markhor. In this respect it offers a striking contrast to the Rocky Mountain goat, in which the summer coat is short; and as its habitat in summer is probably warmer than that of the latter at the same season, the difference in this respect seems inexplicable.

The tahr is a typical Himalayan animal, inhabiting the forest districts of the middle ranges of the chain from the Pir Panjal to Sikhim, and being especially abundant in the lower Wardwan valley, the Kistwar district, and Chamba. Although it is difficult to obtain accurate information as to the ranges of animals in Kashmir, the tahr does not apparently occur in the mountains to the north of that valley, or in the Kaj-nag range.

Tahr inhabit, perhaps, the worst ground on which it is possible for a large mammal to exist; and it is to this that many sportsmen owe the loss or destruction of some of their finest trophies. They are essentially forest animals, and generally prefer steep slopes, more or less clothed with trees, to bare mountain-tops, to which, however, they occasionally wander. Till autumn old bucks keep apart from the herds during summer, generally ascending to higher elevations. The pairing-season occurs in winter; the kids, of which there is usually but one at a birth, being dropped in June or July.

THE NILGIRI TAHR, OR IBEX

(*Hemitragus hylocrius*)

NATIVE NAMES.—*Warri-adu*, OR *Warri-atu*, TAMIL; *Kard-ardu*, CANARESE; *Mulla-atu*, MALABARI

(PLATE iv, fig. 7)

Although it has several local names of its own, while it is commonly known to sportsmen as the Nilgiri ibex, this species may be more appropriately termed the Nilgiri tahr, since it is a relative of the Himalayan species, with which and a third species from Southern Arabia it constitutes the genus *Hemitragus*. The isolated distribution of the present species indicates that at some former epoch conditions permitted the existence of tahr in the country between the Himalaya and the Nilgiris.

In size the Nilgiri tahr is somewhat superior to its Himalayan relative, the bucks standing from 39 to 42 inches at the withers, although the does do not appear to exceed about 35 inches. From the Himalayan species it is distinguished by the generally short and stiff coat, the prominent convexity of the outer surface of the horns, and the presence of only a single pair of teats in the female. The face exhibits a slight concavity on the forehead and a corresponding convexity at the lower part of the nose. With the exception of being lengthened to form a low and stiff mane on the back of the neck and shoulders in bucks, the hair is short, thick, and coarse, probably exhibiting little or no difference between the summer and winter coats. Almost in contact at their bases, the horns of adult bucks are nearly parallel for some distance, after which they become gradually divergent, the curvature forming a bold and regular sweep. Throughout their length they are marked by conspicuous transverse wrinkles, and while the inner surface is nearly in one plane, the outer surface is highly convex: along the front inner angle runs a sharp keel, but the hind surface is rounded off. The general colour is dark yellowish brown (greyer in does and kids), with a dark streak down the back, and becoming paler on the under surface. Old bucks are darker, being sepia-brown, passing into blackish on the face. They have a fawn-coloured ring round the eye, a grizzled grey streak down the side of the face, and a patch of the same behind the eye; but their most conspicuous mark is a large grizzled white saddle-shaped patch on the loins, which in very old bucks turns almost white. From this the patriarchs of the flock take their name of "saddle-backs." The legs, which are blackish brown in front and paler behind, are more or less grizzled in old males.

The largest horns on record have a length of 17½ inches along the front curve, with a basal circumference of 9⅞ inches; the corresponding dimensions of the second best specimen being 17 and 9¾ inches; while a third specimen measures 16¾ inches in length. The largest female horns on record have a length of 12⅜ inches, and a basal girth of 5½ inches.

The Nilgiri tahr inhabits the chief mountain ranges of Southern India, including the Nilgiris, the Anamalais, and the Western Ghats; its range extending from the latter chain nearly as far as Cape Comorin. Although occasionally found at lower levels, these goats are usually met with at elevations of between 4000 and 5000 feet.

Before its numbers had been reduced by shooting, the Nilgiri tahr was met with in flocks which included from half-a-dozen to half-a-hundred head; while in instances where two or more flocks had joined, the numbers might be considerably greater. Although occasionally seen on the upland grassy plateaux characteristic of the hills of South India, these goats prefer the scarps and crags above the forest, where they graze on patches of grass occurring in suitable spots. Their feeding-times are morning and evening, the hottest hours of the day being passed in repose and cud-chewing beneath the shelter of tall rocks. Some of the does act as sentinels, and keep watch so vigilantly that to approach within range requires all the skill of the sportsman. There does not appear to be any definite breeding-season; and it is stated that there are commonly two kids at a birth. If this be true, and also that the Himalayan species has usually but one, the smaller number of teats in the Nilgiri tahr is very remarkable. Leopards, and more rarely tigers, thin the flocks to a great extent; while the packs of dholes, or wild dogs, which hunt on the Nilgiris must likewise take their quota. Of recent years the tahr herds have been protected by law; and their numbers are now steadily increasing.

THE SEROW

(*Nemorhædus sumatrensis*)

NATIVE NAMES.—*Tau-tshiek*, BURMESE; *Kambing-utan*, MALAY; *Sarao* IN THE NORTH-WEST HIMALAYA; *Ramu*, *Halj*, *Salabhir*, KASHMIRI; *Goa* IN CHAMBA; *Aimu* IN KUNAWAR; *Yamu* IN KULU; *Tehr* IN NEPAL; *Gya* AMONG THE BHOTIAS OF SIKHIM; *Sichi* OF THE LEPCHAS.

(PLATE V, figs. 2, 2*a*)

In the case of popular names of animals which, although originally applied to one species, have been expanded so as to include a group of more or less nearly allied forms, there is often a difficulty in deciding the limits to be employed in this more extended usage. No better example of this difficulty exists than in the use of the term "antelope." Originally applied to the blackbuck of India, the name has been in later times used to denote a vast assemblage of horned animals which come under the denomination neither of cattle, sheep, nor goats ; and the question is whether it should be still further extended so as to include the European chamois, the Rocky Mountain goat, and the subject of the present notice. In the cylindrical form of their horns serows are, indeed, much more similar to some antelopes than they are to any of the goats ; but, on the other hand, in their clumsy build, heavy limbs, and stout hoofs, as well as in their habits, they undoubtedly come nearer to the goats. In order to express this dual relationship, they have been called goat-antelopes ; but as that term is cumbrous and inconvenient, it appears preferable to call them by the name by which they are known in the North-West Himalaya, viz. serow, or, correctly, sarao.

This name properly belongs to the Western Himalayan representative of the group, but the Sumatran or Burmese race (whose native name *Kambing-utan* signifies wild goat) is discussed first for the reason that while the latter was scientifically described so early as the year 1801, the Himalayan animal was not made known till 1832, when it was described by Brian Hodgson, the discoverer of so many previously unknown animals and birds of the Himalaya.

Serows are heavily-built, ungainly mountain ruminants, of about the size of an average English donkey, with long, shaggy, coarse hair. Both sexes are furnished with horns, which show little inferiority of size in females as compared with males. The horns are comparatively short, conical, and marked in the lower portion by a number of low, closely approximated rings, and partially interrupted longitudinal grooves. In colour they are jetty black ; and while their direction is at first nearly coincident with the plane of the face, towards the tips they curve slightly backwards, and at the same time diverge to a small degree from each other. Nine and a half inches is the maximum

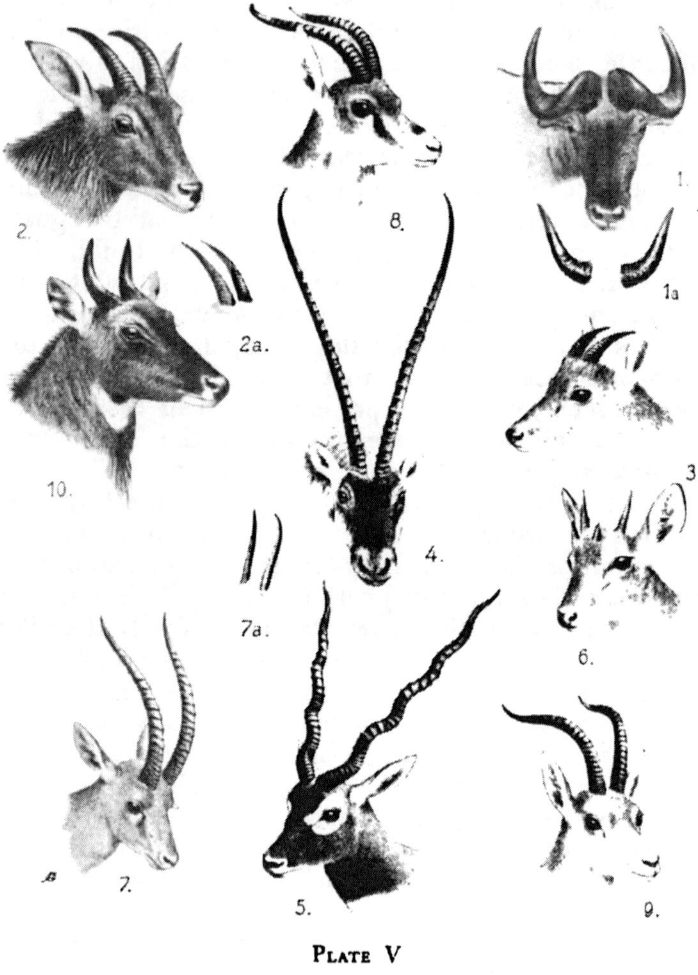

PLATE V

1, 1*a*. Takin.
2, 2*a*. Serow.
3. Goral.
4. Chiru.
5. Blackbuck.
6. Four-horned Antelope.
7, 7*a*. Chinkara Gazelle.
8. Persian Goitred Gazelle.
9. Goa Gazelle.
10. Nilgai.

recorded length of the horns of the typical Sumatran serow.

Serow are further characterised by the proportionately large size of the head, the long mule-like ears, and the short, thickly-haired tail. Face-glands, opening by a small circular orifice below each eye, are present; and the muzzle is bare and moist, like that of cattle. Glands are developed between the hoofs of all four feet, but there are none in the groin. The female is furnished with four teats. The upper cheek-teeth are generally similar to those of sheep and goats. The coarse and rather thin hair on the head and body is of moderate length, but developed so as to form a rather long mane running from the nape of the neck to the withers, which, in some instances at any rate, is white.[1] Since the colour of the Himalayan race of the species is described at some length, it will suffice to say that the typical Sumatran, or eastern, representative of the species (*Nemorhædus bubalinus typicus*) is specially characterised by the lower part of the legs being rufous, instead of white or grey, as well as by the more rufous tinge of the hair generally. Apparently also the size is not equal to that of the largest specimens of the Himalayan race, although small examples of the latter do not exceed the present race in this respect.

Probably there is a complete transition from one race to the other, since a specimen was killed by General A. A. Kinloch near Darjiling, which in point of colour was intermediate between the two. Apparently the geographical range of the typical race extends from Sumatra through the elevated tracts of Siam, Burma, and Assam, to the Eastern Himalaya. It is commonly called the Burmese serow, but as it is typically from Sumatra it is better indicated by the name of that island, if indeed the Sumatran and Burmese animals are inseparable.

In habits the Sumatran serow is doubtless identical

[1] See plate ii. of vol. xxii. of *Jardine's Naturalists' Library*, "Ruminants," pt. 2.

with the Himalayan race, although it inhabits somewhat lower elevations. The red colouring of the limbs indicates that it is a semi-melano as compared with the Himalayan race ; red or tan on the limbs and underparts in association with black above being, as Mr. R. I. Pocock has shown in the case of black-and-tan dogs, the first stage on the road to complete melanism.

The Tibetan representative of the species (*Nemorhædus sumatrensis milne-edwardsi*), originally described by the Abbé David from Moupin in Eastern Tibet, but subsequently recorded by the late Dr. J. Anderson from Yunnan, resembles the Sumatran race in the rufous lower portion of the legs, but differs by the uniformly brownish-black colour of the upper-parts. There is also a woolly under-fur to the coat, which appears to be generally wanting in the other races. Dr. Anderson states that a horn of this serow is generally an indispensable adjunct to the shoulder-bag or haversack of every Kakhyen, Shan, and Chinese peasant of Western Yunnan, from which it is suspended, and serves the purpose of a drill in repairing harness, etc.

Although often considered identical with the typical form of the species, the Arakan serow (*Nemorhædus sumatrensis rubidus*) appears entitled to be regarded as a third local race, distinguished by the extremely red tinge of the coat. It seems also to be unusually small, but further information is needed. It was originally described, as a distinct species, by Edward Blyth in 1863, under the name of *Capricornis rubida*, in his Catalogue of the Bengal Asiatic Society's Museum.

Himalayan sportsmen may often be deceived as to the nature of the game which they are pursuing owing to the circumstance that the name used in one district to denote a certain species is applied in another to a totally different animal. An example of this confusion occurs in the present case, where the serow of the North-West Himalaya is termed tehr in Nepal, where the animal to which that name is generally restricted in natural history is known as jharal. On the other hand, in Chamba the serow figures as the goa, a name properly pertaining to the Tibetan gazelle ; while in the Suleman range the name sarao is applied to the markhor, and in Sind to the wild goat.

As mentioned above, the Himalayan serow (*Nemorhædus sumatrensis bubalinus*) is a local race of the Sumatran species, from the typical race of which it is distinguished by the greyer tone of the coat, and more especially by the circumstance that the lower parts of the legs are white or grey, instead of being of the same rufous tinge as the hair of the body. The maximum recorded horn-measurements are as follows: length, 12¼ ; basal circumference, 6½ ; and tip-interval, 2¾ inches ; these being taken from a Garhwal specimen in the possession of Mr. A. O. Hume. Next to this are examples respectively measuring 12 and 11 inches in length, while there are several specimens varying between 10 and 10½ inches. The height at the shoulder apparently ranges between 33 and 37 or 38 inches, while the weight varies between 120 and 190 pounds.

As regards colour, the Himalayan serow may be described as blackish or dark grey on the upper-parts, with a generally grizzled appearance, owing to the whitish bases of the hairs, the head, neck, and mane being black. On the flanks, buttocks, upper portion of the limbs, chest, and throat, the black of the back passes into rusty red, which in turn gives place on the under part of the body, the inner side of the thighs, and the lower portion of the legs to dirty white or greyish ; the inside of the ears and the front and sides of the chin being likewise white, but of a purer tint. Frequently a black line down the back may be more or less clearly distinguished.

The range of the Himalayan serow extends along the outer and middle Himalaya from Kashmir to the Mishmi Hills, at elevations between about 6000 and 12,000 feet. In Kashmir the animal appears to be found only on the south side of the valley, in the Pir Panjal range, and it does not cross the Jhelam into the Kaj-nag range. It occurs in Chamba, probably on the south side of the Chinab in Pangi, and certainly in Kulu and Nepal, as well as in the interior of Sikhim. As noticed above, it probably passes into the Sumatran race somewhere in the neighbourhood of Darjiling.

Serow share with tahr the notoriety of frequenting the very worst ground the Himalaya can show; and only those who have had practical experience can realise how bad this can be. Not only will a serow go across an almost perpendicular face of rock as easily as if it were horizontal, but it has a habit of choosing ground covered with slate-débris, on which progress is most difficult to the sportsman. A solitary animal, nowhere abundant, it is never found far away from wood, and often takes up its abode in thick forest, or scrub-jungle; the description known as ringal-jungle, which is mainly formed by a long thin reed-like bamboo, being an especial favourite in the Eastern Himalaya. Good accounts of its habits are given by General A. A. Kinloch in his *Large Game Shooting in Thibet and the North-West*, as well as by General D. Macintyre in the volume entitled *The Hindu-Koh*.

From these accounts it appears that serow are in the habit of spending most of the day concealed among the gloomy recesses of the wooded precipitous gorges which form their favourite haunts, from which they usually issue to feed in the evening and early morning, and even then wander but short distances from their head-quarters. Shyness seems to be one of the most characteristic traits of this animal, although when attacked or brought to bay, none displays greater boldness. As an illustration of this, General Macintyre states that when the follower of an English sportsman was proceeding to secure the body of a female serow that had been shot by his master, the male suddenly rushed out from some dense covert in which it had been concealed, and with one butt sent the unfortunate man rolling down the hillside, without giving the chance of a fair shot to the sportsman looking on. This instance shows that although serow are frequently seen alone, they may also be found in pairs. Very little difference in general appearance distinguishes the does from the bucks; and as the former have nearly as large horns as the latter, they are legitimate game to the sportsman. When serow cannot be stalked on their feeding-grounds, they may sometimes be induced to break covert by driving, although not unfrequently the difficult nature of the country renders this method impracticable. When alarmed, serow give utterance to sharp, shrill screams, or shrieks, repeated at short and regular intervals, and much resembling the cries of goral. When first heard, they are decidedly alarming. Many ruminants when suddenly surprised seem to "lose their heads" for a few seconds, and in the serow this momentary bewilderment is especially noticeable, the animal standing stock-still, as if dazed, and this, too, in some instances after it has been fired at. When, however, the animal has got over its bewilderment it starts off with a rush headlong down the precipitous mountain-side in a manner

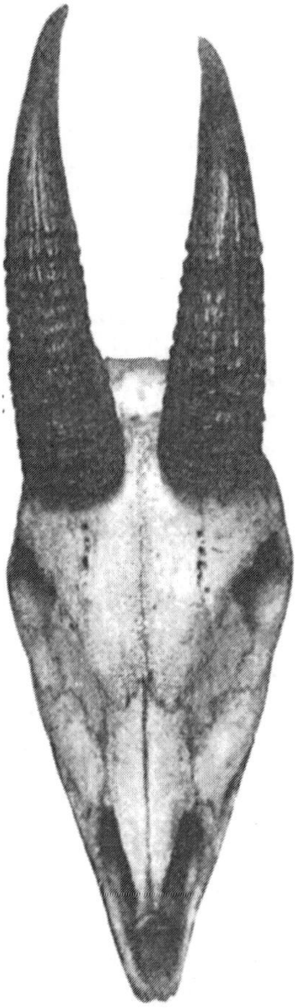

FIG. 23.—Skull and Horns of the Himalayan Serow, from a specimen in the possession of Mr. A. O. Hume.

which generally renders pursuit out of the question. Occasionally the alarm-scream is uttered without any apparent cause. When wounded and charging, the eyes display a peculiar red gleam, which gives an almost fiendish appearance to the animal.

Some difference of opinion exists in regard to the time when the does give birth to their progeny, Brian Hodgson stating that this takes place in September or October, after a gestation of eight months, whereas Leith-Adams gives the time as May or June. Apparently a single kid is produced at a birth.

The Malay serow, although described by Mr. A. L. Butler in the Zoological Society's *Proceedings* for 1900 as a distinct species, is best regarded as the melanistic phase of the ordinary species under the name of *N. sumatrensis swettenhami*. Its general colour is black; the back being strongly and the sides slightly grizzled with grey, while the bases of the hairs are whitish. The lips are greyish white; the hind part of the upper ones, a patch on each side of the lower jaw, and another on the throat being rusty red. The ears are black, tinged with rusty at their bases, and lined and edged with greyish-white hairs. The mane is black with some whitish hairs on the fore portion of the neck and reddish ones near the withers. The head, except the parts mentioned, is black, as are the neck, underparts, tail, and legs, except the inside of the thighs, which is rufous.

The white-maned serow (*Nemorhædus argyrochætes*) inhabiting the mountains of North-Western China, of which a figure will be found in the Zoological Society's *Proceedings* for 1906, may perhaps be considered merely as another local phase or race of *N. sumatrensis*.

THE HIMALAYAN GORALS

(*Urotragus goral* and *U. bedfordi*)

NATIVE NAMES.—*Goral* IN THE NORTH-WEST HIMALAYA; *Pij*, *Pijur*, *Rai* AND *Rom*, KASHMIRI; *Sah* OR *Sar* IN THE SUTLEJ VALLEY; *Suh-ging* OF THE LEPCHAS; *Ra-giyu* OF THE BHOTS OF SIKHIM; *Deo Chagal* IN ASSAM.

(PLATE V, fig. 3)

Owing to the practice of applying the names of European animals to their relatives in other countries, goral are often known among sportsmen as Himalayan chamois; but beyond the fact that they belong to a group of ruminants in some degree serving to connect antelopes with goats, they have really little in common with chamois, from which they differ by the shaggy coat, as well as in the more sombre coloration, and the form of the horns. They are, in fact, near relatives of the serows, from which they are mainly distinguished by the absence of glands on the face, and in certain details of the skull.

In most characters, such as the naked muzzle, the presence of glands in the feet, and of four teats in the female, as well as in the development of horns in both sexes, gorals resemble serows; the absence of face-glands being the chief reason for referring them to a separate group. Very generally the tail is comparatively short (about 4 inches in the Himalayan species), but it attains a considerable length in the long-tailed goral (*U. caudatus*). As a rule, gorals are smaller than serows, but there is a species of the latter from Japan (*Nemorhædus crispus*) not much larger than a goral.

In all gorals the short black horns, which are nearly as large in does as in bucks, are very similar to those of serows, being conical and slightly divergent, curving evenly backwards, and marked for the greater part of their length by somewhat irregular, closely approximated rings, or ridges, partially interrupted by longitudinal groovings. The general form is also goat-like, with the limbs strong and stout. The hair is rather coarse

FIG. 24.—A Himalayan Goral, from a photograph by the Duchess of Bedford.

and shaggy, with a certain amount of woolly under-fur at the roots, and generally shows a tendency to develop into a slight crest along the back of the neck and at the bases of the horns.

The animal here regarded as the typical Himalayan goral is rufous brown in colour, only slightly paler below than on the back, with the face somewhat lighter and more rufous, but darkening towards the horns;

and a white or whitish patch on the chin and throat. Along the back, from nape to tail, runs a conspicuous black streak ; the tail is wholly black above ; and there is a blackish stripe down the front of the legs, which are elsewhere brown.

In the *Fauna of British India* the late Dr. Blanford made no mention of any colour-variation according to season, age, or sex ; but Mr. Sterndale, in his work on the Mammals of India, stated that the does and young are lighter coloured than old bucks. On the other hand, General Macintyre, in his *Hindu-Koh*, observed that the doe is like the buck in appearance, except for her thinner horns ; and he described the colour as uniform greyish brown, with a white throat-patch.

At least three skins in the British Museum conform to the above-mentioned brown type ; but a fourth skin, with part of the skull, in the same collection, which appears to represent a fully adult animal, differs by its decidedly greyish-fawn colour, the absence of a distinct dark dorsal stripe, and certain other details. On the evidence of this one specimen there might be considerable hesitation in admitting the existence of two forms of Himalayan goral. The British Museum possesses, however, a mounted goral-skin, presented in 1897 by the Duke of Bedford, belonging to an animal formerly living in the park at Woburn, and believed to be of Himalayan origin. This specimen agrees precisely with the one last mentioned. Its general colour is light yellowish grey-fawn, suffused with blackish ; the white throat-patch extends largely on to the cheeks ; there is no dorsal stripe ; the muzzle has a dark median streak extending to the level of the eyes ; the tail is blackish only at the base ; and the fore-legs have only a blackish "knee-cap," and the hind ones are wholly rufous fawn. In addition to these striking differences of colour, the ears of this goral are larger than in the typical brown goral, and the horns are more curved and rougher. Both the grey skins seem to be adult, and are apparently those of males. It is difficult to believe that the differences between this form and the typical goral can be explained by season, sex, or age.

If this be so, it must be assumed either that the Himalayan goral exhibits dimorphism, or that there are two local races or species, which must be presumed to inhabit separate areas or different zones of altitude. In the *Zoologist* for 1905 the present writer adopted the latter view; and named the grey Himalayan goral *Urotragus bedfordi*, taking the mounted specimen in the British Museum as the type.

These two forms of goral may be briefly diagnosed as follows :—

1. *Urotragus goral.*—Colour rufous brown, with a white patch on the throat and chin, a black dorsal stripe and tail, and a black stripe down the front of each leg. Horns comparatively straight, and not heavily ringed. Eastern Himalaya.

2. *Urotragus bedfordi.*—Colour yellowish grey-fawn suffused with blackish, the light throat-patch pure white and extending on to the cheeks, no distinct dorsal stripe, a dark streak on muzzle; base of tail and knees blackish, the rest of the legs being fawn. Horns more curved and more heavily ringed than in the last. Western (and in part ? Eastern) Himalaya.

To determine the respective habitats of the two Himalayan gorals must in part be left to others. Judging from its dark colour, it may be suggested that the brown species (*U. goral*) is a native of the damp forests of the Terai, and the grey *U. bedfordi* an inhabitant of drier and colder forests.

Himalayan goral stand from 26 to 28 inches in height at the shoulder, and weigh from about 58 to 63 lbs.

The maximum recorded length of goral horns is 8½ inches, one pair of these dimensions, from Bissahir, being in the possession of Major A. E. Ward, and a second (a female from Dalhousie) in that of Mr. J. Johnston-Stewart. Three specimens measuring 8 inches in length are known, one of them having a basal girth of $3\frac{3}{4}$ inches, and an interval of $3\frac{1}{8}$ inches between the tips; two of these specimens are from Chamba, and the third from Kumaon.

The Himalayan gorals inhabit the outer and middle ranges of the mountains from Kashmir to Bhutan, and are also said to occur in the Naga Hills. In Kashmir they are probably restricted to the ranges to the south of the valley. Although stated to be far from abundant in the Siwalik Hills, in most districts they are common, and not unfrequently found in the neighbourhood of hill-stations. The lowest elevation at which they occur is about 3000 feet, and the highest range about 8000 feet.

Never found away from forest, goral usually associate in small parties of from four to eight head, and where one is seen, others are almost sure to occur; old bucks are, however, solitary for the greater part of the year. Grass-clad hills, or ledges among steep cliffs, and rocky ground in the midst of forest form their favourite haunts; and sometimes the country they frequent is so precipitous that a wounded animal will fall several hundred feet before its body finds a resting-place, General Macintyre mentioning an instance where a goral he had shot fell headlong for a depth of about 1000 feet. Like most Himalayan ruminants, goral usually feed in the morning and evening, taking a long *siesta* during the mid-day heat; but on dull and cloudy days they may be seen abroad at all hours. The period of gestation is about six months, and the kids, of which there is usually one at a birth, are born during May and June. Being such common animals, it is surprising to find that up to the year 1896 only a single example of these gorals had been exhibited in the London Zoological Gardens; at

Woburn Abbey there have, however, been numerous living examples.

In spite of the insignificant character of the horns as trophies, goral-shooting has a considerable attraction for sportsmen, especially those who dislike the weary mid-day halts inseparable from most kinds of big-game-stalking, or who object to sleeping out on the hill-sides. As General Macintyre remarks, on the precipitous and broken ground of the middle Himalayan ranges this kind of stalking is perhaps one of the pleasantest descriptions of sport. When the goral are taking their mid-day nap, the sportsman can nearly always return to his tent for lunch ; and, in any case, he can make sure of a night in bed. In good localities blank days are, moreover, few and far between ; the writer last mentioned having bagged no less than sixty head of these game ruminants during a single season's shooting.

THE BURMESE GORAL

(*Urotragus evansi*)

This species resembles the grey Himalayan goral in the absence of a black dorsal stripe, but differs by the general colour being a more brownish grey, heavily suffused with chocolate-brown ; while there is no white on the cheeks, no dark mark on the upper surface of the muzzle, and the throat-patch is yellowish. The tail is blackish brown throughout ; and the legs are coloured exactly the reverse of those of the typical goral, being dark brown behind and rufous fawn in front. The horns are very small, nearly straight, and almost smooth.

It may be briefly diagnosed as follows : Colour brownish grey-fawn suffused with brown ; throat-patch small and yellow ; no stripe on muzzle or back ; tail and back of legs dark brown, rest of legs rufous fawn. Horns very small. Mountains of Upper Burma and (?) Siam.

In the Zoological Society's *Proceedings* for 1905, Major G. H. Evans communicated the following notes: "These goral, I believe, extend into Siam and are to be found in suitable places on the Siamese side of the Thaungyin River, and also occur, but are more scarce, about the hills at the headwaters of the Me-Ping. As has been recorded in the case of the Indian form, these goral live in parties of four, six, or even a dozen. They inhabit very steep ground and the more precipitous it is the better they seem to like it. They are never to be found at any distance from rugged, rocky ground, even though there may be forest near by. The only time they may be found away from dangerous ground is during the early hours of the morning and late in the evening, when they graze on the grassy patches close by. No doubt when the sky is overcast, as is the case during the rains, or in the cold weather when there is a heavy mist, they feed much later. Apparently they are inclined to remain always about any favourite locality. Their sight seems to be extraordinarily good, and they appear to rely more on this sense than on smell or hearing. The day is usually passed lying on inaccessible ledges of rock about precipices.

"If a goral is startled it jumps up and makes a short sharp hissing or sneezing noise, very often repeated at short intervals. It may be a note of alarm or a call to its mates, for as sure as one calls, if there are any others about (and this is generally the case), it is immediately answered. In Burma, at least, goral are not easily followed, unless by expert cragsmen.

"Goral, when standing about these crags, afford fairly easy shots with high-velocity rifles, but the recovery of a carcase is, as a rule, by no means an easy matter. The shikaris and followers are generally anything but keen on a trip down one of these precipices, and I for one do not blame them. Though they may be adepts in woodcraft, they cannot be anything like the cragsmen (hill-shikaris) met with in the Himalaya. Goral-flesh is not at all bad. From December till May is the best season to hunt these animals, and morning and evening is the best time to find them, as they are then grazing or lying down in places more easily accessible."

THE ASHY TIBETAN GORAL

(*Urotragus cinereus*)

This species, like the next, is one of the numerous animals discovered by the missionary Abbé David in the Moupin district of Eastern Tibet, and described by Professor Milne-Edwards of the Paris Museum. In the type specimen the horns measured 7½ inches in length.

Compared with the next the present species is stated to be larger, and its fur of a more nearly uniform colour, being more distinctly ashy, and less mingled with brown. Moreover, the whitish patches on the throat and on the feet are smaller and less suffused with yellow. More important than all is the greater length and bushiness of the tail, which is not inferior in these respects to that of the Mongolian long-tailed goral (*U. caudatus*). The describer adds that he should have hesitated to distinguish this species from the next were it not for important differences in their skulls, that of the present animal, in addition to other points, being more elongated.

The two animals are stated to be recognised as different from one another by the natives of Eastern Tibet, who affirm that the present one lives at a higher altitude than the next. Both appear distinguishable from Himalayan gorals by the character and colour of the hair, as well as by their longer tails, but further information is required as to whether the two are really distinct.

THE GREY TIBETAN GORAL

(*Urotragus griseus*)

Although it may seem curious to find two nearly allied species in the same district, yet in the opinion of Professor Milne-Edwards this goral is entitled to specific distinction from the preceding. The present species, which inhabits the Moupin district of Eastern Tibet, is nearly allied to the Mongolian *U. caudatus*, from which it is distinguished by its lighter build, shorter tail, and the deeper tint of its fur. The upper surface of the head, together with the nasal region and the chin, is brown with a tinge of maroon ; while the whitish patch on the throat is more prolonged under the jaw than in the Mongolian species. The colour of the upper-parts and flanks is yellowish grey, suffused with brown, the latter tint predominating along the middle line of the back, on the front of the shoulders, and on the fore-legs and thighs. The feet are less light-coloured, while the buttocks and the inner surfaces of the legs are whiter than in the species with which the comparison is made. The height at the shoulder is about 24 inches.

While there are slight differences in the form of the horns, the characters of the skull are said to afford ample means of distinguishing this species from *U. caudatus*.

THE TAKIN

(*Budorcas taxicolor*)

NATIVE NAMES.—*Takin*, MISHMI HILLS ; *Ye-more*, EASTERN TIBET

(PLATE V, figs. 1, 1*a*)

At the present day there are comparatively few animals coming under the designation of big game that have not fallen to the rifle of the British sportsman ; but the strange-looking ruminant known to the natives of the Mishmi Hills, on the northern frontier of Assam, as the takin was till recently an exception to this rule. This seems the more strange seeing that the Mishmi Hills lie within sight of British territory ; they are, however, at ordinary times closed to British sportsmen. It is true that the first known specimens of the takin were obtained by Brian Hodgson (who described the animal) while British Resident at Katmandu ; but these were procured by the aid of native explorers.

The takin is a clumsily-built ruminant, standing about as high as a small mule, the height at the withers being approximately 3½ feet. The most striking feature of the adult is formed by the sharply angulated blackish horns which are present in both sexes, although decidedly smaller in ewes than in rams. In the young they form simple spikes, which in the full-grown animals constitute that portion above the bend. Very characteristic of the animal is the highly arched region of the nose, or chafron, which is specially conspicuous in the skull. The muzzle resembles that of goats and sheep in being vertically grooved, and covered with hair except on one small spot ; the ears are very small and almost quadrangular ; the tail is little more than a stump ; and the limbs are very short and thick, with the lateral pair of hoofs remarkably large. As regards the teeth, it must suffice to mention that these are of the general type of those of sheep and goats, and therefore quite unlike those of oxen. The female has four teats, like the serow and one species of thar. The coat is formed of comparatively short and stiff hair, varying locally in colour from reddish brown with a light saddle to golden yellow on the back, and darker on the face and limbs. In the skeleton the most remarkable feature is the shortness and width of the front and hind cannon-bones; the breadth of which approximates to half the length.

The skull of the takin, of which no complete specimen is known in this country, is remarkable for its great depth in front of the eyes, the highly arched profile, the comparatively short and convex nasal bones, the enormous size of the nose-cavity (probably connected with living at a high elevation), and the smallness and weakness of the premaxillæ, or front upper jaw-bones. It recalls, in fact, to a certain extent the skull of the Theban domesticated goat, in which the vertical depth and the convexity of the profile are still more exaggerated. A still nearer approximation to the form characteristic of the Theban goat is presented by the skull of a large extinct ruminant from the Siwalik Hills of Northern India known as *Bucapra daviesi*, which may have been a near relative of the takin, but more specialised in skull-characters. The least imperfect skull of the takin in the collection of the British Museum was presented by Mr. Claude White, British Resident in Sikhim.

Turning to what naturalists have written regarding the affinities of this strange ruminant, we find the following statement, with the initials J. C. (J. Cockburn), in Sterndale's *Mammalia of India*: "The takin," it is there written, "is essentially a serow with affinities to the bovines through the musk-ox, and other relationships to the sheep, goat, and antelope."

In suggesting affinity with the oxen (bovines) the author was clearly on the wrong tack, seeing that the teeth of the musk-ox (like those of the takin) are of a somewhat different type, and much nearer those of the sheep and goats. This was recognised by Dr. Blanford, who in the *Fauna of India* observed that the takin is "allied to both goats and antelopes; I cannot see the bovine affinities attributed to it."

Some years later (1898) Dr. P. Matschie, of Berlin, supported the view of the relationship of the takin to the musk-ox, basing his conclusions on the shortness and width of the cannon-bones, the shape of the skull and horns, the small and peculiarly formed ears, the nature of the muzzle, the shortness of the tail, the stout, short legs, and the relatively large lateral hoofs. He might have added that, as in serow, the females of both have four teats.

The next to enter the arena was Dr. E. Lönnberg, of Upsala, who, in a paper published in the Zoological Society's *Proceedings* for 1901, disputed the supposed relationship. Dr. Lönnberg, it should be mentioned, does not regard the musk-ox as a near relative of the sheep and goats, but as the sole living representative of a comparatively primitive group, which has become specialised after its own particular style. He points out that the muzzle of the two animals is different, that of the takin having a downward prolongation of the naked area to divide the upper lip after the fashion of sheep and goats, and still more serows. To the form of the ears, tail, and lateral hoofs he attaches little importance; while, as he truly remarks, the horns of the two animals are strikingly different, although he forgot to mention that, as in serows, those of the females in both species are relatively large. He also challenges the statement with regard to the proportions of the cannon-bones; but the measurements given (although no doubt exact) are misleading. When compared with the other bones of the legs, the fore and hind cannon-bones of the musk-ox are indeed remarkably short and wide, although not quite to the same extent as in the takin. And since it is only in these two ruminants and the Rocky Mountain goat (*Oreamnus*) that this very marked shortness of both cannon-bones occurs, it must be regarded as a feature of importance. The wild goat, it is true, has a short front cannon-bone, as Dr. Lönnberg remarks; but then the hind cannon-bone is very long, actually longer indeed than in a wild sheep (*Ovis orientalis*) in which the front cannon-bone greatly exceeds the corresponding element of the goat in length.

In connection with the relationships of the takin it is important to refer to two extinct ruminants, *Euceratherium* and *Preptoceras*, of which the remains have been discovered in certain Californian caverns. That the ancestors of these animals came from Asia is practically certain; and their describers, Messrs. Furlong and Sinclair, are of opinion that they present resemblances both to the takin and the musk-ox, although not nearly related to either. Probably, writes the former, "*Preptoceras* bears somewhat the same degree of relationship to *Ovibos* that *Budorcas* does"; which is perhaps not a very lucid way of putting matters when the nature of the latter relationship is just what we do not know. Still, there seems a probability that the two extinct American ruminants, together with the Rocky Mountain goat and the musk-ox, are all descendants of an Asiatic assemblage of ruminants of which the takin and the serow are Old World survivors. The aforesaid Siwalik *Bucapra* seems, however, to indicate that the takin type was in existence at a relatively early date. Possibly an extinct ruminant from the Pliocene Tertiary deposits of Samos known as *Criotherium* which has curiously bent horns, may be a member of the same assemblage.

On the whole, despite the criticisms of Dr. Lönnberg, it seems probable that Messrs. Cockburn and Matschie were right in their belief as to the existence of some kind of kinship between the takin and the musk-ox, although it is impossible to formulate the nature of the affinity. Possibly the fact that both animals dwell on or near the snow may be additional evidence of their relationship. By means of the Rocky Mountain goat, the takin is probably connected in some way with serows, which are themselves relations of the goats and sheep. This whole assemblage of ruminants once inhabited north-eastern Asia, whence the Rocky Mountain goat, the musk-ox, and the two extinct genera referred to above wandered into the New World, while the takin and serows remained in the old family home.

In 1906, Mr. J. Claude White, Commissioner of Sikhim, had a young takin in his camp which it was hoped might be transported alive to England, although the fates willed it otherwise. Of this specimen a photograph appeared in the *Field* for 11th October 1906. Apart from this and one or two other immature examples, the takin in a living state apparently still remains unknown to Europeans, at all events in the territories bordering British India. Since, however, the range of the takin extends from the country north of Bhutan and the Mishmi Hills through Eastern Tibet into Szechuen and not improbably still farther eastward in China, it is possible that Europeans may have seen the animal in some part of its Chinese habitat.

The little known concerning the habits of the creature is derived from native reports. The small size of the ears is sufficient to indicate that takin, unlike serow, do not live in jungle. Mr. John Cockburn, in Sterndale's *Mammalia of India*, has stated that when at Sadya he was shown by a Mishmi the open spurs inhabited by these animals, and also that their range extends from about 8000 feet to the Alpine region which forms their true habitat. This is confirmed by Mr. White, who has recently stated in the *Field* that takin inhabit the zone immediately below the snow-line ;

and likewise that they are exceedingly fierce in disposition, so much so indeed that the natives (who have to get within short range) find them awkward customers. They generally go about in pairs, each of which may be accompanied by a kid.

The longest known horns measure 24½ inches along the front curve; one pair with these dimensions being in the possession of Colonel John Biddulph, and a second in the Indian Museum, Calcutta. Several examples ranging between 20½ and 22½ inches in length are known. Some difference of opinion has arisen with

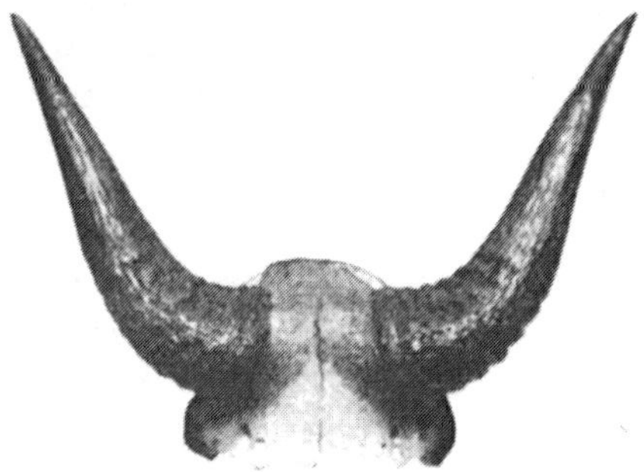

Fig. 25.—Frontlet and Horns of Young Male Takin, from a specimen owned by Mr. A. O. Hume.

regard to the horns of the female. Brian Hodgson described them as similar in form to those of the male, although smaller, but in a paper communicated to the *Proceedings* of the Zoological Society for 1887, Mr. A. O. Hume urged that this was incorrect, and that the female horns are of the type shown in fig. 25. On this subject Captain A. Wilson, of the 14th Gurkhas, wrote as follows from Kohima, Assam, in March 1900: "In *Great Game Records* I saw the head of what was supposed to be a female takin, and as I had seen a good many heads of this animal at one time and another, I thought it strange that a female's head had never come under my notice. My regiment has just been on an expedition into the Mishmi country, and I gave the men instructions to get a female takin head. A good many heads were brought in, but none like the one in the figure, with the exception of very small specimens, which belonged to very young animals." The writer then goes on to say that he consulted Mr. Needham, the political officer at Sadiya, who had seen a considerable number of heads, and who was of opinion that the female horns are similar in shape to those of the male, and that the small singly-curved horns shown in fig. 24 are those of immature animals.

In the typical Mishmi takin the colour of the hair on the head is black, but elsewhere it varies from yellowish to reddish brown mingled with black, being lightest on the back and darkest on the under-parts and limbs.

The precise limits of the geographical distribution of the Mishmi takin are not yet known. Two eastern races of the species have been described, namely the Moupin takin (*Budorcas taxicolor tibetanus*) of Eastern Tibet, and the Kansu takin of North-West China; but whether they are really distinct may be doubtful.

Writing of the younger examples obtained by the Abbé David, Professor Milne-Edwards observed that at this stage of its existence the Moupin takin presents a considerable resemblance to a small, long-haired, and somewhat woolly calf. In colour it is brown-red, more or less dark, passing into black along the middle line of the back, on the cheeks, the upper part of the body, and the feet. The build is less heavy than in the adult, and the horns commence to bud at an early period. With advancing age the coat lightens and becomes in great part yellowish, as in the adult, although the original brown-red colour persists for a long time in front of the withers and in the region of the pelvis. In the adult female the colour is paler and greyer than in the bull; but none of the specimens in the Paris Museum show the coloration of the Mishmi takin.

The same writer also states that if the figures of the skull published by Hodgson be exact, there are also certain differences between the horns of the Moupin and the Mishmi takin. A specimen of (presumably) the Kansu takin in the British Museum has the general colour of the coat (which is longer than in the Mishmi race) of a bright golden yellow, very different from the brownish red of the Mishmi takin.

According to information obtained by the Abbé David from the natives, the Moupin takin frequents the steepest and most thickly wooded declivities of its native mountains, only leaving its retreats to feed during the night. In winter, when the mountains are enveloped in snow, it ascends to the elevated tracts above the forests where no snow falls at that season, finding there an abundance of dry herbage on the slopes exposed to the sun, on which the snows that fall in the summer and autumn have been melted by the solar rays. In these districts takin seem to be fairly common; and they range eastward into the Chinese provinces of Kansu and of Szechuen. Although generally living solitary or in small parties, it is stated to collect during the month of June in herds of considerable size.

THE NILGAI, OR BLUE BULL

(*Boselaphus tragocamelus*)

NATIVE NAMES.—*Nil*, *Nilgao* (male), *Nilgai* (female), *Rojh*, *Roz*, OR *Rojra*, HINDUSTANI; *Ru-i*, DECCANI, MAHRATHI, GUZRATI, etc.; *Guraya* OF THE GONDS; *Murim* (male), *Susam* (female) OF THE HO KOL; *Manu-potu*, TAMIL; *Mairu*, MARAVI; *Kard-Kadrai*, CANARESE.

(PLATE V, fig. 10)

It is unfortunate that the largest of Indian antelopes is so poorly off in the matter of horns that, from the point of view of trophies, it is scarcely worth powder and bullet. This poor horn-development is the more remarkable from the circumstance that the animal is a near relative of the elands, kudus, bongo, and bushbucks of Africa, the males, or in some cases both sexes, of which carry large and graceful horns, while the animals themselves are among the most beautiful of their tribe. No less noteworthy is the fact that in past times eland and kudu, as testified by their fossil remains, were the companions of nilgai on the plains of Northern India ; and the reason for the disappearance of the two former from that country and the survival of the latter forms one of the many unsolved problems presented by zoology. As the nilgai is unknown in Ceylon, it might have been considered a comparatively recent immigrant into India, but since its fossil remains are found at the foot of the Himalaya, and (at a more recent epoch in the valley of the Narbada), while the genus is unknown in any other country, it is evidently an ancient inhabitant of the north of India, which has probably only made its way into the south of the peninsula at a comparatively recent date.

Despite the fact that this sex is fawn-coloured, the name nilgai properly refers to the female, and means "blue cow" ; the word *nil* (pronounced *neel*) being again met with in "Nilgiris," and also as the general term for indigo. Sportsmen generally call the animal "blue bull," which is the translation of the Hindustani *nilgao*.

The nilgai is such a peculiar and ungainly-looking animal that it cannot be mistaken for any other antelope. Like most of its African relatives, it is only the male that bears horns. The horns are smooth, short, nearly straight, and directed upwards and backwards ; the section being triangular at the base, but becoming circular near the tip. The front edge bears a distinct keel, which in old bulls extends forwards and inwards till the bases of the horns are almost in contact.

With a peculiarly long and pointed head, the nilgai has the fore-legs considerably longer than the hind pair; and it is largely owing to this feature that it has such an ungainly and clumsy appearance. Although the neck is ornamented with a mane in both sexes, it is only the bulls that develop a tuft of hair on the throat. The ears are of moderate size, and pointed; there are glands of small size below the full ox-like eyes; the narrow and delicate muzzle is naked and moist; and the tail, which reaches about to the hocks, is tufted with long hairs in its terminal half. The hair of the body is short and somewhat wiry; and it does not appear that the winter coat is appreciably longer than that of summer. Neither does there seem to be that change in colour between the winter and summer coats so conspicuous in most deer.

The general colour of a full-grown blue bull is dark speckled grey, more or less distinctly tinged with either blue or brown; the mane and other tufts of long hair are, however, deep glossy black; and streaks and patches on the ears and face, a gorget on the throat, a narrow streak on each buttock, as well as a ring above and below each fetlock, together with the under surface of the body and tail, are white. The terminal half of the outer surface of each ear, as well as two spots in the interior of the same, are black, as are the horns. In young bulls and cows at all ages the grey of the adult bulls is replaced by rufous brown. A large bull nilgai stands from 13 to 14 hands (4 feet 4 inches to 4 feet 8 inches) at the withers, which are relatively high. Average horns measure about 8 inches along the curve in front, but Mr. Rowland Ward records six specimens exceeding 9 inches in length, the largest (in the possession of Sir E. G. Loder) measuring 9⅞ inches in length and 7¾ inches in circumference. These dimensions are, however, exceeded by the horns of a bull killed by Mr. A. O. Hume in the Aligarh district in the year 1855, which measured 11¾ inches along the front curve, and 9½ inches in basal girth. They were lost during the Mutiny.

The range of the nilgai includes a large portion of peninsular India, from the foot of the Himalaya to the south of Mysore, in Madras, but excluding Assam, Eastern Bengal, and apparently the Malabar coast. The animal is particularly common in many parts of

FIG. 26.—A Female Nilgai, from a photograph by the Duchess of Bedford.

the Punjab, such as the neighbourhood of Jhelam, Guzerat, and the North-West and Central Provinces. In Ceylon, as already said, it is unknown, as it is in the countries to the eastward of the Bay of Bengal; so that it may be regarded as a characteristic Indian animal.

Like so many of the larger *Bovidæ*, old bull nilgai generally prefer a solitary existence for the greater part of the year, although they occasionally collect in parties, sometimes numbering half-a-score individuals, or even more. The cows and calves, as well as the younger bulls, on the other hand, associate in family parties, or, less commonly, in small herds. The cows give birth either to a single calf or twins, and apparently breed every year. Although seldom resorting to thick forest, nilgai specially affect ground covered with thin bush among which larger trees occur at intervals; and are equally partial to open grassy plains with patches of covert into which they can retire. Frequently they may be seen feeding among corn-fields; and this under a burning noonday sun, since the nilgai is an animal of diurnal habits, although sometimes resorting to the shade for a short *siesta*. In districts where they are in the habit of resorting to corn-fields for their daily meal, they display remarkable unconcern at the presence of man; this being largely due to the fact that, as its name implies, the nilgai is regarded by the Hindus as a near relation of the sacred cow, and consequently enjoys immunity from molestation. In deference to these prejudices, shooting these animals by Europeans is prohibited in certain districts. In spite of its semi-sacred character, the flesh of the nilgai is eaten, however, by most of the Hindus of the Deccan, not even excepting those jungle-tribes who regard the gaur in the light of a deity.

On account of the insignificant nature of the trophies it yields, the bull nilgai is not regarded as worthy game for the rifle in most parts of India. Its beef may, however, be useful on occasions to supply a large camp with food; the marrow-bones being a delicacy, and the tongue of good quality. The skin makes excellent leather, the thinner portions of the hide becoming as soft and pliable as sambar-leather, while the thicker skin of the back is suitable for sole-leather.

A writer in the *Asian* newspaper of 21st February 1899 related the following experiences of nilgai-stalking:—"I have frequently found blue bull wild and difficult to approach, requiring a careful stalk to enable one to obtain even a long shot. The first one I saw and killed looked so like the village oxen in whose proximity it was grazing that I had some compunction in shooting it, whilst my companion entirely mistook it for a domestic cow, and thus permitted it to retreat and meet its fate in my direction. My first shot broke the animal's fore-leg, and it was brought to bay after a short chase through the bushes by my fox-terrier, and finished off with another bullet. The next that fell to my rifle was a large, almost black bull, that got up out of a nala close to me in thick jungle, and was immediately shot, for we were in want of meat. I then discovered that the unfortunate creature had a number of dreadful wounds on its back, evidently inflicted by a tiger some time previously ; and it was in such an emaciated condition that the flesh did not appear to be fit for food, although it was eagerly devoured by the jungle-men who were with me."

The same writer then goes on to refer to the extraordinary tenacity of life displayed by nilgai when wounded. "I have frequently," he writes, "experienced considerable difficulty in killing them, and have known one travel far with a heavy and well-placed bullet in the shoulder, which would have been sufficient to kill most animals. On another occasion a sportsman with me shot one of these beasts and proceeded to cut its throat. When the operation had been partially performed, the animal suddenly jumped up and ran some distance, but did not attempt to attack its rash assailant. The blue bull was shot through the lungs, and the release of the blood at the throat had relieved the pressure on the chest, and so enabled the animal to recover for a space." It is added that in the district referred to almost every nilgai killed had one or more bullets, presumably fired by natives, embedded in its body. When the amount of damage these animals, in districts where they are numerous, inflict on crops is borne in mind, it is little wonder that, when religious prejudices do not interfere, war to the death is waged against them.

Man is, however, by no means the only enemy against whom the nilgai has to be on its guard. Tigers, as in the instance quoted above, wound or kill a large number, even of full-grown bulls, while the younger members of the herd fall victims to the stealthy advance of the leopard. Wild dogs, too, probably capture a certain number, especially as they are more easy to run down than are sambar and other large deer.

It must not, however, be inferred from the last statement that nilgai are by any means slow movers. On the contrary, when they are found in country of a sufficiently open nature to admit of their being ridden down and speared, the heavy gallop of even an old bull will call forth the best efforts of a good horse, while on hard ground it is more than probable that a cow in prime condition would get away from her pursuer. However lightly esteemed at the present day, nilgai-hunting (probably on horseback) was a favourite sport of the Mogul emperors of India; and, as we learn from Bernier's account, it was practised by Aurungzeb on his bi-annual progress between Delhi and Kashmir. At that date the animals are stated to have been extraordinarily abundant in certain parts of the country.

Although old bulls can never be depended upon, and are always apt to make themselves disagreeable, nilgai, if captured at a sufficiently early age, can be readily tamed and broken to harness; and if it were worth while, and the animals were sufficiently abundant, there is little doubt that they would make as useful beasts of burden and draught as reindeer.

Like most ruminants which inhabit open and sandy districts, nilgai can exist with but a small supply of water; and it is probable that, in the cold season at least, they drink only every second or third day, and that they could go for a considerably longer period without liquid.

Nilgai were first exhibited alive in England in 1767, when a pair were sent from Bombay as a present to Lord Clive; a second pair being shortly afterwards presented to the then queen. In 1862 Senior Comba introduced a dozen nilgai into his park at Mandria, Italy; and ten years later the herd had increased to 172 head, which roamed at complete liberty over the domain. A small herd is kept by the Duke of Bedford in the park at Woburn Abbey.

THE CHOUSINGHA, OR FOUR-HORNED ANTELOPE

(*Tetraceros quadricornis*)

NATIVE NAMES.—*Chousingha*, *Chouka*, *Doda*, HINDUSTANI; *Bhokra*, *Phokra*, GUZRATI; *Bhirki* AT SANGOR; *Bhir* OF THE GONDS; *Bhirul* OF THE BHILS; *Kotari* AT CHUTIA NAGPUR; *Kurus* OF THE GONDS OF BASTAR; *Konda-gori*, TELEGU; *Kondguri*, *Kaulla-Kuri*, CANARESE; *Jangli-bakri* IN THE DECCAN.

(PLATE v, fig. 6)

It is not a little remarkable that while among the host of antelopes inhabiting Africa not a single species has developed more than the ordinary pair of horns, yet that among the few representatives of the group found in India there should be one with two pairs of these appendages. It is still more remarkable that the only other wild four-horned ruminant in the world is, or rather was (for it is extinct, and only known by its fossilised remains) also an inhabitant of India. The latter animal is the *Sivatherium*, of the Siwalik Hills of Northern India, which is by far the largest of all known ruminants, as the four-horned antelope is one of the smaller. Although it was at one time thought that these two singular ruminants were near relatives, later researches have shown this view to be untenable.

As might be expected, the existence of the extra pair of horns in the present species is indicated by some at least of its native names ; chousingha (*cha*, or *chou*, four, and *singh*, a horn) being the Hindi equivalent of four-horned antelope. In the Deccan, and apparently in some parts of the Madras Presidency, where the front pair of horns is frequently, if not invariably absent, the animal is known simply as *jangli bakri*, or wild goat. By sportsmen it is frequently termed the *chinkara*, a name properly belonging to the Indian gazelle.

Even when the front horns, which are situated between the eyes of the bucks (the does being hornless), are fully developed, they are but poor affairs ; being frequently little more than knobs, while at their best they are not known, with one exception, to exceed 2½ inches in length. Neither are the back horns, which are simple pointed spikes, much to boast of in the way of size, the maximum recorded length being 5 inches. As a rule, the length of the front horns seldom exceeds a little more than half that of the hind pair, but in the exception alluded to the front pair (3¾ inches) slightly exceeds the hind ones (3½ inches) in length. This specimen, which was obtained at Mandla, in the Central Provinces, is in the possession of Captain B. H. Boucher.

Despite their small size, the presence of two pairs of horns renders heads much sought after as trophies. In Madras the front horns are, as mentioned above, seldom developed ; and if it should turn out that in certain districts they are invariably absent, and regularly present in individuals from most other parts, then the two-horned form would be entitled to rank as a distinct local race, or sub-species. If that prove to be the case, the race will have to be known as *Tetraceros quadri-*

cornis sub-quadricornutus. Kathiawar specimens have frequently but one pair of horns.

The chousingha is the Indian representative of the duiker-boks of Africa ; its affinities to the latter being indicated, among other features, by the circumstance that the face-gland takes the form of a narrow deep slit on the side of the face below the eye, that of the duiker-boks forming a narrow bare line perforated at intervals by pores. The muzzle of this antelope is bare and moist, the tail is short, and the female has four teats. In size and build the animal may be compared to a small gazelle, the height at the shoulder being about 25 inches, and the weight some 40 pounds. The general colour of the short and stiff hair is dull rufous brown, becoming whitish beneath, with the muzzle, the outer surface of the ears, and a line down the front of each leg blackish brown, and some white on the outer side of the pasterns. The doe may be distinguished from a female Indian gazelle by the absence of the face-markings of the latter. More difficulty may be experienced in distinguishing between a doe chousingha and a female hog-deer, but the two can always be separated by the absence in the former of gland-tufts on the hind-legs.

The four-horned antelope is exclusively Indian, occurring locally over a great portion of the peninsula, from the foot of the Himalaya southwards. It is unknown both in Ceylon and to the eastward of the Bay of Bengal ; as is true of all the four species of Indian antelopes, namely the nilgai, the chousingha, the blackbuck, and the chinkara. Probably the Burmese countries, from their moist climate, are unsuited to antelopes of this type, which prefer dry, open districts ; but whether the same explanation will account for their absence from Ceylon is not easy to say.

In India the chousingha is to some extent local, being unknown on the plains of the Ganges, and likewise on the Malabar coast of Madras. It has been reported from Sind, and there are skulls in the British Museum from Kathiawar. In the wooded districts of Rajputana it occurs abundantly, and it is equally common in the Bombay Presidency, as well as in the Central Provinces and the northern districts of Madras. Towards the east, in Chattisgarh, Chutia Nagpur, and Orissa, it becomes more rare, as it does in Mysore, where it is only occasionally met with ; but it has been observed on the Nilgiri and the Palni Hills of South-Western Madras. Along the foot of the Himalaya it occurs, in suitable districts, from the Punjab in the north-west to Nepal in the south-east.

The favourite haunts of this little antelope are districts where the ground is hilly and wooded, but not encumbered with thick jungle : a country, in fact, similar to that met with between Rawal Pindi and Muree, after the plains are left. Unlike blackbuck, it is not fond of company, and it is seldom that more than two or three are seen together, while it is frequently solitary. In these unsocial habits it agrees with the African duiker-boks, as it does in its partiality for covert. In constantly keeping in the neighbourhood of water, and in drinking regularly once a day, it differs, however, from the typical duiker-bok, which, is frequently met with far from water ; but in this respect the Natal duiker-bok comes nearer to the chousingha, since that species drinks once daily in cold and twice in hot weather. The pairing-season of the chousingha takes place during the summer rains, the young making their appearance during the following January or February, so that the period of gestation is about six months. From their shyness these antelopes are difficult to approach ; when put up, they start with a peculiar jerky run, which can never be mistaken ; this jerkiness also characterising their walk. The fawns are either one or two in number ; and if taken sufficiently early are easily tamed and make pleasing pets.

Most sportsmen say that the flesh of the chousingha is dry and tasteless, although it may be improved by being well larded with mutton fat; but Dr. Blanford, wrote of it more favourably, although admitting that it is much inferior to that of the chinkara or the blackbuck.

THE BLACKBUCK, OR INDIAN ANTELOPE

(*Antilope cervicapra*)

NATIVE NAMES.—*Ena* (male), *Harina* AND *Mirga*, SANSCRIT; *Haran* OR *Harna* (male), *Harni* (female), *Kalwit* (female) AND *Mrig*, HINDUSTANI; *Kala* (male), *Goria* (female), IN TIRHOOT; *Kalsar* (male), *Baoti* (female), IN BEHAR; *Bureta* IN BHAGALPUR; *Barant* AND *Sasin*, NEPALESE; *Alali* (male), *Gandoli* (female), BAORI; *Badu*, HO KOL; *Bamani-haran*, URIA AND MAHRATHI; *Phandayat*, MAHRATHI; *Kutsar*, KORKU; *Veliman*, TAMIL; *Irri* (male), *Ledi*, AND *Jinkar*, TELEGU; *Chigri* AND *Hule-kara*, CANARESE.

(PLATE V, fig. 5)

Although now in such familiar use as to be an English word, the name antelope appears originally to have been employed to denote a fabulous or semi-fabulous animal; Eustathius, in the fourth century of our era, alluding by this name to an imaginary creature dwelling on the banks of the Euphrates, which was reported to entangle itself in bushes with its horns, and to saw down trees with the same weapons. As to the origin of the name there is some degree of doubt, but it has been suggested that it is a derivation from *Pantholops*, the old Coptic title for the mysterious unicorn. Whatever be its derivation and origin, it is certain that by early English writers and subsequently by the French naturalist Buffon the name antelope was applied to the present species; and although, both in its original form and as the Latinised *Antilope*, the term has been extended so as to include all the ruminants commonly known as antelopes, yet it is to the Indian blackbuck that it properly belongs, and it is to that species alone that the scientific title *Antilope* is now restricted. Properly, therefore, the blackbuck ought to be known as *the* antelope, although, according to present usage, if employed at all, the latter name must be qualified by the prefix Indian.

Although so common, the blackbuck is one of the most graceful of all antelopes; and its elegant, spirally twisted black horns have long been in use in the courts of Indian rajas as handles to the *chowris*, or yak-tail fly-whisks. It is one of the few antelopes in which the male differs markedly from the female in colour; the others being the nilgai and certain kinds of African bushbucks and kobs. The black livery assumed by old bucks of this species is indeed a specialised feature; fawn being the original colour of all antelopes of this group. In addition to being the sole representative of the genus *Antilope* (in its restricted sense), the blackbuck is likewise the type of a large group, or subfamily, of antelopes which includes, among others, the saiga of the Russian steppes, the Tibetan chiru, the gazelles, and the African springbuck and impala. All the members of this group are small or medium-sized antelopes, generally of graceful and slender build, always with narrow, hairy, sheep-like muzzles, usually with more or less short tails, and invariably with narrow, high-crowned cheek-teeth resembling those of sheep. With the exception of the majority of the gazelles and the springbuck, horns are normally developed in the bucks alone. From the gazelles (as indeed from all other representatives of the group), the blackbuck is sharply differentiated by the beautiful spiral horns of the bucks and the sable coat donned by adult members of that sex. Very characteristic is the large size of the face-glands, which open by a linear slit, and during the rutting-season are constantly everted by the bucks. Glands are likewise present in all the feet, as also in the groin; and the does, as in other members of the group, have a single pair of teats. The hoofs are delicate and sharply pointed, and the knees furnished with tufts of stiff hairs.

In height the blackbuck stands about 32 inches, and its average weight is about 85 pounds. The long and slender corkscrew-like horns of the bucks, which arise near together on the forehead, are cylindrical and divergent, but display great individual variation in the degree of divergence. Their spiral is, however, always comparatively close; and the ridges, or rings, which encircle the horn, extend from the base (where they are more approximated than elsewhere) nearly to the tip. Usually the number of turns in the spiral is from three to four, but five is by no means uncommon, and in the unique example shown in fig. 27 the number reaches six. In this specimen, which belongs to Mr. A. O. Hume and was obtained in the Delhi district, the length, measured in a straight line, is 28¼ inches, and the interval between the tips 17¾ inches. The former dimension is only known to be exceeded in the case of a specimen once in the possession of General Sir Bindon Blood, in which the length is stated to be half-an-inch more. In horns of over 20 inches in length the interval between the tips varies from a minimum of 13½ to a maximum of 24½ inches. Throughout the greater part of the Indian peninsula blackbuck horns rarely exceed 22 inches in length, from 16 to 20 inches being a fair measurement for good specimens. Rajputana and Hurriana are the districts where the longest horns are generally met with. In exceptional instances does develop horns, which are somewhat irregular in shape, and generally curve more or less backwards.

In does of all ages and in younger bucks the colour

of the head, upper-parts of the body, and outer sides of the limbs is yellowish fawn, while the under-parts are white ; a pale band runs in the fawn a short distance above the sharp line of division from the white. In old bucks the colour of the upper-parts is blackish brown, passing almost into black in aged individuals ; the nape of the neck is, however, always brownish rufous, and the front and sides, as well as the face, with the exception of an irregular white patch round each eye, are blackish brown. With the acquisition of the black coat, the light lateral streak disappears from the flanks of old bucks. Information is required as to the age at which bucks begin to acquire their sable dress, and also as to whether this is done by all. A mounted specimen from Madras in the British Museum, which appears to be adult, exhibits scarcely any trace of blackness, and the writer has been informed that such a condition is common in Southern India. Colonel Heber Percy states, indeed, in the "Badminton Library," that many full-grown bucks with good heads in all parts of India never seem to turn black at all, although the master-buck of a herd is always so at the proper season. He adds, on the authority of Major Fitz-Herbert, that the master-buck, with the change of coat that takes place after the rutting-season in the spring, turns brown, regaining his full sable hue at the close of the rains. While he is in the brown dress he resigns the charge of the herd to a younger buck, who remains black. Other observers believe that all the bucks become more or less brown during the hot weather.

The blackbuck is exclusively Indian, occurring locally from the foot of the Himalaya to the neighbourhood of Cape Comorin, but not crossing the Palk Strait into Ceylon. In a transverse direction its range extends from the Punjab to Lower Assam, while its southern limit appears to be Point Calimere ; it is unknown on the Malabar coast to the south of the neighbourhood of Surat, as it is in the swamps of the

Ganges delta, which are unsuited to its habits. It is, however, not absolutely unknown in Lower Bengal,

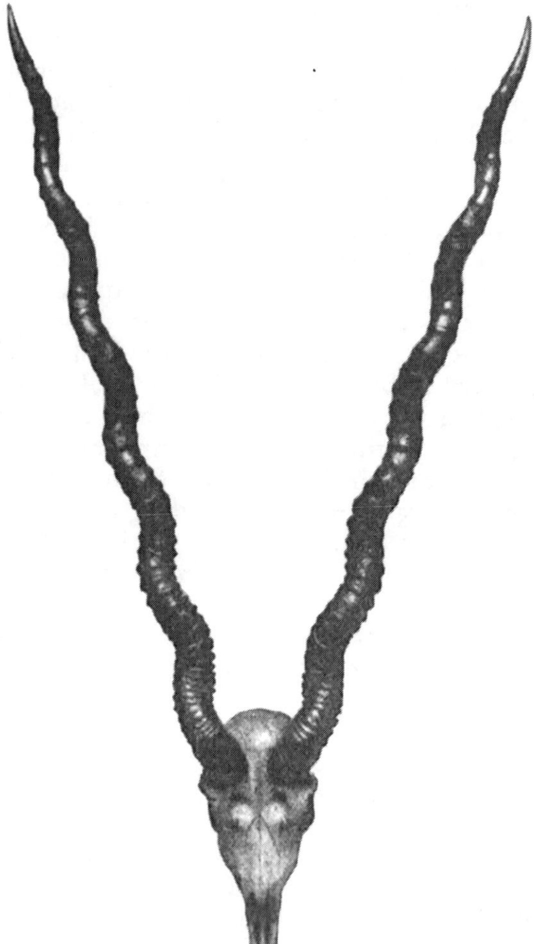

FIG. 27.—Skull and Horns of the Blackbuck, from a specimen in the possession of Mr. A. O. Hume.

since it frequents plains in the neighbourhood of the coast in Midnapore, as it does those of Orissa. The

Jhelam and the rivers joining it to flow into the Indus appear to form the northern boundary of the Indian antelope in the Punjab. The species is most abundant in the North-West Provinces, and on the confines of the Indian desert between Rajputana and the Punjab, where, as already mentioned, it grows longer and finer horns than in the south ; but even in these districts it is only locally and apparently capriciously distributed, being unknown in many places apparently in every way suited to its habits. The Mattra district and the neighbourhood of Meerut are well-known centres for buck-shooting.

Although often found in the *churs*, or islands covered with long grass in the river-valleys, as well as on the banks of the latter, blackbuck are essentially inhabitants of open plains, avoiding hilly and forest-clad districts. No other Indian ruminant occurs in such extensive herds, and although it is difficult to credit the statement that in the Hissar district the numbers in a herd were estimated at between 8000 and 10,000, yet there is no doubt that in old days these were very large indeed. More commonly the herds consist of from about ten to thirty, or even fifty does, attended by a single master-buck, who does not, however, remain constantly in charge. The pairing-season takes place in February or March, the time varying somewhat according to locality. The young may be either one or two in number, and as they may be seen of all ages at all seasons, it would almost seem as if the period of gestation were not constant, although this is unlikely. Not unfrequently during the pairing-season the master-buck separates a particular doe as his special companion, whom he will not allow to rejoin the herd till the period is over. Young fawns are frequently concealed by their dams among grass or bushes ; and occasionally adults, especially if wounded, will resort to such covert.

The short grass which partially covers so much of the plains of India, as well as various kinds of cereal crops, afford the chief food-supply of the Indian antelope, grazing taking place at all hours of the day, although the herd frequently enjoys a period of repose during the hottest time. Whether blackbuck ever drink is a matter on which there is a difference of opinion, but that they can exist without taking liquid seems demonstrated by the occurrence of a herd on a narrow spit of land between the Chilka Salt-Lake in Orissa and the sea, where for thirty miles the only fresh water obtainable is derived from wells. Exception has been taken to this statement, and the suggestion made that there may be irrigation canals or troughs of water used for cattle. The spot is, however, I believe, perfectly barren. That there is nothing improbable in the statement is evident from the fact that several kinds of antelopes in the Kalahari Desert of South Africa never drink for at least many months in succession.

When a herd of blackbuck is frightened and starts off to escape from intruders, its members invariably take a number of leaps high in the air, after the manner of springbuck. After continuing these gambols for a few hundred yards, the entire herd settles into a gallop, the speed of which, except under special conditions, easily ensures escape even from the swiftest greyhounds. Occasionally, indeed, blackbuck have been pulled down by greyhounds on ordinary ground; and on heavy sand, as in parts of Orissa and the Punjab, as well as on the soft rich pastures of Point Calimere, to the south of Trichinopoli, they can be taken by dogs with no great difficulty, as they also can in other districts when the ground is soft and holding after heavy rains. Blackbuck have, too, occasionally been speared by riding down, but it requires a horse with speed and power of endurance to effect this; an ordinary horse frequently having considerable difficulty in overtaking a wounded buck. The flesh of this antelope is of good quality, although inferior to that of the chinkara.

If captured young, blackbuck can easily be tamed, but old males are apt to be spiteful, especially during the pairing-season. During this season they walk about with a peculiar mincing gait, the head being thrown back so that the horns lie on the back, and the face-glands widely opened. At such seasons bucks frequently utter a peculiar short grunt, the only other sound the species produces being a hissing by the does. When in this state of excitement, old bucks are dangerous both to human beings and to other animals in their neighbourhood.

The wariness of the species varies in different districts according to the amount of disturbance to which the herds are subjected. In districts where there is little shooting the herds may be approached within a hundred and fifty yards or less; while they will frequently allow natives with carts or oxen on their way to and from ploughing to come comparatively close. Natives are, indeed, always allowed to approach nearer than Europeans, and sportsmen sometimes don the native dress in order to get within range. Solitary master-bucks are always more difficult to approach than those with the herds, and to stalk these successfully demands all the skill and ingenuity of the sportsman. When engaged in combat for possession of the does, old bucks are less wary than usual. In stalking a herd, the plan usually recommended is to walk round in a semicircle, gradually closing in, and taking only side glances at the quarry, till within range, when the shot should be immediately delivered standing. If two sportsmen are working together, from opposite sides of the herd, the stalk is rendered much easier. On the approach of an intruder, some of the does will often begin to leap into the air, but this by no means implies that the herd is about to seek safety in flight. A horse, led by a native groom, or sais, which can be ridden to within stalking distance, will be found an invaluable auxiliary in buck-shooting.

The Blackbuck, or Indian Antelope

The natives of India have many—for the most part unsportsmanlike—ways of capturing blackbuck. The most celebrated is the capture by trained hunting-leopards, or chitas, which are taken out blindfold in a cart, and slipped at their quarry when the vehicle has approached as close as practicable. The hunting-leopard either secures his prey by a single rush (the speed of which is almost incredible), or, if he fail in this, gives up the pursuit in disgust. Another method is to place snares at intervals over a considerable area of ground, and then to drive the herd across it, when animals of all ages and both sexes are taken. A less common plan is to send a number of tame bucks, upon whose horns snares are tied, into the herd, when the master-buck challenges the intruders, and during the fight that ensues is frequently caught himself.

Colonel Heber Percy describes a method of stalking by means of a grass-screen and a tame buck and doe held in check by a long string. When the sportsman and his attendant come within a convenient distance of the herd, they set up the movable screen, which is furnished with a hole through which the muzzle of the rifle can be thrust, and take up their position behind, crouching down on their knees. Meanwhile the decoy buck and doe are incited to walk out in front of the screen, and soon attract the attention of the master-buck, who advances to challenge the intruding rival and carry off the doe. He is, however, somewhat curious and anxious with regard to the screen, and endeavours by a flanking movement to ascertain what is concealed behind. To obviate this the screen must be constantly shifted round in accordance with the movements of the buck, till he comes sufficiently near to afford a shot. It is said that the decoy buck should not be too old, or the herd-buck may be afraid to challenge him.

A white blackbuck is preserved in the Hon. Walter Rothschild's museum at Tring.

THE CHIRU, OR TIBETAN ANTELOPE

(*Pantholops hodgsoni*)

NATIVE NAMES.—*Tsus* (male), *Chus* (female), *Chiru* AND *Chuhu*, TIBETAN

(PLATE V, fig. 4)

Most fabulous animals appear to have a living prototype, and there seems considerable probability that the present species may be the one to which the legend of the unicorn owes its origin. At any rate this was the opinion of Brian Hodgson, to whom we are indebted for first making known the chiru, and who gave it the name of *Pantholops*, as being an ancient title of the unicorn. There has long been a tradition to the effect that the unicorn came from Tibet, and the long slender horns of the chiru, if seen in profile, might give rise to the idea of a unicorned animal. It is further remarkable that in Tibet itself there still exists a belief in the existence of a unicorn, even in districts where the chiru itself is a familiar animal. Possibly, as General Macintyre suggests in *The Hindu-Koh*, the legend may be based on a chiru that had lost one horn.

Whatever may be its relation to the fabled unicorn, the chiru is an interesting and peculiar member of the antelope tribe. As shown by the structure of its skull and teeth, it belongs to the same group as the blackbuck and the gazelles, although its nearest relative appears to be the saiga of the Russian steppes. A male chiru stands from about 31 to 33 inches at the shoulder, and is distinguishable from all other antelopes by the long, erect, slightly curved, and sub-lyrate black horns, puffy nose, hairy muzzle, thick coat of soft and almost woolly hair, and short bushy tail. The puffiness of the nose is due to a protuberance situated by the side of each nostril, which marks the position of a large lateral chamber, or sac, in the latter; this being perhaps designed to assist respiration at high altitudes. Another peculiarity of the chiru is the great development of the inguinal glands, which form tubes, running up a considerable distance into the body. Glands are present between the hoofs of both fore and hind feet; but there are none on the face below the eyes. The horns of the bucks, which rise close together a short distance above the eyes, and are remarkable for their fine grain, are compressed from side to side, and carry a number of bold transverse ridges on the front surface for the greater part of their length, but are smooth behind; their general shape has been already mentioned, but it may be added that they curve slightly forwards at the tips. Chiru-horns are remarkable for their constancy in size and shape; the largest pair on record are the property of Mr. A. O. Hume, and measure 27¾ inches in length along the curve, with a basal circumference of 6⅛ inches.

The coat is so thick and upright as to feel almost like the wool of a South Down sheep, and thus forms an efficient protection against the winter cold of the elevated regions to which the animal is restricted. There is considerable variation in the colour of bucks. In a specimen, probably from Ladak, figured by Dr. Blanford in the *Zoology of the Second Yarkand Expedition*, the whole of the upper-parts and outer sides of the limbs are pale fawn-colour (light rufous brown), while the under side of the head and neck is greyish white, and the inner surface of the ears, a streak down each buttock, the belly, and the hinder half of the inner surface of the upper portion of the limbs are white. The whole of the face below the horns, and the front surfaces of both limbs are dark brown or black. On the other hand, in a mounted buck from the north of Sikhim exhibited in the British Museum the fawn-colour only occupies the middle of the back, the parts in front and behind this being dirty white; while on the fore-limb the black band commences on the side of the chest and extends on to part of the outer side of the leg, although in the hind-leg the whole outer surface, as well as the front, is black. In both specimens the black is continuous over the whole of the face; but in a head from Changchenmo figured in Kinloch's *Large Game Shooting in Tibet, etc.*, the black is patchy, and does not extend continuously over the face, the same condition obtaining in a head from the same district presented by Mr. Walter Rothschild to the British Museum. About the same amount of black is noticeable on the face of a buck shot in Ladak by Major Powell Cotton, but the dark stripe on the fore-leg is narrower than usual, partially interrupted, and stops short at the upper pastern, instead of descending to the hoof, while in the hind-leg the dark markings are wanting. Since there is no evidence that these variations are local peculiarities, they must for the present be regarded as individual. They are nevertheless decidedly noteworthy.

Although General A. A. Kinloch, who was one of the first sportsmen to describe the chiru in its native haunts, states that the females have short horns, other observers have shown that this sex is hornless. The does, which have two teats, lack the black markings of the bucks.

The skull of a chiru is remarkable and unmistakable on account of the great relative size of the aperture and cavity of the nose.

Although the chiru was first made known to science in 1826 and more fully described by Brian Hodgson eight years later, it was comparatively little known to sportsmen before the appearance of General Kinloch's book on big game shooting in 1869. It is there stated that although horns had been previously brought by traders to Naini Tal and Darjiling, it was not till some few years before 1869 that the animal had been killed by an English sportsman. The fortunate individual appears to have been the late Mr. Wilson, of Mussorie, a well-known "Shikari," who shot chiru on the Changchenmo river, in North-Eastern Ladak. Since that time Changchenmo has become a favourite hunting-ground for this antelope, which has also been killed farther eastwards, in the neighbourhood of the Manasarowar Lake, and elsewhere.

Chiru are confined to the arid districts of Tibet lying beyond the snowy range of the Himalaya, but their exact limits are not yet ascertained. Westwards they extend into North-Eastern Ladak, and they have been obtained in Hundes, across the Niti Pass, as well as in Northern Tibet. Probably they inhabit the whole Tibetan plateau. From 13,000 to 18,000 feet are the elevations at which they are commonly found in Ladak, but at times they doubtless ascend to higher elevations. Although they are not unfrequently called snow-antelope, this is by no means a satisfactory name, as the greater part of the country in which chiru are found is free from snow in summer, and does not receive a great amount even in winter. In Ladak favourite haunts of chiru in summer are the grassy flats bordering the plains of the Changchenmo river, where the present writer made his acquaintance with the species. They are also to be found in other parts of the Changchenmo valley, where deep ravines lead from the higher grounds to the river valley.

At the time of his visit the present writer used to see only some half-dozen chiru on the plain at once, but cannot recollect whether there were females among them. General Kinloch states, however, that at the date of his trips to Changchenmo does were hardly ever seen there, and that although he met with herds of from sixty to seventy bucks, on only one occasion did he recognise a doe among them, and this in three visits. On the other hand, Mr. Darrah, in his *Sport in the Highlands of Kashmir*, mentions on one occasion having seen a party comprising three does and two bucks in

Changchenmo ; and General Macintyre likewise tells of having seen mixed herds. Owing to the reluctance of sportsmen to shoot them, specimens of female chiru are rare in collections.

The writer's own experience of the difficulty of getting within range of chiru on the Changchenmo flats is confirmed by General Kinloch, who states that he frequently found it a good plan to drive them. The banks above these flats are very steep, and as it is only in certain places that the chiru can ascend them, if the sportsman places himself in the most favourable of these paths, and sends a native to drive the game towards him, he will stand a chance of getting a shot, when it would be impossible by stalking.

July and August are the best months for shooting in Changchenmo, as the river-flats are then free from snow and carry an abundant crop of grass, to which the chiru descend for grazing in the morning and evening. In the early part of the summer, according to the observations of the last-named sportsman, the chiru apparently frequent the higher and more exposed plains and slopes, on which the snow cannot lie. As the snow which has accumulated during the winter on the river-flats melts, the antelopes gradually descend. At no time of the year do they frequent precipitous ground. After their morning feed on the flats in summer, they seek higher and more exposed situations in which to pass the day until it is time to descend again for the evening meal. When reposing for the day, they are reported to excavate deep hollows in the stony ground, in which they lie with only their heads and horns exposed to view.

Like all Tibetan animals, chiru appear to depend as much on sight as on smell to warn them of the approach of enemies. According to Brian Hodgson, who seems to have derived his information from native reports, chiru pair in winter, and the does give birth to their fawns (of which there is but one at a time) in the summer. In summer they are much troubled with bots, and their skins are then difficult to preserve in good condition. The Ladakis, who, like most uneducated people, endeavour to find a reason for every peculiarity of structure they do not understand, have a theory that, when pursued, the chiru inflate their inguinal glands with air, and are thus enabled to increase their speed ! General Macintyre describes the flesh of these antelopes as tender and juicy.

The chiru has never been exhibited alive in England ; and it is doubtful if it would survive the journey to the plains of India.

THE GOA, OR TIBETAN GAZELLE

(*Gazella picticaudata*)

NATIVE NAMES.—*Goa* OR *Ragao*, TIBETAN

(PLATE V, fig. 9)

Of the three species of gazelle found within the limits of the area treated of in this book, one has horns in both sexes, while in the other two the females are hornless. The goa is one of the two latter, and is specially distinguished by a white disk on the buttocks, surrounding the tail, and the peculiar and sharp backward curvature of the horns of the bucks, which are not distinctly hooked at the tip, and have somewhat the shape of a native Indian scimitar, or *talwar*. Another peculiarity of the goa, which is, however, shared by its larger relative the Mongolian gazelle, is the absence of the dark and light face-streaks occurring in most members of the genus. The tail and ears, as compared with those of more typical gazelles, are short. Another peculiarity is the absence of the usual face-glands below the eyes, the position of which is indicated by naked spaces. The tufts of long hairs at the knees, present in so many gazelles, are likewise wanting in the goa. In winter the hair becomes long and soft, but the summer coat is much shorter. The black horns of the bucks have the transverse ridges less strongly marked but more crowded together than in other Asiatic gazelles, their number reaching to between twenty-five and thirty in old individuals. Fourteen and a half inches is the longest length recorded for goa-horns: this measurement being that of a pair from Hanle, in Spiti, belonging to the Hon. Walter Rothschild. There are numerous examples ranging between 13 and 13½ inches in length.

A full-grown goa stands from 24 to 25 inches at the shoulder. In winter the colour of the hair on the head and back is light sandy fawn, with a grizzly tinge due to the pale tips of the hairs; but the summer coat is more distinctly grey. The under-parts are white, with the line of division from the fawn of the back not very strongly marked; on the buttocks the white area forms a large patch, including the tail, and round this disk the fawn of the back assumes a more rufous tint than elsewhere. The tip of the tail is dark rufous brown or black; and it was from this feature that Brian Hodgson gave to the goa the name *picticaudata*.

The goa, sometimes miscalled the Tibetan ravine-deer, has much the same geographical distribution as the chiru, being restricted to the Tibetan plateau, where it is met with at elevations between 13,000 and 18,000 feet. It likewise frequents the same kind of ground as the latter, avoiding rocky and steep localities, and selecting undulating plains and gently sloping valleys. In early summer goa are found in small herds, which apparently include animals of both sexes and of all ages; but by September, or somewhat earlier, the old bucks separate themselves from the herds, and go about in small parties of from two to four or five head. Although difficult to approach, goa are unlike many

Himalayan ruminants in that, when fired at, they do not go straight away, but, after running for a certain distance, stop and begin to feed again, thus affording the sportsman a second chance. When running off, the white hairs of the rump-patch are partially erected and expanded, in the same manner as in Japanese deer; the white patch in both cases serving as a guide for the members of a herd to follow their leaders in flight. The grey summer-coat renders goa difficult to detect, and affords them the best protection at the season when the ground is free from snow. In their winter dress they may accord better with a snow-clad landscape.

In regard to goa-shooting, Mr. H. Z. Darrah, in *Sport in the Highlands of Kashmir*, recommends the sportsman who is on the ground in late summer to avoid the herds, and confine his attentions to the small parties of old bucks. If these are seen moving towards ground where there seems to be a chance of getting within range, the sportsman should make a circuit, and endeavour to intercept them. Under other conditions, it is preferable to advance straight towards them in the hope of driving them out into the open. Lastly, whether at short or long range, a shot should be taken whenever an opportunity presents itself, as, owing to the habit already mentioned, in the event of a miss, there is no fear of the game taking themselves beyond hope of pursuit. Large herds, when on open ground, will let nothing approach within 400 yards; and it is impossible to drive them on to broken ground, for the reason that they refuse to go.

The goa's chief enemies, other than man, are probably the snow-leopard, the Tibetan lynx, the wild dog, and the Tibetan wolf, the same animals likewise preying on the chiru. The fawns of both species are doubtless also carried off more or less frequently by eagles.

THE GOITRED GAZELLE

(*Gazella subgutturosa*)

NATIVE NAMES.—*Ahu*, PERSIAN ; *Kik* OR *Saikik* AND *Jairan*, TURKI

(PLATE V, fig. 8)

Although resembling the goa in the absence of horns in the female, the goitred gazelle is a very different animal, easily distinguished by a peculiar dilateable swelling in the throat of the bucks, the absence of a large white patch on the buttocks, the longer tail, the form of the horns, which are lyrate, with the tips somewhat turned inwards, and the presence of glands on the face below the eyes, and of more or less distinct dark face-markings. In the dilateable larynx, which produces the swelling in the throat, the species is in fact nearly allied to the rather larger Mongolian gazelle, from which it differs in possessing face-markings, as well as by the greater length of the tail, which is crested with black or blackish-brown hair, and the longer horns.

The goitred gazelle is one of those ruminants in which the summer and winter coats are very different, owing to the much greater length and shagginess of the latter, so that there is considerable difference in the appearance of the animal at the two seasons. In the bucks the lyrate horns diverge near the base, and have the tips turned inwards and converging, so that in a side view they present a not very strongly marked S-like curvature ; and the ridges on the horns are pronounced, and vary in number from sixteen to twenty-five. In the long winter coat the colour is paler than in summer, but the general coloration is as follows :—The upper-parts are rufescent sandy, while the under-portions, parts of the inner and front surfaces of the legs, and the buttocks up to but not including the tail, are white; the white and the fawn being distinctly defined, and separated by a darker band both on the flanks and the buttocks. In the winter coat the face is also often more or less white, and always shows a longitudinal stripe of fawn below each eye, while there may be a more or less distinct dark nose-streak. In old animals these dark face-markings differ from those of other members of the genus except the Marica gazelle of Arabia (in which the females are horned) in that the central dark band, when present, is interrupted on the forehead, which is thus pure white. In the summer coat of the typical race there is a pale line above the dark band on the flanks. The tail, which is of the length obtaining in ordinary gazelles, and thus unlike the stump to which it is reduced in the Mongolian species, is blackish brown or black on the upper surface. From 24 to 27 inches is the approximate shoulder-height.

Such is the general description of the species, but there are at least three local races of *Gazella subgutturosa*; and it is owing to the existence of these local forms that the animal is called the goitred gazelle instead of Persian gazelle. The reason for this is that if we call the species the Persian gazelle, and then speak of one variety as the Yarkand, and a second as the Altai gazelle, it looks as though we were dealing with three distinct species. By the other plan the species is designated as the goitred gazelle, while its races are respectively distinguished as the Persian, Yarkand, and Altai goitred gazelles.

It is to the typical or Persian race (*G. gutturosa typica*), as the only one found within the area treated of in this volume, that attention is directed. Fig. 28 represents a buck from Tehran, in the winter coat, which was living in the park at Woburn Abbey in 1899, and is now mounted in the British Museum. The condition of the horns, in which the ridges are unworn and continued right down to the base, shows that the animal is adult, although not aged. The height at the withers is about 24 inches; and the horns are relatively long and carry fully twenty ridges. When photographed, there was a short but distinct dark streak on each side of the face from the eye towards the angle of the mouth, but none along the middle of the face, which is white. At the time of its death these lateral marks had almost disappeared, leaving the whole face white. This slight development of the face-markings seems characteristic of adult bucks of the Persian race in Persia itself. In younger bucks and in does of all ages these markings are more developed, the cheek-lines being longer and broader, and the frontal line likewise conspicuous. The whole face is greyish, and the hair of the upper-parts darker and greyer.

The head of a male shown in plate v, fig. 8, which was obtained by Mr. T. W. Greenfield in Baluchistan and presented by him to the British Museum, differs from the Woburn Abbey buck by the stronger development of the face-markings. The horns, which indicate an animal of approximately the same age as the latter, are of nearly the same relative length, and carry about the same number of ridges. The strongly defined face-markings comprise one frontal and two cheek streaks, as in does; the former terminating some distance above the muzzle in the shape of an inverted V. For the greater part of their length these streaks are bright fawn-colour, passing into a blackish brown patch near the middle of their length. In spite of this fuller development of the face-markings, this specimen should perhaps be assigned to the typical race, although showing an approximation in the feature mentioned to the Yarkand form.

Two pairs of horns presented in 1889 by Dr. Aitchison to the British Museum apparently indicate that it is the Persian race which is found in

Afghanistan. Dr. Aitchison brought home living specimens of this gazelle, which he presented to the London Zoological Gardens; and a descendant of one of these is stated to form the subject of the plate of the Persian gazelle in the *Book of Antelopes*, although it would seem that the artist has largely used the

Fig. 28.—Persian Goitred Gazelle at Woburn Abbey, from a photograph by the Duchess of Bedford.

British Museum specimen of the Altai race in making the figure.

If the foregoing determinations are correct, the typical Persian race of the goitred gazelle is an inhabitant of the Caucasus, Asia Minor, Persia, Baluchistan, and Afghanistan, although its northern limits are not defined. *Gazella subgutturosa typica* is found everywhere in the Persian highlands, from an elevation of about 3000 to some 4000 feet above the sea-level, but is unknown in the plains bordering the

Persian Gulf and the Arabian Sea, while in the central deserts of the country it may be more or less replaced by *G. bennetti*. With the exception that it is more of a desert animal, its habits are apparently very similar to those of the ordinary Indian gazelle. The late Sir O. B. St. John states that, like the ghor-khur, it especially affects the salt-deserts, and is thus probably able to exist for long periods without drinking. It appears to breed in the sheltered valleys at the foot of the hills, and is commonly seen in small parties of from three to half-a-dozen head. When it has a fair start, the Persian gazelle will get clear away from the fleetest greyhounds ; but if suddenly roused when reposing in a hollow, or when the ground is heavy from rain, bucks may be pulled down by good dogs. In Baluchistan its habits are doubtless similar.

The Yarkand race of the species (*G. subgutturosa yarcandensis*) was described in 1879 by Dr. W. T. Blanford in the *Scientific Results of the Second Yarkand Expedition*, where a coloured plate is given of a group in the summer dress. These specimens came from the neighbourhood of Yarkand and Kashgar. In the original description the Yarkand gazelle was stated to differ principally from the typical Persian gazelle in the much darker face-markings, and the smaller divergence of the horns of the bucks. It was also said to be probably larger, although not much importance was attached to this point, on account of a presumed variation in size of the typical race. The largest number of ridges on any of the Yarkand horns is fourteen. The colour of the upper-parts is described as light rufous brown (fawn). In the coloured plate the face-markings are represented as strongly developed, the middle one running right up the forehead, where it splits to terminate at the base of each horn ; between the dark bands, with the exception of a narrow streak, the greater part of the face is fawn-coloured like the back, so that there is an absence of white on the

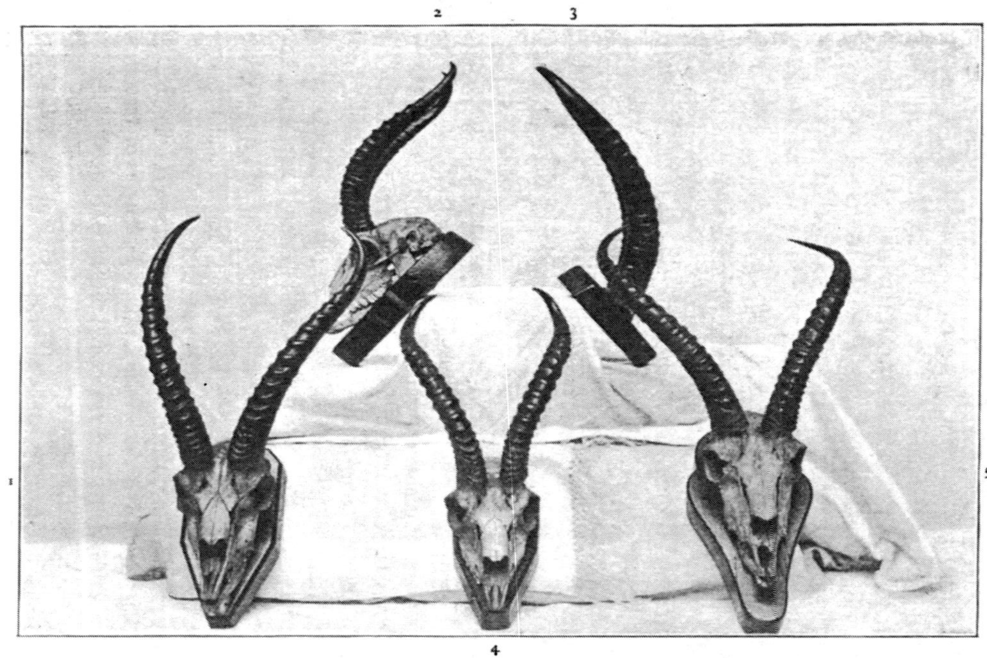

FIG. 29.—Skulls and Horns of Yarkand (1, 2, 5) and Persian (3, 4) Races of the Goitred Gazelle. From specimens in the collection of Mr. A. O. Hume.

forehead. The white on the buttocks is represented as extending more on to the sides than is the case with the typical Persian gazelle in winter dress.

The horns in a number of skulls of this gazelle collected by the late Mr. Dalgleish in Yarkand and presented by Mr. Hume to the British Museum are longer and stouter than those of the typical Persian gazelle, and specially characterised by the less numerous ridges, which seldom exceed sixteen. The degree of divergence of the horns varies, and does not seem to be of much importance. A pair from Yarkand in the possession of Mr. Hume measures 16 inches in length along the curve and 5 inches in basal circumference.

It thus seems that the Yarkand gazelle is a well-characterised race, distinguished from the typical Persian gazelle by superior size, the longer and less numerously ridged horns, the more pronounced face-markings, the fawn-coloured forehead, and the greater amount of white on the buttocks. An approach to the Yarkand race is, however, so far as face-markings are concerned, made by the representative of this gazelle from Baluchistan; while a Persian skull presented by Dr. Blanford to the British Museum has horns more like those of the Yarkand race than is usually the case.

The skulls shown in fig. 29 came from Eastern (Chinese) Turkestan, two of them being from Lob Nor, on the western border of that territory near the Gobi desert. They are thus within the distributional area of the present species; that of the Mongolian gazelle being Northern and Eastern Mongolia. They are, moreover, much longer than typical horns of that species, and apparently present no characters by which they can be distinguished from those of the present animal. Moreover, the nasal bones of these skulls have the notched terminal extremities by which the goitred gazelle may be distinguished from both the goa and the Mongolian gazelle, in which the terminal extremities of these bones are entire. The same notching of the nasals is observable in the unusually long-horned skull from Kuldja shown in fig. 30. The range of the Yarkand goitred gazelle apparently extends from Eastern Turkestan to Lob Nor and the confines of the Gobi desert.

FIG. 30.—Skull and Horns of the Yarkand Gazelle from Kuldja, in the possession of Sir E. G. Loder.

Gazella subgutturosa also ranges into the Altai, where it is represented by a third local race. An adult buck presented to the British Museum in 1891 by Mr. St. George Littledale, and shot in the Sair, or Saiar Mountains, in the Great Altai on the north-western border of Mongolia, nearly due east of a point midway between the Semipalatinsk and the Semirechinsk Altai, in latitude 86° E., longitude 47° N., is considerably larger than the typical Persian race, standing about 27 inches at the shoulder. The advanced age of this specimen is indicated by the nearly smooth, slightly wrinkled band at the base of the ridged portion of the horns; the ridges themselves being somewhat worn and about twelve in number. Compared with the above-mentioned Baluchi head of the Persian race, it seems evident that the horns are of a perfectly distinct type. In the few ridges on the horns the Altai goitred gazelle comes nearer to the Yarkand race, although the horns are shorter. Moreover, with the exception of a pale fawn-coloured streak running from below each eye, the face is devoid of markings and nearly white; this distinguishing the Altai animal markedly from the Yarkand race. Although larger than a mounted specimen of the Persian race, the Altai buck has shorter horns. It has also shorter hoofs, but this difference may be due to the nature of the ground on which the animals lived.

The following notes on the habits of this race were furnished by Mr. A. O. Hume. "In Yarkand and Kashgar they are found throughout the forest belt, and in the deserts bordering these for some thirty miles or so on either side of these belts. Wherever there is cultivation they may be found in its neighbourhood. They cannot remain anywhere very far from water, for they drink regularly, and their paths to the water through the desert and through the jungle can always be distinctly traced; but they cross the desert north of the Tarim to the high-road and the cultivation about it, and so are found northwards to the base of the Thian-Shan. Though often seen in the desert, where they sleep out in the open in the daytime, and where they spend the night, they resort to the forest or jungle or the edges of cultivation morning and evening, to graze and drink. They never ascend the mountains, though they may be found in the outer ravines of these, and their range may be said to be from 3500 to 5000 feet, or perhaps at Kilian to 6000 feet."

THE CHINKARA, OR INDIAN GAZELLE

(*Gazella bennetti*)

NATIVE NAMES.—*Chinkara*, *Chikara*, AND *Kalpunch*, HINDUSTANI ; *Phaskela* IN THE NORTH-WEST PROVINCES ; *Ask*, *Ast*, AND *Ahu*, BALUCHI ; *Khazm*, BRAHUI ; *Kalsipi* OF THE MAHRATTAS ; *Tiska*, *Budari*, AND *Mudari*, CANARESE ; *Sankhali* IN MYSORE ; *Porsya* (male), *Chari* (female), BAORI ; *Burudu-jinka*, TELEGU

(PLATE V, figs. 7, 7*a*)

Although the chinkara must have been known to Anglo-Indian sportsmen at least since the commencement of the last century, it was not recognised as a distinct species till the year 1831, having previously been confounded with the Arabian gazelle. In the year mentioned it was named *Antilope bennetti* by Colonel Sykes in honour of Mr. E. T. Bennett, at that time secretary of the Zoological Society of London ; and when the gazelles were separated from the genus *Antilope* to form a group by themselves the species changed its name to *Gazella bennetti*. By many sportsmen this gazelle is commonly spoken of by its Hindustani title of chinkara, and no better name could be desired ; but, unfortunately, it has also acquired the name of "ravine deer," which is one of the worst misnomers in existence, as if there are two groups of animals which ought not to be confounded, they are antelopes and deer.

The chinkara is a more typical gazelle than either of the species hitherto described ; that is to say, it agrees with the majority of the members of that group in leading characters, so that it has to be distinguished by comparatively minute details, but as the chinkara is the only one of the more typical gazelles inhabiting India, there is no difficulty in its identification.

From both the goa and the goitred gazelle the chinkara differs in that the doe is furnished with horns. The fact that the horns of the bucks do not turn in at the tips serves at once to distinguish the species from the goitred gazelle (from which it also differs by the absence of the swelling in the throat of the bucks), while the want of a large white tail-patch (to say nothing of the difference in the curvature of the horns) separates it from the goa.

In size this species is approximately equal to the Persian race of the goitred gazelle, the height being about 23 or 24 inches at the withers and 26½ inches at the rump; while a buck weighs about 50 lbs., and a doe from 10 to 15 lbs. less. Although from 10 to 12 inches is the average length of the horns of bucks, and their basal girth about 4 inches, specimens respectively measuring 14½ and 15 inches in length are recorded, the longer of these having a basal circumference of 5 inches. Female horns are smaller, 8 inches being apparently the longest on record.

In bucks the horns are nearly straight, showing a small lateral divergence when viewed from the front, but with a slight S-like curvature when seen from the side, with the tips bending somewhat forwards. Generally the number of ridges on each horn is fifteen or sixteen, but there are seventeen or eighteen in the specimen shown in fig. 31; and it is stated that there may be as many as twenty-five. In the female of the Indian race the horns are devoid of ridges.

The face has distinct glands, opening by small apertures below each eye; and the knees are furnished with the usual tufts of stiff hairs.

The chinkara has the usual gazelle face-markings

well developed ; the general colour of the upper-parts is light chestnut, becoming somewhat darker at the junction with the white of the flanks and buttocks, although not showing either a distinct dark lateral band or a pale band ; while the chin, chest, under-parts, and a streak on the sides of the buttocks are white, the white stopping short of the root of the tail. The tail is dark brown or black ; but the knee-tufts are somewhat variable in colour, although frequently dark brown. The face has a whitish streak running down each side, externally to which is a rufous stripe, while the middle, from the roots of the horns to the nostrils, is dark rufous, sometimes with a dusky patch above the nose.

Fig. 31.—Head of the Chinkara, from a specimen shot by Mr. L. M. le Champion.

In Sind and the Indian desert the chinkara assumes a paler tone, as is commonly the case with desert animals ; and if this difference be considered worthy of subspecific distinction, the desert form should be known as *Gazella bennetti christyi*.

The range of the chinkara extends from the plains and low hills of North-Western and Central India through Baluchistan to the eastern shore of the Persian Gulf. The Baluchi and Persian form differs, however, in certain characters of the female, and is referred to a distinct race. The Indian, or typical race (*G. bennetti typica*), unless the pale Sind variety be separated, is found in suitable localities over a considerable area of the peninsula, being met with all over the Punjab, Sind, Rajputana, the North-West Provinces, and the Bombay Presidency, with the exception of the Western

Ghats and the Konkan. In Central India it occurs as far east as Palamow and the western portion of Sarguja ; in the Central Provinces it has been met with as far to the eastward as Seoni and Chanda ; while it also occurs in Hyderabad territory, and in the Madras Presidency to some distance south of the Kistna valley, having been recorded from Anantapur, to the south of Kurnul, as well as in the north of Mysore.

The chinkara is allied to the Arabian and Muscat gazelles (*G. arabica* and *muscatensis*), as well as to the Dorcas gazelle (*G. dorcas*) of North Africa.

In general habits the chinkara is similar to the majority of the members of its genus, being generally found in small parties of from two to half-a-dozen individuals, although on rare occasions as many as from ten to twenty may be seen in company. Seldom frequenting alluvial plains, and avoiding cultivated land to a greater extent than the blackbuck, the chinkara is partial to more or less sandy, open tracts of uncultivated lands, especially those cut up by ravines ; the sand-hills of the Indian desert being favourite resorts of the species. It is, however, by no means confined to open country, being often met with in thin bush or tree-jungle ; while, where the country is suitable, it may be found on the tops of hills. Grass and the leaves of bushes and shrubs form its chief nutriment ; and although partial to the luscious grass growing in the neighbourhood of water, it is believed by some observers never to drink, being often found during the hot season where there is no water except in deep wells. Even in places where water is found, Dr. Blanford states that he never saw the footprints of gazelles among those of animals that came to drink at the pools. The writer of a review of the original edition of this work in the *Asian* newspaper disputes this opinion in the following words :—" I have seen a chinkara," he writes, " in the act of drinking, when I was waiting one evening for a panther, near a pool of water. In one locality during a drought, the gazelles used to troop down in numbers to the wooden troughs by the wells, as evidenced by their tracks. There were regular beaten paths made by their footmarks, and they drank under cover of darkness."

This gazelle is much troubled, during the rainy season, in Harriana, at any rate, by bots under the skin at the root of the tail; and the following incident, for the truth of which the anonymous author must be responsible, appeared in the *Asian* newspaper of 7th November 1899:—"While out shooting in the Harriana district during the month of February a couple of years ago, I was greatly interested and amused by the antics of a fox and a herd of chinkara I was stalking. I had got behind a hay-rick about 50 yards from the herd, when I observed a fox cautiously creep out from his burrow and stalk the buck nearest me. On getting to within about a yard of the buck, the fox crouched and commenced shaking himself from side to side just as a cat does preparatory to springing. The buck prepared to meet the attack by coming to the charge, but hardly had he done so, when the fox sprang at him and caused him to give a big bound to one side. These tactics over, the fox promptly started sniffing about and greedily devouring something he found. The operation I have described above was repeated about a dozen times with different members of the herd, when I cut the proceedings short with a shot. I rolled over the buck I fired at, and getting to the place where he lay hunted about to ascertain what the fox had been devouring. I found several whitish grubs, about the size and appearance of a newly formed chrysalis of the wild silkworm, lying about, and was at a loss to know how they came there till the buck I had shot was skinned. I then discovered about fifty or sixty of these grubs [bots] all along the spinal column under the skin, the larger ones partly protruding. Indeed, the skin, when it was removed and stretched, looked as if a charge of No. 1 shot had been put into it.

"Here then was the mystery of the performance I had witnessed. The whole thing seemed quite clear to my mind and prearranged. The fox gave the chinkara a start to make him bound, and the act of bounding, by tightening the skin, expelled the mature bots, and so provided him with a dainty morning meal, while it rid the chinkara of a painful and troublesome pest. I shot some five or six more chinkara after this, and they were one and all similarly infested with those bots, while curious to say four blackbuck I shot were quite free from them."

According to the observations of Sir Walter Elliot, chinkara bucks fight after the manner of rams, running at one another from a short distance, and striking their heads together with great violence. When alarmed, the chinkara stamps smartly with the fore-feet, like a sheep, at the same time uttering a loud hiss, whence it derives its Canarese name of *Tirka*. Does may often be seen followed by a pair of fawns; but neither the pairing-time nor the duration of gestation is definitely known, although the reviewer just quoted states that the fawns are in some cases at any rate born in winter.

The flesh of the chinkara is of excellent quality for the table, being much superior to that of the blackbuck; and as the species is so frequently found in broken ground, where stalking is comparatively easy, it affords very pretty shooting with a small-bore rifle, although the smallness of the mark renders accurate shooting essential. In spite of their general wildness chinkara do not go far when disturbed, so that with patience a shot is in most cases obtainable. On the fringe of the Indian Desert, where covert is scarce, a steady shooting horse, or, still better, a riding camel, is often essential to enable the sportsman to get within range. Fidgety and restless at times, and even when feeding constantly switching their tails from side to side, these gazelles when frightened invariably start off at once at a racing gallop, without the preliminary bounds so characteristic of their cousin the Indian antelope. Their speed is so great, and their endurance so marked, that it is seldom that they can be overtaken by dogs, although such a feat has been occasionally accomplished. The natives of certain parts of India were formerly, at any rate, in the habit of hunting the chinkara with the aid of the saker falcon, the bird being first flown at the animal, so as to strike it on the head and render it confused, when the greyhounds were slipped to rush in and pull it down.

Whether the Baluchi chinkara is entitled to rank as a distinct race may be open to doubt, but as it has received a name, it may be alluded to as *Gazella bennetti fuscifrons*. It was originally named by Dr. Blanford in 1873 on the evidence of a female head obtained by Sir O. B. St. John at Jalk, in Northern Baluchistan. Its claim to distinction is that the horns of this sex are distinctly, although not very prominently, ridged or ringed, and that the darker portions of the face are dark brown instead of rufous. When the male was discovered, it was found not to differ perceptibly from the ordinary Indian chinkara, except that the horns are a little more curved backwards, and slightly more lyrate when viewed from the front. From Baluchistan the chinkara extends to the head of the Persian Gulf in the neighbourhood of Bushire. There it inhabits the low country, as it does in Baluchistan, not ranging above the 3000 feet level, where it is replaced by the goitred gazelle, easily recognised, even at a comparatively long distance, by its lighter colour.

THE HANGUL, OR KASHMIR STAG

(*Cervus cashmirianus*)

NATIVE NAMES.—*Hangul*, *Honglu* (male), *Minyamar* (female), KASHMIRI ; *Barasingha*, HINDUSTANI

(PLATE vi, fig. 1)

From other representatives of the typical ruminants the majority of the deer tribe are distinguished by the cranial appendages of the males taking the form of antlers, which are periodically shed and again renewed, and in most Asiatic species are more or less branched. In no deer dealt with in the present volume are the hinds normally provided with antlers ; while in the few species in which these appendages are lacking in both sexes, the bucks are provided with long sabre-like upper tusks projecting below the margin of the lip. In the latter respect these uncrowned species resemble chevrotains, or mouse-deer, from which, however, they are distinguished by important anatomical features. The mode of replacement and growth of antlers, as well as their structural difference from horns properly so called, have so often been described, that a repetition on this occasion is unnecessary. It may be observed, however, that in the species in which they eventually attain a more or less complex development, the antlers are more simple in the young than in the adult ; their complexity increasing year by year till a certain period of life, after which they commence to degenerate, or "go back."

Most deer are characterised by the marked difference between the colour of the winter and summer coats ; the general tone of the former being some shade of grey or brown, while that of the latter is chestnut or rufous. Among species exhibiting this colour-change in great perfection are the American

PLATE VI

1. Hangul.
2. Shou.
3. Thorold's Deer.
4. Indian Sambar.
5. Malay Sambar.
6. Chital.
7. Swamp-Deer.
8. Thamin.

white-tailed deer, and the roes, the latter being remarkable for the circumstance that the white rump-patch, which forms so conspicuous a feature in so many of the tribe, is generally developed only in the grey winter coat. This white rump-patch is apparently for the purpose of facilitating recognition of the direction taken by the members of the herd when in flight. Other aids to recognition are afforded by the glands with which deer are so abundantly provided. Most deer have a pair of glands on the face below the eyes, while in the muntjac there is also a pair of frontal glands on the forehead. In addition to those on the face, the majority also have glands situated between the main hoofs, while there may likewise be either one or two glands on each hind-leg, the position of which is indicated by a tuft of hair differing in length and frequently also in colour from that clothing the rest of the limb. The most common of these glands is situated on the outer surface of the hind-leg some distance above the foot, and is known as the metatarsal gland. Less common is the tarsal gland, situated on the inner surface of the hock, or tarsus.

Stags are subject to outbursts of sexual excitement during the pairing-season, when they lose their timid and retiring habits, and become some of the most vicious and dangerous of all animals, especially in captivity. During this period of excitement the males of the larger kinds utter a peculiar call or roar, intended as a challenge to their rivals for the mastery of the herd.

In the typical genus *Cervus*, of which the hangul is a member, the antlers of the stags are large and complex, rising at an acute angle to the middle line of the forehead, projecting at first from the plane of the latter, and then continued upwards nearly in that plane. They are supported on comparatively short, permanent, and skin-covered pedicles (longer in young than in adult animals), and are furnished with a brow-tine, while they are never regularly forked at their first division. Three is the minimum number of tines met with in the antlers of this genus. There are other distinctive features of the group, of which mention may be omitted on the present occasion.

The deer of the genus *Cervus* may be divided into five subgeneric groups, of which three are met with in

FIG. 32.—Hangul Stag at Woburn Abbey, photographed by the Duchess of Bedford.

the area treated of in the present volume. In the typical group (to which belong the larger species, inclusive of the hangul) the antlers are rounded, and usually bear five or more tines, among which there is generally a bez (second) and always a trez (third). In adult stags the coat is more or less completely devoid of spots, and has a large light-coloured rump-patch generally surrounding the tail; but in the young it is marked with rows of light spots.

The hangul, as it is called in its native country,[1] may be regarded as the Kashmir representative of the

[1] Kashmiri shikaris only apply the term *Barasingha* to this deer when addressing Europeans.

European red deer. The antlers are usually five-tined, with the brow-tine (which is often shorter than the bez) generally starting at some distance above the burr. The fourth and fifth tines, which are often approximately equal, form a terminal fork, which is placed somewhat obliquely to the long axis of the head. The antlers are rounded throughout, and also bowed outwards at first and then inwards, so that the fifth tines of opposite sides are inclined towards one another. The legs are thicker than in the red deer, with the tuft of the metatarsal gland larger, coarser, and placed somewhat lower down. In height a full-grown stag stands from 4 feet to 4 feet 4 inches at the withers. The tail is relatively short, and the light rump-patch, which is nearly white, is small, and does not extend on to the upper surface of the buttocks, thus excluding the tail. In winter the general colour varies from brown to liver-colour, the individual hairs being speckled; the light area on the inner sides of the buttocks is dirty white, with a dark line on its outer border, which runs down the inner side of the thigh, and stands out in contrast to the general body-colour. The flanks and limbs are somewhat paler than the back; the upper surface of the tail is black; and the lips and chin are white, and the inner surfaces of the ears whitish. In the summer coat the general colour is lighter and more rufous, with most of the underparts whitish, although posteriorly brown in stags. At this season hinds, and sometimes also stags, show traces of spotting on the flanks and back. The fringe of elongated hair on the throat is comparatively short, and not markedly darker than the rest of the coat. The light spots of the fawns are stated to be retained till the third or fourth year. The cry of the stags in the pairing-season is a prolonged squeal, unlike that of the red deer, but approximating to that of the wapiti. In the whiteness of the light rump-patch and its dark-coloured edging the hangul departs from the red-deer type to approach the group of Asiatic deer known as sikas, as it also does to a certain degree in its comparatively simple antlers.

The maximum recorded lengths of antlers are 48½ and 47 inches, one of three examples with the latter dimension showng a tip-to-tip interval of 21, and a second of 30 inches.

FIG. 33.—Hangul Stag, with the antlers in velvet, from a photograph by the Duchess of Bedford.

Hangul inhabit the forests of the vale of Kashmir and some of the neighbouring valleys, such as Maru-Wardwan, Kishtwar, Badrawar, and Tilel, but further information is required with regard to the exact limits of their distribution in the vale of Kashmir itself. It is well known that hangul are to be met with throughout the range forming the north-eastern barrier of the valley, as well as that at its south-eastern extremity. In the *Deer of All Lands* it is stated that they are unknown on the Pir Panjal range, forming (with the Kaj-nag to the west of the Jhelam) the south-western barrier of the valley; and a practically similar statement is made by Mr. Dauvergne in a paper on the big game of Asia published in the *Bulletin* of the Paris Museum of Natural History for 1898. His words (p. 200) are that the distribution of these deer is limited to *toutes les montagnes autour de la vallée au nord*, together with Kishtwar and some adjacent districts. Consequently the Pir Panjal and Kaj-nag ranges are excluded from the habitat. The present writer has seen hangul on the Marbal Pass, situated on a northern spur of the eastern extremity of the Pir Panjal; and as this is the route to Kishtwar it comes within their ordinary range, and in no wise invalidates the above statements. He has, however, been shown a note by an English sportsman, in which it is stated that about forty years ago (at which time Mr. Dauvergne was resident in Kashmir) hangul were seen near the Pir Panjal Pass, which is almost in the centre of the range. Possibly these were only stragglers, but in any case this point would appear to be their extreme western limit on this side of the valley, as the writer has never heard of their occurrence west of the pass last-named or in the Kaj-nag.

In summer hangul may be met with as high as from 9000 to 12,000 feet above sea-level, but in winter they descend to the valley of Kashmir, which is in some places not more than 5000 feet above the sea. The herds resorting to the western end of the vale of Kashmir pass northwards in summer into the adjacent Tilel Valley, through which runs the Kishan-ganga, some of them crossing that river to wander into the mountains of southern Astor. On the other hand, those from the northern and eastern flanks of the Kashmir Valley retire to the slopes of Haramuk, the great peak in the northern mountain-barrier. At the eastern end of the vale the deer appear to migrate much less than do those at its western extremity, finding a suitable summer climate at the sources of the tributary valleys, or nalas ; their favourite summer resorts being the birch-forests, which grow immediately above the pine-zone.

Towards the end of September, when the antlers of the stags are clean, hangul descend from the birch-forests, and the old stags commence to call. Formerly they are stated to have called throughout the day, but now do so only in the mornings and evenings, commencing late in the afternoon. During the pairing-season the old stags frequently show themselves in the open glades with their harems of hinds, and are then easy to approach. They wander frequently from one patch of forest to another, so that a spot abounding in deer one week may be deserted the next. By the latter part of October the calling generally ceases, and the stags become less bold, and are consequently more difficult to discover. When, however, they are driven down by the winter snows into the open ground of the vale of Kashmir, they are once more easily approached, and in former times numbers were ruthlessly slaughtered by the villagers when driven down by the storms of winter to seek shelter at low levels. The fawns are generally dropped during the month of April.

An account of hangul-stalking will be found in General M'Intyre's work, *The Hindu Koh.*

The Yarkand stag (*Cervus yarcandensis*) was at one time believed to be only a race of the hangul, but it is entitled to rank as a perfectly distinct species. Not only do its antlers, as shown by a series of specimens in the British Museum, differ markedly from those of the Kashmir stag, but the coat of the Yarkand stag is distinctly reddish in place of grey, and has much less black on the under-parts and hindquarters ; while the tail is entirely rufous instead of mainly black on the upper surface, and the rump-patch is larger and orange-coloured. The terminal fork of the antlers (fig. 34) looks directly forwards, the fifth tine is usually larger than the fourth, and in

Fig. 34.—Skull and Antlers of Yarkand Stag, from a specimen in the British Museum.

some specimens, as in the one here figured, the upper part of the antler is more curved forwards, somewhat after the manner obtaining in the shou. In all these respects the antlers are more shou-like than are those of the hangul.

THE SHOU, OR SIKHIM STAG

(*Cervus affinis*)

NATIVE NAME.—*Shou*, BHOTIAS OF NEPAL AND DARJILING

(PLATE vi, fig. 2)

Although its magnificent antlers are not uncommon in collections, few British sportsmen have seen the shou alive; and in Europe it is chiefly known by skulls and antlers, although the British Museum possesses one mounted head. Of the general appearance of this stag our chief knowledge is derived from two coloured sketches formerly belonging to its describer, Brian Hodgson, and now preserved in the library of the Zoological Society of London.

Shou-antlers (fig 35) present the same marked bend at the third tine and the inward inclination of the long fifth tine so conspicuous in the Kashmir hangul, in addition to which they are also abruptly bent forward above the third tine, so that when suspended in the ordinary position the upper portion overhangs the skull. As in the hangul, there are usually five points; but the brow-tine seems to be less constantly longer than the second, and is closer to the burr than is often the case in the Kashmir species. More important is the circumstance that the terminal fork is placed at right angles to the axis of the head, so as to look directly forwards; and the fifth tine is nearly always markedly larger than the fourth. Judging from the size of its skull and antlers, the shou must apparently fall little if at all short of the stature of the wapiti. As regards coloration, accurate information is a desideratum. The mounted head in the British Museum, which has suffered by fading since it was presented more than half a century ago by Brian Hodgson, is pale rufous brown. A somewhat similar colour, which extends over the whole of the rump, is displayed in one of the sketches noticed above; but in the second of these, which not improbably shows the animal in its winter garb, the general hue is considerably darker, and there is a large light rump-patch, which includes the tail.

The largest shou-antlers on record are the pair shown in fig. 35, which measure 55¾ inches in length, 6½ in basal circumference, 17¼ between the tips, and a pair of similar length in the British Museum. In nearly all cases at least one antler has five well-developed points, but occasionally its fellow may have four, six, or seven points. Considerable uncertainty has prevailed with regard to the precise habitat of the shou. Dr. Jerdon (who erroneously thought it might be identical with the great stag of Siberia) stated that it inhabited Eastern Tibet and the Chumbi Valley on the Sikhim side of Tibet. Dr. Blanford, on the other hand, wrote that "it is not found in Sikhim nor in the Chumbi Valley immediately east of Sikhim, but apparently in the next valley to the eastward, Mr. Hume was assured, he tells me, that the area inhabited by *C. affinis* is drained by streams running northward to the Sangpo." From information furnished by Mr. Claude White, Commissioner of Sikhim, it appears that Jerdon was practically right; the range of the species, including some portion of the upper Chumbi Valley and some of the adjacent valleys in Bhutan.

In a letter to the *Field* of October 27, 1906, Lieut.-Col. H. A. Iggulden stated that the range of this deer "is certainly not restricted to the Chumbi Valley and the adjacent valleys of Bhutan, though, perhaps, it may be more numerous in those districts than elsewhere.

"My own observations and inquiries on this matter may be of interest to naturalists, for whilst in Tibet with the military expedition of 1903-1904 I made inquiries regarding this stag, and saw a considerable number of skulls and horns at various places between our boundary on the Talep Pass and Lhasa. I came to the conclusion that these deer are not found to the

FIG. 35.—Skull and Antlers of Shou Stag, from a specimen in the possession of Mr. A. O. Hume.

west of a line drawn north and south between Shigatse and the northern point of Sikhim. They are never found in Sikhim itself, as the climate there is too damp, though one or two may possibly at times have crossed the boundary. There are a fair number in the Chumbi and branch valleys, which are well wooded, though they are probably more plentiful in some of the northern Bhutanese valleys.

"After leaving the Chumbi Valley these deer are not again encountered until the Tsangpo or Bramaputra Valley is reached, where there are some herds of them in a valley to the north of the Kamba Pass, which were said to be protected by the Dalai Lama, and were consequently unmolested. They also inhabit the high mountains on both sides of the Bramaputra for many miles to the east, probably as far as the unexplored Bramaputra Falls. I next definitely heard of them existing in the bare hills to the north-east of Lhasa, and was told that they were occasionally seen and killed some few miles from that city.

"During the seven weeks we spent at Lhasa I was fortunate enough to procure two very fine shou or 'shaow' heads, which I purchased from some natives, who said they were shot about forty miles east of Lhasa up the Khichu Valley, and as they had the flesh and skin on them intact, they could not have been brought from very far. Unfortunately these heads had been decapitated close to the skull, but I was able to bring them to England. They both measure close on 50 in. one having thirteen points, the other the normal ten. I may also mention that I saw three or four heads with more than ten points, so that the accepted idea that this deer never carries more than ten points is not borne out by fact, though ten is undoubtedly the normal number. This deer was also said to exist in the Kham country, which is some way to the east of Lhasa."

If these Lhasa shou are completely isolated from the typical Chumbi-Bhutan animals, they probably indicate a distinct race of the species.

THOROLD'S DEER, OR THE LHASA STAG

(*Cervus albirostris*)

(PLATE vi, fig. 3)

Although a member of the typical group of the genus *Cervus*, Thorold's deer is distinguished from its relatives by its white muzzle, lips, and chin, the reversal of the hair on the withers, which forms a kind of hump, and is directed forwards, and the comparatively simple antlers, which lack the bez-tine, and have but four or five points each.

In size this deer is very nearly the same as the hangul. The antlers, which, as already mentioned, lack the bez-tine and carry either four or five points, are much flattened and have the beam suddenly bent back at the trez-tine (which, owing to the absence of the bez, is the second of the series). The brow-tine springs from the beam some distance above the burr; the trez-tine is situated nearly in the plane of those above it, the tine immediately above the trez being larger than any of the rest. The antlers differ widely from those of the hangul and shou in that the terminal fork is parallel to the long axis of the head, as in wapiti. The tail is short, and included in the large light rump-patch. The colour is dark brown, with the hairs minutely speckled, scarcely lighter on the underparts than on the back. The rump-patch, which extends down the inner sides of the thighs, is pale ochrey buff, without any white below the tail, but bordered with blackish in front. The face is somewhat darker than the back, the inner surface of the ears whitish, while the muzzle, lips, and chin are white. The hair is coarse and brittle; and the metatarsal gland, which is covered with still coarser hair, is situated about halfway up the cannon-bone.

In the formation of the antlers this deer appears to

display indications of affinity with the sika deer, from which it may indicate a connecting link towards wapiti. The antlers of the stags are smooth and nearly white. Those of the mounted specimen in the British Museum have a length of 38 inches along the outer curve ; but these dimensions are much exceeded by a pair brought home after the Tibet expedition, which measure 47 inches.

This deer was first described by Col. Przewalski ; the two specimens subsequently obtained by Dr. W. G. Thorold in the neighbourhood of Lhasa being named *C. thoroldi*, under the impression that they belonged to a new species. The two examples in question were killed at a spot about 200 miles to the north-east of Lhasa, at an approximate elevation of about 13,500 feet above sea-level. They were found in snow among brushwood growing just above the upper limit of forest.

Local races of wapiti (*Cervus canadensis*) occurs in Turkestan, the Altai, the Thian Shan, and Manchuria and Amurland ; the Manchurian wapiti (*Cervus canadensis xanthopygus*), serving in some degree to connect red-deer and wapiti. With a short wapiti-like tail, and antlers of the wapiti-like type, although smaller in proportion to the head, and with an inferior development of the fourth tine, this deer turns bright foxy red in summer. When the antlers are five-tined they may be distinguished from those of the hangul and shou by the terminal fork being parallel to the axis of the head. Neither of these deer, nor any of the sika deer, are, however, met with in the area treated of in this volume.

THE SAMBAR

(*Cervus unicolor*)

NATIVE NAMES.—*Sambar* OR *Samar*, HINDUSTANI ; *Jarao* (male), *Jurai* (female), NEPALESE ; *Maha* IN THE TERAI ; *Meru* AMONG THE MAHRATTAS OF THE GHATS ; *Ma-ao* AND *Mauk* OF THE GONDS ; *Saram* OF THE HO-KOL ; *Kadave* AND *Kadaba*, CANARESE ; *Kennadi*, TELEGU ; *Kadumai*, TAMIL ; *Gona*, *Rusa*, CINGALESE ; *Gous*, *Gaoj*, AND *Bhalongi* (female) IN EASTERN BENGAL ; *Khat-khowa-pohu*, ASSAMESE ; *Sacha* IN THE DAPHLA HILLS ; *Tshat*, BURMESE ; *Takhau*, *Hseukhau*, AND *Kheu* OF THE KARENS ; *Rusa* AND *Rusa-etam*, MALAY

(PLATE vi, figs. 4 and 5)

Despite the comparatively simple form of its antlers, and its somewhat shaggy appearance, the sambar must be reckoned as the finest deer found in India proper. In size and bulk it considerably exceeds all the rest ; and for solid massiveness its rugged antlers, of which the outer surface presents a curious resemblance to the bark of a wych-elm sapling, are perhaps unsurpassed by those of any other member of the *Cervidæ*. Magnificent specimens of these antlers are preserved in the British Museum and in many private collections, the equals of

FIG. 36.—Sambar Stag at Woburn Abbey, photographed by the Duchess of Bedford.

which it would be difficult, if not impossible to find at the present day, when comparatively few stags are allowed to attain the age necessary for the full development of these splendid appendages.

The sambar, in common with a number of more or less closely allied species inhabiting the Oriental, or Indian, region, differs so markedly, not only in the form of its antlers, but in many details of structure and colouring, from the members of the red-deer group, that it may be taken as the type of a second group, for which the name rusine deer (from the Malay name for deer) is a convenient designation. With the exception of a small species supposed to be from the Philippines, and described as *C. tavistocki*, the rusine deer are characterised by the relatively simple antlers, which are cylindrical, and have usually only three tines, owing to the absence of both the bez and the trez; each antler, after giving off a brow-tine immediately above the burr, or coronet, consisting of a beam terminating in a simple fork. Although the coat of the adult may be either uniformly coloured or spotted at all times of the year, it never has the large light-coloured rump-patch of the red-deer group, nor does it exhibit that marked difference in colour according to season which is so striking in most members of that group. Several species (like the sambar) have the throat and neck more or less heavily maned; and in most cases the ears are large and the tail comparatively long.

The Indian sambar (the typical representative of a widely spread species with many local races, whose full title is *Cervus unicolor typicus*) is a large and somewhat heavily built deer, attaining a height of at least 5 feet 4 inches at the withers, and characterised by its long and almost uniformly dark-coloured coat, heavily maned throat and neck, large spreading ears, evertible face-glands, and thick bushy tail. The long and massive antlers have a peculiarly rugged exterior, and the two tines of the terminal fork are usually approximately

FIG. 37.—Head of the Indian Sambar.

equal in length, and when unequal, it is generally the front one which is the shorter of the two, while the hind one springs from the posterior aspect of the beam, and does not form the direct continuation of the axis of the latter. The space enclosed between the antlers is generally U or V shaped, and the bony pedicles on which they are supported are relatively short. In colour the sambar is usually almost uniform dark umber-brown, but there is a considerable amount of individual variation ; some specimens, especially hinds (which are paler than stags), tending more or less decidedly to greyish or yellowish. Old stags may become almost black ; and in lighter-coloured males the face, mane, and the upper surface of the tail are black or blackish. On the under surface of the body the hair is but little paler than on the back ; but in the stags the chin, the inner portion of the buttocks, the under side of the tail, and the inner surface of the upper part of the limbs are more or less distinctly chestnut ; this colour sometimes extending on to the sides of the buttocks, and occupying the whole of the lower portion of the legs. On the head and neck the hairs are uniformly coloured, but those on the hind half of the body may have yellow tips. Young fawns are uniformly red, without light spots, but apparently with a black tail and a stripe of the same colour down the middle of the back. The broad ears of the adult are equal to about half the length of the head, which has a nearly straight profile and is of considerable relative length.

Sambar-antlers vary much in length and stoutness, the longer specimens being frequently inferior in girth to shorter examples. Very rarely are there more than the normal three tines to each, although occasionally, as in two examples in the British Museum, a fourth point may be added (see fig. 38). The longest recorded specimen is from Bhopal, and measures 50⅛ inches, with a basal girth of 9⅜ inches. Next to this comes a single antler from Khandesh, of which the length is 48 inches, and

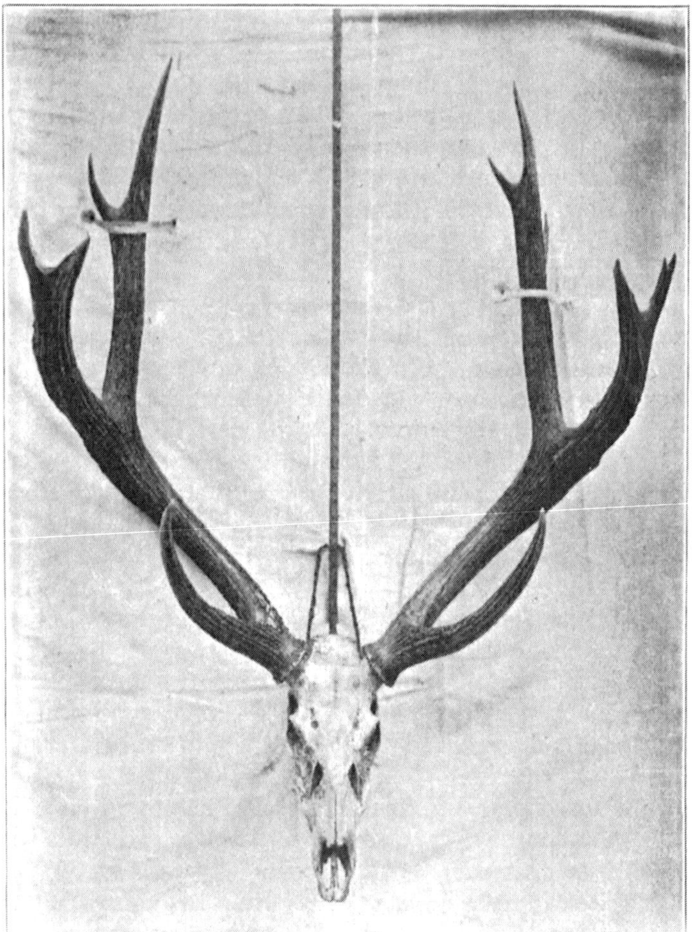

FIG. 38.—Skull of Indian Sambar with abnormal antlers, from a specimen in the possession of Mr. R. McD. Hawker.

the girth above the brow-tine 7 inches. Specimens measuring $46\frac{7}{8}$, $46\frac{1}{2}$, and $45\frac{1}{2}$ inches in length are also recorded, one of which has a basal girth of 9 inches. A stag will weigh about 600 lbs. "live weight," and about 410 lbs. "butcher's weight."

The forests of India and Ceylon, especially those in hilly districts, form the habitat of the typical sambar. Eastwards the limits of its range are perhaps formed in Assam by the Bramaputra, on the farther side of which the Malay race probably occurs. From its smaller size, the Ceylon representative of the sambar should probably be regarded as a race apart. Throughout the open plains of the Punjab, Sind, and Western Rajputana a forest-dwelling animal like the sambar is, of course, unknown. In the outer ridges of the Himalaya, where its western range does not seem to be ascertained, sambar may be found as high as 9000 or 10,000 feet above sea-level, and they are commonly met with on the summits of the Nilgiris and other ranges in Southern India, as well as at Newera Ellia in Ceylon. Although, as already mentioned, hills form their favourite resorts, these deer may be met with on river-flats.

Sambar generally associate in small herds or family parties, and, like all forest-dwelling animals, are impatient of the rays of a tropical sun between early morning and evening, seeking shelter in the deepest and most sequestered parts of the forest during the hottest hours. In the Siwaliks the resting-place may, however, be under an isolated tree. Whenever such are to be found in the vicinity of their haunts, sambar select forests on the higher grounds for the mid-day siesta. Whether they require water every day is still a question ; but it is well known that they are frequently in the habit of travelling long distances in search of that element. Unlike the members of the red-deer group, wild sambar do not shed their antlers regularly every season ; and in many parts of India and Ceylon these appendages are dropped by the stags only every second or third year. Such, at any rate, is the testimony of those who have had opportunities of studying these deer in their native wilds. March is stated to be the month in which the shedding generally takes place in the plains, while in the Himalaya April is the more usual season. In the plains the master-stags call during October and November, and during that season these deer collect in larger herds than at other times of year. The call of the stags is a loud metallic bellow, to which the hinds reply by a kind of grunting low. The fawns in the plains of India are born during June and July, and it is rarely that twins occur. In the herd of sambar at Woburn Abbey the fawns are, however, produced at all times of the year, the same being the case with the shedding of the antlers, which appear to be dropped annually; and it may be suggested, that with these sambar the time of shedding the antlers depends on the season of the year at which each individual came into the world. Whether this irregularity in the season of birth and the consequent difference in the time of year at which the antlers are shed is due to the abnormal environment of the Woburn herd, or whether it can in any degree be matched in a state of nature, remains to be proved. During the pairing-season old stags stalk about with erected tail, outstretched muzzle, and everted face-glands, and are by no means pleasant-looking animals; while in captivity, at any rate, they are highly dangerous.

With regard to sambar-stalking, it is stated in the *Badminton Library* that "the sportsman should be on his ground just before daylight, and work slowly through the forest at the edge of the feeding-grounds, taking the bottom of the hill if there are crops on the plain below. Presently, if there are any sambar about, he will hear their trumpet-like call, and, creeping on, see two or three dark forms moving among the trees. . . . If the sportsman fails to intercept any stags on their return from their feeding-grounds by working along the base of the hill, he should next ascend the hill and try the cup-like basins which are so often found near the summits. . . . The above applies chiefly to the isolated hills which rise out of the plains in Central India; in ranges like the Siwaliks the best plan is to walk along the top of a ridge, examining the ravines below, and in the grass on the crest of these ridges will often be found places where sambar have been lying down under the trees, the 'form' being carefully chosen so that the shade of the tree will be over it during the hottest part of the day."

In some parts of India stalking sambar, or other species of deer, is difficult, and in such spots driving is considered by some sportsmen admissible. In regard to this practice an article may be quoted from *The Asian* newspaper of January 16, 1900. In reply to the question whether, when stalking is impossible, driving is permissible, the writer asks, Where is it impossible to stalk deer? "During a considerable experience," he observes, "extending from the Himalayas to Southern India, we have seen no such impossible ground, with the exception of parts of the Terai and Assam, where elephants are a necessity. The Himalayas, the Siwaliks, the Satpura Hills of the Central Provinces, and the mountains of Southern India, all afford ideal stalking ground, and driving for deer in their forests is inexcusable and unsportsmanlike. The ground may be difficult, steep, dangerous, and rocky; but where a deer can climb, a man can climb also. The jungle may be dense, and the foliage luxuriant, but the sportsman content to wander all day in the forest, rifle in hand, on the chance of obtaining a shot, accompanied only by one or two men, is sure to meet with ultimate success, although he will probably not bring to bag so many animals as the man who lurks behind a tree or rock, and has the game driven up to him.

"And it is in this that the gist of the matter lies. The real sportsman is ready to undertake any amount of labour in order to bring his game to bag, and the more trouble and toil he expends in its pursuit the more does he value his quarry and the trophy it yields, whilst he does not gauge success by numbers. But

FIG. 39.—Frontlet and Antlers of the Malay Sambar, from a Burmese specimen in the British Museum.

the other kind of hunter thinks only of killing his animal, and cares not in what manner it is slain, so long as it falls to his rifle, preferring that method of procedure which entails the least possible trouble and exertion. A few miles' drive or ride from camp or station; a comfortable place in the shade of a tree whilst the beat is being arranged; and a shot from ambush, perhaps at a few yards' distance, at an unfortunate sambar, the whole process occupying a few hours—this is the acme of sport to the lazy man whose sole object is to shoot the game. . . . But the true sportsman scorns such methods ; his pleasure is found in wandering over the hills and through the forest from daybreak to sunset, keeping every sense on the alert, and pitting his knowledge of wild animals and jungle-lore against the cunning of the denizens of the woods."

The representative of the sambar met with in Burma, Eastern Assam, and Kachar, differs sufficiently from the typical form to be regarded as a local race, although not as a distinct species. Consequently, for the name of "equine deer," often applied to this race, the title of Malay sambar is preferable, as serving to emphasise its specific identity with the Indian animal.

Nearly rivalling the latter in respect of size, the Malay sambar (*Cervus unicolor equinus*, plate vi, fig. 5) usually has shorter and thicker antlers, in which the hind or inner tine of the terminal fork is considerably inferior in length to the front or outer tine, while it springs as a kind of spur from the inner margin of the beam, of which the outer tine forms the direct continuation. The brow-tine, too, is in most instances of proportionately greater length. On the average, the general colour appears to be darker than in Indian sambar, approaching to black or slaty grey in the old stags ; there is frequently a light flesh-coloured ring round each eye, and the ears are relatively smaller, and often show a whitish margin. In some cases the lower portion of the legs shows a tendency towards dirty white, and the tail seems to be more bushy than in the typical race. The fawns are foxy red in colour, with the upper surface of the tail and a line down the back black or blackish, and in many instances, although by no means invariably, they are spotted on the hind-quarters.

Although typical antlers of this race (fig. 39) are

very distinct from those of the Indian sambar, there are examples in which the distinction is less clearly marked. Antlers measuring 30⅛ and 29⅝ inches in length, with respective basal girths of 4⅜ and 6 inches, have been recorded.

The range of the Malay sambar apparently extends from Assam (probably eastward of the Bramaputra) into Burma, and then on to the Malay and other countries lying beyond the area of which this volume treats.

THE CHITAL, OR INDIAN SPOTTED DEER

(*Cervus axis*)

NATIVE NAMES.—*Chital*, *Chitra*, and *Jhank*, HINDUSTANI; *Chatidah* IN BHAGALPUR; *Boro Khotiya*, BENGALI; *Buriyah* IN GORAKHPUR; *Lupi* AND *Kars* OF THE GONDS; *Darkar* OF THE KORKU; *Pusta* OF THE HO-KOL; *Sarung*, *Saraya*, *Jati*, AND *Mikka*, CANAREE; *Dupi*, TELEGU; *Pali-man*, TAMIL AND MALABARI; *Tic Muha*, CINGALESE.

(PLATE vi, fig. 6)

The sambar and the chital in India and the greater and lesser kudu in Somaliland offer an analogy in their respective habits, the sambar and the greater kudu inhabiting hill-forests, while the chital and the lesser kudu frequent for most part the lowlands, although the chital sometimes betakes itself to hilly ground. Both species of kudu frequent dense and often almost impenetrable thorn-jungle, and are accordingly furnished with enormous ears, capable of catching the largest possible amount of sound. They are probably also to a considerable extent nocturnal animals. The same is the case with the Indian sambar, which is likewise a forest animal, and the ears are accordingly large. On the other hand, in the chital, which is to a great extent diurnal and frequents more open country than sambar, the ears are relatively small and narrow. The

Fig. 40.—Head of Chital Stag.

remarkable difference in coloration between the sambar and the chital may likewise be attributed to difference in environment, the sombre hues of the former affording protection in the obscurity of the forest, while the bright tints of the latter are more in harmony with the brilliancy of its inanimate surroundings.

The Chital, or Indian Spotted Deer

By sportsmen this deer is commonly called axis, a name applied by Pliny (and adopted from him by Belon) to an Indian animal which there is every reason to believe is the present species, of which indeed it forms the scientific title. For ordinary purposes it is, however, preferable to adopt the Hindustani name chital, of which spotted deer is a translation.

With the exception of a darker species from the Philippines, the chital is the only rusine deer spotted with white at all seasons of the year. Indeed it is, with the above-named exception, the only deer that is as fully spotted in winter as in summer, fallow-deer losing all spots in the former season, while these generally tend to disappear at the same season more or less completely in the Japanese deer and its larger relatives.

Fig. 41.—Chital Hind at Woburn Abbey, photographed by the Duchess of Bedford.

In size the chital may be described as medium, the height at the withers usually ranging between 36 and 38 inches. It has a rather long and pointed head, elongated limbs, and a generally light and gracefully built frame. There seems no decided seasonal difference in the colour of the coat, of which the general hue is light rufous fawn, marked all over the body with large rounded spots, which tend to arrange themselves in longitudinal lines along the back and immediately above the white of the under surface of the body. A dark stripe runs from the nape of the neck to the tip of the tail, on each side of which the spots form at least one well-marked line. The chin, the upper part of the throat, the inner surface of the ears, the under parts of the body, the inner surface of the limbs, and the lower side of the tail, are white like the spots. The head, which is darker on the face than elsewhere, is fawn, usually marked in stags with a brown chevron on the forehead (fig. 40) and also has a blackish band above the naked area of the muzzle. The antlers, (fig. 40) which are supported on short pedicles, are long, slender, and moderately rugose. The rather long brow-tine is given off from the beam nearly at a right angle; the front or outer tine of the terminal fork considerably exceeds the hind, or inner one, in length, and forms the continuation of the line of the beam, from the inner side of which springs the hind tine. The space enclosed between the two antlers is more or less distinctly lyrate; and sports, or snags, are frequently given off near the point of origin of the brow-tine. The ears, as already mentioned, are moderate-sized and narrow; and the face-glands, of which the position is marked by tufts of reddish hairs, are likewise of medium development. The rather long and pointed tail is evenly haired throughout; and there is no long hair on the neck and throat, this feature largely contributing to the neat appearance of the chital as contrasted with the sambar.

The longest chital antlers on record measure 38¼ inches in length along the outer curve, with a basal girth of 4¾ inches, and a tip-to-tip interval of 19½ inches. Many examples ranging in length between 35 and 37½ inches in length are known, among which the maximum tip-to-tip interval is 25¼ inches. Chital antlers, unlike those of the red deer group, attain their maximum complexity in the third year, after which they continue merely to increase in size year by year until the period of decline is attained.

Where chital and fallow deer are herded together in parks, the observer may be puzzled to distinguish between the hinds of the two species when in the summer coat. The following points of distinction are accordingly quoted, with some verbal alteration, from the *Gardens and Menagerie of the Zoological Society*, by Bennett. "In both, the colour of the back and sides is fawn spotted with white; a deep brown or blackish band occupies the middle line of the back; and an almost continuous white line passes along either side of the belly between the limbs. But the head, which in the fallow deer is of a uniform greyish brown, is marked in the chital by a broad dusky spot on the forehead, and a line of the same colour extending along the middle of the nose. The chin and throat of the chital are pure white, while in the fallow deer they are of nearly the same colour with the chest and under surface of the body, which are both of a greyish hue. The buttocks of the fallow deer are occupied by a broad white patch, separated from the fawn of the back and sides by a black band; and the tail is black above and white beneath. In the chital the buttocks are of the same colour with the adjacent parts, and the tail is tawny above and white beneath, with a narrow blackish border towards the tip."

The chital is one of the most characteristic animals of India and Ceylon, to which it is confined, and where it is widely distributed. It is absent from Assam, and the plains of Sind, the Punjab, and Western Rajputana, which are unsuited to its mode of life. Although to a great extent a plain-loving animal, it is found along the foot-ranges of the Himalaya from the neighbourhood of the Sutlej as far west as Nepal, but does not extend into Sikhim; on these outer hills it may be found as high as about 3500 or 4000 feet above sea-level in a few localities. It is common in the Bengal Sandarbans, as indeed it is in nearly all parts of India and Ceylon suitable to its habits; and in such localities it may almost be regarded as an integral component of Indian jungle-scenery.

Compared with the typical Indian race Ceylon chital, although similar in general characters, differ not only by the more slender and lighter antlers, but likewise in several details of coloration. The ground-colour of the coat is, for instance, a yellower and purer fawn, while the white spots on the body are smaller, and may be described as flecks rather than spots. On the head the brown markings present a less decided contrast with the fawn area, while the forehead is almost wholly brown instead of showing a more or less well defined dark chevron between the eyes, as is usually the case in the large chital of the mainland. The chevron, it is true, is present in the Ceylon animal, but its distinctness is largely obscured by the dark patch in the middle of the forehead. Ceylon chital, I am told, rarely have antlers exceeding 27 inches in length.

Hodgson recognised two forms of chital in India, *Axis major* and *Axis minor* or *medius* (for he uses both these names), the latter distinguished by its inferior size, and being a native of the southern provinces of the peninsula. The smaller form, which has never been properly defined, has been assumed to be common to Ceylon ; but there is no evidence that such is really the case, and consequently (especially in view of the fact that the smaller mainland form is still undefined) I have regarded the Ceylon animal as a distinct race, with the name of *Cervus axis zeylanicus*.[1]

In Ceylon sportsmen attribute the small size of the antlers of the chital to the lack of lime in the soil. This, however, can scarcely be regarded as a *vera causa* since there are many sandstone districts in India where these deer grow good antlers. Rather must we attribute the diminution in the size of the antlers in the Ceylon chital to that general dwarfing which is very common in island forms.

The near neighbourhood of water is essential to this beautiful species ; another requisite being the proximity of covert into which it can retire for repose. Chital are, perhaps, the most gregarious of all Indian deer,

[1] This name was published in the *Field* for 1905, vol. iv, p. 947.

the herds frequently including hundreds of individuals, among which there is at least one master-stag. As is the case with most animals associating in large herds, chital are to a considerable degree diurnal, feeding for several hours after sunrise, and being on the move some time before sundown. Where there is a sufficiency of covert, the neighbourhood of human habitations is no detriment to their presence, provided they are not too much disturbed; and in such localities they frequently do much damage to standing crops. Bamboo-jungle, where there are open glades dotted with isolated clumps, in the immediate vicinity of water, forms some of their favourite haunts. They both graze and browse, and are good swimmers, taking readily to water. Their ordinary cry somewhat resembles a kind of bark, but they also utter a shrill alarm-scream. Although in India most of the fawns are dropped during the cold weather, many are born at other times of the year; and this implies a corresponding irregularity in the shedding of the antlers, which apparently occurs in each buck at a time of year depending upon the season in which it was born. It is stated in the *Badminton Library* that the irregularity in the time of shedding the antlers is more marked along the foot of the Himalaya than in Central India, where the majority of the stags have these appendages free from velvet in January, and shed them about January.

Chital are chiefly hunted by stalking; and the sportsman's best chance of escaping detection when he comes unexpectedly on a herd; is to stand motionless, when, if suitably clothed, he may be mistaken for a tree-stump, whereas if he attempts to crouch he will be detected. This remark applies, of course, to other kinds of game.

Chital have been acclimatised for more than fifty years in some French and German parks; and the Duke of Bedford possesses a herd at Woburn Abbey, which is, however, kept in an enclosure.

Hinds of all deer are marvellously clever at concealing their young; but no better instance of this trait is on record than one that occurred among a small herd of chital kept by Mr. W. H. Ravenscroft at Colombo, Ceylon, in 1883. One of the does had given birth to a fawn in a small enclosure near the house of its owner; and on the second day after the birth she was seen quietly feeding between four and five in the afternoon, but unaccompanied by the fawn. Mr. Ravenscroft, with half-a-dozen servants entered the enclosure to search for the fawn. The ground within the enclosure, which was about a quarter of an acre in extent, and devoid of covert, except at one end, where there were a few cinnamon-bushes and a single good-sized tree, was carefully examined, without any trace of the missing fawn. So too, was an area of some extent outside the fence (through which it was thought the fawn might have crept), but with a similar result. Next morning the doe and fawn were seen together. A man was set to watch, who informed the owner that one afternoon he saw the pair go into the bushes, and the doe come out alone after a few minutes. It thus appeared that for eight or ten days the mother regularly put her offspring to bed about half-past four in the afternoon, and concealed it so successfully that although the owner knew within a few feet the place where it lay, he never succeeded in finding it.

It is well known that during the pairing season red-deer stags occasionally get their antlers so locked together that they are unable to extricate them and thus perish miserably. It might have been thought that the simple form of the antlers of the chital would not lend themselves to such interlocking; but that this is not the case is proved by a pair of skulls picked up many years ago in the Central Provinces, in which the antlers were immovably locked.

THE PARA, OR HOG-DEER

(*Cervus porcinus*)

NATIVE NAMES.—*Para*, HINDUSTANI, SINDI, AND PUNJABI ; *Dodar* IN ROHILCUND ; *Khar laguna* IN THE NEPAL TERAI ; *Nutrini haran*, BENGALI ; *Will-muha*, CINGALESE ; *Darai* OR *Dayai*, BURMESE.

(PLATE vii, fig. 1)

The para is the smallest of the Indian rusa-like deer, its height at the shoulder commonly ranging between 25 and 29 inches. Certain characters in the skull distinguish this species from the sambar and chital (which belong to the sub-genus *Rusa*), and it is accordingly referred to a distinct sub-genus, *Hyelaphus*. The general build is low and heavy, with the legs and face comparatively short ; and it is perhaps from this characteristic massiveness of make that the title of hog-deer is derived. The antlers, which in adult stags are considerably longer than the head, are supported on relatively tall pedicles from the skull, and are fairly stout, although less rugose than in the sambar. The brow-tine is short, the beam of great length, and the hinder, or inner tine of the terminal fork somewhat shorter than the outer one.

The hairs on the back have pale tips, but are not banded with rings of different shades. Full-grown hog-deer in winter dress are generally bright, shining rufous or yellowish brown in colour, somewhat speckled over with a lighter shade owing to the pale tips of the hairs ; a peculiarity being that the hair on the lower surface of the body is considerably darker than that of the back. In the summer coat, on the other hand, the general tint is distinctly lighter, and, during at least the early portion of the season, a variable number of very pale brown or white spots make their appearance. In some individuals, as in the buck shown in fig. 43, the entire body is thus dappled ; but in other instances the spotting may be restricted to a couple of rows on each side of the dark streak on the back. The ears, which are well covered with hair on the outer surface, and are white internally, are rather large ; and the tail, of which

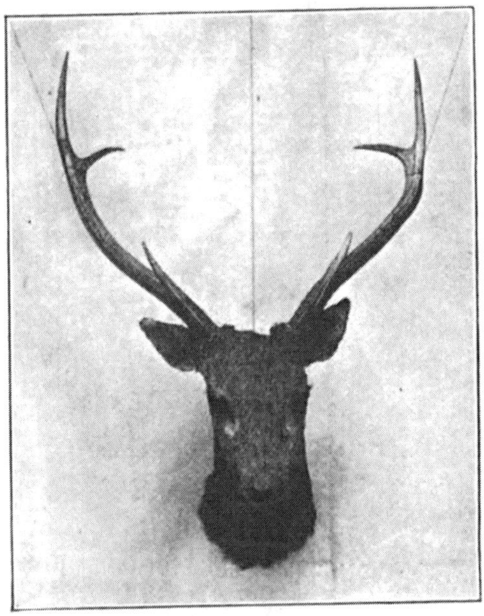

FIG. 42.—Head of Hog-Deer Stag, from a specimen in the possession of Mr. H. C. V. Hunter.

the lower surface is white, is proportionately long ; the throat is devoid of mane ; the face-glands are less developed than in the sambar ; and the colour of the tufts of hair on the metatarsal glands is lighter than that of the rest of the leg. Antlers measuring 23¼ and 21¾ inches in length have been recorded, the longer pair having a basal girth of 3⅞ inches.

Unlike sambar, which dwell in hill-forest, para inhabit river-flats, where they prefer tracts with grass of

PLATE VII

1. Hog-Deer.
2. Muntjac.
3. Tenasserim Muntjac.
4. Tibetan Tufted Deer.
5. Musk-Deer.
6. Meminna, or Indian Chevrotain.
7. Indian Wild Boar.
8. Pigmy Hog.

moderate height; but they are occasionally found in forest. In India the species seems restricted to the plains of the Indus and Ganges valley, its reported occurrence in the peninsula proper being unconfirmed. On this vast plain its range extends from Sind and the Punjab, through Assam and Sylhet, into Burma; the southern limit on that side of the Bay of Bengal being

FIG. 43.—Hog-Deer Stag in summer dress, from a photograph by the Duchess of Bedford.

apparently Tenasserim. Its occurrence in Ceylon is due to importation.

Hog-deer live mainly by grazing, and are therefore suited for turning out in parks, on account of not damaging trees and foliage. Numbers have been turned out by the Marquis d'Hervey at St. Denys, and by Monsieur Pays Mellier at Pataudière; and the species also thrives in the Duke of Bedford's park at Woburn.

The para is to a considerable extent nocturnal, and since it generally dwells among grass of sufficient height to conceal its body, it is easy to see why it retains the large ears of its relative the sambar. Unlike the latter, it is unsociable, never collecting in herds, and generally found solitary, except in the pairing-season, when two or three individuals go together. The antlers are generally shed in April, the pairing-season takes place in September or October, and the fawns make their appearance in the following May or June.

Hog-deer are somewhat ugly movers, running with the head carried low. They are frequently put up when pig-sticking on grass plains, and afford a good run. In Dera Dun and the sub-Himalayan Terai these deer are generally shot from elephants while beating large tracts of grass when larger game is not on the move. The does lie so close as almost to be kicked up by the feet of the elephants ; but the bucks are more alert, and rise sooner, so that the best chance of shooting them is to ride on one flank somewhat in advance of the line of elephants, or to take up a position on foot in a place to which they are likely to bolt. To the novice shooting such comparatively small and quickly moving animals from elephant-back will be found by no means an easy matter.

THE SWAMP-DEER, OR BARASINGHA

(*Cervus duvauceli*)

Native Names.—*Barasingha* and *Maha*, Hindustani ; *Baraya*, *Gonr*, and *Ghos* in the Nepal Terai ; *Jhinkar* in the Kyarda Dun ; *Goin*, Sindi ; *Goin-jak* (male), Gaoni (female) in Central India ; *Bara-Nerwari*, and *Sal-Samar* in Mandla ; *Bhelingi-pohu*, Assamese.

(Plate vi, fig. 7)

Were it not that the name is so frequently misapplied to the hangul, the Hindustani title barasingha (*anglicè*, twelve-tined) would be the best designation

Fig. 44.—Head of Swamp-Deer Stag, from a specimen in the possession of Mr. H. C. V. Hunter.

for this species; but in view of this possible confusion it seems better to employ an English name, using barasingha merely as an alternative title—and as the name swamp-deer, although not free from objection, is in general use, it seems the most convenient.

With the exception that it retains in most instances a line of whitish spots on each side of the dark dorsal

FIG. 45.—Swamp-Deer Stag, with the antlers in velvet, photographed by the Duchess of Bedford.

streak, the swamp-deer is as uniformly coloured as the sambar, and, like that species, exhibits no marked seasonal change in the colour. Indeed this feature appears to be common to all deer of the rusine and rucervine groups; the latter (rucervine) being the one to which the present species and two other allied Oriental deer belong.

The rucervine deer are best distinguished by the form of the antlers, which are more complex than those of sambar, and at the same time different from those of the red-deer group. Another feature is the absence or rudimentary condition of the metatarsal gland and tuft. As regards the antlers, which may be either rounded or flattened, they lack both bez (second) and trez (third) tines, and have the beam forked (often symmetrically) at a variable distance above the origin of the brow-tine, and one or both branches of this fork again dividing at least once, so that the minimum number of points on each antler is four, while there are frequently six, and in some cases eight or more. Another feature is that the brow-tine is either given off at a right angle to the main beam, or forms an uninterrupted continuation of the curvature of the latter. Although the fawns are more or less spotted, the coat of the adults is in most cases nearly uniformly coloured, and shows no light rump-patch. The neck is slightly maned, the face long, and the tail rather short; while the face-glands attain only moderate development. The group is represented by three allied species of relatively large-sized deer, one of which is restricted to India, while the second (*Cervus schomburgki*) inhabits northern Siam, and the third is found in Burma and countries lying still farther east.

The swamp-deer is a somewhat stoutly-built species, standing from about 3 feet 8 inches to 3 feet 10 inches at the withers. The muzzle is rather long and narrow; and the hair of a moderate degree of fineness, with a tendency towards a woolly nature. In the summer coat the general colour of the upper-parts is bright rufous brown, frequently, at least, with a broad brown streak, bordered on each side by a line of whitish spots, down the middle of the back, and with a less distinct trace of spotting on other parts. The throat, the inner surfaces of the thighs, and the under-parts generally are white or whitish, while the lower surface of the tail is white. In winter the general colour is yellowish brown, with the under-parts paler. Hinds

FIG. 46.—Head of Swamp-Deer Stag with antlers of an abnormal type, from the *Proceedings of the Zoological Society* for 1899.

at all seasons are somewhat lighter in colour than the stags; and the fawns are spotted all over with white. The metatarsal gland is wanting.

In their typical form the antlers of the swamp-deer cannot be mistaken for those of any other species.

They are smooth and flattened, with the relatively long brow-tine springing from the beam almost at right angles. Above the point where this tine is given off the beam remains undivided for about half the length of the antler, when it divides into a regular fork, both branches of which are of equal calibrè, and each usually simply forked, although the outer branch may exceed the inner one in length, and carry three or more tines. Small supplemental snags not unfrequently occur on the upper surface of the brow-tine, but that tine never forks, while "sports" at its junction with the beam are seldom seen.

Such is the typical form of antler characteristic of the swamp-deer, but among a series of heads obtained by Major C. B. Wood in 1899 in the Central Provinces, the one shown in fig. 46 departs widely from this type, while the others, although less markedly abnormal, exhibit a variation in the same direction. In these antlers the long and much-curved brow-tine arises at more than a right angle from the beam, which is also much curved ; so that a little more and the two would form a continuous curve. The forking of the beam likewise occurs at a point higher up than usual, and the inner or posterior branch of the fork is thinner and shorter than the outer or anterior branch, which curves forward in continuation of the line of the beam, and gives off two snags from its sharp hind or upper surface, serially continuous with the small hind branch of the main fork. In fact, the whole antler (especially on the left side, where the hind branch of the main fork is not subdivided) is in many respects more like that of one race of the thamin than of a typical swamp-deer, this being especially shown by the nearly cylindrical shaft of the beam. If all swamp-deer from the Central Provinces presented this type of antler, they would be entitled to rank as a distinct local race, but other specimens obtained by Major Wood indicate that this is not the case, although they depart to a certain degree from the normal in the direction of the aberrant type.

A length of 41 inches, with a basal circumference of 5½ inches, is the "record" for swamp-deer antlers.

As already mentioned, the swamp-deer is restricted to the Indian mainland, being unknown in Ceylon as well as in the countries lying to the south of the Assam valley, which forms its limit in this direction. Westward the range of the species is continued along the foot of the Himalaya to the Kyarda Dun, beyond the Jumna. From the eastern Sandarbans of Bengal the swamp-deer is met with in a few localities in the Indo-Gangetic plain as far as Bahawalpur and Rohri in Sind, as well as locally through the great tract between the valleys of the Ganges and the Godaveri, as far eastwards as the Mandla district. It is likewise numerous in the upper portion of the valley of the Narbada, as well as southwards to the neighbourhood of Bastar. In the Central Provinces the limits of the areas inhabited by this deer correspond to the tracts of sal-forest.

Avoiding thick forest, swamp-deer, which subsist by grazing, affect the outskirts of woods and grassy plains with scattered trees; the vicinity of water being essential. In such localities they are found during the cooler months of the year in herds, which in some instances are of great extent. In the spring the members of these herds disperse; single stags being met with on the grass plains of Assam during March with their antlers in velvet. These deer are at least as diurnal in their habits as chital; and the pairing-season appears to take place in the latter part of October.

Where the ground on which they are found, as in parts of Central India, is open, swamp-deer may be stalked; but in the high grass of the Nepal Terai and Assam they are commonly shot from elephants.

THE THAMIN, OR ELD'S DEER

(*Cervus eldi*)

NATIVE NAMES.—*Sangnai*, OR *Sangrai*, MANIPURI ; *Thamin*, OR *Thameng*, BURMESE

(PLATE vi, fig. 8)

The thamin, or Burmese representative of the swamp-deer, was formerly placed in a genus by itself, under the name of *Panolia* ; and is hence sometimes spoken of as the "Panolia deer." Its relationship to the swamp-deer was, however, gradually recognised ; but it was not till the description of the above-mentioned head of the latter species obtained by Major Wood that the closeness of the relationship was realised. It is somewhat remarkable that it was not till 1842 that the thamin was definitely made known to science, although there is a possibility that a deer described five years earlier may have belonged to this species.

The thamin stands about 3 feet 9 inches in height at the shoulder, and has a coat of coarse hair, which becomes shaggy in winter, when it forms a kind of mane on the throat of the stags. Thamin differ from all other deer (with the exception of Major Wood's specimen of the swamp-deer) by the curvature of the antlers. These are cylindrical and rugose, with the long and arched brow-tine forming the continuation of the curve of the beam, which is set at right angles to the pedicle, so that the entire antler is approximately bow-shaped. For the greater part of its length the beam is undivided, having at first a backwards, then an outwards, and finally a forwards curvature ; but towards its termination it is simply forked, each fork corresponding to the main fork in swamp-deer antlers. In old animals the outer tine of the terminal fork is larger and more complex than the inner one ; the number of terminal points varying from as few as two or three to at least eight or ten. In this respect, however, there is considerable local variation. In the Burmese thamin (*Cervus eldi typicus*) the antlers are cylindrical to their summits, with few or no additional points on the prongs of the main fork, and a long brow-tine. On the other hand, in the Siamese thamin (*C. eldi platyceros*) the front or larger branch of the

Fig. 47.—Group of Burmese Thamin, from a photograph by the Duchess of Bedford.

main fork is considerably flattened, and carries a large number of snags on its sharp hind edge, and the brow-tine is relatively shorter. It is in this race that the antlers make a close approximation to Major Wood's specimen of the swamp-deer. In both races one or more prominent snags are usually developed at the point of junction between the brow-tine and the beam, that is to say, immediately above the pedicle ; and it is a general feature of the species that the antlers of opposite sides are unsymmetrical when compared with one another. In the Burmese thamin, with which alone this book is concerned, the colour of the winter dress of the stags is uniformly dark brown above (occasionally with a few light spots near the middle line of the back) and white or whitish beneath; the throat-fringe, which sometimes shows a white gorget, is darker than the rest of the coat, and there is usually some white on the chin, around the eyes, and on the margins of the ears. In summer the colour of the stags changes to fawn above and pale brown on the under-parts. At all times hinds are a paler rufous fawn; and very young fawns are usually spotted with white on the hind-quarters. The Siamese race of the thamin is more rufous-coloured, and more or less distinctly spotted at all seasons of the year. In general bodily form thamin are like swamp-deer, having the same short tail, but retaining more or less distinct traces of the metatarsal gland and tuft.

In the Manipur valley, which is one huge swamp, the thamin have developed a peculiar modification in the foot which enables them to walk with ease in such ground. In the Burmese thamin the under surface of the hind-pasterns is covered with hair in the ordinary manner, and the animal walks entirely on the main hoofs, keeping the pasterns much elevated. In the Manipur thamin, on the other hand, the under surface of the pastern is covered with a very hard, bare skin, which immediately above each hoof has almost the consistency of horn, and is practically continuous with the hoof itself. Moreover, so far as can be determined from comparison with a mounted specimen of the Burmese form, the pasterns are considerably longer than in the latter. In walking, according to the account given by Major C. S. Cumberland, the foot is much bent, so that the animal walks on nearly the whole of the under surface of the pasterns, and thus gains a firm support on the yielding morass.

Assuming this feature to be constant (as Major Cumberland believes to be the case), the Manipur thamin appears entitled to rank as a distinct local form, for which I have proposed the name *C. eldi cornipes.*

Apart from this point, the modification is of special interest as indicating a mode by which ruminants may adapt themselves to a life in swamps. In the well-known instance of the sitatunga antelope of Africa, a sufficiently large surface of support is afforded by a lengthening of the hoofs; in the present case the hoofs remain of the normal length, and support is obtained by the animal walking on the under surface of the hardened pasterns. It is, in fact, an incipient instance of the reversion of a digitigrade animal to the plantigrade progression of its swamp-dwelling ancestors.

Thamin are found on all flat alluvial tracts in the countries to the east of the Bay of Bengal, ranging from Manipur through Burma and Tenasserim into the Malay Peninsula.

The largest pair of thamin-antlers recorded measures 42 inches along the outer curve (exclusive of the brow-tine), with a basal circumference of 5, a tip-to-tip interval of 29, and a maximum width inside of 24 inches. The corresponding dimensions of the second largest specimen are 41, 5½, 27⅝, and 36 inches. Both came from Burma, the former having two points on one side and three on the other, while the latter has five in both antlers.

Thamin are very similar in their mode of life to swamp-deer, congregating for at least a portion of the year in large herds, and frequenting low, flat country, where they at all times avoid thick forest and dense bush-jungle, although frequently resorting to open tree-jungle. To a great extent they are grazing animals, feeding largely on wild rice; but they also browse on the leaves of certain trees. When disturbed, hinds give vent to a kind of barking grunt, while the cry of the stags is a louder and longer sound of the same nature. The pairing-season lasts from the middle of March to the middle of May, and the fawns, of which there is but one at a birth, are dropped in October and November, when they find shelter among wild rice. The fawn often remains with the hind till its second year. In Manipur the stags begin to drop their antlers in June, although in Lower Burma the shedding is deferred till the latter part of August or beginning of September. During the dry season, which lasts from the middle of February till the latter part of April, thamin betake themselves to salt-swamps, and, except for dew, must apparently exist without fresh water.

In Upper Burma, where they are fairly common, thamin are driven by beaters, but in Lower Burma they are sometimes shot, in native fashion, with the aid of lanterns at night. In addition to the sportsman and his rifle-coolies, the party on such an expedition includes a lantern-carrier and a man with bells and rings on a stick. On arrival at the spot selected, a fire is kindled after dark, and a kind of incantation-ceremony performed, in the course of which the various members of the party, together with the rifles, should pass through the smoke. The lantern, which consists of an earthenware pot with a hole in one side, and is used as a search-light, is then lit, the bells are jingled, and on the approach of a stag, the light is turned full in its eyes, by which it becomes so dazed as to offer an easy shot.

A large herd of thamin is kept at the present time by the Duke of Bedford in an enclosure in the park at Woburn, where these deer, like chital and barasingha, have become thoroughly acclimatised.

THE MUNTJAC

(*Cervulus muntjac*)

NATIVE NAMES.—*Kakar*, HINDUSTANI ; *Ratwa*, NEPALESE ; *Karsiar* OF THE BHOTIAS ; *Sikku* OF THE LEPCHAS ; *Maya*, BENGALI ; *Gutra* (male), *Gutri* (female) AND *Bherki* OF THE GONDS ; *Bekra* AND *Bekar*, MAHRATHI ; *Kankari*, *Kard-kari*, *Kond-kari* AND *Chali*, CANARESE ; *Kuka-gori*, TELEGU ; *Kalai* AND *Katu-ardu*, TAMIL ; *Weli* AND *Hula-muha*, CINGALESE ; *Hugeri*, ASSAMESE ; *Gyi*, BURMESE ; *Kidang*, MALAY ; *Jangli-bakri*, COMMONLY IN SOUTHERN INDIA.

(PLATE vii, fig. 2)

Although the term "muntjac" is one in regard to the origin of which there seems no clue (it was used by the German naturalist Zimmermann so long ago as the year 1780 as the name of the present species) it is so convenient a designation for the small deer of the genus *Cervulus*, since it serves to mark their distinctness from the members of the genus *Cervus*, that its retention is advisable. Some writers, apparently basing their objection on the fact that muntjac is not the native name of any member of the group, prefer the title rib-faced deer, or barking deer, but such a designation fails to emphasise the structural difference between the present group and more typical deer.

Muntjacs in the wider sense of the term are small deer inhabiting India and some of the neighbouring countries, easily recognised by the peculiar structure of the skull and antlers of the bucks. The antlers, which do not normally exceed half the length of the head, are two-pointed, and consist of a short brow-tine, and a beam, of which the tip is inclined inwards ; the two forming an acute angle at their junction. These antlers are supported on long, slender bony-pedicles, often but little shorter than the antlers themselves, and frequently longer; the pedicles being continued downwards on the forehead of the skull as sharp ridges, converging towards the middle line as they descend, but never actually meeting. In the does tufts of bristly hair and short prominences mark the position occupied by the pedicles of the antlers in the bucks. With advancing age the pedicles of the antlers of the bucks become shorter and thicker than in youth, when they are sometimes longer than the skull. The typical members of the group have a pair of glands in the skin of the forehead situated on the inner side of each of the supporting ridges of the antler-pedicles; and the face-glands beneath the eyes are likewise well developed. On the other hand, the metatarsal glands and tufts are wanting. An important feature is the large size of the upper tusks of the bucks, which project beyond the level of the upper lips, although they do not grow from persistent pulps.

The Indian muntjac, kakar, or barking-deer, as it is called, is a reddish-coloured deer, standing from about 20 to 22 inches in height at the withers. It has a relatively short tail, comparatively short and fine hair, and no tuft of bristly hairs on the crown of the head between the pedicles of the antlers. In adult bucks the general colour (apparently at all seasons) is uniform foxy or chestnut red, darker on the back, and paler on the lower surface of the body. The face and limbs are brownish; and a distinct black line runs down the inner side of the pedicles of the antlers, to be continued for some distance down their supporting ridges. The chin, upper portion of the throat, hind part of the abdomen, and the inner side of the thighs, together with the lower surface of the tail, are white; and there is a whitish mark above the hoofs on the front surface of each leg. Females are coloured practically the same as males, with the exception that tufts of bristly black hairs mark the position of the antler-pedicles of the latter. The fawns are spotted.

I have seen examples of dark-coloured muntjacs, in which the back was nearly black, and the rest of the hair very dark brown; a skin of this type, obtained near Darjiling, at an elevation of about 5000 feet, was brought home by Mr. M. G. Jukes, and Dr. C. Hose states that dark-coloured muntjacs are not uncommon in some of the mountainous districts of North Borneo. This abnormal coloration would therefore seem to be an instance of the melanism frequently met with among animals inhabiting subtropical mountain forests, and cannot be regarded as indicative of a local race.

Indian muntjac antlers seldom exceed 6½ inches in length, with the brow-tine only about 1½ inches; but a specimen from Mussuri measures 7½ inches in length, and an exceptionally long pair from Java rather more than 10 inches. In 1899 Mr. R. E. Holding (*Proc. Zool. Soc. London*, p. 295) described and figured a large pair of muntjac antlers picked out of a cargo of horns from Singapore. These are characterised by their great size and massiveness, and the shortness and stoutness of the supporting pedicles. The antlers measure 9 inches in length, and the brow-tine 4¾ inches, while the pedicles have a girth of 3½ inches. Any doubt as to their being really muntjac-antlers is dispelled by the frontlet and antlers of a muntjac from Pahang, Malay Peninsula, shown in fig. 48, in which the antlers measure 7 inches in length, and are remarkable for their stoutness and great lateral compression, and consequent great antero-posterior depth; the pedicles being also short and stout. This specimen, which was collected by Dr. C. Hose, is in the British Museum. It may be added that a pair of muntjac antlers from Java, recorded in *Records of Big Game*, measures 10¾ inches in length, whilst another pair from Java mentioned in the same work measures 8⅝ inches. I presume a third pair in the same list from Singapore, belonging to

Sir E. G. Loder, is Mr. Holding's specimen, although the length is given as 9½ inches. With the exception of one pair in the same list, of which the length is provisionally stated to be 8½ inches, no Indian muntjac antlers with which I am acquainted equal these dimensions.

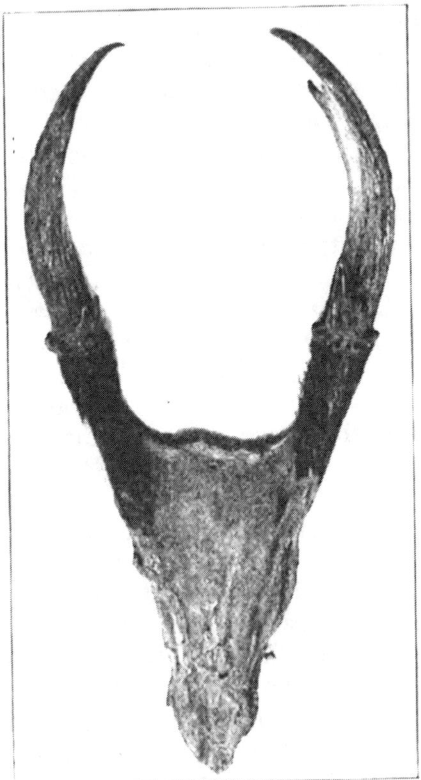

FIG. 48.—Frontlet and Antlers of the Malay Muntjac.

In 1904 Mr. D. H. Allen presented to the British Museum the skull of an old male muntjac picked up in the Thouagyen Forest, Amherst District, Burma, the antlers of which are almost identical with those of Dr. Hose's specimens, showing the same massiveness and marked flattening of the inner surface. The dimensions of the left and larger antler are as follows: Length along outer curve, 6¾ inches; girth above burr, 4⅛ inches; maximum width of inner surface, 1⅜ inches.

The combined evidence of these specimens tends to show that Burmese and Malay muntjac commonly attain an antler-development unparalleled in the Indian *Cervulus muntjac*; and it therefore seems legitimate to regard the former as representing a distinct race. So far as I am aware, none of the scientific names usually regarded as synonyms of the Indian animal were originally applied to Burmese or Malay specimens. The name *C. pleiharicus* was, indeed, proposed by Mr. Kohlbrügger in 1896 for the Bornean muntjac, but I have no means of knowing that this is identical with the Burmese-Malay animal. I have therefore proposed to designate the latter as a distinct race, characterised by its large and massive antlers, under the name of *Cervulus muntjac grandicornis*.[1]

The true or Indian muntjac, inclusive of local races, ranges from the outer Himalaya to Cape Comorin; and is also found in Ceylon, and extends eastwards through Arracan and Burma into the Malay Peninsula, and so onwards to the Malay islands and the coast districts of China. Muntjac from the south of India are smaller than those from the more northerly districts; while, as noted above, those from the Malay Peninsula and islands are larger.

Like the majority of the smaller deer, muntjacs are unsociable creatures, passing the greater portion of their time in solitude, although seeking the society of a mate during the pairing-season. More than a pair are seldom seen in company, although three, and even four, have been observed together. Muntjac only leave the thick covert in which they dwell for the sake of drinking or of feeding on the grass of the adjacent glades; and as they are strictly nocturnal, they are scarcely ever seen except when driven from their retreats. When walking quickly, they move their limbs in a peculiarly stilted and deliberate manner; but, when running, scuttle along with the head carried low and the hind-quarters elevated, the same mode of progress being followed when creeping through thick covert.

The pairing-season, in the more northern districts of the country, takes place in January and February for the

[1] *The Field*, vol. civ. p. 780, 1904.

most part; and when such is the case, the fawns, of which one or two make their appearance at a time, are dropped in July or August. In other districts there seems no regular pairing-season, and fawns are produced at any time of year.

The hoarse, bark-like cry, from which the name kakar is derived, is uttered not only by the bucks in pairing-time, but, under the influence of alarm, at any season of the year; during the pairing-time it is most commonly heard in the morning and evening, although occasionally it may startle the traveller after darkness has fallen. During their contests with one another the bucks appear to rely upon their long upper tusks, rather than upon their antlers. In spite of their tendency to coarse feeding, muntjac yield a venison superior to that of most Indian deer.

I have tried to shoot kakar by having the jungles on a hill-side beaten; but since these little deer are solitary, it is seldom that they come near the sportsman, if there be only a single gun in the field, consequently the sport is by no means exciting or satisfactory. In places where they are numerous, the best plan is to walk them up in covert when they are on the feed in the evening or the early morning.

Muntjac have long been acclimatised in France; and at Rambouillet they survived the severe winter of 1879-1880 with only the shelter of an open shed. They run wild in the Duke of Bedford's coverts at Woburn Abbey.

Muntjac in India are stated to shed their antlers in May and renew them in August; but a head of a Tibetan muntjac which came under my notice leads me to think that the shedding is not annual. In this specimen (shot in a wild state) the antlers are so worn and polished that the external surface has become abraded, leaving the hard white inner layer, which has been polished to such an extent that it resembles ivory. Such wearing seems unlikely to have been caused within less than a twelvemonth; and the inference is that the antlers cannot be annually shed. The statement that muntjac can move their upper tusks seems doubtful.

THE TIBETAN MUNTJAC

(*Cervulus lachrymans*)

Since this species is closely allied to the last, and occurs in districts where European sportsmen seldom penetrate, a few lines in regard to it will suffice. In size it is inferior to the Indian muntjac, standing only 19 inches at the shoulder; and while having face-markings similar to those of the latter, it is distinguished by a difference in general colour, which is bright rufous brown, with the hairs on the back speckled, the head and neck being yellowish brown, or even yellow.

This muntjac was first discovered in Moupin, Eastern Tibet, whence its range extends into Central and Southern China.

THE TENASSERIM MUNTJAC

(*Cervulus feæ*)

(Plate vii, fig. 3)

Very different from both the preceding species is the rare Tenasserim muntjac, in which the general colour, instead of being some shade of chestnut, is sepia-brown, while the tail, which is comparatively short, is black above and white below. It agrees, however, with the Indian muntjac in the absence of a tuft of hair between the pedicles of the antlers. The upper part of the face is very brilliantly coloured, being bright yellow from above the level of the eyes, with the exception of a black V running along the inner borders of the face-ridges to terminate on the brown of the nose; and the front surface of the thighs is conspicuously marked with a white line. Unlike the Indian muntjac, this species has no glands on the forehead.

This muntjac was described from a male, obtained about 1888 in the mountains to the south-east of Maleyit, in Tenasserim, and preserved in the Museum at Genoa. In many respects it forms a link between the Indian species and the hairy-fronted muntjac (*C. crinifrons*) of Eastern China, which is a larger plum-coloured species, distinguished by a crest of long coarse hairs on the crown of the head, almost completely concealing the pedicles of the antlers.

THE TIBETAN TUFTED DEER

(*Elaphodus cephalophus*)

(Plate vii, fig. 4)

The tufted deer, of which the Tibetan representative alone comes within the purview of this volume, are connected with the muntjacs by means of the hairy-fronted species to which a passing reference has just been made. They derive their title of tufted deer from the crest of long and dense bristly hair crowning the summit of the head; while their scientific name of *Elaphodus* refers to the long sabre-like tusks in the upper jaw of the bucks. The two latter features are common to the hairy-fronted muntjac, and the short antlers are similarly supported on long ridges; but the species of *Elaphodus* are distinguished from *Cervulus* by the pedicles of the antlers diverging inferiorly instead of converging, while they are not continued down the face as ridges. The tips of the tusks of the bucks are not turned outward in muntjac fashion, while the hair is extremely coarse and comparatively long. The lateral hoofs are much smaller than in muntjac, being quite rudimentary. The fawns differ from those of the chestnut-coloured muntjacs in being spotted only along the middle line of the back; but since the young of the plum-coloured muntjacs are unknown, this character cannot at present be regarded as one of generic importance. Tufted deer have broad, rounded

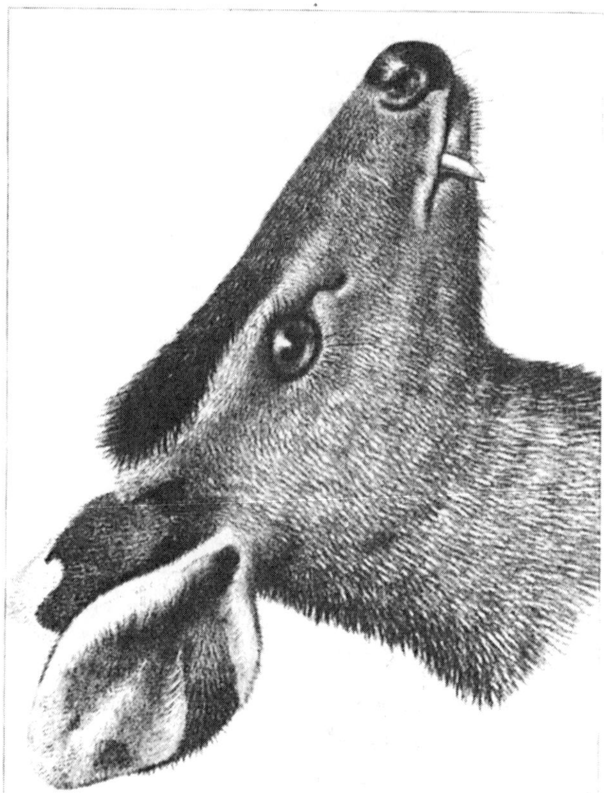

FIG. 49.—Head of Michie's Tufted Deer, from *Proc. Zool. Soc. London*, 1876.

ears, of which the outer surface is thickly haired, and a tail of moderate length.

In the Tibetan species, which may be compared in size to the Indian muntjac, standing about 22 or 23 inches at the withers, the general colour is deep chocolate-brown, the hairs on the fore part of the body having brown tips with a white ring below, whereas farther back this white ring is absent. Consequently the region of the shoulders is finely speckled, but the hind-quarters are uniformly coloured. The crest forms a nearly black horse-shoe on the forehead, bordered above each eye by a line of grey; the ears show a large amount of white internally and on the inner margin, and the lower surface of the tail and the inner sides of the thighs and buttocks are likewise white.

This little deer inhabits the mountains of Moupin, in Eastern Tibet, but is replaced in the east of China by a closely allied species, of which the head is shown in fig. 49, while another representative of the group inhabits the mountains bordering the Ichang valley.

THE KASTURA, OR MUSK-DEER

(*Moschus moschiferus*)

NATIVE NAMES.—*Kastura* AND *Mushk*, HINDUSTANI; *Raos* OR *Rons*, KASHMIRI; *La* AND *Lawa*, TIBETAN; *Ribjo*, LADAKI; *Bena* AND *Masakneba* IN GARHWAL AND KUMAON.

(PLATE vii, fig. 5)

As the animal now to be discussed is very different from true deer, and is only admitted within the family *Cervidæ* on sufferance, it would be better if it were called either by its Hindustani name of kastura, or simply musk, dropping altogether the affix "deer," but custom is hard to overcome, and since the name musk-deer is current, it would be hopeless to attempt its abbreviation.

From all the true deer mentioned in this volume musk-deer differ by the absence of antlers in both sexes; but as a similar feature also obtains in the case of the Chinese water-deer, this alone would not suffice to differentiate the present animal from other members of the family *Cervidæ*. As a matter of fact, the structural features by which the musk-deer is separated from the latter are chiefly connected with the skeleton and the soft internal organs, and detailed reference to them would be out of place on this occasion. It must accordingly suffice to mention that such structural differences do exist, among them being the presence of a gall-bladder, which is never developed in true deer.

As regards general appearance, the musk-deer might be taken, if its long tusks be disregarded, for a female antelope just as well as for a female deer; but the sabre-like upper tusks of the bucks are a feature unparalleled among hollow-horned ruminants. In the extremely large size of the lateral hoofs, which are capable of being spread out so as to secure an additional foothold, the musk-deer is peculiar.

In build musk-deer are stout and heavy, if not clumsy, the rump being raised above the level of the fore-quarters, while the hind-limbs are longer than the front ones, which, however, are also of considerable length; both pairs being thick. The coarse and thick hair, which is minutely waved, is extremely brittle and pith-like, and serves as a protection against the cold of the animal's habitat. The ears are large; and although much smaller in females, the upper tusks attain great development in bucks. From other *Cervidæ* musk-deer differ by the absence of face-glands below the eyes; and the metatarsal and tarsal glands found in so many deer are likewise wanting. The tail is reduced to a mere glandular rudiment; but whereas in the bucks it terminates in a small tuft, in the does it is covered uniformly with hair. A gland in the skin of the abdomen of the bucks secretes, at least during the pairing-season, the well-known powerful scent from which the animal derives its name.

In height the musk-deer stands some 22 inches at

the rump, and about a couple of inches less at the withers. On the upper part of the head and body and outer surface of the limbs the prevailing colour is some shade of rich dark brown, more or less mottled and speckled with grey, and in immature individuals displaying traces of spots, generally arranged in lines. The speckled appearance of the coat is due to the coloration of the individual hairs, which are white for the basal three-quarters of their length, then ringed with white, and terminating in a blackish tip. The under surface of the body and the inner sides of the limbs are whitish, and there may be a single or double white spot on each side of the throat. In regard to details of coloration there is, however, a considerable individual variation, some skins being paler and others more yellow than ordinary ; in addition to which there may be splashes of black or golden red on the upper-parts, while the under surface may be either golden yellow or white.

Being forest-dwelling mountain animals, musk-deer are restricted in the Himalaya to the wooded ranges, where they are usually found at elevations of about 8000 feet, or higher, during summer. So far as present information goes, the western limit of the range occurs somewhere about the neighbourhood of Gilgit ; the species is unknown in the barren districts of Dras, Zanskar, and Ladak, but farther west, probably in the neighbourhood of Sikhim, extends northwards into the forest districts of Eastern Tibet. It has also a wide distribution in Central and Northern Asia.

As musk-deer yield a product valuable to man, which can be obtained from no other source, they are objects of eager and incessant pursuit, which would in all probability have already resulted in their extermination, were it not for the circumstance that they frequent country where concealment is comparatively easy. As it is, however, the numbers of this animal have been seriously reduced in the more accessible parts of its habitat; although the enactment of game-laws in certain districts may do something towards its rehabilitation. The contents of a "pod" of musk weigh about one ounce.

In wandering among the birch-forests which clothe

FIG. 50.—A Young Musk-Deer, from a photograph by the Duchess of Bedford.

the mountains of Kashmir for a certain height above the belt of pines, especially in early spring, when the snow still lies deep between the silvery stems, the traveller will, from time to time, be startled by a little animal of the size of a roe getting up suddenly at no great distance away, and starting off in a series of enormous bounds, after having taken from ten to twenty of which, it will turn round to gaze at the disturber of its haunts—a habit which too often leads to its destruction. The creature that has thus bounded off is a musk-deer, which has either been gathering a meal from the dead grass buried beneath the snow or the lichens growing on the surrounding tree-stems, or has been sleeping in its "form." For musk-deer, like hares, appear to have regular resting-places, in which they lie up for the greater part of the day, being mainly nocturnal in their habits. Although the birch-forests and the higher portion of the pine-zone form their principal haunts in Kashmir, they may be seen farther eastwards at considerably lower levels, at times even among the rhododendron-forests, which in spring clothe the sides of many of the outer Himalayan valleys with a blaze of colour.

Musk-deer appear enabled to maintain a firm foot-hold on smooth and slippery boulders or faces of rock by means of the peculiar conformation of their hoofs, which are unlike those of other ruminants. As already mentioned, the lateral hoofs, which are more or less completely rudimentary in most ruminants (if not altogether wanting, as in the pala antelope and the giraffe), in the musk-deer vie in length and mobility with the main pair ; and it would seem that by widely spreading these hoofs a grasp of the surface of the rock is obtained. These large lateral hoofs also appear to act as a kind of break, by preventing the animal from slipping when descending a frozen snow-slope, or an inclined face of rock. In the fore-legs the toe-bones supporting the lateral hoofs are supplied with special muscles and tendons which have become aborted by disuse in most other ruminants.

The food of the musk-deer varies, it seems, according to season, probably including dried grass and lichens during the winter, and leaves of trees and flowers in summer. When wounded or captured musk-deer often utter piercing screams, but under ordinary circumstances they are comparatively silent, although sometimes giving vent to loud hisses as they stand gazing on an intruder into their lonely and silent domains.

For the greater part of the year musk-deer are solitary, but in January the buck seeks the company of a single doe, with which it remains during the pairing-season. In June the fawns make their appearance, and although one is the usual number at a birth, there are occasionally twins. In this respect musk-deer are unlike Chinese water-deer, which are also devoid of antlers and provided with long upper tusks in the males; the number of the young produced by the doe of the latter being as many as half-a-dozen. Fawns arrive at maturity rapidly, and are capable of reproducing their kind within their first year.

Sportsmen are in the habit of estimating the fineness of the musk-deer they shoot by the length of their tusks. In the largest specimen on record the tusk projects 3¼ inches beyond the jaw-bone; while two examples are known in which the length is 3 inches. The only apparent difference between the sexes when seen in the field is the presence of the long upper tusks in the males, and to recognise the absence or presence of these weapons in a momentary glance requires some degree of practice. With these weapons the bucks engage in combats with one another during the pairing-season, specimens being sometimes killed in which the hair has been ripped off in long lines. The brittleness and stiffness of the hair renders the skin of little value, although from its peculiar nature the cold-resisting power of the fur must be great.

In musk-deer shooting the usual plan is to walk up to the game, when either a small-bore rifle or a shot-gun may be used. Less sportsmanlike is the method of driving; while the plan followed by the natives of Garhwal of catching them by means of long net-fences, provided at intervals with gaps in which are set running nooses, is to be deprecated from all points of view.

The musk-deer inhabiting Kansu has already been separated as a distinct species (*M. sifanicus*), and possibly, when large sets of specimens are available for comparison, the Himalayan musk-deer may be divisible into local races. A skull in the British Museum indicates that the range of musk-deer extends as far east as Amurland.

THE MEMINNA CHEVROTAIN

(*Tragulus meminna*)

NATIVE NAMES.—*Pisura*, *Pisora*, AND *Pisai*, HINDUSTANI AND MAHRATHI ; *Jitrai-haran*, BENGALI ; *Gandwa*, URIA ; *Yar*, HO-KOL ; *Kuru-pandi*, TELEGU ; *Kuram-pani*, TAMIL ; *Kur-pandi*, CANARESE ; *Meminna* AND *Walmaha*, CINGALESE.

(PLATE vii, fig. 6)

Among the errors of popular natural history none is more persistent or difficult to eradicate than the belief that the little animals known as mouse-deer, or chevrotains, are members of the deer tribe, or *Cervidæ* ; for they are really very like diminutive hornless deer, such as the Chinese water-deer and the musk-deer. Superficial resemblances are, however, not to be trusted ; and when the anatomy of the chevrotains is examined, there are found important features by which they are distinguished from typical ruminants, such as deer.

It is true they have no upper front teeth, and that they ruminate, or "chew the cud," and also that their stomachs are divided into compartments ; but the compartments are three instead of four in number, and the fibula or smaller bone of the second segment of the hind-limb is complete and free from the tibia or larger bone, instead of incomplete and more or less united with the latter. All the bones of the lateral toes are likewise complete, whereas some of them are imperfect or even wanting in true ruminants. Then, again, if the ankle-joint be examined, it will be found to contain one bone more than in the latter group, in which two of the original elements are fused together. In the structure of their cheek-teeth chevrotains resemble, however, true ruminants, as they do in possessing "cannon-bones," although in the African genus *Dorcatherium* it is only in one pair of limbs that the two component elements unite to form a cannon-bone.

All Oriental chevrotains are small, delicately built animals, with elevated hind-quarters, and slender limbs. They inhabit forests, and are of shy and skulking habits. From their larger African relative they are distinguished by having cannon-bones in both limbs. The head is long and pointed, with comparatively small and rounded ears, a large portion of the narrow muzzle bare and moist, and no glands below the eyes; glands being likewise wanting between the hoofs and in the groin. There are no appendages comparable either to horns or antlers, but the males, as in musk-deer and the Chinese water-deer, are furnished with long sabre-like tusks, capable of inflicting severe wounds in their combats with one another. The tail is more or less short, the hair is fine and close, and the females are provided with four teats. In walking, chevrotains have a peculiar stilted gait, treading only on the tips of the hoofs; the legs having such a rigid appearance that it is a common idea there are no joints to the knees.

The meminna is distinguished by being spotted and streaked with white, as well as by the chin and throat being completely covered with hair, instead of showing a bare glandular area; while the tail is shorter than in other species, and there is only a small bare patch on the hind-leg in the neighbourhood of the hock. In height the animal stands from about 10 to 12 inches at the shoulder ; the length from the nose to the root of the tail varies from 18 to 22 inches, the tail itself measuring only an inch, or an inch and a quarter ; the weight is from five to six pounds. In colour the upper-parts are rich brown (darker in some individuals than in others), speckled with yellow, the individual hairs being brown at the roots and black at the tips, below which they are ringed with yellow, thus causing the speckled appearance of the coat. The sides of the body, from the shoulder to the rump, are marked with longitudinal rows of white or buff spots, which tend to form streaks about half-way down ; and the inner surface of the ears, a streak above each eye, three broad stripes on the throat and chest, together with the under-parts, are white.

The range of this chevrotain is limited to the forests of Ceylon and Southern India at elevations not exceeding about 2000 feet above the sea ; its northern extension including Orissa, Chutia Nagpur, the eastern division of the Central Provinces, and the Western Ghats to the northward of Bombay. Its reported occurrence farther north requires confirmation. The animal is evidently a member of the Malay fauna ; and the group, as is attested by the occurrence of fossilised remains of extinct species in the sub-Himalaya, must have existed in Northern India at a time when Ceylon formed a portion of the peninsula.

Meminna is the Cingalese name of the species, and is mentioned by Robert Knox in a work on Ceylon, published during the reign of Charles II. :—"Deer," it is there written, "are in great abundance in the woods, from the largeness of a cow to the smallness of a hare, for there is a creature in this land no bigger than the latter, though every part rightly resembleth a deer ; it is called *Meminna*, of a grey colour, with white spots and good meat." Although now commonly known by Europeans as mouse-deer, Sir Emerson Tennent states that in his time it was called "moose-deer" in Ceylon, "moose" being probably a corruption of the Dutch word *muis*, equivalent to mouse. He likewise suggests that the title musk-deer, by which these animals are also known, is traceable to the same origin, but it seems more probable that it was given from their superficial resemblance to the true musk-deer. Sir Emerson Tennent mentions that in 1847 he saw in Ceylon a pure white chevrotain.

In Central India the meminna usually takes up its abode among jungly rocks, from which it never ventures out into the open, and in the crevices of which it spends the hot midday hours, and produces its young. Consequently it is but seldom seen, and when encountered at once makes for its rocky haven. The young, of which there are generally couplets, are beautiful little creatures, so delicate and fragile that they seem scarcely fitted to endure the hardships of the world. They are born towards the end of the rainy season, or the commencement of the cool season ; the males consort with their partners only during the pairing-season, which takes place about June or July, spending the rest of the year by themselves. Both sexes feed in the evenings and early mornings, and the only sound they are known to utter is a feeble bleat.

As they carry no trophies worth talking about, chevrotain offer little attraction to the sportsman. They may be killed either with a shot-gun or the rook-rifle.

THE NAPU CHEVROTAIN

(*Tragulus napu*)

NATIVE NAME.—*Napu*, MALAY

In common with its smaller Malay relative, the napu, or larger Malay chevrotain, is distinguished from the meminna by its uniformly coloured body, and the presence of a naked glandular area on the throat, as well as of another bare tract on the hind surface of each hind-leg in the neighbourhood of the hock; the tail, too, is longer, measuring about 3 inches. In height the animal stands about 13 inches at the shoulder, the length to the root of the tail being about 28 inches. The general colour of the upper-parts is yellowish or rufous brown, becoming greyer on the flanks, the tail being brown above and white below. A distinctive feature is the presence of five white bands on the throat and chest, of which one is median, while the other four form oblique lateral pairs.

The geographical range of the napu extends from the southern districts of Tenasserim through the Malay Peninsula to the islands of Java, Sumatra, and Borneo. The island forms of both this and the kanchil have received in many cases distinct specific names, but they can scarcely be regarded as more than local races, and consequently need not be further noticed.

THE KANCHIL CHEVROTAIN

(*Tragulus javanicus*)

NATIVE NAMES.—*Yun*, BURMESE; *Kanchil*, MALAY

In this work it will suffice to state that the lesser Malay chevrotain, as this species is frequently called, is chiefly distinguished from the napu by its inferior size, and the presence of only three white stripes on the throat and chest. Of these stripes, the central one is situated within an arrowhead-like brown mark, while the other two form a pair on each side of the latter. As in the napu, the distinctness of these markings shows considerable variation. The maximum length, from nose to root of tail, attained by this species is 18 inches. The distribution is very similar to that of the napu, but includes Cochin-China and Cambodia.

THE INDIAN WILD BOAR

(*Sus cristatus*)

NATIVE NAMES.—*Suar*, *Barha*, AND *Bad* OR *Bura Janwar*, HINDUSTANI ; *Dukar*, MAHRATHI, GUZERATI, AND SINDI ; *Hikh*, BALUCHI ; *Guraz* AND *Kuk*, PUNJABI ; *Pandi*, TAMIL AND TELEGU ; *Katu-pani*, TAMIL ; *Paddi* OF THE GONDS ; *Bir Sukri*, HO-KOL ; *Kis* OF THE HILL-TRIBES OF RAJMEHAL ; *Handi*, *Mikka*, *Jevadi*, *Kari-jati*, CANARESE ; *Sukaram*, MALABARI ; *Waluru*, CINGALESE ; *Banel*, NEPALESE ; *Ripha* AND *Phak* OF THE BHOTIAS OF DARJILING ; *Sarao* IN THE DAPHLA HILLS ; *Bali* AND *Techim* OF THE MISHMIS ; *Sniang* IN THE KHASI HILLS ; *Vak* IN THE GARO HILLS ; *Omar* AND *Hono*, KACHARI ; *Kubak*, *Tharo*, *Kashag*, *Mengi*, AND *Vak* OF THE NAGAS ; *Eyeg*, ABOR ; *Mu*, KHAMTI ; *Ok*, MANIPURI ; *Vu*, KUKI ; *Vhu*, AKA ; *Wa*, SINGPHO ; *Tau-wet*, BURMESE ; *Kalet*, TALAIN ; *Hto* OF THE KARENS ; *Mu* IN THE SHAN STATES ; *Babi-utan*, MALAY.

(PLATE vii, fig. 7)

The Indian wild boar is one of the gamest of all four-footed animals, never giving in without a gallant struggle for life, and invariably fighting bravely to the bitter end ; and if not actually the first, "pig-sticking" is one of the finest and most exciting of all Indian field-sports, calling into play all the bodily activity and skill of horse and rider, and making no inconsiderable demands on the nerve and coolness of the latter. The element of danger is, indeed, by no means lacking in this pastime; and if pig-sticking takes a secondary place among Indian sports, it is only by tiger-shooting that it is excelled. Nor are tangible trophies wanting to reward the sportsman, for although boars' tusks are not to be compared with horns or antlers, yet, in their way, they are handsome objects, and capable of being worked up as accessories of several useful or ornamental articles.

Since every one is familiar with a pig, and a wild boar is nothing more than a pig that has not been shorn of its natural glories by the effects of domestication, it will be unnecessary to discuss in what respects the members of the family *Suidæ* differ from other hoofed mammals, or how the pigs of Europe and Asia are distinguishable from the bush-pigs and wart-hogs of Africa.

The characters by which the Indian wild boar is differentiated from the wild boar of Europe are so trivial, that it is only by naturalists that they are appreciated. The near relationship of the two species is shown by the shape of the lower tusks; the transverse section of these forming a triangle of which the hind surface is only slightly narrower than the front one, while the outer surface has but half the breadth of the one first named. The importance of this apparently trivial feature is referred to later.

Adult Indian wild boars not unfrequently stand from 33 to 36 inches in height at the shoulder, and it is even stated by Mr. F. B. Simson that a very old individual killed in Bengal (where large boars are far from uncommon) fell little short of 38 inches. In length a boar will measure about 5 feet from the muzzle to the root of the tail; the length of the latter being from 8 to 11 inches or more. From 200 to 300 pounds, or even more, may be given as the weight attained by the Indian wild boar; and that the European species runs to about the same bulk is attested by a specimen killed in Spain by the Duc d'Orléans, the weight of which was 302 pounds. It is comparatively seldom that lower tusks of the Indian species, when removed from the jaw, measure more than about 9 inches along the outer curve, but specimens measuring 10, $10\frac{1}{2}$, $10\frac{5}{8}$ inches are known; and these dimensions are exceeded by two tusks (one malformed), the respective lengths of which are given by their owner as $14\frac{3}{8}$ and $14\frac{3}{4}$ inches.

The Indian wild boar is a taller and more scantily haired animal than its European relative, but with a strongly developed crest or mane of long bristles running from the nape of the neck down the back; and it is also stated that the tail, which reaches nearly to the hocks, is more thickly tufted at the tip. The Indian species lacks the woolly under-fur commonly found in the European *Sus scrofa*. An important distinction is to be found in the greater length and complexity of the last lower molar tooth in each jaw of *S. cristatus*; the length of this tooth generally exceeding the combined length of the two molars immediately in front. The general colour of the coarse and bristly hair of the adult is black, more or less mixed with rusty brown or whitish; the tint being browner in young, and greyer in aged individuals. It may be added that there are neither a distinct whitish streak on the side of the face nor warts on the head. As in other wild representatives of the genus *Sus*, the new-born young are light yellowish-brown, marked with longitudinal stripes of dark brown. Occasionally, in thick forest and jungle, herds of wild pigs are met with in which the general colour of the hair is brown, instead of black; but there is no evidence that this difference indicates a distinct local race.

The Indian wild boar (*Sus cristatus typicus*, to give its full title) is found from the Himalaya, where it ascends to a considerable elevation, throughout India, Ceylon, and Burma. Whether the wild swine of Baluchistan and Afghanistan belong to this species, or to the

European *S. scrofa* (which is probably found in Persia) is not determined, although Dr. Blanford considered that such might be the case. The same remark applies to the wild swine of Kashmir. Under these circumstances it has not been considered necessary to introduce *Sus scrofa* as a member of the fauna treated of in this volume.

To a considerable extent the Indian wild boar is nocturnal, hiding in thick covert—it may be long grass, cultivated crops of grain or sugar-cane, bushes, or, more rarely, forest—during the greater part of the day, and issuing forth to feed in the morning and evening. The extent to which pigs are nocturnal varies, however, according to the degree in which they are disturbed; and in certain districts they may be seen feeding till comparatively late in the day. On moonlight nights they remain out for hours; and in cultivated districts the damage they do to growing crops by turning up the soil with their snouts is extensive. The "sounders," as the herds in which they associate are commonly termed, are composed exclusively of sows, immature boars, and young; the old boars spending a solitary existence. The number of individuals in a sounder does not ordinarily exceed ten or a dozen, although occasionally as many as a score, or more, may be seen in company. The solitary old boars are extremely awkward animals to encounter; and the natives of certain districts of the Himalaya have a saying that it is as easy to face a tiger as one of these veteran swine. Although mainly vegetable-feeders, wild swine by no means restrict themselves to a diet of this description, being, in fact, more or less omnivorous. Not only will they make a hearty meal off carrion, but in Assam they are stated to be in the habit of digging up the fish which take refuge in the mud of the river-beds during droughts. If they have a partiality for one kind of vegetable food more than another, it is for the roots and tubers of plants growing in moist situations; and they prefer marshy situations, such as the banks of *jhils* and tanks, to dry ones, wallowing in mud being a pastime among pigs of all descriptions.

Pigs increase with great rapidity, the period of gestation being only about four months, so that there is time for the production of a couple of litters a year; the number of young in which is generally from four to six. In certain districts, at all events, Indian swine are in the habit of forming a rude kind of shelter of grass, in which the sows are reported to place their offspring for security; while occasionally old boars resort to these refuges. The flesh of young porkers is excellent eating, but since cooks in India are for the most part Mohammedans there is great difficulty in getting it dressed for table, and the carcase is usually made over to the *saises*, or grooms, and other low-caste Hindus.

At the first burst, a wild boar starts off at a rattling pace, but he is not long-winded, and is sooner or later caught up by the horseman unless the ground is very bad, nor are the sows much, if at all, superior in speed and wind to the boars. When brought to bay, old boars fight in the most determined manner, charging at every horse that comes in their way, and inflicting terrible wounds with their formidable lower tusks by a side sweep of the head. A competent observer has given it as his verdict that there is not a bolder animal in the world than a wild boar. Not that boars are specially vicious by nature, for if unmolested they generally leave the passer-by alone; but when once roused, they "mean business." Even the tiger cannot attack them with impunity, there being several instances on record where "stripes" has come off worst in such an encounter. But it is not every boar that displays the same amount of boldness and courage, nor indeed of speed; and it is stated that while the comparatively lightly-built and "leggy" animals of the Deccan and the Punjab possess the greater capacity for speed, the heavier and more massive boars from the swampy districts of Bengal are the best fighters.

Wherever the country is suitable for riding, "pig-sticking" is the only legitimate sport connected with *Sus cristatus.* As this sport has been described over and over again with a detail which would be impossible in this volume, the reader may be referred to the numerous works on the subject, among which may be mentioned Mr. F. B. Simson's *Letters on Sport in Eastern Bengal*, and a well-known volume by Mr. J. Moray-Brown.

In the Himalaya and the hills of Ceylon, where riding is impossible, the wild boar is, however, occasionally shot, or (in Ceylon) hunted with hounds. Of the latter sport a vivid and interesting account is given by Sir Samuel Baker. When boar-hunting in the hill-forests of Ceylon that sportsman followed the hounds on foot, and tackled the boar at bay with the hunting-knife alone. Comparatively few would, however, care to follow his example in this respect; and the spear is the weapon generally chosen to give the *coup de grâce* in this exciting and dangerous kind of sport. Sir Samuel expressed great admiration for the general "cuteness" of the Indian wild boar, stating that not only is it a fierce antagonist, but that it is a creature which always knows its own mind and acts up to its own convictions, never hesitating in a course on which it has once determined. If it decides to go forward, nothing will stop it; while, on the other hand, if it determines to break back, not even a serried line of elephants will check its mad rush. Giving a sharp jerk of its mobile snout, first to one side and then to the other, it dashes headlong through the line, leaving its mark even upon the tough hide of the legs of the elephants, should they attempt to bar its progress.

In regard to its powers of scent, the same author makes the following observations :—"I have frequently seen a pig making apparently direct for my position, but it meets a small jungle-path upon which some person has been walking. The pig at once halts, smells the ground, and waits, listening attentively and making up its mind. It may be that it determines to go forward; if so, it starts off at its best pace; but should it declare for a retreat, it waits, listens for the advance of the line of beaters, and quietly hides in the densest bushes. At last, with shouts sufficient to scare away every animal for miles around, the beaters arrive; you know the pig is there, but nobody has yet discovered it. Just as the beaters have brought their line in good order to the extreme margin of the jungle, there is a sudden outburst of shouts and yells, a rush in all directions; screams and halloes; sticks going upon all sides; a few short angry grunts, and a rattling of loose stones, explain that the boar has broken back through the line of beaters."

Lower Siam and the central part of the Malay Peninsula are inhabited by a wild pig near akin to the Indian species, but of inferior size, with smaller and nearly naked ears, which are devoid of a fringe of hair, and less complex last molars. Although described as a separate species, it may best be termed *Sus cristatus jubatus*. Still smaller is *S. cristatus jubatulus* from Pulo Teratau and perhaps other islands off the west coast of the Malay Peninsula. A small pig from Kisserain Island, Mergui Archipelago, may be the same as the last.

In past times Northern India was inhabited by two gigantic pigs (*Sus giganteus* and *S. titan*), one of which was apparently nearly as large as a good-sized mule, although shorter in the legs. Both were allied to the warty pig (*S. verrucosus*) of Java, as is shown by the section of the lower tusk.

The wild pig discovered by the Abbé David in the forests of Moupin, Eastern Tibet, described by Professor A. Milne-Edwards, of the Paris Museum, as a *Sus moupinensis*, is stated to show relationship with the wild swine of Europe and Southern Asia. It is probably not entitled to rank as a species by itself, but whether it should be regarded as a local race of the Indian species, or be affiliated to the European *S. scrofa*, is at present uncertain.

THE ANDAMAN AND NICOBAR WILD PIGS

(*Sus vittatus andamanensis* AND *S. v. nicobaricus*)

The larger islands of the Bay of Bengal and the Malay Archipelago are the home of a group of wild pigs near akin to *S. cristatus*, and in some cases indistinguishable externally from the island races of that species. They are, however, easily separated by the much simpler form of the last molar tooth in each jaw; the upper one having only two transverse ridges and a small terminal heel. The section of the lower canine of the boars is similar to that of *S. cristatus*; a character distinguishing them from *S. verrucosus* of Java. The group is typified by *S. vittatus* of Sumatra, and although its various representations in other islands and in the Malay Peninsula have been described as distinct species, it is preferable to regard them merely in the light of local races.

The two smallest representatives of the groups are the Andaman and the Nicobar wild pigs (*S. vittatus andamanensis* and *S. v. nicobaricus*). The former, which appears to be chiefly distinguished from the latter by its smaller size, stands about 20 inches in height, and has blackish hair, with a brownish tinge on the mane. *S. v. peninsularis* of Johore and other parts of the extremity of the Malay Peninsula is a considerably larger member of the group.

The *S. verrucosus* group does not occur within our limits.

THE PIGMY HOG

(*Sus salvanius*)

NATIVE NAME.—*Sano-banel*, NEPALESE

(PLATE vii, fig. 8)

Its diminutive size serves to distinguish the wild pig inhabiting the sal-forests of the Terai-land at the foot of the Himalaya in Nepal, Sikhim, and Bhutan, from all its relatives, although structurally it does not appear to differ essentially from other members of the genus *Sus*. The females have only three pairs of teats, instead of the six pairs found in other pigs ; a feature which might be regarded sufficient to justify the reference of the pigmy species to a genus by itself. In this case it would be known as *Porcula salvania*, a name proposed by its describer Brian Hodgson, on the supposition that it had one pair of molars less in each jaw than ordinary swine.

In size the pigmy hog does not surpass a hare, the height of a full-grown boar not exceeding a foot, and the length from the muzzle to the root of the tail being only about 26 inches. The tail is short, measuring only about an inch and a quarter ; and the ears are small and naked. Although there is no distinct crest, the hairs on the hind part of the neck and the middle of the back are slightly longer than on other regions of the body. The general colour of the adult is brown or blackish brown, owing to a mixture of brown and black hairs ; but the young are marked with longitudinal rufous stripes on a brown ground, with the under-parts white.

Hodgson describes the pigmy hog as living in herds of from five to twenty head among the tall grass-jungle of the Terai ; the old boars associating with the herd. Since they only come into the open at night, these pigs are rarely seen, and still more rarely shot.

THE INDIAN LION

(*Felis leo guzeratensis*)

NATIVE NAMES.—*Sher*, *Babar-sher*, AND *Singh*, HINDUSTANI ; *Untia-bagh* (camel-coloured tiger), GUZERATI ; *Sawach* IN KATHIAWAR ; *Shingal*, BENGALI ; *Suh* (lion), AND *Siming* (lioness), KASHMIRI ; *Rastar*, BRAHUI.

(PLATE viii, fig. 1)

As this volume makes no pretence to be a natural history, it will be unnecessary to indicate in what respects Carnivora differ from Ungulata, to which the foregoing pages are devoted. Neither is there any occasion to refer to the distinctive characteristics of the *Felidæ*, or cat tribe, of which the lion stands first on the list, since such details are to be found in natural history works. Moreover, the lion itself is such a well-known and familiar animal, that detailed description of its external features and colour would be superfluous.

The tiger being the great Indian cat *par excellence*, while the lion occupies a similar position in the fauna of Africa, it is apt to be forgotten that the latter has equal claims to be regarded as an Asiatic animal, and that although verging on extinction in India, it is still comparatively abundant in parts of Persia and Mesopotamia, as it probably once was in India, where, however, its range seems to have been restricted to the central and north-western districts.

That it was once a familiar animal in India is proved by the frequency with which its name has been adopted by distinguished native families, as exemplified by the names Ranjit Singh, and Ranbir Singh among the Sikh chieftains of the Punjab, and Sher Ali among the Mohammedan rulers of Afghanistan.

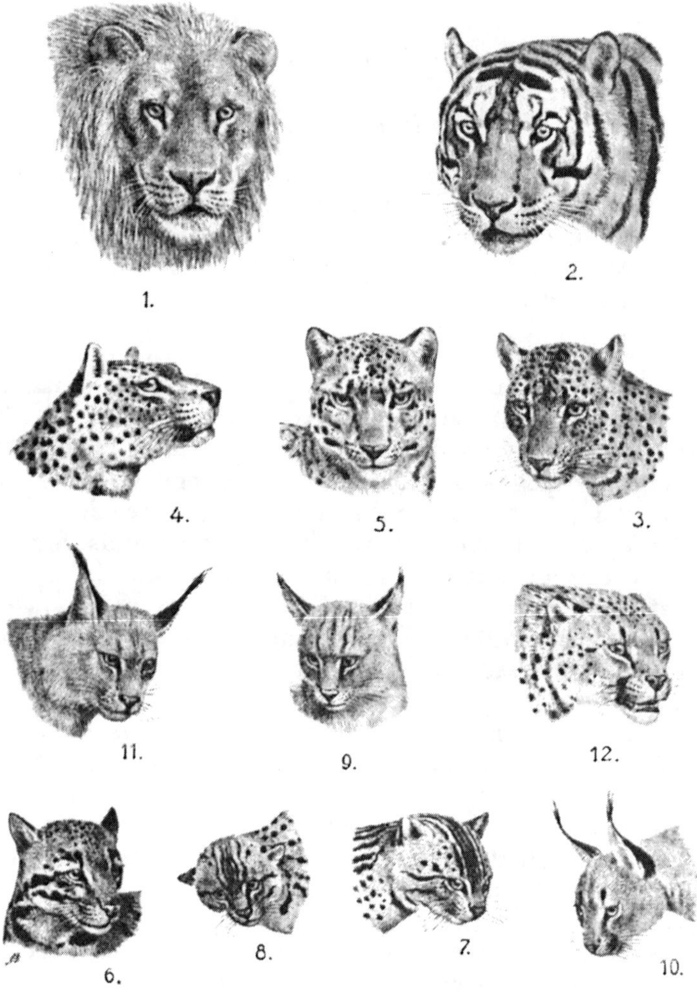

Plate VIII

1. Indian Lion.
2. Tiger.
3. Leopard.
4. Persian Leopard.
5. Snow-Leopard.
6. Clouded Tiger.
7. Fishing-Cat.
8. Leopard-Cat.
9. Jungle-Cat.
10. Caracal.
11. Tibetan Lynx.
12. Hunting-Leopard.

As regards Afghanistan and Baluchistan, lions are now unknown in both, neither does there seem to be historical evidence of their former existence in these states.

The last stronghold of lions in India is the peninsula of Kathiawar, forming part of the district of Guzerat, and bounded on the south by the Gulf of Cambay and to the north by the Gulf of Kutch ; but they also lingered to a recent date in Kutch itself. Not very many years ago natives also from time to time reported the occurrence of an occasional lion in Central India ; and a few undoubtedly lingered in the wilder districts of Rajputana, especially to the south of Jodhpur, in Oodeypur, and around Mount Abu, where they were once common. In Kathiawar the last haunt of lions is the forest covering the Gir range of hills, which extend for about forty miles in the southern part of Kathiawar, parallel with the coast at a distance of about twenty miles inland. Twenty years ago it was believed that not more than a dozen lions survived in this forest, and, to ensure the preservation of the race, lion-shooting was prohibited ; the preserve being closely maintained, as the impression prevailed that in later years the number had decreased.

About 1902 Lord Curzon projected a lion-hunt in the Gir forest, but as the result of representations abandoned the expedition. This probably helped to foster the belief in the increasing rarity of the Indian lion ; but there is evidence that it is much more numerous than has been supposed. There also appear to have been misapprehensions as to his habits, due to the fact that few persons besides native trackers have penetrated the Gir forest to any extent, which is much denser than generally supposed.

Somewhat later Lord Lamington, when Governor of Bombay, organised a lion-hunt in the Gir forest ; the two divisions of his party shooting in places about twelve miles apart. In a short time they accounted for four lions, but unhappily Major Carnegy, of the Political Department, was attacked by a wounded lion and killed before his companions could despatch the beast, and the hunt was in consequence brought to a premature close.

Going back to earlier days, we find in the *Oriental Sporting Magazine* for 1832 over the signature of "Collector," whose address is given as Baroda, a full account of two sportsmen shooting a large lion off elephants; and in the *Bengal Sporting Magazine* of October 1838 a writer signing himself "Kattywar" states that he shot eleven lions between the 14th and 24th of May, to which three more were added between the 19th and 27th of July. Throughout the later volumes of the *Bengal Sporting Magazine*, the *India Sporting Review* and the revived *Oriental Sporting Magazine*, which followed it, there are occasional articles descriptive of lion-shooting; and in the *Asian* for June 30, 1885, Colonel Martin related how he and General Travers killed two lions on a hill to the west of Goona in Gwalior in 1860, and two years later he and Colonel Beadon at Patulghur, some seventy miles north-west of Goona, bagged no less than eight. One of the last lions killed in Central India was shot by Sir Montague Gerrard at Cheen Hill, nine miles from Goona, on Waterloo Day 1872; and in the *Asian* of April 7, 1893, mention is made of another shot by Colonel Hill in 1873. In Guzerat—exclusive of Kathiawar—the last survivor is said to have been killed in 1888. Since that date there have been no lions elsewhere than in the Gir.

In the wild district between Saugor and Jhansi lions were by no means very uncommon about forty years ago. In 1866 two engineers engaged in the construction of the railway between Allahabad and Jabalpur shot one close to the line; and about thirty years before lions were comparatively common in the Ahmedabad district, while in the first and second decades of the last century they were to be met with in Sind and as far to the east as Palamow and Rewa.

A lion shot by Lord Harris had a fine mane, and thus disproves the story long current among naturalists as to the maneless character of the "lion of Guzerat," which arose from the description of an immature specimen. If the absence of mane is not a distinctive feature of the Indian lion, it is possible that a claim to racial distinction may be drawn from the colour of the mane, unless indeed too few specimens are now in existence to render the point certain. The present writer has never heard of the occurrence of a black-maned Indian lion; and in the *Badminton Library* Lieut.-Colonel Heber Percy states such animals are unknown. As black-maned lions are common in Somaliland and other parts of North-Eastern Africa, if it could be proved that all Indian lions were tawny-maned, there would be *primâ facie* evidence of their right to be regarded as the representatives of a local race. Some light may be thrown on the point by the Persian lion, which will probably be found indistinguishable from the Indian; and if Persian lions are all tawny-maned, it may be inferred that the same will be the case with their Indian representatives. *Felis leo guzeratensis* is the distinctive title of the Indian lion.

The Indian lion seems to be inferior in size to the lion of many parts of Africa, and more nearly equal to the small Somali race. On the other hand, it should be remembered that when an animal is on the verge of extermination its surviving members are scarcely likely to attain the maximum dimensions of their race. Consequently the Indian lion may once have been a larger animal than it has shown itself in modern times; although the analogy of the lions of Persia and Somaliland is against this view.

A lion killed many years ago by Captain Smee measured 8 feet 9½ inches in length before skinning;

one mentioned in the *Delhi Gazette* as having been shot in Central India was only 8 feet 7 inches; while the specimen mentioned above as described in the *Oriental Sporting Magazine* for July 1876 reached 9 feet 3 inches. A specimen shot by Lord Harris was still larger, its length being 9 feet 7 inches; but one killed by Colonel Fenton measured 9 feet 5 inches. As lions of considerably over 10 feet in length have been obtained, even in Somaliland, it will be obvious that none of the above-mentioned specimens can be regarded as really large animals. The length of the skull of Lord Harris's specimen is only 13¼ inches, whereas a Somali lion-skull of 15 inches is on record, and a South-East African example reaching 16½ inches is known.

A pair of Asiatic lions exhibited in the Surrey Zoological Gardens were brought home from Basra, at the head of the Persian Gulf, in H.M.S. *Boyne*, by the captain of which vessel they were presented to George IV., and on arrival were deposited in the Royal Menagerie at Exeter Change. They were described as relatively small, with hair of a pale fawn-colour.

Lions being inhabitants of more or less open, dry, and sandy districts, a large portion of India, such as the Assam Valley, the sub-Himalayan Terai, the sal-forest of the Narbada, the swamps of Lower Bengal, and the greater part of Madras, are totally unsuited to their habits; and their limited geographical distribution in the country is thus easily accounted for. The same cause may explain their absence from the countries to the eastward of the Bay of Bengal. When less uncommon than it now is, the Indian lion was said to avoid, as a general rule, heavy forest, preferring sandy hills covered with thin scrub and grass, among which it might be stalked on foot with the danger attached to tiger-shooting under similar conditions. According to native reports, lions in India were always in the habit of selecting one particular bush or tree for their midday place of repose, so that when one was known to be in the neighbourhood its discovery was an easy matter. This may have helped considerably in the diminution in its numbers which has taken place during the last century.

The following account of the habits of the Indian lion is from a sporting writer:—"He seeks the loneliest spot for his midday sleep, and, when disturbed, does not slink away like the tiger, but walks or runs upright, without any attempt to hide himself. He avoids man more than either the tiger or the leopard, and never lives near a village or hamlet. The lion is fond of his kind, and moves in family parties, three generations being sometimes found in one party." Whatever may have been the case when its numbers were few, there is no doubt that after having been so long undisturbed the Gir lion has become unusually bold. A couple of them were recently seen in the vicinity of Junagarh city, and carried off cattle from places close to a number of buildings. There are stories of their having carried off within the last year or two cultivators working on patches of ground in the jungle.

In the valleys of the Tigris and Euphrates lions often resort to reedy swamps for covert, and in the neighbourhood of Shiraz enter reed-brakes and oak-forest for the purpose of preying upon the droves of swine which find shelter and food in such localities.

The male lion, it may be added, is the only member of the *Felidæ* adorned with the flowing mane on the head and fore-quarters which adds so much to the grandeur of its appearance; the tuft on the tip of the tail being another distinctive peculiarity. It is likewise the only species that is polygamous. The lioness, in general form, is much more like a tiger; to which animal the present species is very closely related; although from the occurrence of faint spots in the cubs it is evident that the ancestor of the lion was a spotted instead of a striped animal. An important difference in regard to the relations of the bones of the face distinguishes the two species. In the skull of a lion the nasal bones, which form the roof of the chamber of the nose, terminate superiorly on the forehead on the same horizontal line as do the upper extremities of the maxillæ, or upper jaw-bones. In the tiger's skull, on the other hand, the nasals reach considerably higher on the forehead than the maxillæ.

The lower jaws of the two animals are also distinguishable by the contour of the lower border of each lateral half. These are by no means the only differences. Compared with that of a tiger, the great upper carnassial, or flesh-tooth, of the lion has the tubercle near the front extremity of the inner side markedly smaller ; the lion in this respect approaching nearer to the great extinct sabre-toothed tigers than does its striped relative.

An interesting paper on the occurrence of the lion in Greece during the historic period, by Dr. A. B. Meyer, appeared in *Der Zoologische Garten*, vol. xliv. pp. 65-78, 1903 ; a translation being published in the Smithsonian Report for the same year, pp. 661-667.

To the *Journal* of the Asiatic Society of Bengal for 1867 Dr. W. T. Blanford contributed some important notes on the distribution of the lion in India ; while in the *Proceedings* of the same Society for 1881 Prof. V. Ball directed attention to a forgotten record of the occurrence of the lion in Palamow.

THE TIGER

(*Felis tigris*)

NATIVE NAMES.—*Bagh* (tiger), *Baghni* (tigress), AND *Sher* (tiger), *Sherni* (tigress), HINDUSTANI; *Nahar* OR *Sela-vagh*, HINDI OF CENTRAL INDIA; *Babr*, PERSIAN; *Mazar*, BALUCHI; *Shink*, SINDI; *Padar-suh*, KASHMIRI; *Patayat-bagh* AND *Wahag*, MAHRATHI; *Go-vagh*, BENGALI; *Tut* AND *Sad* OF THE HILL-TRIBES OF RAJMEHAL; *Garumkula* OF THE KOLS; *Lakhra* OF THE URAONS; *Krodi* OF THE KONDS; *Kula* OF THE SOUTHALS AND KORKUS; *Puli*, TAMIL, TELEGU, MALABARI, AND GONDI; *Puli-redda-puli* AND *Peram-pilli*, TAMIL; *Pedda-puli*, TELEGU; *Perain-puli* AND *Kudua*, MALABARI; *Kuli*, CANARESE; *Nari* OF THE KURGS; *Pirri* AND *Bursh* OF THE TODAS OF THE NILGIRIS; *Tag*, TIBETAN; *Tukt*, OR *Tuk*, BHOTIAS; *Sathong*, LEPCHA; *Keh-va* OF THE LIMBU; *Schi* OF THE AKAS; *Matsa* IN THE GARO HILLS; *Kla* IN THE KHASI HILLS; *Sa*, *Ragdi*, *Tekhu*, AND *Khudi*, NAGA; *Humpi*, KUKI; *Sumyo* IN ABOR; *Su*, KHAMPTI; *Sirong*, SINGPHO; *Kei*, MANIPURI; *Misi*, KACHARI; *Kya*, BURMESE; *Kla*, TALAIN; *Khi*, *Botha-o*, AND *Tupuli*, KARENS; *Htso*, SHANS; *Rimau*, *Arimau*, OR *Harimau*, MALAY.

(PLATE viii, fig. 2)

As the wolf looms large in the nursery-stories and fairy tales of Europe, so the name of the tiger is writ large in the folk-lore of the natives of India and the Malay countries. The Hindu believes that an additional lobe is added yearly to the liver of the tiger, and that his claws, if arranged together in a circle and hung round the neck of a child, are a sure preservative against evil. In most parts of the country the tiger is

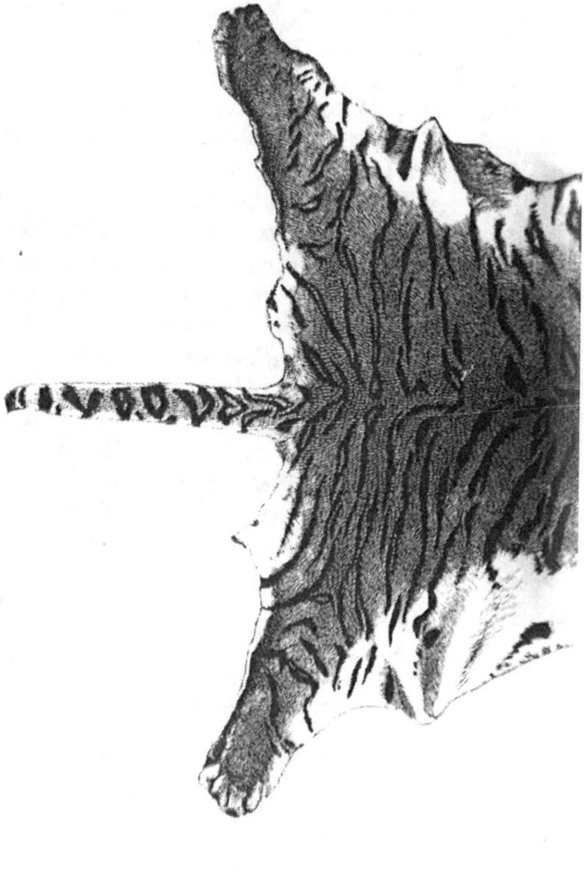

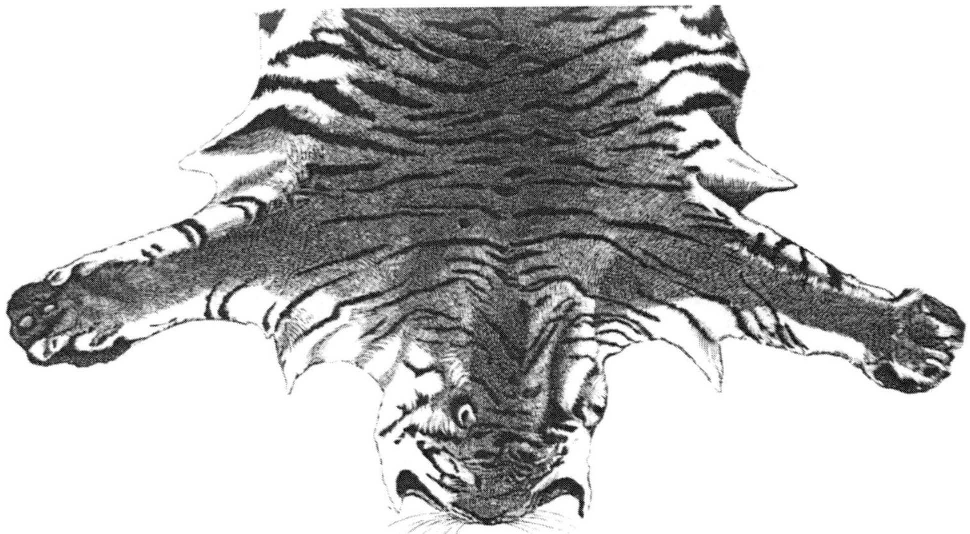

Indian Tiger Skin.

never alluded to by its proper name, but spoken of as "the Uncle," "the Great One," and other respectful epithets. Among the Malays there is a deeply ingrained belief that those versed in occult arts are capable of transforming themselves at will into tigers; as there is in the existence of "ghost-tigers" (*rimau kramat*), which latter are invulnerable and recognisable by having one foot smaller than the other. The most curious of these legends is, however, one relating to the origin of the tiger's stripes. A boy, so runs the story, of an incorrigibly bad disposition, was once soundly thrashed by his schoolmaster, with the result that he was transformed into a tiger, who to this day carries on his hide the mark of the stripes with which he was beaten.

Now it is these same stripes which form the most characteristic external feature of the tiger; no other member of the feline tribe being so conspicuously marked in this manner, although a sombre-hued approximation to this type of coloration is presented by the wild cat of Europe and one phase of the domesticated "tabby." It was long held that the stripes of the tiger were developed in order to harmonise with the vertical streaks of light and shade to be seen in an Indian grass-jungle; but it should be remembered that the Siberian tiger, which is similarly marked, inhabits a totally different kind of country, and since the tiger appears to be a comparatively recent immigrant into the peninsula of India, it is evident that an explanation is required of the use of its coloration which will apply equally to all phases of its existence. If there be, indeed, any preferential claim for one part of its habitat rather than another, this preference is due to Central Asia.

From the reports of sportsmen and travellers as to the almost invisibility of zebras when standing in the open, even at a comparatively short distance, the truth would appear to be that the colouring of the tiger is for the purpose of rendering it as inconspicuous as possible when wandering in the gloaming in search of prey. It has been remarked that a tiger shooting out suddenly from the dark jungle on to an unexpecting bullock appears to the spectator more like a puff of grey smoke than anything else in nature, so harmoniously do its colours fade into a grey when seen by the faint light of early dawn or late evening.

A less noisy, but apparently a stronger and more active animal than the lion, the great striped cat of Asia is represented by four local races. Firstly, there is the typical Indian, or Bengal tiger (*F. tigris typica*), a large, long-limbed, long-bodied, lithe, and lanky animal, in which, with the exception of the short ruff on the throat, the fur is uniformly short and somewhat stiff throughout, with the black stripes (frequently double) generally numerous, and the colour of the fur a rich orange or rufous fawn. In the Caspian provinces of Persia and the Caucasus the tigers, on the other hand, run smaller and are more roughly haired; this small Persian race (*F. tigris virgata*) possibly entering the western confines of the area treated of in this volume. The Manchurian tiger (*F. tigris mongolica*), which ranges into Korea, is characterised by its large size, heavy build, short and thick limbs, and the length, fineness, and thickness of the fur, which seems less highly coloured, and may be less fully striped than is generally the case in the Indian race. The head and muzzle of the Manchurian tiger have likewise a different appearance from those of its Indian cousin. This, however, is to be expected, for, in the case of a species with a wide geographical range, when there are two or more local races whose respective habitats differ considerably in respect to climate, it is a rule that the race inhabiting the colder climate is more heavily built than the one from a hotter region. The Transcaspian tiger has been described by Dr. Satunin as a fourth local race, under the name of *F. tigris septentrionalis*.

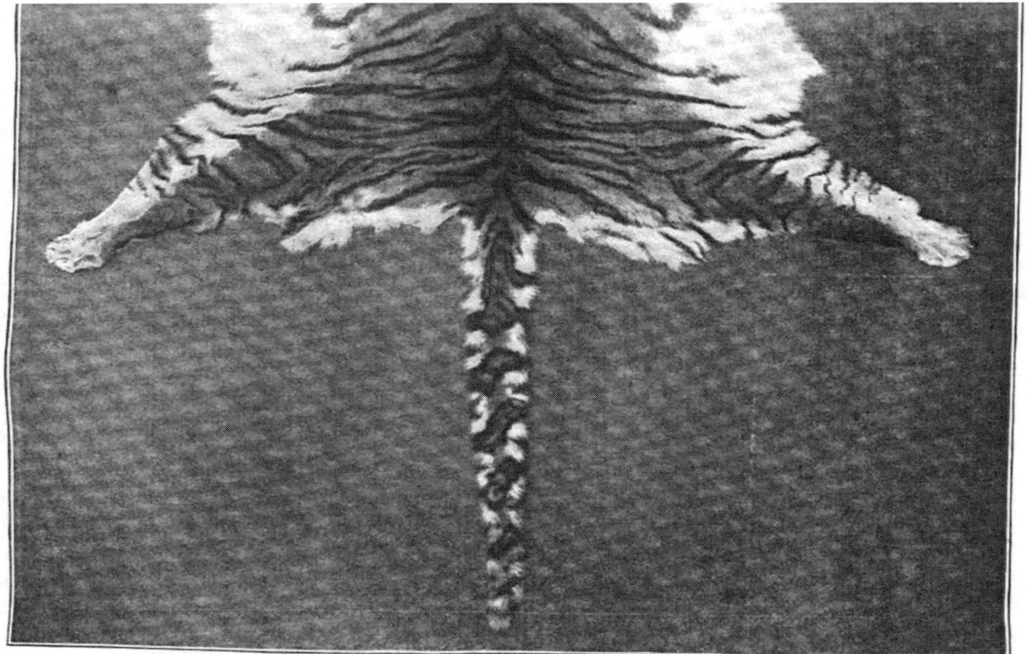

Manchurian Tiger Skin.

The Tiger

The geographical range of the tiger extends from the Caucasus through Northern Persia, India, Assam, Burma, and the Malay Peninsula to the Malay Islands, China, Manchuria, Amurland, and Korea. The species is, however, absent from Ceylon; and since there is geological evidence to prove that the latter island was connected at no very remote epoch with the mainland of the peninsula, there is strong presumptive evidence that the tiger is a comparatively recent immigrant from the north or east into India itself. Another inference is that the Palk Strait, separating Cape Comorin from Ceylon, is beyond the ordinary swimming powers of the tiger. In India tigers are found from Cape Comorin to the Himalaya, ascending in the latter range to an elevation of about 7000 feet above sea-level; but they are unknown in Afghanistan and Baluchistan.

There is considerable variation in the richness of the ground-colour of the fur of Indian tigers, and occasionally specimens are met with in which the colour is creamy buff, with the stripes only showing somewhat darker in certain lights; but in most instances there is no information whether these white tigers were true albinos.

A white tiger was exhibited alive at Exeter Change about 1820; a second was killed at Poona about 1892; in March 1899 a white tiger was shot in Upper Assam and the skin sent to Calcutta, where a fourth specimen was received about the same time. The Maharaja of Kuch-Behar also possesses a white tiger-skin. In regard to the third specimen, the property of Mr. W. J. Consadine, Major H. G. C. Swayne wrote as follows: —"The colour of the skin is like that of a polar bear, with the faintest lines to indicate stripes. The ground-colour is bright creamy white, exactly like a polar bear; the darker lines, representing stripes, are about the dull white of a rather dirty white cat which has been out all night on the roof."

Many years ago a black tiger was found dead near Chittagong.

In old days exaggerated ideas were prevalent with regard to the maximum length attained by the tiger; but when criticism was brought to bear on the question there is little doubt that scepticism was pushed too far, and the dimensions underrated. Unfortunately, the measurement of length is not always taken in the same manner; this being sometimes the interval between the muzzle and the tip of the tail in a straight line, and in other cases the length of the same interval following the curves of the head and body. The latter method, commonly known as "sportsman's measurement," is the one usually adopted, and was doubtless employed in the under-mentioned instances. Measured in this fashion, full-grown tigers commonly range between 9 and 10 feet, and tigresses between 8 and 9 feet; but larger animals undoubtedly occur at times. The two largest mentioned in *Records of Big Game* respectively measure 10 feet 7 inches and 10 feet 6 inches. These, however, if we credit sportsmen whose testimony should be above suspicion, by no means approach the maximum.

In the *Asian* newspaper for February 1896 Mr. Moray Brown published the following list of unusually large tigers, omitting mention of such as fell short of 11 feet. "Firstly, we find the late Sir J. F. Yule stating that he has killed tigers of 11 feet odd inches twice or thrice. Colonel George Boileau killed a tiger at Muteareah in Oudh well over 12 feet before the skin was removed, and of quite exceptional size. The Hon. J. R. Drummond, sometime Commissioner of Rohilkund, stated that he never saw a 12-foot tiger, though he shot one of 11 feet 9 inches, measured as he lay on the ground before being padded. Colonel D. G. Stewart states that the largest tiger he ever saw measured 11 feet ¼ inch. General Sir H. Green observed that the biggest tiger he ever assisted in

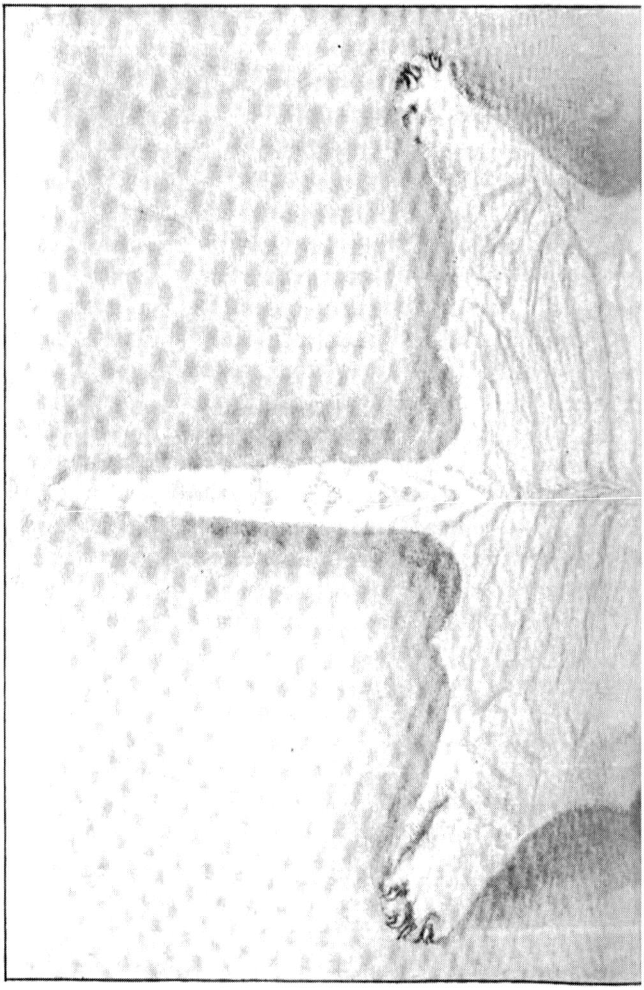

White Tiger Skin.

killing was one shot near Surat, which was 11 feet 11 inches, measured as it lay, and whose skin when pegged out was 12 feet 4 inches. Sir H. Green shot one himself which measured 10 feet 11 inches. Mr. C. Shillingford, whose experience extended over thirty-five years, during which period he shot more than two hundred tigers, states that in 1849 he shot the largest tiger he had ever seen, which measured, as it fell, 12 feet 4 inches. This tiger was very old, with short hair and light in colour. Mr. Shillingford shot another of 11 feet 10 inches, and in 1855 one of 11 feet 4 inches. Mr. Cumming shot one at Rohinipore of 11 feet 4 inches, one at Kaladearah in 1865 of 11 feet 2 inches, and one at Gour in 1871 of 11 feet 2 inches. Finally, Sir Charles Reid informed Sir Joseph Fayrer that he had shot in the Dun a tiger which measured 12 feet 3 inches before the skin was removed."

To the above may be added a supplemental list furnished by Mr. F. A. Shillingford (nephew of the above-mentioned gentleman of the same name) to the same journal for August 1896. It is there written :— "On March 20, 1866, my neighbour, the late Mr. Henry Cave of Gondwarah, Purneah, shot a tiger 11 feet, measured on the ground, where he fell, and the hunt is described in the *Oriental Sporting Magazine* for July 1868. On December 13, 1867, at Bankacot, about four miles from this factory (Kolassy, Purneah), I accounted for a tiger 11 feet, measured about three hours after death. On October 18, 1868, my brother, the late Mr. J. Shillingford, shot a tiger 11 feet. On November 3, 1868, Mr. J. Shillingford shot the largest of his many large tigers at Tappra, in the Kosi Duars, measuring 11 feet 5 inches. On April 18, 1870, Mr. W. DeCourcy shot a tiger 11 feet 1 inch; while on April 19, 1871, Mr. J. Shillingford shot one of 11 feet."

Some years ago Mrs. Lawrie-Johnstone shot in the Duars a tiger of which the skin when removed measured

12 feet 5 inches in length; indicating that the animal could scarcely have measured less than 11 feet 1 inch.

The following dimensions and weights of tigers have been furnished by the Maharaja of Kuch-Behar.

	Ft. Ins.	Ft. Ins.	Ft. Ins.	Ft. Ins.	Ft. Ins.	Ft. Ins.	Ft. Ins.
Total length . .	10 1½	10 0	9 10¼	10 3	10 0½	10 1	10 2½
Do. of body .	7 1½	6 11	6 11½	7 1½	6 11	6 11	7 0
Girth behind shoulders	54	52	54	52	54½	52¾	48½
Upper arm . . .	29	26	29	29	27½	26½	26½
Forearm . . .	21	21	19	19¼	20	20	20
Head	40½	36	39½	36½	38	37	38½
Height at shoulder .	44¾	40	40	40½	38	36¼	38½
		Lbs.	Lbs.	Lbs.	Lbs.	Lbs.	Lbs.
Weight . . .	?	520	508	487	493	496	500

Of number 1 the Maharaja wrote that "this is undoubtedly the biggest and heaviest tiger I have shot or seen shot. Unfortunately I was unable to weigh him, as we had no scales with us, but he must have weighed close on 600 pounds."

So much literature has been devoted to the habits of tigers and tiger-shooting, that it would be almost waste of space to recapitulate the leading points in connection with the former subject, while the latter will be left almost alone.

Speaking generally, it may be said that, apart from certain minor differences according as to whether individual animals come under the designation of game-killers, cattle-lifters, or man-eaters, tigers as a rule are solitary and unsociable animals, although the male and female associate more closely during the pairing-season. Whether the union be permanent or temporary, it is certain that tigers are monogamous. When more than two tigers are seen in company, the party is usually, if not invariably, a family one. It has already been stated that tigers are less noisy animals than lions; and it may be added that they are as fully nocturnal in their habits as the latter, and perhaps more so. Intolerance of the direct rays of the summer sun is one of the most marked traits of the Indian tiger; this supporting the view that the animal is a comparatively recent inhabitant of the more torrid portions of its habitat. In this connection may be mentioned the extraordinary length and thickness of the fur of Indian tiger-cubs—a provision against cold totally unnecessary in their present environment, which may be inherited from an ancestor whose home was in the bleak north.

Water is essential to tigers, and the necessity for frequent access to this element curtails their wanderings in the hot season, when pools are few and far between. At other seasons tigers are, however, great wanderers; and it is noteworthy that when one tiger occupying a definite "beat" is killed, its place is almost immediately filled by a successor. Grass-jungles, swamps, and forests are the resort of tigers; but, failing these, clefts or caves in rocks, ruined buildings, or dry nalas afford amply sufficient shelter to the striped robber. Although, like lions, tigers are unable to climb, their presence in a district is made evident by the marks of their claws on the tree-stems, which extend as high as they can reach when standing on their hind-legs.

The falsity of the popular idea that tigers spring upon their victims from a distance, and after killing them by a blow from one of the fore-paws, or by tearing at the throat with the claws, suck their blood, was demonstrated by Mr. G. P. Sanderson, in *Thirteen Years among the Wild Beasts of India*. From the accounts of natives the same sportsman came to the conclusion that the tiger clutches the fore-quarters of its victim with its paws, one of which is generally thrown over the shoulder, while with the jaws it seizes the throat from below, and turns it upwards and over, so as to dislocate the vertebræ of the neck: sometimes giving additional weight to the wrench by jumping to the opposite side of the stricken animal.

This explanation was for some time generally accepted; but in a communication to the *Asian* newspaper of July 12, 1895, Mr. F. A. Shillingford raised objections to certain details of the attack as described by Mr. Sanderson. His observations are as follows:—"Tigers, as a rule, always roar when charging or fighting in self-defence, but there are exceptions to the rule. In the latter case it would appear that a very savage tiger, in order to wreak his vengeance without fail on the intruders, lies low and attacks without warning. The well-known feint of an attack, termed by the natives *bhagocha*, made by tigers to demoralise a line of beaters, and thus effect an unchallenged retreat, is always accompanied by the loudest roar they can emit. It seems almost impossible to picture a tiger seizing by the neck from below without first closing with his victim. He must turn his neck round until his open jaws face upwards, in order to grip from below, and this can hardly be accomplished without the purchase of his paws on the shoulders, and this, in my opinion, is what occurs in the generality of cases. There are instances in which you see fang-marks both at the back and in front of the neck, but the former, I take it, is a mere preliminary grip of an obstreperous victim, quickly followed by the fatal clutch below. That the tiger always breaks the neck I do not believe. Let any one open the jaws of the skull of a tiger and then look at the neck of a full-fed buffalo, and he will see this. The expanse of the open jaws would only cover a bunch of the muscles of the neck, and with this grip it seems absurd that the animal could give the fatal wrench that dislocates the neck. In the case of a bull-buffalo, such as are sometimes killed, it seems doubtful whether the neck of the aggressor or of the victim is the tougher. That the necks of animals, especially cows, are often broken, may be due to the fall in the struggle, but the idea that tigers systematically set to wrenching their necks, appears untenable. That tigers approach their victims stealthily and without noise is natural, but in the moment of victory they may roar occasionally to terrify their prey into succumbing sooner. This was exemplified in the case of a planter, seated on an easy-chair outside his bungalow, being startled in his reverie by a loud roar to the left, and on looking round he saw some 500 yards off a tiger struggling with a bullock in a field. The tiger killed the bullock, and retreated into the jungle before guns could be got ready."

In the *Fauna of British India*, Dr. W. T. Blanford, while accepting the view that tigers generally kill their prey, when of large size, by breaking the neck, suggested that in the case of very large beasts, like gaur and buffalo, which they are unable to overthrow, they occasionally hamstring them, most likely by a blow from the paw, although this is not certain. Dr. Blanford was acquainted with two instances where buffalo were thus hamstrung. At a later date, in the *Journal of the Bombay Natural History Society*, Mr. C. W. Allan, writing from Burma, stated that on several occasions he has come across sambar, tsaine (Burmese bantin), gaur, and domesticated buffalo that have been hamstrung by tigers, the method adopted being seemingly to stalk the victim and bite one of the hind-legs immediately above the hock, thus severing the tendon and breaking the bone, apparently by one bite. Subsequently the other leg is treated in the same way, after which the victim is seized by the throat and killed. Although the writer referred to had never apparently seen a tiger actually make this mode of attack, he states that, according to native accounts, it is the ordinary method by which these animals kill their prey in Burma, and he asks what is the experience of sportsmen in India on this point. From Mr. Allan's account it may apparently be taken that tigers do, as a rule, kill large game in Burma by hamstringing them, while in India this method appears to be the exception rather than the rule. Further information as to the method in which the attack is made is, however, desirable, for although a tiger may well sever the hock-tendons of a gaur by biting, it seems difficult to understand how it could break by this method the lower ends of the two leg-bones immediately above the hock. If there is direct evidence of this being done the fact must be accepted ; but if there is not, Dr. Blanford's supposition that the attack is made by a blow from the paw would seem more probable.

A remarkable, and apparently inexplicable difference between tigers and leopards is exhibited by the manner in which they break up their prey ; a tiger invariably commencing to devour his victim at the hind-quarters, whereas a leopard turns his attention at the commencement of his meal to the chest and fore-quarters.

In the condition of their food tigers are by no means particular, and they have been observed gorging on putrid carcases, from which the vultures have been driven away by their appearance on the scene. In many cases, they will consume almost the whole of the animal which affords the meal, rejecting neither skin nor bones, except such of the latter as are too large or too solid to be devoured. Neither do they limit themselves to any particular kinds of animal as food, for tigers have been known to kill and eat bears, leopards, and even individuals of their own species. Colonel F. T. Pollok states, for instance, that he has known of cases in Assam where, after a contest between two of these animals, the victor has made a meal off the body of the vanquished. An instance is also known of a tiger having killed a young individual of its own species over a dead bullock, and eaten the former in preference to the latter. One reason for regarding the tiger as more active and powerful than the lion is that on every occasion when a contest has taken place in a menagerie between two of these animals, the tiger has come off victorious.

Man-eating tigers, which are generally females, are perhaps the most wary of all the members of the species.

Although it is probable that some man-eaters have taken to their particular line from being disabled by old age from pursuing more active prey, it is certain that this is not the case with the majority, which are often in the best condition. Rather is the acquisition of the habit to be attributed to the boldness acquired by cattle-lifting tigers, which on some particular occasion summon up courage to attack the herdsman. Having once discovered how much easier it is to kill a man than a cow, such tigers ever afterwards practise man-eating to a certain extent, although only a limited number confine themselves exclusively to a diet of human flesh.

Several instances are on record where young elephants have been killed by tigers, and in the *Asian* of May 15, 1900, a writer instances a case where, although the evidence is circumstantial, an adult elephant appears to have fallen a victim.

After first mentioning that he was disinclined to attach credit to the statements of the natives as to the manner in which the elephant in question came by its death, the writer states that, accompanied by some friends, he visited the spot where the encounter had taken place. His description of the scene that met his eyes is as follows :—

"The place where the remains of the elephant lay showed that a hard struggle had gone on between the elephant and a tiger, or a couple of tigers for aught we knew. The high grass-jungle where the elephant was hobbled and let loose at night for grazing was trodden and trampled down for about 40 square yards. The elephant was hobbled, and therefore could not run away from its assailants, and its cries of distress and shrill trumpetings were heard by the villagers a couple of miles off. The rope-hobbles were still on its legs, and the half-severed ear and the holes on the skin of its neck indicated the attack of a tiger, and left no doubt in my mind that the beast was done to death by a pair of tigers, which must have tackled her from both sides at the same time, and buried deep their fangs in her jugular veins and finished her off quickly. The skin did not seem to have been injured much, and it lay like a pall, or rather a tarpaulin, covering the whole skeleton."

The ordinary cry of the tiger is stated to be very similar to the lion's roar, but is much less frequently uttered, tigers never standing and emitting roar after roar for an hour together after the manner of lions in Africa. When surprised, a tiger springs up with a loud "woof"; while, when angered, it gives vent to a growl. Different from all of these is the hoarse guttural sound of a charging tiger, repeated two or three times during the short furious rush. Although occasionally reaching as many as six, the number of tiger-cubs in a litter usually varies between two and five; but two is the most common number, and three the next. In all cases of twins the cubs are respectively male and female. Now it is a well-known fact that tigresses are much more numerous than tigers, and it would be an interesting matter to ascertain whether, in the case of triplets, two of the cubs belong to the female sex. Even, however, if this should prove to be the case, it may be doubtful if the occurrence of triplets is sufficiently common to account for the disparity in the numbers of the two sexes. The cubs require about three years to attain full growth, the greater portion of this time being spent with the female parent, which does not appear to breed more frequently than every second, or possibly every third year.

Many years ago, in the *Journal* of the Asiatic Society of Bengal, I described the lower jaw of a tiger containing a small additional molar tooth (or rather the socket for the reception of the same) behind the carnassial or flesh-tooth. In a recent issue of the *Zoologischer Anzeiger* Mr. Hilzheimer (who appears to be unacquainted with the foregoing case) recorded a precisely similar abnormality in a tiger's skull. The occurrence of such a supernumerary tooth is a matter of considerable interest as showing a reversion to the early extinct cats, such as *Pseudælurus*, in which the occurrence of a molar behind the lower carnassial tooth is normal. Among the hundreds of skulls of tigers, lions, and leopards in the possession of sportsmen, there must almost certainly be some showing a similar abnormality, and records of such an occurrence would be of interest.

Tiger-shooting may be divided into four main classes, namely, shooting from elephants, driving with beaters to sportsmen posted in trees, sitting up over the "kill" to await the return of the murderer, and walking up on foot. The last is certainly the most dangerous, and probably therefore the most exciting sport, fatal accidents being frequent. The least exciting of the four is the sitting up over the "kill," on a *machan*, or platform, built in some convenient tree; but where the forest is dense, or elephants are unobtainable, it is frequently the only practicable mode. In districts where beating is the custom, natives are usually chary of giving any information as to the whereabouts of "stripes," partly in order that they themselves may not be impressed to take a share in the *honk*, or drive, and partly from the fear that if they do so, they will fall victims either to the wounded tiger, if it escapes, or to its companion, upon whom the office of *vendetta* is supposed to devolve. Here it may be repeated that in many parts of India natives never mention the tiger by its proper title, but use some other term, as, for instance, the name of the jackal; this being due to superstition that the mention of the name will lead to the death of the speaker.

Beating is practised in Central and Southern India, where tigers are commonly found in densely-wooded ravines, of which the banks are often high and precipitous. On the other hand, beating with elephants is chiefly employed in the tall grass-jungles of the Terai and Assam, where any other mode would be almost impracticable. In the swampy Sandarbans of Lower Bengal, where the tigers lead a semi-aquatic life, they must either be walked up on foot, or shot from a *machan*, unless the sportsman is lucky enough to "pot" his game from a boat.

THE LEOPARD

(*Felis pardus*)

NATIVE NAMES.—*Chita*, *Sona-chita*, *Chita-bagh*, *Adnara*, AND *Tendwa*, HINDUSTANI ; *Palang*, PERSIAN ; *Diho*, BALUCHI ; *Suh*, KASHMIRI ; *Tidua* AND *Srighas* IN BUNDELKAND ; *Gorbacha* OR *Borbacha*, DECCANI ; *Karda*, *Asnea*, *Singhal*, AND *Bibia-bagh*, MAHRATHI ; *Tenderwa* AND *Bibla* AMONG THE BAURIS OF THE DECCAN ; *Honiga* AND *Kerkal*, CANARESE ; *Teon-kula* OF THE KOLS ; *Jerkos* IN RAJMEHAL ; *Burkal* AND *Gordag* OF THE GONDS ; *Sonora* OF THE KORKUS ; *Chiru-thai*, TAMIL ; *Chinna-pali*, TELEGU ; *Pali*, MALABARI ; *Kutiya*, CINGALESE ; *Bai-hira*, *Tehr-he*, *Goral-he*, OR *Ghor-he* IN THE SIMLA DISTRICT ; *Sik*, TIBETAN ; *Syik*, *Syiak*, OR *Sejjiak*, LEPCHA ; *Kajengla*, MANIPURI ; *Misi-patrai* AND *Kam-kei* OF KUKI ; *Hurrea-kon*, *Morrh*, *Rusa*, *Tekhu-Khuia*, AND *Kekhi*, NAGAS ; *Kya-lak* OR *Kya-thit*, BURMESE ; *Klapreung*, TALAIN ; *Kiche-phong* OF THE KARENS ; *Rimau-bintan*, MALAY.

(PLATE viii, figs. 3 and 4)

Among many instances of uncertainty as to the proper application and signification of names in natural history, perhaps no greater confusion exists than in the case of the large spotted cat scientifically known as *Felis pardus*. This animal was known to the ancients by the names *pardalis* and *panthera*, respectively Anglicised into pard and panther. At the same date the animal now known as the hunting-leopard was designated *leopardus*, or leopard, from the idea that it was a hybrid between the lion and the pard. As time went on, the name "pard" fell into disuse, and the term leopard became transferred from the animal to which it originally belonged to one of the varieties of *Felis pardus*; panther being retained for another phase of the same animal, on the supposition that there were two kinds of these spotted cats.

This transference of the name leopard to *Felis pardus* left the animal to which it originally pertained without a popular title of any kind; and the Hindustani name chita (meaning spotted or speckled) was consequently made to do duty for the latter. Such a restriction seems, however, unjustifiable, for although by the natives of Central and Upper India the latter title is applied indifferently to *Felis pardus* and *Cynælurus jubatus*, on most occasions on which it is employed the former animal will be the one designated. Sometimes if a native wishes to particularise the exact kind of chita to which he may be referring, he will distinguish *Felis pardus* either as sona-chita (golden chita) or chitabagh (spotted tiger), but on ordinary occasions chita suffices.

One way out of the difficulty is to avoid the use of the name chita altogether, and to call *Cynælurus jubatus* the hunting-leopard, and to restrict the term leopard to *Felis pardus*. Another element of confusion arises from the fact that Indian sportsmen are convinced of the existence of two species of large spotted cats, in addition to the hunting-leopard, which they respectively call leopard and panther. It is, however, certain that these animals are at most only varieties of a single species, of which they may indicate a larger and a smaller race; and it is accordingly proper to use only a single English name for this species, although the existence of two Indian races, if proved true, may be indicated by designating one the lesser and the other the larger Indian leopard; the name "panther" being allowed to fall, so far as possible, into oblivion.

The next point is the definition of the leopard. Under this term are included all varieties of large ring-spotted cats inhabiting the Old World, with the exception of the snow-leopard, of which the distinctive features are pointed out later. From the hunting-leopard, the present species, in addition to the difference in general form and the structure of the claws, is distinguished by the circumstance that a certain proportion of the spots on the back and sides form large circular broken rosettes, while all those of the former animal are smaller and solid. The only other cat with which the leopard is liable to be confounded is the jaguar of the New World; the latter being generally recognisable by the presence of a small black central spot to each rosette, of which there is no trace in the leopard, and a difference in the length of the tail.

In size the leopard is variable; the extremes of length ranging from less than six to as much as eight feet. The general ground-colour of the upper-parts varies from olive through rufous to pale yellow or brownish yellow, and that of the under-parts from yellow to white. The black spots on the head and lower part of the limbs are small and solid; and such solid spots may be continued on to the neck and shoulders, as well as in a double line down the middle of the hind part of the back, while the greater portion of the outer surface of the limbs may occasionally be solid-spotted. Over a larger or smaller extent of the upper surface of the body and outer side of the upper portion of the limbs the spots take the form of rosettes, consisting of a black, and frequently interrupted ring with a pale centre, which may or may not be darker than the general ground-colour. On the under-parts the spots are solid, and often lighter-coloured than those of the back, being generally also larger and more irregularly shaped than those on the head. On the upper surface of the tail the spots are elongated and light-centred ; but towards the tip of the upper surface they assume the form of broad transverse bars, the under surface of the tail-tip being uniformly yellowish or white.

Marked local differences in form and in the length of the tail and hair are likewise noticeable, the Manchurian race being a more heavily built and longer-haired animal than the leopard of Bengal.

The distribution of the leopard includes the greater part of Africa, Asia Minor, the Caucasus, Syria, Palestine, Persia, Baluchistan, Afghanistan, a large part of Central Asia, India, Assam, Ceylon, Burma, the Malay Peninsula, Siam, China, Manchuria, Java, and Sumatra. With such an enormous geographical range, it is only natural to suppose that the leopard should be divisible into a considerable number of local races. The first point in connection with these races is to indicate which is the typical *Felis pardus* of Linnæus, by whom the species was named. In the *Systema Naturæ* the first reference is to the figure of an African representative of the species, and this might be taken to indicate that the typical leopard is the African form ; but at the conclusion of his notice Linnæus gave the habitat of the species as *in Indis*, and since the description indicates that all the spots on the upper surface are ringed, it accords better with the Indian than with the African animal.

African leopards are collectively characterised by the spots being numerous and comparatively small, and more especially by the circumstance that the whole or the greater portion of those on the fore part of the body—that is to say, about as far back as the hind side of the shoulders—are in the form of irregular solid spots, the rosettes not making their appearance till behind the shoulder-blades. Frequently these solid spots tend to continue some distance down the middle line of the back ; and the majority, if not all of the spots on the limbs, are of the solid type, although larger than those on the shoulders. These features are well displayed in fig. 51. As a rule, the middle line of the back is marked by a broad dark streak, and the centres of the rosettes are elsewhere not conspicuously darker than the general ground-colour. In a few skins the rosettes all over the body tend to break up into small irregular spots ; and it is occasionally difficult to decide whether a particular skin is Indian or African, although there is no difficulty at all in determining the locality of a series.

Another point is that there are no black leopards in Africa, although occasionally specimens are met with on the high grounds of South Africa in which practically the whole of the rosettes are broken up into minute, widely separated spots, while the ground-colour is darker than usual and the middle line of the back almost completely black. In one such specimen the semi-blackness of the back extends over the whole of the upper-parts, although the spots are still more or less distinctly visible. African leopards generally appear to be comparatively small, and in Somaliland there is a pigmy race (*F. pardus nanopardus*) in which the length of flat skins of males is less than six feet, while those of females are still smaller.

In East African specimens the ground-colour of the skin is generally light golden tawny, with the under-parts and the inner surface of the limbs white. On the other hand, leopards from the moist forest region of the west coast are darker, the ground-colour of the upper-parts being olive tawny, and that of the lower parts yellow tawny.

In the year 1777 Erxleben applied the name *Felis leopardus* to the African leopard, and in the absence of any evidence to the contrary, it may be permissible to consider this typified by the East African leopard, which should then be known as *F. pardus leopardus*.

FIG. 51.—Skin of an African Leopard, from Dr. Bonavia's *Studies in the Evolution of Animals.*

If there were only these two phases to deal with, the West African might be separated as a distinct race, but since both agree in the general arrangement of their spots, and thereby differ from the Asiatic representatives of the species, such a classification does not adequately express the relationships of the different modifications; and it would require a quadrinomial system to properly indicate the distinctions.

Indian leopards (fig. 52) have the spots larger, less numerous, and more widely separated than in their African representatives, while the rosettes extend forwards on the back as far as the hind region of the neck, and likewise reach some way down the upper region of the limbs. The middle line of the back never forms such a conspicuously dark streak as in African leopards, and in many skins there is no appreciable darkening in this region at all. Individual specimens, more especially in the Malay countries, may, however, be completely black, the spots and rosettes then being visible only in certain lights. Frequently the centres of the rosettes on the back are appreciably darker than the general ground-colour. As regards the length of the fur and the thickness of the tail, Indian and African leopards are very similar; the fur on both body and tail being short and close.

As the Indian leopard appears to be the typical representative of the species, its full title will be *Felis pardus typica*. But Indian leopards are by no means precisely alike, the lesser form, which is the one generally met with in the plains of the Peninsula, being characterised by the relatively small size of the rosettes, the pale ground-colour, and the absence of darkening in the central area of the rosettes, generally accompanied by a relatively long tail and short head. On the other hand, in the larger Indian leopard of the damp forest-regions of Bengal, Assam, the Terai, Burma, and probably the Malay countries, the ground-colour tends to reddish, the central areas of the rosettes are darker

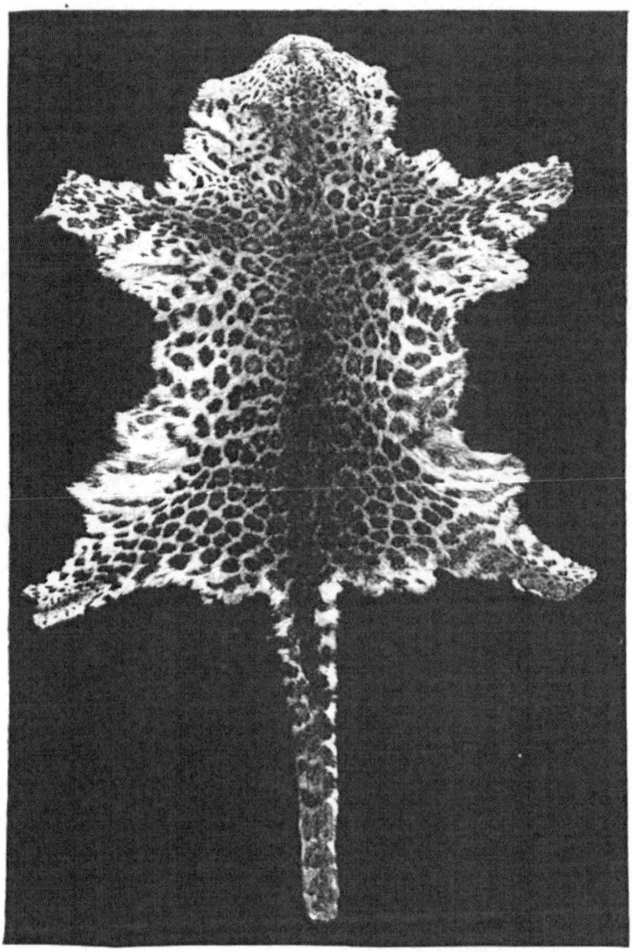

FIG. 52.—Skin of an Indian Leopard.

than the rest of the fur, and the tail is relatively short and the head long. A mounted example of this type is exhibited, in a crouching attitude, in the British Museum. Although in a large series it may be difficult to assign individual skins and skulls to one or the other, if the two forms are, as a whole, distinguishable and restricted to particular localities, they are undoubtedly entitled to recognition.

The Indian race of the leopard (whether in both of its two phases is uncertain) probably extends into the Malay countries and the south of China; but in Baluchistan, Persia, etc., it is replaced by a distinct race, of which the characteristics are given below. In Manchuria the species is represented by *F. pardus villosa*, of which a mounted example is exhibited in the British Museum; this being much more distinct than any of the other local races of the species, and presenting the extreme divergence from the small-spotted African race. In general massiveness of build the Manchurian leopard is indeed very similar to the tiger of the same region, having stout and somewhat clumsy limbs, a relatively short and broad head, and long, thick fur. The spots are much larger and more widely separated than in Indian leopards. The ground-colour of the fur is pale sandy, but the light centres of the rosettes, especially on the back, are much darker than the general body-colour. The solid spots of the head are continued on to the region of the shoulders, and thence down the whole of the fore-limbs, similar solid spots reappearing on the hind-legs. These large spots are widely separated from one another, and nearly circular in shape, and thus markedly different from the small, closely-crowded, and irregular solid spots on the fore-quarters of African leopards, while they are equally different from the annulated spots occurring in the same region in the Indian representative of the species. The dark rings are, in fact, much less broken up than in either the Indian or African races. A leopard-skin from

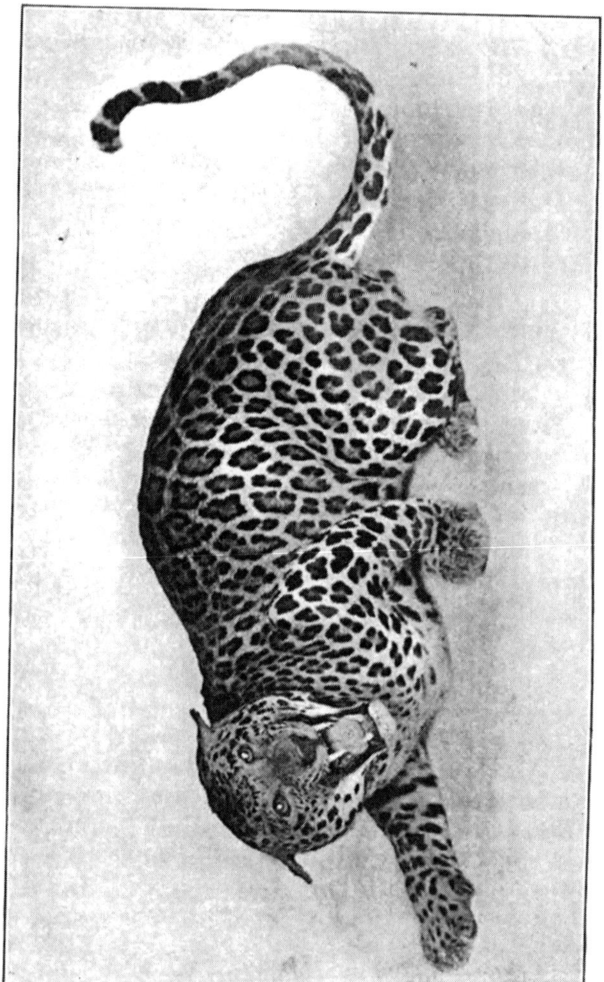

FIG. 53.—An Indian Leopard.

Shensi, Northern China, presented to the British Museum by Father Hugh, seems, however, to be intermediate between the Manchurian and the larger Indian race ; having the long hair and thick tail of the former, but resembling the latter in the rich tawny ground-colour of the fur, and also in the prevalence of rosettes, especially on the hind-quarters.

Black leopards are not entitled to be regarded as a distinct race, being merely specially coloured individuals of the larger Indian leopard, which is found not only in Bengal, but apparently also in Burma and the Malay countries. Hot, moist forest districts are those most favourable to the development of melanism among leopards, Travancore and the south of India generally being the regions on the west of the Bay of Bengal where these "sports" are most common, while to the east they are still more abundant in Lower Burma and the Malay countries. In a paper contributed to the *Zoologist* for 1898 Colonel F. T. Pollok has suggested that the reason for the prevalence of melanism in the latter district is that the leopards habitually prey on gibbon apes, and that their dark colour renders them more inconspicuous than if they were spotted. He even goes so far as to say that under such conditions a leopard of the ordinary colour would starve ; but this implies that all Malay leopards are black, which is certainly not the case, and it is also more than doubtful whether, in the case of an animal creeping along the arm of a tree, a uniformly black colour would not be more conspicuous than the ordinary spotted coat of the leopard. A white (albino) leopard has been recorded by Buchanan Hamilton.

The most essential difference between the habits of the leopard and the tiger is the facility with which the former can ascend trees ; indeed, in some of the forest-districts where it preys largely on monkeys, it may become almost completely arboreal. This arboreal habit renders the leopard more cunning than a tiger, since, when approaching a "kill," it is stated to invariably scan the boughs above, whereas a tiger only does this when it has learnt caution from having been fired at from above on a previous occasion. It has been already mentioned that whereas a tiger commences its meal by tearing at the hind-quarters of its victim, a leopard begins operations on the fore-quarters and viscera.

Leopards are on the prowl for prey throughout the night, dogs being their favourite victims in the neighbourhood of human habitations, while, as already stated, in many forest-districts they subsist chiefly on monkeys. When a leopard takes to man-eating, it is even more to be dreaded than a tiger with similar propensities, since it will frequently not hesitate to burst through the frail walls of native huts and seize the inhabitants as they lie asleep. Colonel Pollok states that in certain portions of the Nizam's dominions the average deaths from man-eating leopards reached one *per diem*, while in others it was as many as two daily. Even shikaris posted on platforms (*machans*) in trees have been carried off by the stealthy approach from behind of the very animals for which they were lying in wait.

In many parts of India the favourite haunts of leopards are rocky, scrub-clad hills, containing numerous clefts and caverns, in which they make their lairs. Water is less essential to their well-being than is the case with the tiger, and they are not unfrequently found in completely dry districts in India, while in Somaliland they commonly dwell in such situations. In India, at any rate, leopards are generally found in pairs, and the cubs are born during February or March, the number in a litter being usually from two to four, although Colonel Pollok states that he has heard of as many as seven. In leopard-cubs the spotting is much less distinct than in the adult, and the general colour brownish; this being precisely the reverse of what occurs in the lion. As a rule, leopards are silent animals, although when charging they utter a short growl; but when on the prowl they occasionally give vent to a harsh cry, quite different from the roar of a tiger, and somewhat intermediate between a grunt and a cough.

Although leopards were at one time hunted by the troopers of the Central Indian Horse by beating them out from patches of sugar-cane during the rainy season with the aid of a pack of dogs, and then spearing them, while they are often speared by parties of two or three mounted Europeans, the more general plan is either to watch for them by night in a *machan* over a tethered bait or a "kill," or to drive them from covert with a line of beaters. Machan-shooting is weary work, and requires a large stock of patience on the part of the watcher. As leopards usually go in search of water between seven and eight in the evening, and again between five and six in the morning, it is at such times that they most frequently approach the bait; the majority of tethered baits being seized between the time of sunset and an hour after. In the dim twilight the spots of the leopard harmonise so exactly with the speckled shade of the surrounding foliage that unless the watcher make the best use of his eyes, the marauder will be only too likely to have sprung upon the bait before its presence is even suspected.

The following hints on machan-shooting are given by a writer in the *Asian* newspaper of February 27, 1900:—

"If you have had a kill, go early to your *machan*, and take the precaution to have the kill securely tied or hung to some fixed object, or you may find the leopard carry it off without giving you a chance. If you are to sit over a live goat, see first that the *machan* is so constructed as to give you the advantage of rising ground if there be any. Take care that the rope of the goat is not too long, or you will find it difficult to get a shot from your circumscribed look-out hole. If there is a little moonlight expected after dusk, try and arrange your *machan* so as to have the light falling from behind you on to the goat. Recollect the shadow cast by the moon. It is not always easy to distinguish the shadow from the substance of the goat, and the same is of course true of the leopard. Take your time in aiming, and if the leopard is inextricably mixed up with the goat, wait. Eventually the leopard will conquer the goat and give you a steady shot while sucking the blood from the neck.

"Don't fancy the leopard will not come, once you have made up your mind to sit up. Some are exceedingly crafty and suspicious, and do not fail to observe the goat most carefully. Often the goat ceases bleating simply from an access of fear; it has seen, heard, or scented the leopard. You will often see it, after standing or lying carelessly, suddenly assume a rigid position, gradually moving its head round, and sometimes by the action of its legs unmistakably indicating that the foe is about. The goat will sometimes stamp on the ground and emit little snorts. Of course occasionally this may only indicate a hyæna, or a pig, or the insignificant mongoose, or a hare, but never neglect such indications. As to using slugs, I think you will do well to have a smooth-bore loaded with buck-shot; but stick to your rifle to the last possible moment. Slugs do not always penetrate between the ribs and reach a vital part, and they seldom leave a bloody trail. I have rarely found my .500 Express fail even when it was impossible to see the sights."

In a work on the animals of Russia and Asia, published in 1811, the Russian naturalist Pallas gave the name *Felis panthera* to the leopard of the Caucasus; and although he appears to have regarded it as identical with the true *F. pardus* of Linnæus, yet according to modern usage his name is entitled to stand for the Persian and Caucasian race of the species. The name of this race will consequently be *Felis pardus panthera.* It should be added, however, that in 1856 the French naturalist Valenciennes gave the name of *Felis tulliana* to the Persian leopard (ignoring the priority of the name *panthera*); and in consequence of this the race is frequently known as *F. pardus tulliana.* If it were possible to distinguish the Caucasian from the Persian leopard (which does not seem to be the case), the name *F. pardus panthera* would stand for the former and *F. pardus tulliana* for the latter.

The geographical range of the Persian leopard (plate viii, fig. 4) appears to extend from the Caucasus and Anatolia through Persia and Baluchistan to the hills of Sind. This race may be distinguished from the Indian leopard by its longer fur, thicker tail, and certain details of colouring; being in these respects in some degree intermediate between the latter and the snow-leopard. A skin of this race from the Caucasus was described by myself in the Zoological Society's *Proceedings* for 1899; the description being accompanied by a coloured plate. From the small size of this plate the animal does not appear very markedly different from an ordinary Indian leopard, but when skins of the two are laid side by side, the distinction is apparent. Compared with an Indian leopard's skin the Caucasus specimen is distinguishable by the irregular formation and small size of the rosettes, in which the centres are not appreciably darker than the general ground-colour, as they are in the larger form of the Indian race. From the head to the shoulders the spots are solid, somewhat like those of the African leopard. The fur, which is relatively long all over the body, becomes still more markedly so on the under surface, where it is white, with large solid elongated spots, widely separated from one another. In this respect the specimen is decidedly nearer to the Indian than to the African race, in the latter of which the spots on the under surface are generally so large as to leave only a network of light ground between. In the double line of solid elongated black spots down the middle of the hind half of the back, there is, however, an approximation towards the African type. The long and bushy tail, the terminal third of which is black and white only, is strikingly like that of the snow-leopard.

It would be of interest to ascertain in what part of India the Persian race is replaced by the Indian, and likewise whether there is a complete gradation between the two. The writer once purchased a leopard-skin in Kashmir which, although evidently nearer to the Persian than to the Indian race, may have indicated a partial transition between the two. A mounted specimen of the Persian leopard, obtained from Astrabad, in Persia, and presented by Colonel Beresford-Lovett in 1882, is exhibited in the British Museum. In the thick, furry tail, as well as in general colouring, it presents a marked contrast to the crouching specimen of the larger Indian leopard exhibited in the same case.

THE OUNCE, OR SNOW-LEOPARD

(*Felis uncia*)

NATIVE NAMES.—*Ikar*, *Zig*, *Sachak*, AND *Sah*, OF THE BHOTIAS; *Bharal-hē* OF THE TRIBES NORTH OF SIMLA; *Thurwagh* IN KUNAWAR.

(PLATE viii, fig. 5)

Although sometimes confounded with the long-haired Persian race of the leopard, the white or snow-leopard is a distinct species. It was formerly regarded as very rare, but skins may now be frequently seen in the windows of the London furriers, and a few years ago a specimen was exhibited in the Zoological Society's Menagerie. By Anglo-Indian sportsmen the animal is almost invariably designated snow-leopard; but by the older travellers and naturalists it was commonly termed the *Ounce* or *Onza*,—names said by Buffon to be corrupted from *Lynx* or *Lunx*, of which the present species was supposed to be a relative. The same name occurs again in the scientific title of the jaguar, *Felis onca*. The name *Bharal-hē*, given to the snow-leopard by the hill-tribes to the north of Simla refers to its partiality for the blue sheep or bharal.

The snow-leopard is specially characterised by the length and thickness of the fur, which attains its maximum development on the tail. The ground-colour is white, and the black spots, except on the head, are larger and more ill-defined than in the leopard, forming interrupted and somewhat irregular rosettes, with the light areas inside rather darker than the general ground-colour. On the head and limbs, as well as in the terminal third of the tail (where they form rings), the spots are solid, that is to say, without light centres; and on the under surface of the body there are comparatively few, and these somewhat ill-defined. A dark longitudinal streak runs from near the middle of the back to the root of the tail; and the black external surface of the ear is marked by a large yellowish spot.

The snow-leopard stands about 24 inches at the shoulder; and, although precise dimensions are difficult to obtain, its total length would appear to range between 6 and 7 feet, or rather more. In a specimen of which the length was 6 feet minus half an inch, the tail measured 36 inches; but this appendage had also a similar length in an example of which the entire length was 6 feet 4 inches. The skull, which measures from 6 to 7 inches in length, may be distinguished from that of the leopard by the more swollen palate, and the shorter nasal bones, approximating in the latter respect to that of the lion.

The snow-leopard, as its name implies, is essentially an inhabitant of high mountains, and is found on all the elevated ranges of Central Asia, occurring not

Fig. 54.—The Snow-Leopard.

only in the neighbourhood of the snowy range of the Himalaya, as well as in Ladak and Tibet, but extending in a north-westerly direction to Gilgit, Hunza, and Nagar, and being likewise met with in Turkestan, Trans-Baikalia, Amurland, and North-Western China. Its reported extension into Persia is, however, more than doubtful, and its alleged occurrence in the Caucasus is due to specimens of the Persian variety of the leopard having been mistaken for this species. Although usually found at elevations above 8000 feet (and probably ascending to 18,000 or 20,000 feet), in winter it descends as low as about 6000 in the Gilgit district.

Beyond the fact of its living for the most part in open, and frequently snow-clad, country (for which its colour is no doubt specially adapted), there does not appear to be much calling for special mention in the habits of this species, although our information on this subject is far from being as full as desirable. Comparatively few specimens are seen by European sportsmen, and still fewer bagged. The present writer once had a good view of one of these animals ascending a hill at some distance off in Ladak, and Mr. Darrah relates how on one occasion in the same district he suddenly came across a snow-leopard lying on a rock, although only the head and a portion of its thick tail were visible. This animal had recently killed a bullock, of which the carcase lay near by, and, after the manner of the Indian leopard, it returned to the "kill" in the evening, although Mr. Darrah was not fortunate enough to add its skin to his trophies.

Away from the neighbourhood of human habitations the prey of the snow-leopard comprises bharal, shapo, young argali, ibex, and probably an occasional chiru and goa gazelle. Near villages, however, or in the vicinity of Tatar encampments, the animal turns its attention to domesticated sheep, goats, ponies, and occasionally, as in the instance mentioned above, cattle.

Whether it displays the same partiality for dog-flesh as the ordinary leopard is not recorded, but if so it must have some difficulty in gratifying its taste, as the mastiffs which guard Tibetan encampments and villages, and are the only dogs in the country, are awkward customers for even a leopard to kill and carry off.

THE CLOUDED TIGER

(*Felis nebulosa*)

NATIVE NAMES.—*Pungmar* AND *Sarchack* OF THE LEPCHAS; *Zik* OF THE LIMBU OF NEPAL; *Kung* OF THE BHOTIAS; *Lamchitia* OF THE KHAS TRIBE OF NEPAL; *Thit-kyoung*, BURMESE; *Arimau-dahan*, MALAY.

(PLATE viii, fig. 6)

A much rarer animal than the last is the beautiful but smaller cat commonly known as the clouded tiger, although sometimes designated clouded leopard. Its Malay name means "tree-tiger." Most of the little known of this species in the wild state is derived from native sources, which are frequently more or less untrustworthy; but it appears to have been seen in its natural haunts by Dr. Charles Hose in Borneo.

The clouded tiger is essentially a Malay animal, inhabiting the Malay islands and peninsula, and thence extending through Burma into Assam and the Sikhim and Nepal Himalaya. It has a special claim on the interest of the naturalist on account of the unusually great relative length of its upper tusks, or canines, which in this respect come nearer to those of the extinct sabre-toothed tigers (*Machærodus*) than is the case in any other living member of the cat tribe.

In size the clouded tiger may be compared to a small specimen of the leopard, its length ranging between 6 and 6½ feet, of which from 2 feet 6 inches to about 3 feet is taken up by the long, thickly-haired tail. The colouring may be regarded as a modification of the type found in the snow-leopard; for if we imagine the dark rosettes of the latter diminished in number and extended in size, so as to form large blotches with dark margins and centres of a somewhat deeper shade than the general ground-colour, we should have the "clouded" pattern met with in the present species. The ground-colour is some shade of pale yellowish-grey, upon which are dark blotches or patches of a couple of inches or more in diameter; these being frequently edged in part, especially on the hind border, with black. In aged individuals the blotches themselves tend more or less completely to disappear, leaving little or nothing more than their broken black margins. The upper surface of the head is ornamented with solid black spots; and two broad black bands, separated by narrower streaks or rows of elongated spots, run from the ears to the shoulders, to be continued as more or less ill-defined lines of oval spots along the middle of the back. The cheeks have the two black stripes so common among the smaller cats, and the margins of the upper lip may be also black, while the black of the outer surface of the ear is frequently relieved with a central grey spot. The tail is ornamented with a series of dusky rings, frequently imperfect on the sides, and connected along the upper surface of the basal portion by a dark, longitudinal stripe. Typically the tail is of great relative length—frequently nearly as long as the head and body—but in Formosa there is a shorter-tailed race of the species, known as *Felis nebulosa brachyurus*.

As is indicated by its Malay name, the clouded tiger is arboreal, and its food appears to consist of small mammals and birds, for which it lies in wait on the branches of trees. In Borneo it occurs both on the plains and in the mountains up to an elevation of

5000 feet, and in the Himalaya it ranges up to about 7000 feet. If taken young, it can be easily tamed, and it has been several times exhibited in the London Zoological Gardens.

The marbled cat (*Felis marmorata*) of the Eastern Himalaya, which may be described as a miniature replica of the present species, can scarcely claim to be regarded as a game animal.

The same type of colouring is presented by Fontanier's cat (*Felis tristris*) of East Central Asia ; and in the opinion of the present writer this type of colouring may indicate affinity between all the members of this group and the ocelot cats of tropical America.

THE GOLDEN OR BAY CAT

(*Felis temmincki*)

Of somewhat inferior size to the clouded tiger (length of head and body 31 inches, of tail 19 inches), the golden cat is distinguished by its uniformly coloured coat, which, except on the face, lacks both stripes and spots. The colour varies from bright rusty red to dark brown or grey, the cheeks and forehead being streaked with white and brown, and faint traces of spotting occasionally showing themselves on the flanks and the under surface of the body. The range of this cat extends from Nepal and Sikhim, in the Eastern Himalaya, at moderate elevations, through the hills of Tippera, to Burma, and so by way of the Malay Peninsula to Borneo.

This species has been regarded as the ancestor of the Royal Siamese domesticated breed ; but, in the opinion of Mr. R. I. Pocock, the theory is improbable.

THE FISHING-CAT

(*Felis viverrina*)

NATIVE NAMES.—*Banbiral*, *Bardeen*, *Khupya-bagh*, AND *Bagh-dasha*, HINDUSTANI; *Mach-bagral*, BENGALI; *Handun-diva*, CINGALESE.

(PLATE viii, fig. 7)

It has long been a matter of speculation why domesticated cats should display such a marked partiality for a fish-diet, and yet be so averse to wetting their feet; and the problem is rendered no easier of solution by the fact that the present species (which slightly exceeds its domesticated relative in size) is endowed with the same taste, and has no hesitation in taking the necessary steps to gratify this desire. Nor has this fishing habit escaped the notice of the natives of India, its Bengali name being the equivalent of its English title.

The fishing-cat is a spotted species, of somewhat larger dimensions than the under-mentioned leopard-cat, from which it differs by the grizzly grey fur of the body being marked by longitudinal lines of partially connected dark brown spots, replaced on the hind-quarters by smaller black spots. The short and bushy tail, which is about one-third the length of the head and body, is marked above by transverse bars of dark brown. Very characteristic of the species is the narrowness of the nasal bones of the skull, which form a sharp ridge.

This cat, which also inhabits the south of China and the island of Formosa, is found in Ceylon, India, Lower Burma, and Tenasserim. In India it has been recorded from the Indus Valley, the outer Himalaya, Nepal, Assam, and Bengal, and it may possibly occur also on the coasts of Malabar and Travancore, although it appears to be absent from the Central Provinces.

In order to exercise its fish-catching propensities this species generally takes up its residence in marshy situations, on the banks of swamps and rivers, where it also feeds on the large snails known as *Ampullariæ*. In spite of its comparatively small size, it is a vicious creature, frequently levying toll on poultry and such domesticated quadrupeds as it is able to destroy.

THE LEOPARD-CAT

(*Felis bengalensis*)

NATIVE NAMES.—*Chita-billa* (spotted cat), HINDUSTANI ; *Ban-biral*, BENGALI ; *Wagati*, AMONG THE MAHRATHAS OF THE GHATS ; *Thit-kyoung*, ARAKANESE ; *Kye-thit*, *Thit-kyuk*, AND *Kya-gyuk*, BURMESE ; *Kla-hla* OF THE TALAINS AND KARENS ; *Rimau-akar*, MALAY.

(PLATE viii, fig. 8)

Of all the smaller Indian felines the leopard-cat is perhaps the most abundant and most generally distributed. Compared with the fishing-cat it is a smaller and more "leggy" animal, being, in fact, somewhat inferior in size to an ordinary domestic cat, but with proportionately longer limbs. As regards colour and markings, it is extremely variable, and consequently difficult to describe ; but since there is no other species with which it is liable to be confounded, the description need not on the present occasion be detailed. As a rule, the ground-colour of the fur of the upper-parts varies from yellowish grey to bright yellow ; and on this are dark brown spots and streaks, which also extend on to the white under-parts, while the extremity of the long tail is marked by black transverse bars. The majority of the dark markings take the form of more or less elongated spots, but there are a couple of dark bars on the inner side of each fore-leg, as well as two horizontal cheek-stripes, of which the lower may be joined with a horizontal throat-band, while there may be other more or less ill-defined stripes across the lower part of the throat and chest. On the forehead two pairs of longitudinal stripes run backwards over the head to the hind part of the neck ; and the middle pair of these stripes, which may be separated for some distance by other markings, is frequently continued down the back as a double row of spots. In addition to these dark markings, there is generally a white streak running from the inner side of each eye to the forehead ; and likewise a large whitish spot on the outer surface of each ear, the remainder of which is black. From 22 to 26 inches is the general length of the head and body of this little cat, while that of the tail varies between 11 and 12 inches, or sometimes a little more.

Doubtless this widely-spread species will eventually be found to be divisible into local races, of which more than one may be found in India itself. As a matter of fact, several names have already been proposed for different colour-phases of this highly variable cat. Such distinctions have, however, little interest for the average sportsman, and may accordingly be dismissed without further notice. In Southern India and Ceylon there is a smaller species known as the rusty-spotted cat (*Felis rubiginosa*), which, in addition to having one pair of teeth less in the upper jaw, is distinguished by the middle pair of the four longitudinal dark streaks on the forehead being continued as two simple slightly divergent lines or rows of spots between the shoulders, whereas in *F. bengalensis* there are never these two lines alone. The upper surface of the tail is also devoid of spots in *F. rubiginosa.*

In addition to an extensive range in China and the Malay countries, the leopard-cat extends from Burma through Assam to India, where it is found from the foot of the Himalaya to Cape Comorin, although apparently unknown in Ceylon. If its absence from the latter island be a fact, the species would appear to be a member of the Malay fauna which has entered India at a comparatively recent epoch. It is to a great degree a nocturnal and arboreal animal, frequently taking up its quarters in a hollow tree, and feeding upon small mammals and birds ; in disposition it is extremely savage and spiteful.

THE MANUL CAT

(*Felis manul*)

NATIVE NAME.—*Manul*, TIBETAN

The wild cat inhabiting the arid deserts of Ladak and Tibet and thence northwards through Mongolia to Siberia, is a species agreeing approximately in size with the preceding, but differing from all others met with in the area of which the present volume treats by its thick coat of long and soft fur, and short tail. The general colour is pale whitish or yellowish grey, with a few indistinct dark markings on the head and upper portions of the limbs, and some more clearly defined but widely separated narrow black transverse barrings across the hind-quarters, the tail being likewise ringed with black. From behind each eye a white streak, between a pair of black ones, runs downwards and backwards, and behind each ear is a black mark. The under-parts are white. About 21 inches is the usual length of the head and body, and that of the tail 10 inches.

Unlike the majority of smaller cats, which dwell in forest or jungle, the manul makes its home among barren rocks, in the crevices of which it rears its offspring. Its prey comprises various small mammals and birds, especially the rodents known as picas; and its thick fur affords an adequate protection against the winter cold of its habitat.

In the *Annuaires du Musée Zoologique* of the Academy of Sciences of St. Petersburg for the year 1904 (pp. 495-506) Dr. Const. Satunin, of Tiflis, published a paper on the manul, which he made the type of a new genus, *Trichælurus*, on account of certain peculiarities in the skull, being apparently unaware that a separate genus name had been proposed for it many years previously by the Russian naturalist Severtzoff. According to Dr. Satunin, the typical *F. manul* ranges from the Western Siberian steppes and the mountain ranges of Transcaspia (including the Kopet-dagh, Murgab, and Tedshen) as far east as Lake Baikal. East of Lake Baikal in Siberia and all over Mongolia the typical form is replaced by the so-called *F. manul mongolica*, represented in Wolf's figure in Elliot's *Monograph of the Felidæ* (plate x). As the name *mongolica* is preoccupied (*see* p. 296), this race may be called *F. manul satuni*.

Nearly related is *Felis nigripectus* of Hodgson, which Dr. Satunin regards as a distinct species, the skull, and especially the nasal bones, presenting peculiar characters. This cat, which ranges all over Tibet, has been recorded from Ladak.

The suggestion has been made that the manul is the ancestor of the Persian breed of domesticated cats; but it differs from all the latter in that the pupil contracts to a nearly circular disk, instead of to a slit; while the ears are smaller and set lower on the sides of the head, and the markings are of a different type.

THE DESERT-CAT

(*Felis ornata*)

A short notice must suffice for this cat, since it is one of those species of which the claims to admission in a work devoted to "game" are doubtful, its size being approximately the same as that of a domesticated cat. It resembles the jungle-cat in the presence of a few long stiff hairs on the tips of the ears, forming incipient pencils, but these hairs are brown instead of black; and it is further distinguished from that species by the greater length of the tail, which reaches to the hocks, by the ears being coloured like the rest of the head, and by the fur being marked by numerous roundish black spots on a pale yellow ground. The under surfaces of the paws are black; and the terminal half of the tail is ringed with black; the cheeks are marked by a pair of horizontal brown stripes; and there are two black transverse bands on the inner surface of the fore-arm, the outer surface of the limbs also showing dark cross-bars.

The desert-cat inhabits open, sandy districts in North-Western India, extending from Banda, through the North-West Provinces to Agra, Sambhar, and Sind, where it is comparatively common.

The species was long regarded as nearly allied to the jungle-cat, but Mr. R. I. Pocock (*Proc. Zool. Soc. London*, 1907, p. 165) considers that its affinities are really with the African wild cat (*Felis ocreata*), which is itself near akin to the European wild cat (*F. catus*). In Bokhara the group is represented by the steppe-cat (*F. caudata*), which was shown by Prof. Martorelli in 1895 to be an ally of *F. ocreata*.

THE JUNGLE-CAT

(*Felis chaus*)

NATIVE NAMES.—*Jangli-billi*, HINDUSTANI ; *Khatas*, HINDUSTANI AND BENGALI ; *Bamberal*, BENGALI ; *Gurba-i-kuhi*, PERSIAN ; *Baul* AND *Bhaoga*, MAHRATHI ; *Berka* IN RAJMEHAL ; *Mant-bek*, CANARESE ; *Kada-bek* AND *Bella-bek*, WADARI ; *Katu-pundi*, TAMIL ; *Jurka-pilli*, TELEGU ; *Cherru-puli*, MALABARESE ; *Kyoung-tset-kun*, ARAKANESE.

(PLATE viii, fig. 9)

The jungle-cat is a widely-spread species, ranging from North Africa and the Caucasus through Syria, Palestine, Transcaspia, Asia Minor, Persia, Baluchistan, and Afghanistan, to India, Ceylon, Assam, Burma, and North-West China. In size it somewhat exceeds an ordinary domestic cat ; and it is easily distinguished from other species by the almost or completely uniform tawny colour of the fur of the body, and the extreme shortness of the tail, which is less than a third of the total length. The ears are tipped with a few long black hairs, scarcely sufficient to form a distinct pencil. Their presence serves, however, to indicate the affinity of the jungle-cat to the lynxes, with which it agrees in the characters of the skull and teeth. Another special feature is in the more or less reddish colour of the backs of the ears. The length of the tail varies from a third to two-fifths of that of the head and body. There are remarkable local variations in the size of the teeth and the colour of the fur.

The colour of the head and upper-parts of the body varies from sandy or yellowish grey to greyish brown, the back being darker than the flanks, often with a rufous, and more rarely a dusky tinge. Although the head and body are generally of a uniform colour, there are usually dusky bands across the limbs ; and in some skins reddish stripes on the cheeks and a band of the same tint on the chest may be observed. More rarely indistinct vertical rows of spots or wavy lines may be detected; and the occurrence of a black specimen has been recorded in India. The under surface of the body is tawny or reddish white; the foot and ankle are brown beneath; the tail has a black tip, and several black rings in its terminal third; and the ears generally have black tips, and although often foxy red, may be more or less grizzled.

In 1898 Mr. W. E. de Winton pointed out, in the *Annals and Magazine of Natural History*, that the species may be divided into several local races. As it was first described upon the evidence of specimens obtained from the neighbourhood of the Caspian, it is evident that this region is the home of the typical jungle-cat (*Felis chaus typica*); and the same race extends into the Caucasus, Turkestan, and Persia, while it may not improbably also occur in Baluchistan and Afghanistan. From this typical race the Indian jungle-cat (*Felis chaus affinis*) may be distinguished by its slighter build, somewhat longer tail, and the bright foxy-red colour of the back of the ears, which contrasts with the tawny of the rest of the head. The skull is proportionally narrower, and the teeth are relatively smaller, and less crowded together. On the other hand, the Egyptian jungle-cat (*Felis chaus nilotica*), which closely resembles the typical race in form and colour, although of rather superior size, is distinguished by the darker and more grizzled ears, the colour of which does not form a bold contrast to that of the rest of the head, as in the typical and Indian races, in both of which the ears are foxy red, although brighter in the latter than in the former.

Another race (*Felis chaus pallida*) occurs in North-Western China, distinguished by its pale colour; but the most remarkable of the local races seems to be the one from Palestine (*Felis chaus furax*), in which the teeth are so disproportionately large as to be little inferior in this respect to those of a small female leopard. Concerning this feature, Mr. de Winton remarks that "there is as little difference between the teeth of the Palestine chaus and those of a female leopard as there is between those of the European wild cat and the Indian chaus—in fact, the flesh-teeth are actually larger than those of the ocelot, and had the separate teeth been found fossil, they would have been put down to an animal of the size of a leopard. Therefore in this group of cats we have all the intermediate steps in size between the teeth of *Felis catus* (wild cat) and *Felis pardus*, though the animals themselves do not vary greatly in size and are not much larger than the former."

The Indian jungle-cat presents nothing calling for special notice in its habits. It is very generally distributed over India, from a considerable elevation in the Himalaya to Cape Comorin, and it appears to be equally abundant in Ceylon and Burma. Himalayan skins may be distinguished from those obtained in the plains of India by the greater length of the fur.

This cat is less strictly nocturnal than the majority of its kind, Jordon mentioning that he has known one spring out and seize a peacock as it fell to the gun, while the present writer has seen a specimen walk out of a maize-field at midday. It is a destructive creature to the smaller kinds of game, both furred and feathered; and it occasionally directs its attentions to domesticated poultry. From three to four kittens is the usual number in a litter; and the female is said to breed twice a year. It has been stated that hybrids between this species and domesticated cats are by no means rare in India, but Mr. R. I. Pocock, who has made a special study of the subject, is of opinion that the evidence in favour of such crossing is untrustworthy.

THE CARACAL

(*Felis caracal*)

NATIVE NAMES.—*Siyah-gush*, PERSIAN ; *Karakal*, TURKI

(PLATE viii, fig. 10)

The names *Siyah-gush* and *Karakal* both refer to the black ears of this animal, which form one of its most distinguishing features, when viewed from behind, *siyah* meaning black in Persian, and *kara* having the same signification in Turki. Other instances of the employment of the same words occur in *Siyah-posh*, for the black-clothed Kafirs of Central Asia, and *Karakorum* (black sand) as the name of a pass on the route to Yarkand. The caracal has a wide geographical distribution, ranging from Africa through Palestine, Arabia, Syria, the Taurus, Mesopotamia, and Persia, to Baluchistan and India, and also occurring in Transcaspia. In Ceylon it is unknown ; and in India, where it is everywhere rare, it is more abundant, as might have been expected, in the western districts, such as Sind, Kutch, and the Punjab, although it is met with over a great part of the peninsula, in suitable localities. It is unknown in the Eastern Himalaya and Bengal, as it also is on the Malabar coast. By Vigne it was stated to occur in the Upper Indus Valley, and he gives *ech* as its Ladaki name ; but this term is evidently the same as *ee*, which is commonly used for the Tibet lynx ; and if the animal was seen by that traveller in Baltistan and Ladak, it was probably in a state of captivity.

The caracal forms a connecting link between the jungle-cat and the true lynxes ; its ears resembling those of the latter in being furnished with large tufts of long black hairs at their tips, although its tail is much longer, and the throat and chest lack the distinctive lynx-ruff. Still the caracal is more of a lynx than a cat, its skull and teeth being decidedly lynx-like. In size it is intermediate between the jungle-cat and an ordinary lynx ; but it is of remarkably slight and slender build, the limbs being proportionately long, and the tail, which reaches down to the hocks, about equal to one-third the length of the head and body. The height at the shoulder varies from 16 to 18 inches, the length of the head and body from 26 to 30 inches, and that of the tail between 9 and 10 inches.

No one can fail to recognise a caracal at the first glance, its lynx-like ears, uniformly red colour, and comparatively long tail rendering it unmistakable. With the exception of the outer surface of the ears, a pair of spots on the upper lip, and sometimes others on the face, as well as, in some instances, the tip of the tail, which are black, and two pairs of pale spots in the neighbourhood of the eyes, the whole of the upper-parts and limbs are uniformly reddish, varying from rufous fawn to brownish rufous. On the under-parts the colour varies from pale rufous to white, the inside of the ears being likewise white. Although it is rarely that traces of spotting can be detected on the back and sides of adult individuals, pale rufous spots are generally more or less in evidence on the light under surface of the body, and in newly-born kittens the whole coat is distinctly spotted. Individuals inhabiting desert districts are probably paler-coloured than those which live among grass and scrub.

The caracal may be regarded as a member of that section of the Indian fauna which attains its maximum development in Western Asia and Africa. Always frequenting more or less open country, it sometimes takes advantage of the cover afforded by bushes and long grass, but never that of forests. Perhaps its most distinguishing trait is its agility, by which it is enabled to capture birds on the wing at a height of several feet above the ground, springing at them as they fly over its head, and knocking them over with a blow of one of its fore-paws. It likewise possesses a speed which falls little short of that of the hunting-leopard. Taking advantage of these attributes, the native chieftains of India have long been in the habit of training caracals to capture the smaller deer and antelope, as well as hares, cranes, peafowl, etc. According to Vigne, who travelled in Kashmir and India between the years 1836 and 1840, the number of tame caracals then kept by some of the chiefs was very large. Pairs of these animals were frequently matched against one another to kill the greatest number out of a flock of pigeons feeding on the ground, the caracals springing suddenly into the midst of the flock and knocking down the birds before and as they rose to fly. In the wild state various kinds of game-birds, together with gazelles, hares, and the smaller deer, form the chief prey of caracals; the habits of which are, however, still imperfectly known.

THE LYNX

(*Felis lynx isabellina*)

NATIVE NAMES.—*Patsalan*, KASHMIRI; *Ee* OR *Ech*, LADAKI; *Tsogde*, BALTI

(PLATE viii, fig. 11)

Although frequently regarded as a distinct species, there can be little doubt that the Tibetan lynx (*F. lynx isabellina*) is merely a pale-coloured race of the ordinary lynx of Northern Europe and Asia, especially since there appears to be a more or less complete transition between the two forms in the Gilgit district. Desert animals, in harmony with their environment, are always of a more sandy, or "isabelline," tone of colour than their relatives inhabiting grass-clad or forest districts; and since the lynx of Scandinavia and other parts of Northern Europe is a forest-dwelling creature, while its representative in Ladak and Tibet has to be satisfied, for the most part, with bare rocks as a dwelling-place, it is only natural to expect that there would be a marked difference in colour between the two.

Lynxes are the most aberrant representatives of the genus *Felis*—so aberrant, indeed, that they are often assigned a genus to themselves. From the caracal, which is their nearest relation, lynxes differ by the abundant frill, or ruff, of long hair fringing the throat, which helps to give them their peculiar and striking appearance, and likewise by the shortness of the tail, which does not nearly reach so low as the hocks. The coat is more or less distinctly marked with small solid black spots, and the pads of the feet are clothed with a variable amount of hair. A generally "stilty" appearance, due to the relatively long legs and the short tail, is characteristic of lynxes. The tufts of long black hairs surmounting the pointed ears have been already alluded to under the heading of the caracal; and certain characters distinctive of the skull will be found described in works of a more scientific nature.

In the Tibetan lynx the general colour of the thick and soft fur is pale sandy grey, or isabelline, with the under-parts white, and the extremity of the tail, the margins, tips, and tufts of the ears, together with a variable number of hairs in the throat-ruff, black. In the summer coat the whole tawny area is ornamented with black spots; but in winter these disappear from all parts except the limbs and flanks, and sometimes even there. In rare instances black spots may be noticed on the white under-parts in the summer. The Tibetan race is further characterised by the relative shortness of the hair on the toes.

This race inhabits the plateau of Eastern and Western Tibet, and certainly extends into Baltistan; but its exact geographical limits are impossible to define, because, when we descend lower down the valley of the

Indus, to the neighbourhood of Gilgit, where there is a certain amount of forest, the lynxes begin to assume a more rufous tinge, and thus pass imperceptibly into the typical European form in which the colour may occasionally be rusty red. Seeing that in Scandinavia the lynx is a forest-dwelling animal, it is not a little remarkable that in the Kashmir territories the animal seems never to be found on the forest side of the snowy range in Kashmir itself, but is restricted to the bleak and arid country on the Ladak side of the passes. It is true that the creature has a Kashmiri name, but the same is the case with several animals not found in the vale of Kashmir ; Kashmiris being frequent travellers into the adjacent districts, and often receiving consignments of skins from Ladak and other places.

Throughout its habitat the Tibetan lynx is a rare animal, seldom seen, and still more rarely shot. Cubs are, however, occasionally taken by the natives of Ladak, Spiti, and Hanle ; and the writer once made the acquaintance of a tame specimen belonging to the Governor of Ladak. Tibetan hares and blue pigeons form the chief prey of the lynx in Ladak, although it also levies toll on the smaller domesticated animals of the Tatars. In capturing pigeons the tame lynx just mentioned displayed an agility comparable to that described in the case of the caracal.

Lynx-cubs, of which there are generally two or three in a litter, are beautiful little "fluffy" creatures ; and in Ladak are generally born in a crevice among rocks.

In the province of Kham, South-East Tibet, there is stated to be a distinct race of lynx—*Felis lynx camensis*.

The Canadian lynx is another race of the ordinary species, but the Spanish lynx (*Felis pardina*) and the American red lynx (*F. rufa*) are distinct.

THE HUNTING-LEOPARD

(*Cynælurus jubatus*)

NATIVE NAMES.—*Chita* AND *Laggar*, HINDUSTANI; *Yuz* AND *Yuz-palang*, PERSIAN; *Chitra* OF THE GONDS; *Chita-puli*, TELEGU; *Chircha* AND *Sivungi*, CANARESE.

(PLATE viii, fig. 12)

Neither of the two popular names in common use for this interesting animal is altogether satisfactory. The Hindustani *Chita*, which, like its Gond equivalent *Chitra*, means spotted, is, as mentioned above, applied in many parts of India to the leopard; and with regard to the name "hunting-leopard," there is the great objection that the creature is not a leopard, either in structure or in coloration, being in fact the only existing member of the cat tribe that is unquestionably entitled to be classed in a genus apart from all the rest. To some of the older writers the animal was known as the guepard; and, whatever may be its origin, this name is unobjectionable, but since it has become obsolete, it would be hopeless to attempt its revival. Of the other two names, hunting-leopard seems less liable to lead to confusion.[1]

From all the species—both cats and lynxes—included in the genus *Felis*, the hunting-leopard is distinguished by the circumstance that it is unable to withdraw its claws entirely within the margins of their protecting sheaths, so that the points remain exposed. The body is more slender, and the limbs are proportionately longer and slighter than in any of the species of *Felis*; the animal being obviously cut out for racing much more decidedly than are any of the latter. There are likewise certain distinctive features

[1] See above under the heading of Leopard.

connected with the skull and the upper flesh-teeth, which may be passed over without special mention.

In place of being called the "hunting-leopard," the animal might have been better designated the "hunting-serval," since the black markings on its fur take the form of solid spots like those of the African serval, instead of the rosettes distinctive of the leopard. In size and form the species may be compared to a long-legged, slender-bodied leopard, with short and rounded ears, a tail somewhat exceeding half the length of the head and body, the hair of the neck rather elongated, so as to form an incipient mane (whence the name *jubatus*), that on the under surface of the body rather longer and shaggier than elsewhere, and the fur as a whole somewhat coarse. On the upper-parts of the head and body, as well as the outer surface of the limbs, the ground-colour varies from tawny to bright ruddy fawn, while on the under-parts it is paler, and devoid of the round black spots with which it is elsewhere ornamented ; the chin and throat, which are buffish white, being also unspotted.

Towards the extremity of the tail the spots tend to coalesce so as to form incomplete rings. The outer surface of the ears is black, except at the base and on the margins, where it is tawny. From the outer angle of each eye a black streak runs to the lip, this being continued, either as a continuous line or a row of spots, from the inner angle of the eye to a point just below the ear. The cubs have a coat of long and uniformly grey hair, but on turning this back more or less distinct traces of spots are noticeable on the shorter under-fur.

The geographical distribution of the hunting-leopard is very similar to that of the lion. Unknown in Ceylon and on the Malabar coast, the species ranges from the confines of Bengal through Central India and Rajputana to the Punjab, whence it extends through Baluchistan and probably parts of Afghanistan to

Persia, Russian Turkestan, Transcaspia, and so on through Syria and Palestine to Africa, where it ranges as far south as the Cape. According to Dr. Satunin, it is not found in the Caucasus. Further observations are required as to the southern limits of the range of the hunting-leopard in India.

Although much has been written with regard to the training and employment of the hunting-leopard for the purpose of capturing blackbuck and other animals by the natives of India, little has been said about the creature in its wild state; and since this has been repeated over and over again in works of natural history, a short notice will be sufficient in this place. The favourite haunts of the Indian hunting-leopard are low, isolated, rocky hills, whence it can obtain an unrestricted view of the surrounding plains, and mature its plans for stalking the blackbuck, gazelles, deer, and other animals which form its prey. These felines hunt in couples, and creep up to within a certain distance of their intended victims, when they make a sudden rush at a terrific pace, which, whether successful or otherwise, is the final effort, the pursuit being abandoned if the quarry is not overtaken during the first spurt. Occasionally, instead of a single pair, it is said that a whole family will join in the stalk and subsequent rush. After a successful foray the hunting-leopard indulges in such a gorge that it generally requires two or three days' repose and quiet before again taking the field. Before each chase these animals repair to some favourite tree, upon the bark of which they sharpen and clean their claws. The cubs are carefully trained by their parents in stalking and taking their prey; and so essential is this parental instruction that, according to native reports, cubs that have not been thus taught are of no use for hunting. Consequently the trained individuals kept by the chiefs for the latter purpose are captured when full-grown. The method of hunting with these tame animals has been so often described, that there would be nothing gained by its repetition.

Hunting-leopards never attack man, and very seldom carry off or molest domesticated animals. Considering that on ordinary ground the best English greyhounds have not a chance with blackbuck, the speed of the hunting-leopard during its final rush must be tremendous. This speed can, however, only be maintained for a very short distance, and a well-mounted horseman can come up with a hunting-leopard after a comparatively short run, when it generally permits itself to be speared without vigorous resistance, although at times requiring to be driven out from the covert in which it has taken refuge. If the statement by Jardine that these animals were formerly kept by the Moghul emperors in thousands for sporting purposes is to be relied upon, it would seem that they must have been more numerous than is the case at the present day, when they are comparatively rare.

A full-grown hunting-leopard stands about 2½ feet in height at the shoulder, and has a total length of about 7 feet, 2½ of which is accounted for by the tail alone.

THE INDIAN CIVET

(*Viverra zibetha*)

NATIVE NAMES.—*Khatas*, HINDUSTANI (in common with several small Carnivora); *Mach-bhondar*, *Bagdos*, AND *Puda-ganla*, BENGALI; *Bhran* IN THE NEPAL TERAI; *Nil-biralu*, NEPALESE; *Kung* OF THE BHOTIAS; *Saphiong* of the LEPCHAS; *Kyoung-myeng* (horse-cat), BURMESE; *Tangalong*, MALAY.

Although commonly called cats or civet-cats, the civets and their allies the palm-civets are very different animals from the *Felidæ*, forming the related family *Viverridæ*. Civets, in place of the short, "smug" faces of the cats, have long, sharply pointed muzzles, which implies the possession of a larger series of teeth. And not only are the teeth of the members of the civet tribe more numerous than those of the cats, but they are likewise different in structure, being less completely adapted for rending flesh.

The civets of the genus *Viverra*, which with the exception of the fossa (*Cryptoprocta*) of Madagascar, include the largest representatives of the family to which they belong, are distinguished by the grooved upper lip, the long, ringed tail, the absence of tufts on the ears, the black gorget on the throat, the long and loose character of the fur, which is generally elongated into a kind of crest down the back, and the short and partially retractile claws. They walk on the tips of their toes, and, with the exception of the "pads," the sole of the foot is hairy. These animals are furnished with a pouch in the groin which secretes the strong perfume from which they derive their name (or which derives its name from them).

The present species, also known as the large Indian civet, is larger than the other members of the group inhabiting the country, the length of the head and body being about 32 inches, and that of the tail 8 inches. Its most distinctive feature is the banding of the whole length of the tail by alternate dark and light rings. The general colour is dark hoary grey, frequently with a more or less decided brownish or reddish tinge, the sides of the body being often uniformly coloured, but in other instances marked with transverse cloudy dark bars ; the crest, like the gorget on the throat, is black, but the front and sides of the throat, as well as the chest, are white. Not unfrequently there is a dusky band above and another below the gorget, and when the second of these is developed, it joins a horizontal streak running from behind the

PLATE IX

1. Binturong.
2. Striped Hyæna.
3. Tibetan Wolf.
4. Indian Wolf.
5. Wild Dog.
6. Panda.
7. Short-tailed Panda.
8. Himalayan Brown Bear.
9. Blue Bear.
10. Himalayan Black Bear.
11. Bruan, or Malay Bear.
12. Aswal, or Sloth-Bear.

ear. The upper portion of the limbs shows dark barrings externally, but their lower parts are uniformly blackish brown, or black.

The range of this civet includes Burma, Assam, the Eastern Himalaya, and Bengal. In Sikhim and Nepal it ascends to a considerable elevation above the sea-level; and it is for the most part solitary, hiding in thick covert during the day, and wandering in search of food by night. Although unable to climb, it takes readily to the water, and frequently makes its lair in a hole in the ground. All animals that it can kill, as well as eggs, seem acceptable as food to the civet, which not unfrequently does considerable harm to domesticated poultry. Since the skin is of little value, the animal offers slight attraction to the sportsman.

Three smaller species of civet inhabit India and Burma. In addition to these there are, in the Eastern Himalaya and Burma, the graceful and beautifully coloured linsangs (*Linsanga*), while various species of palm-civets, or toddy-cats (*Paradoxurus*), as well as mongooses (*Herpestes*), are to be met with all over the country. None of these can, however, be regarded as game animals, even in the widest sense of that term.

THE BINTURONG

(*Arctictis binturong*)

NATIVE NAMES. — *Young*, ASSAMESE; *Myouk-kya* (monkey-tiger), BURMESE; *Untarong*, MALAY

(PLATE ix, fig. 1)

Although prehensile tails, by means of which their owners sling themselves to branches, are common among the marsupials of Australia, the ant-eaters, and monkeys of South America, and the opossums of both divisions of the New World, for some unexplained reason such a power in the caudal appendage is not in fashion in other parts of the world. The binturong, or, as it should be correctly called, untarong, is, however, one of the few exceptions to this rule, and for this, if for no other reason, is worthy the attention of the sportsman. It is, indeed, the only prehensile-tailed mammal of any size found throughout the three great continents of the Old World.

The binturong may be compared in size and general appearance to a large, long-tailed, shaggy black cat, with tufts of elongated hair to its pointed ears. And since it cannot be confounded with any other animal, this comparison will suffice. It may, however, be added that, instead of walking on its toes, after the manner of a cat, the binturong applies the whole under surface of the hind-foot to the ground, like a bear. In most specimens there is a more or less marked tendency to a grey grizzling, and in Borneo there is a distinctly grey phase. The length of the head and body ranges between 28 and 33 inches, and that of the tail between 26 and 27 inches.

The distributional area of the binturong extends from the Malay Islands and Peninsula through Borneo to Assam. Although Dr. W. T. Blanford doubted its alleged occurrence in the Eastern Himalaya, Mr. W. L. Sclater states that it is found as far west as Simla. However this may be, there is no doubt that the animal is a Malay type.

The binturong has been from time to time exhibited in the London Zoological Gardens ; and as it is purely nocturnal, it is mainly from these captive specimens that the little we know of its mode of life has been gleaned. It is always found in forests, and is probably for the most part, if not completely, arboreal. Captive individuals have demonstrated the prehensile power of the tail, and have likewise indicated the omnivorous tastes of the creature. As to its breeding-habits, there is opportunity for sportsmen to enlighten naturalists, as there is to ascertain the truth of the assertion that the binturong utters a weird and piercing cry.

THE STRIPED HYÆNA

(*Hyæna striata*)

NATIVE NAMES.—*Lakar-bagha*, *Lakar-bagh* OR *Lakra*, *Jhirak*, *Hondar*, *Harvagh*, AND *Taras*, HINDUSTANI; *Taras*, MAHRATHI AND SINDI; *Cherak*, SINDI; *Aptar*, BALUCHI; *Renhra* OF THE GONDS; *Hebar-kula*, HO-KOL; *Derko-tud* IN RAJMEHAL; *Dhopre*, KORKA; *Kirba* AND *Kut-kirba*, CANARESE; *Dumul-gundu* AND *Korna-gundu*, TELEGU; *Kalu-thai-korachi*, TAMIL.

(PLATE ix, fig. 2)

Hyænas are among the few animals for which no one has a good word to say; and it must be confessed that they are attractive neither in personal appearance nor in habits. Nevertheless they are useful creatures, being some of the most efficient of all scavengers, since their powerful cone-like teeth enable them to crack bones of considerable calibre, and thus devour skeletons which are left by other animals. In return for these benefits, the striped hyæna, when captured, is cruelly maimed and tortured by some at least of the natives of India.

Although there may be some confusion between the spotted African hyæna and the hunting-dog of the same country, no one in India is likely to mistake a hyæna for any other animal, or to fail to recognise one when met with, either alive or dead. Consequently, there is no need to describe the features by which these animals are distinguished from cats and civets on the one hand and dogs and wolves on the other. Neither is it necessary to record in detail the specific characters of the striped species, seeing that it is the only representative of the group in India. As regards the first point, it will suffice to mention that these animals are classed in a family by themselves—the *Hyænidæ*—and exhibit certain indications of affinity with the *Felidæ* and *Viverridæ*, as they also do with the *Canidæ*. No one who has examined a hyæna's skull will have failed to recognise the enormous biting power indicated by the great vertical ridge or wall of bone running down the middle of the temporal region, or the bone-crushing capacity of the (premolar) teeth immediately behind the tusks, which, instead of the compressed form they exhibit in cats and dogs, have assumed the shape of blunt truncated cones, admirably adapted for the purpose for which they are intended. So great, indeed, is the power of its jaws, that a hyæna is credited with being able to crack the leg-bone of a horse at a single snap.

Compared with its spotted African cousin, from which it is distinguished by the characters of its skull and teeth, as well as by external appearance, the striped hyæna is a comparatively small beast, standing about 26 inches and measuring about 3½ feet from the tip of the snout to the root of the tail, the tail itself averaging 1½ feet in length. The general colour of the untidy and shaggy fur, which is elongated into a semi-upright crest or mane along the neck and back, is dirty grey, marked with a number of narrow transverse tawny or blackish stripes on the body and limbs.

Not extending into the countries lying east of the Bay of Bengal, unknown in Ceylon, and comparatively rare in Lower Bengal, the striped hyæna ranges over the greater portion of the peninsula of India, and thence westward through South-Western Asia, including Bokhara and Arabia, to the Caucasus and North and East Africa. It belongs therefore to the western element in the fauna of India, and while fossil remains of more or less nearly related species occur in the Pliocene rocks of Northern India, others indistinguishable from this species have been recorded from those of England and other parts of Europe. Both the Asiatic and the African representatives of the species have been divided into local races, which need not, however, be noticed in this place.

As a rule, Indian hyænas prefer open country, especially of a hilly nature, for their resorts, and are seldom seen in forest, although they may take cover in grass or bushes, or even sugar-cane. Rocky ravines are perhaps the places most generally chosen by these skulking, cowardly animals for retirement during the day, and here they make their lairs among crevices and clefts in the rocks, or in holes dug in the soil by their own exertions. Except on the comparatively rare occasions when one is driven from covert during a beat, or a belated individual encountered returning to its lair in the early dawn, hyænas are rarely seen by the sportsman, who seldom takes much trouble in looking after them, as they yield little in the way of trophies. The skin is valueless, and there are not many sportsmen who set much store on the skulls of these animals. Sometimes hyænas are ridden down and speared by mounted men, and the sport they then afford is by no means to be despised. It is not that they have any great speed; on the contrary, they are soon outstripped even by an ordinary horse, but from their frequent doubling and turning they are difficult animals with which to get to close quarters, so that the run is generally of considerable length. Few sportsmen have, however, practised hyæna-spearing; and to the majority these animals are a nuisance, from their propensity to gnaw and otherwise damage skulls, skins, or other edible articles (including boots) left unguarded within their reach at night. Sometimes a hyæna summons up courage to enter the open door of a tent on a hot night, when the occupant may be startled by the glare of its green eyes as it stands in the doorway.

Generally the striped hyæna is solitary, prowling at night in search of the carcases of animals killed by Carnivora bolder than itself, or of those which have succumbed to disease; and it is reported that these animals have no compunction in devouring the body of another member of their own species, if it should come in their way. A large proportion of their food is formed by the skeletons of animals whose flesh has been partially devoured by larger Carnivora, and the bones subsequently picked nearly clean by vultures and jackals. The gnawed ends of such bones are not unfrequently left by the hyænas at the entrances of their dens, the situation of which is thus revealed to the passer-by. Although seldom, if ever, killing healthy wild animals, hyænas not unfrequently take toll of domesticated sheep, goats, and dogs. The sound of the shrill, weird cry of this species, almost impossible to describe in words, when once heard at night will not readily be forgotten.

THE WOLF

(*Canis lupus*)

NATIVE NAMES.—*Gurg*, PERSIAN; *Gurk*, BALUCHI; *Kharma*, BRAHUI; *Ratnahan*, KASHMIRI; *Chanco*, TIBETAN.

(PLATE ix, fig. 3)

The European wolf, of which the Tibetan wolf and the wolves of North America are local races, is so well known that no detailed description is necessary. It is one of the largest wild representatives of the dog tribe, or *Canidæ*, standing about 2 feet 4 inches at the shoulder, and usually measuring from 3 feet 6 to 9 inches from the muzzle to the root of the tail, the length of the tail varying from 15 to 16, or if the hair at the tip be included, some 3 inches more. The general colour of the long thick fur of the upper-parts and outer surfaces of the limbs is some shade of yellowish or reddish grey, frequently more or less mingled with black, wholly black individuals being by no means uncommon, and the tail being not unfrequently black-tipped. The under-parts and inner surfaces of the limbs are whitish. A soft woolly under-fur, of which the general colour is slaty or light brown, is developed at the base of the longer hairs.

Within the area treated of in the present volume the ordinary or typical race of the wolf is probably met with in the northern part of the Punjab, and certainly in the west of Sind and in Baluchistan, whence it ranges into Persia and doubtless also into Afghanistan. Probably it likewise extends into the valley of Kashmir, although it is replaced on the Ladak side of the range forming the northern barrier of that valley by the Tibetan race. Information is required as to the wolf of the Gilgit neighbourhood; but it will probably be found that somewhere in this district there exists a transition between the typical and the Tibetan races of the species.

To withstand the intense winter cold of the bleak altitudes at which it dwells, and at the same time to harmonise with its physical surroundings, the wolf of Ladak and Tibet (*Canis lupus laniger*) has developed a woolly character in its fur, and has also become paler than ordinary examples of the European race. So pale, indeed, is the colour of the fur that, as shown by a specimen from Ladak in the British Museum, it may be best described as whitish grey. As in the case of the ordinary wolf, individuals are, however, occasionally seen in which the entire coat is black, more or less grizzled with grey in the region of the snout.

According to Ladaki reports, black individuals of the Tibetan wolf, known to the natives as *chanco nagpo*, and apparently by no means uncommon, are bolder and more aggressive than ordinary pale-coloured specimens;

and since a similar idea is current with regard to black leopards, it would be interesting to find out whether this belief is founded on fact. These wolves are seldom encountered by European sportsmen, General Kinloch and Mr. Darrah being among the few who have seen them. According to an account given by the former, it appears that chanko are usually found singly or in pairs, and that, in summer at any rate, they never collect in packs after the manner of the wolf in Siberia. They are in the habit of prowling round the flanks of the flocks of the natives, watching their opportunity to attack and carry off sheep when the guardian mastiffs are occupied elsewhere, General Kinloch being of opinion that they prefer the capture of domesticated animals to the chase of wild ones. Mr. Darrah, however, records that the body of a shapo shot by himself was soon devoured by these animals. General Kinloch tamed a pair of cubs, which were brought to England in 1868.

THE INDIAN WOLF

(*Canis pallipes*)

NATIVE NAMES.—*Bheriya*, *Gurg*, HONDAR; *Nekra* AND *Bighana*, HINDUSTANI; *Bagyar*, SINDI; *Landga*, GONDI AND DECCANI; *Tola*, CANARESE; *Toralu*, TELEGU.

(PLATE ix, fig. 4)

According to Mr. W. E. de Winton (*Proceedings of the Zoological Society of London* for 1899), some misconception has occurred with respect to the Indian wolf of the Deccan on account of its having been confused with the European wolf of the Punjab and Sind; the animal figured in Dr. Mivart's *Monograph of the Canidæ* as the Indian wolf being, for instance, the European wolf of North-Western India. The Indian wolf, like the American coyote, is in reality in some degree intermediate between true wolves and jackals. In point of size it is larger than the Indian jackal (*Canis aureus*), but in this respect very similar to the large Egyptian jackal (*Canis lupaster*). Between the skulls of the latter and that of the Indian wolf there is in fact no practical difference in point of size, although the Indian animal is distinguishable by its larger and heavier teeth, the difference being especially noticeable in the case of the upper carnassial, or flesh-tooth.

In addition to being smaller than the European species, the Indian wolf is also slighter in build, with little or no woolly under-fur. In length the head and body are about 3 feet, against 3½ feet in the European species. The general colour of the fur is greyish fulvous, usually showing a more or less distinct tinge of brown, and in some instances mingled with black on the back. Although it has been stated that rufous-coloured skins have been seen, all the specimens in the British Museum are browner than those of the European wolf, and of an earthy-grey colour, and it is not improbable that the rufous-coloured skins assigned to the present species were really referable to the latter animal. On the back the tips of all the hairs are black, and near the skin coarser white hairs are mingled with the ordinary fine brown fur. As a rule, the hairs on the tail are black-tipped, and the fur of the under surface of the body is dirty white. Cubs are sooty brown in colour, with a conspicuous spot of white in the centre of the chest, which disappears in the course of a few weeks, when a dark gorget, which likewise vanishes before the attainment of maturity, is developed.

The typical locality for the Indian wolf is the plateau of the Deccan, from which locality it was first described by Colonel Sykes in 1831. From the Deccan it ranges over a considerable portion of the Indian Peninsula, although not extending into the foot-ranges of the

Himalaya nor to the Trans-Indus districts of the Punjab and Sind. Indeed it is doubtful if it reaches the Indus in the Punjab, since a skull from the Salt Range has been referred to the European wolf. The Indian species appears to be unknown on the Malabar coast, and is far from common in Bengal. In Ceylon it is unknown, as it is in the countries to the east of the Bay of Bengal; but it has also been recorded from Arabia. Open plain country forms its usual resort, and it is rarely met with in hills or forest.

Except that it never collects in large packs after the manner of its European cousin in many parts of Russia and Siberia, the Indian wolf appears to be similar in its general mode of life to the former, so that there is nothing in this respect calling for notice. Although preying largely on the smaller domesticated animals, the Indian wolf appears to be a terrible foe to black-buck, while even man himself is by no means exempt from its attacks. In attacking adult human beings it appears that two or more individuals are in the habit of joining forces; but in carrying off children from villages—to which the great bulk of the mortality from these animals is due—a single wolf is able to do the business by himself.

When caught in the early morning in a more or less gorged condition, the Indian wolf may sometimes be ridden down and speared by a well-mounted man, but at other times, although not appearing to be going at any great pace, it will easily keep ahead of the fleetest greyhounds till the latter succumb from exhaustion. When their "earths" are known, wolves may sometimes be smoked out and shot; but these animals afford little sport, and are regarded rather in the light of "vermin" than "big game."

Since the last remark applies with still greater force in the case of the Indian jackal, it has not been deemed necessary to include that species in the present volume.

THE DHOLE, OR WILD DOG

(*Canis* [*Cyon*] *sumatrensis*)

NATIVE NAMES. — *Jangli-kutta*, *Ram-kutta*, *Son-kutta*, AND *Ban-kutta* IN HINDUSTANI ; *Kolsun*, *Kolasna*, *Kolasra*, AND *Kolsa*, MAHRATHI ; *Reza-kutta* AND *Adavi-kutta*, TELEGU ; *Shin-nai*, MALABARESE ; *Eram-naiko*, GOND ; *Tani*, HO-KOL ; *Vatai-karau*, TAMIL ; *Ram-hun*, KASHMIRI ; *Siddaki*, LADAKI ; *Bhaosa*, *Bhansa*, AND *Buansu* IN THE HIMALAYA ; *Hazi* AND *Phara*, TIBET ; *Paoho*, BHOTIA AT DARJILING ; *Sa-tum*, LEPCHA ; *Tau-khwe*, BURMESE ; *Anjing-utan*, MALAY.

(PLATE ix, fig. 5)

The wild dogs of Asia, which are generically distinct from the African hunting-dog, are distinguished from domesticated dogs, wolves, jackals, and foxes by the absence of the last pair of teeth in the lower jaw, so that the total number of teeth is forty instead of forty-two. Additional points of distinction are the relatively shorter muzzle, the slightly convex (instead of straight or concave) profile of the face, and the greater number of teats possessed by the female, these forming either six or seven pairs in place of the usual five. The presence of long hairs between the naked pads on the soles of the feet is another character in which the wild dogs differ from more typical wild *Canidæ*.

Whether these points of distinction are sufficient to justify the separation of the wild dogs as a genus (*Cyon*) apart from the wolves and jackals, may be a matter of opinion. As a compromise, they may be regarded as a subgenus, when the full title of the present species will be *Canis* (*Cyon*) *sumatrensis*. The Malay wild dog, it may be mentioned, was described in 1822 as a variety of domesticated dog, under the name of *Canis familiaris*, var. *sumatrensis*; and since this name is earlier than any of the others[1] applied to either the Indian or the Malay race, it must according to modern rules of nomenclature stand for the species.

In regard to the name "wild dog," commonly applied to these animals, Dr. Blanford has remarked that it is a misnomer, "for in every important detail in which the genus *Cyon* differs from *Canis*—in the form of the skull, the dentition, and the number of mammæ—domestic dogs agree with the latter and not with the former." The name, it is further suggested, has probably been applied to the members of the present group on account of their hunting in packs, their handsome appearance, and their courage. It is, however, a translation of the Malay *anjing-utan* and the Hindustani *jangli kutta*; and this we venture to think is its more probable origin. The name "dhole" has been employed by Colonel Hamilton Smith and some other writers, although it is not the name by which these animals are known to the natives of the countries they inhabit.

These wild dogs are confined to Asia, where their range includes Central Asia as far north as the Altai, Amurland, and the island of Sagalien, while to the southward it embraces India, Burma, and the Malay Peninsula and Islands, with the exception of Celebes and the Philippines. No representative of the group has been found either in the north of China or in Japan.

The Malay race of the wild dog appears distinguishable from its Himalayan and Indian representatives by its smaller size and slighter build, the limbs being decidedly more slender. The colour also seems to be a brighter tinge of red, and the tail, of which the tip is black, is stated to form a smaller brush. From Himalayan specimens of the Indian race, the Malay race also differs by the absence of a woolly under-

[1] A still earlier name is *Canis javanicus*, but it is uncertain to what animal it was applied.

fur at the base of the long hairs of the coat, but as the same absence characterises Indian skins, this feature cannot be reckoned as distinctive of the former.

The Malay wild dog is known to occur in Sumatra, Java, the Malay Peninsula, and Tenasserim, while it has been reported from Borneo. It has, however, yet to be determined whether the wild dog of Northern Burma is identical with the present or the following race ; and it may be regarded as certain that when a full series of specimens is obtained, a complete transition will be found in the districts between Tenasserim and Assam from the one to the other.

Whether the wild dog of India and the Himalaya is specifically the same as its Malay representative is a point on which naturalists are not agreed. A compromise is to regard the two as local races of a single species, when the name of the Malay race will be *C. sumatrensis typicus*, and the Indian *C. sumatrensis deccanensis*. Both differ from the wild dog of the Altai and other parts of Central Asia (*C. alpinus*) by the circumstance that the upper cutting, or carnassial, tooth is longer than the combined length of the two molars behind it, instead of shorter. From the analogy of the distribution of other animals, it might have been supposed that the wild dog of the Himalaya and Tibet would be nearer to the Altai than to the Indian form ; but this is not the case, and the Tibetan and Indian animals, which agree in the relative size of their teeth, are regarded as identical. The typical Deccan wild dog lacks, however, the under-fur of the Himalayan and Tibet specimens.

In general appearance and build the Indian wild dog (like its Malay representative) is more like a jackal than a wolf, the limbs being proportionately shorter than in the latter. The tail forms a good brush. In length the head and body of a full-grown male measured between 37 and 38 inches, while the tail, inclusive of the hair, measured between 14 and 15 inches. The colour is as follows :—Upper-parts generally rusty red, varying to rufous grey, or light brownish grey, paler below. In place of being uniform, the colour is variegated by dark tips to the hairs on the back. The under-fur, when present, varies in colour from light brown to dull rufous on the upper-parts, and has light-coloured, coarser hairs intermixed ; the longer hairs are light rufous, with dark rusty red tips. The terminal portion of the tail is black, very rarely with the extreme tip whitish. Young animals are sooty brown throughout. From the typical Malay race of the species, the Indian wild dog appears distinguishable by its somewhat superior size and more powerful build, as well as by the less bright ferruginous tint of the fur.

The Indian wild dog has a comparatively wide geographical range, extending from Eastern Tibet to Cape Comorin, although unknown in Ceylon. It has been recorded from Gilgit, Ladak, Spiti, Nepal, Kashmir, and the Western Himalaya generally. Its absence from Ceylon suggests that it did not reach the mainland of India till after the separation of that island.

The wild dog is a ferocious and gregarious animal, hunting its prey in packs, which usually comprise from six to a dozen individuals, although occasionally as many as a score. In the plains of India and the outer ranges of the Himalaya it dwells in forests, but in Tibet it must necessarily be an inhabitant of more open country. The destruction it inflicts on deer, wild sheep, and chiru antelope is great ; and wherever its footprints are to be met with in Ladak, the sportsman may as well give up hope of killing game. Even the tiger and the Himalayan black bear are stated to occasionally fall victims to the attack of these bloodthirsty marauders, and the mangled remains of a tiger have in one instance been found lying side by side with the bodies of three wild dogs. In the Himalaya ibex form a large proportion of the prey of these animals ; and it has been stated that the serow is the only creature capable of withstanding their attacks, sometimes even transfixing its assailants with its sharp and powerful, although short horns, which are admirably adapted for stabbing. Possibly, too, the dense and long coat of the serow may stand it in good stead when repelling attacks of this nature. Instances are on record where wild dogs have succeeded in pulling down not only such large animals as the sambar, but even domesticated Indian buffalo. Although freshly-killed flesh is the general diet of these animals, it is probable that, as in the case of most other Carnivora, a meal of carrion forms an occasional variety. Since they generally avoid the neighbourhood of human habitations, the toll levied by wild dogs on domesticated animals is less than in the case of many other Carnivora; but they at times kill sheep, goats, and cattle, while, as already mentioned, they occasionally venture to attack the buffalo. They display great sagacity during the breeding-season by driving their prey to the neighbourhood of their dwelling-places before giving it the *coup de grâce*, so that there should be the least possible trouble in carrying the supply of food to the spot where it is required.

In some instances at least wild dogs breed in a kind of warren, where several females associate together, one such breeding-place having been discovered near Simla. Winter is the breeding-season, the young being usually produced in holes or clefts among rocks from January to March. From two to four is the usual number of cubs produced in a litter, although there may be as many as half-a-dozen.

Although wild dogs generally hunt in the daytime, it is probable that sometimes at least they are on the move during the night. It has been asserted that, when in pursuit, they "give tongue," like hounds, but this is denied by an observer who saw a pack in full chase. Others state that these animals howl at night.

In captivity wild dogs appear very difficult to tame, if indeed they are not absolutely untameable. It is true that when taken young they display a certain amount of docility during the earlier months of their captivity, and will even play with domesticated dogs, but with advancing age their wild nature reasserts itself with its original force, and they become spiteful and dangerous.

THE PANDA

(*Ælurus fulgens*)

NATIVE NAMES.—*Wah*, *Ye*, AND *Nigalya-ponya*, NEPALESE; *Thokya*, *Thongva*, AND *Sankam* OR *Saknam*, LEPCHA; *Wakdonka* AND *Woker*, BHOTIA.

(PLATE ix, fig. 6)

There are several names used in natural history, of which the origin is unknown, among these being "panda," which is the title by which the present animal was called when exhibited alive in the London Zoological Gardens. It is certainly not current among the native tribes in the districts where the animal dwells, by some of whom it is called *Wah*, or *Thongwa*; and were it not that panda has come into general use, one of these would be a better title. The origin of a name, so long as it be concise and euphonious, is not, however, of much consequence, and as panda fulfils both these conditions, it may continue to be employed. The alternative names red cat-bear and Himalayan raccoon, are both open to objection.

The panda is one of the most beautifully coloured of all mammals, and in size and shape somewhat recalls a cat, although it may be distinguished by the circumstance that in walking it applies the whole sole of the foot to the ground. Cat-like features are displayed by the rounded form of the head, the short and broad face, in which the eyes are directed forwards, and the small rounded ears. The limbs are short and stout, with the feet and their pads completely covered with fur, and the large claws sharp and capable of partial retraction within protecting sheaths. The long, thick, soft coat has a woolly under-fur, and the well-haired cylindrical tail, which is rather more than two-thirds the length of the head and body, is marked by rings paler than the general colour of the fur, its tip being black. The prevailing colour is rich rusty red, frequently somewhat paler on the back than elsewhere, and always lighter on the forehead ; the under-parts of the body and the inner surface of the limbs are for the most part black, although brownish in places, and the outer side of the ears is often sable, although sometimes dark red. With the exception of a red stripe running down from the eye to the angle of the mouth, and sometimes also of a line from the forehead to the snout, the face and lips are white, as are also the margins and inner surface of the ears. The claws are white, and the soles of the feet whitish or whitey brown. The length of the head and body varies from 20 to 24, and that of the tail (exclusive of the hair at the tip) from 16 to 17 inches, the weight ranging between 7 and 9½ pounds. Individuals are occasionally met with in which the black tends to invade the upper-parts.

Very curious are the teeth of the panda, which at first sight recall those of hoofed herbivorous mammals, the tusks being small and weak, and the molars with a complicated arrangement of cusps on their grinding surfaces. Closer examination shows that these latter teeth are essentially similar in general structure to those of the American raccoons, and thus unlike those of other Carnivora.

The panda has a somewhat remarkable distribution, inhabiting the Eastern Himalaya, at an elevation between about 7000 and 12,000 feet, as far westwards as Nepal, and extending eastwards through the mountainous districts of Assam into Yunnan, but being unknown in the Malay countries. In the *Annals and Magazine of Natural History* for September 1902, Mr. O. Thomas described from Szechuen a larger form of panda, under the name of *Ælurus fulgens styani*.

For a long time the panda was regarded as representing a family group by itself, although its resemblance to the American raccoons had been pointed out by Brian Hodgson and Edward Blyth, the latter of whom classed it among the raccoons. In 1869, when the first living specimen brought to England was exhibited in the Zoological Gardens, Mr. A. D. Bartlett remarked how closely this animal resembled the American kinkajou (one of the raccoon family) in habits, while at the same time Sir W. H. Flower demonstrated its anatomical relationships with the raccoons; and in the *Fauna of British India*, Dr. W. T. Blanford definitely classed the panda with raccoons in the family *Procyonidæ*. Remains of a larger species of panda have been discovered in rocks of Tertiary age in England and Hungary.

Like all animals of the Eastern Himalaya, the panda is a forest-dwelling creature, making its lair either in hollow trees, or, as some have suggested, in crevices of rocks; but it is by no means purely arboreal, as it frequently descends to the ground for the purpose of feeding. Neither is it by any means exclusively nocturnal, although it passes a considerable portion of the day in slumber, its chief feeding-times being morning and evening. Generally two, sometimes with their offspring, are found in company; and, as might be assumed from the structure of its teeth, the species is mainly a vegetable-feeder, although it eats eggs, and probably also insects and grubs. Since it is dull of hearing and sight, and apparently not endowed with an acute sense of smell, while its means of defence are feeble, the panda is not difficult to capture, and examples are frequently taken by the Lepchas in the neighbourhood of Darjiling. Nevertheless, it is seldom brought to England; and up to 1896 only two examples had been exhibited in the London Zoological Gardens, namely, the one presented in 1869, and a second purchased in 1876. Pandas have, however, been kept in the Zoological Gardens at Calcutta.

Ordinarily the panda utters a faint kind of squeak, which has been compared to the chirp of a bird; but in the pairing-season it indulges in loud, unearthly cries, and when angered it will hiss and spit like a cat. The young, of which there are generally two at a time, are born in spring.

THE SHORT-TAILED PANDA

(*Æluropus melanoleucus*)

(Plate ix, fig. 7)

The remarkable black-and-white bear-like animal from Eastern Tibet, of which the head is shown in plate ix, fig. 7, was long regarded as a member of the family *Ursidæ*, since in general form, and especially in the shortness of the tail, it has a marked resemblance to a small bear, although with a shorter and more rounded head. When first described, some idea of the relationship of this animal to the Himalayan panda was entertained; and it was for this reason that it was named *Æluropus*. This presumed relationship has been confirmed by Sir E. Ray Lankester, who is of opinion that the animal is a near relative of the true panda and has only a remote kinship with bears.

The first knowledge of the existence of the short-tailed panda was derived from the travels of the Abbé David in Eastern Tibet; the specimens brought home by that explorer from the district of Moupin and now exhibited in the Paris Museum of Natural History, being long the only known examples of this animal in Europe. In 1896 two skins, with portions of the skeletons, were, however, procured by Mr. Rothschild, one of which is in the museum at Tring, while the second is exhibited in the British (Natural History) Museum. Three years later other examples were brought to England by Mr. F. W. Styan from Szechuen, North-West China.

Apart from its curious colouring, and the greater width and shortness of its head, the short-tailed panda is very like a small bear. It is true that it has a distinct tail, instead of a mere vestige of that appendage, but this alone would not justify its separation from the bear family; neither would the fact that the soles of the feet are clothed with fur, instead of being naked, necessarily involve such separation, seeing that there is a thin coating of hair on those of the polar bear. The skull and teeth, as well as the bones of the skeleton, are, however, so essentially unlike those of a bear, and approximate so closely to those of the Himalayan panda, that there can be little question as to the nearness of the relationship between the two animals.

The head and skull of most bears are long and narrow, with a nearly straight or little-arched profile; and the upper cheek-teeth likewise conform to this type, being considerably longer than broad. In the short-tailed panda, on the other hand, the head and skull are comparatively short and wide posteriorly, with a remarkable convex and sloping profile, while the upper cheek-teeth have broad, nearly square crowns, with a curiously complicated arrangement of cusps and ridges on their grinding surfaces. In all these respects the present animal approximates to the Himalayan panda, from which it differs by having forty instead of only thirty-eight teeth. It is true indeed that the skull of the Malay bear makes some approach to the panda type in its relative width and shortness, but the teeth are still typically ursine. Both kinds of panda have six pairs of lower cheek-teeth, of which in the Himalayan species four are premolars and two molars, whereas in the short-tailed panda there are three pairs of premolars and three molars. In possessing three lower molars the latter differs from other members of the raccoon family and resembles bears ; but this extra pair of teeth may perhaps be regarded merely as an indication of closer affinity with the common ancestor of raccoons and bears than is possessed by other members of the *Procyonidæ*.

Although its feet are bear-like, the short-tailed panda is perhaps less completely plantigrade than bears. In size it may be compared to a small Kashmir bear. The fur is long and thick, and the general colour creamy white, with the ears, rings round the eyes, the shoulders, and the limbs jetty black.

The width of the skull implies great jaw-power, and the structure of the cheek-teeth indicates that the creature feeds on vegetable rather than animal diet ; this inference being confirmed by such meagre reports as we possess of its habits. As it is stated to be a vegetarian, subsisting chiefly on roots and the young shoots of bamboos, it is evidently an inhabitant of forest districts, and not of open plateau. In winter its peculiar type of colouring would not improbably render it inconspicuous when walking in snow among tree-stems ; but in summer it would apparently be just as conspicuous, and it has been suggested that its colouring, like that of skunks, is of what is known as the warning type.

Further information is, however, required with regard to these points, as well as with respect to the limits of the geographical range of this most remarkable animal.

THE BROWN BEAR

(*Ursus arctus isabellinus* and *U. a. shanorum*)

NATIVE NAMES. — *Barf-ka-rinch* AND *Lal-bhalu*, HINDUSTANI ; *Kunia-haput*, KASHMIRI ; *Drengmo*, BALTI ; *Drin-mor*, LADAKI ; *Brabu*, KISHTAWARI ; *Dab*, NEPALESE ; *Tom-khaina*, TIBETAN.

(PLATE ix, fig. 8)

Although often showing a white collar or gorget on the throat, bears, as a rule, are uniformly coloured animals, distinguishable from the short-tailed panda by the form of their molar teeth, which are long and narrow, with the last in the upper jaw elongated, and exceeding in length the one in front.

The snow, or red bear, as, by literal translation of its Hindustani names, the Himalayan animal is called by sportsmen, cannot be regarded as more than a local race of the brown bear of Europe, distinguished (especially when young) by its generally paler fur and its somewhat inferior size. Usually the colour of the long winter coat is pale creamy brown, or isabelline fawn, in fairly young individuals, and these sometimes show a white gorget, stated to be also visible in older individuals immediately after the assumption of the short summer fur. Very old animals, more especially males, become, however, much darker, and sometimes have a silvery tinge, owing to the tips of the hairs becoming white. The skull of the kunia-haput, as this bear is called in Kashmiri, is characterised by the elevation of the forehead, so that in a profile view an obtuse angle is formed immediately in front of the eyes ; another feature being the distinct hollow at the junction of the nasal with the frontal bones. As a rule, the claws are pale-coloured, or even white.

Most Kashmir brown bears do not exceed 6 feet in

length, and may be less than 5 feet, although General Kinloch and General Macintyre record old animals measuring about 7 feet to the root of the tail, and Dr. Leith-Adams has stated that, as an exceptional instance, he saw one which measured 7½ feet.

In the Himalaya the brown bear ranges from Afghanistan at least as far east as Nepal, but is unknown in the outer portions of the range, as it is in the arid districts to the north of the forest-region of Kashmir and adjacent districts. It extends, for instance, into the Tilel valley, and so on to Astor and Gilgit, but is unknown in Dras, Suru, Zanskar, and Ladak, as it apparently is in Upper Baltistan. In Kashmir it is, I believe, not found in the Pir Panjal range, or on the southern flank of the Kajnag. Westward of Afghanistan this race probably passes into the Syrian brown bear (*Ursus arctus syriacus*), which is found in the mountains of Persia, as well as in the country from which it takes its name, and is of greyer tone of colour.

For the most part the brown bear in Kashmir and the adjacent valleys lives at a considerable elevation, frequently hibernating in the zone of birch-forests, which grow at a higher elevation than pines; and in summer its feeding-grounds are generally on the open grassy hills above the forests, where it may be seen grazing (for these bears do graze) close to flocks of sheep and goats. In autumn it will, however, often descend to the higher villages for the sake of feeding on grain and walnuts, and will sometimes come even as low as the valley of Kashmir itself, especially in the Lolab district, which forms the north-western extremity of the valley, General Macintyre mentioning that in the Kashmir valley he once shot an old bear making a meal off the putrid carcase of a cow. These bears also come low down into the valley in spring, when the mulberries, of which they are remarkably fond, are ripe. Whether at the level of Kashmir itself these bears remain active all the year round is difficult to ascertain, but in the higher valleys in the neighbourhood, such as Tilel and Wardwan, they hibernate for a long season, not venturing forth till the snows begin to melt in March, April, or May. When they first come forth from their winter lairs, which may be either clefts in rocks or hollow tree-trunks, their coats are in splendid condition; but in the late summer and autumn, when the animals have become very fat, the fur is in a most dilapidated condition, and the skin not worth the trouble of stripping from the carcase. The supply of fat accumulated during the summer and autumn is completely consumed during the winter slumber and fast, the animal coming forth in the spring as thin as the proverbial herring. To the female the winter fast must be an especially trying time, as it is during hibernation that the cubs, usually two in number, are born. In the higher valleys the mother-bear is generally to be seen in spring accompanied by two cubs, the father of the family usually wandering about by himself at some distance off. When they first venture abroad among the birch-forests the ground is still to a great extent covered with snow, and it is probable that their food consists largely of bark, twigs, and moss; but as soon as the grass grows they take to grazing.

Few things edible seem to come amiss to a Kashmir brown bear; the partiality of these animals for grass, grain, fruit, and an occasional meal of carrion has been already mentioned, and they are also fond of grubbing for ants and the bulbs of the lily-like plants which grow in profusion in the valleys around Kashmir above the forests. They are reported to occasionally kill sheep and goats, and an instance is on record of an old bear killing a couple of its younger brethren and partially devouring their bodies.

As a rule, these bears are by no means vicious or quarrelsome, although occasionally a coolie, generally through his own foolhardiness, is mauled by one, while sometimes a European sportsman gets to closer quarters than is pleasant. This, however, is generally owing to the practice of shooting uphill at a bear; the rule being to get above the animal on the hill-side, and shoot downwards, when, after being hit, it will roll away from the sportsman. When two bears are feeding peaceably side by side, and one is wounded by a bullet, it will generally, with a loud grunt of rage, turn furiously on its companion, which it evidently considers the aggressor, and the pair can then in most cases be bagged by the sportsman.

Thirty years ago bears were extraordinarily numerous in Tilel, and the writer is almost afraid to say how many he has seen in a day; but at the present day their numbers are greatly diminished. To the beginner bear-shooting is exciting enough, but it soon begins to pall, since, with due precautions to prevent them from winding the sportsman, these animals can be approached to within a short distance, and killed outright at the first shot. Near the upper end of the Tilel valley I once succeeded in getting within about 20 yards of a brown bear, and killing it stone-dead with a smooth-bore bullet, which broke one of the vertebræ of the neck. When after ibex, Kashmiri shikaris are much put out if their masters turn aside for the sake of a bear.

General Macintyre gives the following account of the behaviour of a pair of cubs whose mother he shot. "As I considered," he writes, "the youngsters quite big enough to take care of themselves, I aimed deliberately at the old lady and let drive; she rolled a short distance down the hill, and, after a few struggles and groans, expired. The two cubs at first merely stood up on their hind-legs and gazed about them with much apparent astonishment; but on seeing their mother lying motionless below, they at once ran down to her, when their behaviour was such that I felt quite sorry I had shot her. The anxiety they plainly evinced, as they ran grunting and sniffing about their defunct parent, was quite touching. Even on observing us as we approached, they seemed unwilling to leave her. When they at last made up their mind to do so, they merely retired into an adjacent patch of wood, where they continued their whining lamentations, occasionally venturing out a few yards to stand upright and watch us as we ruthlessly stripped their dam of her hairy coat, and did not take their final departure until we gave chase, thinking we might capture them. Although too small to shoot, they were quite knowing enough not to allow themselves to be caught."

In the *Proceedings* of the Zoological Society for 1906, Mr. O. Thomas described the skin and skull of a bear from the Shan States, sent home by Lt.-Col. A. Alcock, then Superintendent of the Indian Museum, Calcutta. This bear lived for a short time in the possession of Mr. Rutledge, an animal dealer, who on its death presented the body to the Indian Museum. No bear had previously been recorded from this part of Asia; and the specimen proved to be a member of the *Ursus arctus* group, apparently nearly allied to *U. a. yesoensis*, of Hokkaido, the northern island of Japan, but evidently representing a different race, which it was proposed to call *Ursus arctus shanorum*. This bear is small in size, with the general colour dark brown; the hairs of the sides being tipped with grey, and an ill-defined dark line running down the middle of the back. The skull is of the long, narrow, vaulted shape of that of *U. a. yesoensis*, but much smaller, with the nasals abruptly and strongly narrowing in their posterior half. The breadth across the postorbital processes is unusually small; the palate is narrow; and the premaxillæ do not extend back to the level of the back of the tusks or canines. The teeth are remarkably short and broad in outline, the first premolar being very broad and heavy, nearly as broad as long, with low cusps and a low broad internal lobe; while the first molar is rather shorter, and yet actually broader, than in *yesoensis*.

The lower teeth are similarly broader throughout, the last molar being unusually wide and square in shape, and not narrowing behind.

From the Hokkaido brown bear the Shan race is distinguishable by its inferior size, and its smaller and somewhat differently proportioned cheek-teeth, as described above.

Other specimens of this race of brown bear would be of great interest.

THE BLUE BEAR

(*Ursus pruinosus*)

(PLATE ix, fig. 9)

For years naturalists had a vague knowledge of the existence of at least one species of bear in Tibet, but it is only in comparatively recent times that the present one has become fully known. In the year 1853 Mr. Edward Blyth published a brief notice of a bear-skin obtained by Dr. A. Campbell from Tibet, and suggested that if it proved distinct from the Himalayan black bear (of which he thought it might be a variety) it should be known as *Ursus pruinosus*, from its generally hoary colour. In 1892 the British (Natural History) Museum received the skin and skull of a small bear from Tibet, now exhibited in the mammal gallery, the skull of which showed that the animal had nothing to do with the Himalayan black bear, but was somewhat more nearly allied to the brown bear, although differing remarkably in colour. The animal (fig. 55), which was not quite adult at the time of its death, appeared to have been in the winter coat; the hair on the back and flanks being long, but elsewhere shorter. Although all the hair is black at the base, much of it is white in the terminal half, and the whole colouring is unlike that of any other bear. On the face and fore-part of the body white is the prevailing colour, although in places there are some black hairs, which are more

Fig. 55.—The Blue Bear, from the specimen in the British Museum.

strongly developed about the forehead, ears, and the fore-part of the nape of the neck. On the hind portion of the nape is a pure white band, or collar, followed by a nearly black transversely elliptical patch above the shoulder-blades. Over the rest of the body the hair is mingled black and white, so as to present a bluish tinge ; and the hind-legs are similarly coloured, although the lower halves of the fore-limbs are almost completely black. The claws, which are of moderate length, are white.

The structure of the skeleton seems to indicate that this bear is specifically distinct from the brown bear ; but there is some doubt whether it ought to bear the name *Ursus pruinosus*, and if this doubt be confirmed, it should be known as *U. lagomyarius*—a name applied by Colonel Przewalski to a bear from Tibet. Information is required as to the size attained by this bear, the specimen in the British Museum being not quite mature.

Probably the blue bear is found in the forest-districts in the neighbourhood of Lhasa, but on this point, as well as in regard to its habits, there is no information.

A noticeable feature of this bear is the curious approximation it makes to the type of coloration obtaining in the short-tailed panda of the same country. This is especially shown by the presence of the pure white band on the hind part of the nape of the neck, followed by the black patch between the shoulder-blades, and less so by the tendency to blackness on the ears and crown of the head. Possibly this similarity in the colouring of the two may be due to their living under similar conditions.

In 1897 the writer had the opportunity of seeing a bear-skin obtained by Mr. Neil Malcolm in Tibet, which is described in the *Proceedings* of the Zoological Society for that year. This skin differs considerably from that of the blue bear, showing much less white on the back and shoulders, and having black (instead of nearly white) ears. It has a rufous band down the middle of the back, which is not observable in the latter.

It seems not improbable that this and other skins of a similar type which have come under the writer's notice indicate the existence of a representative of the brown bear in Tibet. Indeed, on the supposition that the blue bear is a distinct species, the presence of such an animal is almost essential in order to link up the Himalayan with the Shan brown bear.

THE HIMALAYAN BLACK BEAR

(*Ursus torquatus*)

NATIVE NAMES.—*Rinch* OR *Rich* AND *Bhalu*, HINDUSTANI ; *Mum*, BALUCHI ; *Siyah-haput*, KASHMIRI ; *Sanar* AND *Hing-bong*, NEPALESE ; *Dom*, BHOTIA ; *Sona*, LEPCHA ; *Magyen*, LIMBO ; *Situm*, DAPHLA HILLS ; *Situm*, ABOR ; *Mapol*, GARO HILLS ; *Muphur* AND *Musu-bhurma*, KACHARI ; *Vumpi*, KUKI ; *Sawom*, MANIPURI ; *Hughum*, *Thagua*, *Thega*, *Chup*, *Sevan*, AND *Sapa*, NAGAS ; *Wek-won*, BURMESE.

(PLATE ix, fig. 10)

Although a member of the genus *Ursus*, and possessing the same number of front teeth as the brown bear, the *Siyah-haput*, as the Himalayan black bear is called by Kashmiri shikaris, is a very different animal from the former, distinguished by its black colour and conspicuous white gorget, as well as by the form of the skull and cheek-teeth. It is often called *Ursus tibetanus*, but since it does not occur in Tibet, that name, although earlier, is discarded in favour of the one given above.

With the exception of the gorget, or inverted crescent, on the chest, the ends of which are prolonged upwards in front of the shoulders, and the chin, both of which are white, the fur of this species is usually black throughout ; although in some specimens the upper lip is whitish, and in others the nose, and, it is stated, also the paws, may be rusty brown. Unlike that of the snow-bear, the fur at all seasons is short and comparatively harsh, although sometimes showing a waved appearance. On the withers, indeed, it is somewhat longer, this being most marked in the winter coat, when the appearance of a low hump is given. There is no wholly under-fur at the base of the hairs. The rather large ears are fringed with elongated hairs, and the comparatively short but curved and strong claws are black. As a rule, this species seems to be larger and heavier than the snow-bear, although not attaining the maximum length of the latter, and it is larger than the sloth-bear of the plains. An old male has been recorded to measure 6 feet 5 inches in length from the muzzle to the root of the tail ; but ordinary examples run from about 5 feet 6 inches to as little as 4 feet 8 inches in length, exclusive of the 3-inch tail. From 200 to 250 pounds is given as the usual weight, but this is probably exceeded by old animals in autumn.

Although it is unnecessary to refer in detail to the characters of the skull, it may be mentioned that the median ridge on the hind half of the upper surface is less developed than in skulls of the Himalayan brown bear, and that the profile forms a more regular curve, the abrupt descent in the region of the eyes characteristic of the latter being absent.

The range of the Himalayan black bear extends from the confines of Persia through Baluchistan, the Khirtar range on the western border of Sind, and Afghanistan to the forest-regions of the Himalaya, whence it is continued into Assam, Mergui, and Pegu, and thence to the south of China, Hainan, etc. There are statements as to the occurrence of this bear in the plains of Assam and Lower Bengal, but these (especially in regard to Bengal) require confirmation. Information is also required as to the limits of its range in the forest-regions of the Himalaya, although this probably includes the greater part of the middle and outer ranges. The species is found all over the Kashmir valley, as it is in Kishtwar and Chamba, but whether it occurs in the upper part of the Maru-Wardwan and Tilel valleys is difficult to ascertain. I have never seen it in Tilel, and it never extends into the treeless districts north of Kashmir; but the mum, or mumh, of Baluchistan, which Dr. Blanford identified with the present species, apparently inhabits open and more or less desert districts, where its mode of life must differ considerably from that of the Kashmir black bear. From 9000 to 10,000, or even 12,000 feet, is given as the elevation to which these bears ascend in the summer in the Himalaya, while they are stated to descend in winter to 5000 feet or even less. They are common in summer in many parts of the Kashmir valley, the greater portion of which is not much over 5000 feet above sea-level.

Kashmiri shikaris are more afraid of the black bear than they are of its brown relative; and although this may be partially due to the fiercer disposition of the former, it also seems attributable to the different kinds of country in which the two animals are stalked. A brown bear when hard hit while grazing on a grassy hill-side can scarcely fail to roll headlong down the slope. On the other hand, a black bear when wounded on the comparatively flat ground of a forest has no such involuntary means of avoiding an encounter with its aggressor. Apart from this, there is no doubt that a far larger number of Kashmiris are mauled by black than by brown bears; although this is due to the fact that it is the former species which chiefly ascends fruit-trees in the Kashmir valley. Thirty years ago it was quite common to see three, four, or even more, black bears up a single mulberry or walnut tree; and the Kashmiri coolie thought nothing of ascending the same tree, armed with nothing better than a stout *lathi* (cudgel), in order to drive off the robbers. Consequently, either by falling to the ground in the endeavour to escape, or from a direct encounter with an enraged bear, these people frequently received frightful injuries, from which, however, in most instances they completely recovered.

Black bear stalking in the forests bordering the valley of Kashmir requires more care than is expended in approaching the brown bear on the open hills above, the senses of sight and hearing being more developed in the black than in the brown species. Many of these forests are very dense, so that it requires the eye of a practised shikari to see the dark forms of the bears while searching for chestnuts on the ground without the party being detected by the vigilant animals. Another method of shooting is by beating the small patches of forest found in many Kashmir *nalas*, when the bears march out deliberately in single file, with their curiously sedate steps and solemn expression of countenance, offering in most cases easy shots to the sportsman, who may, however, be deterred from taking aim by a tendency to laughter. To behold a family party of five black bears walking solemnly out of covert, one after another, is indeed a comic sight; and still more ludicrous is it to see one of these animals descending—stern-forwards—a fruit-tree in which it has been disturbed, and looking downwards every now and then over one shoulder to see who is below. Shooting them in the fruit-trees is perhaps taking a rather unfair advantage of the bears, but is still often practised. Black bear shooting, although rather more exciting than stalking the brown species, is, however, by no means a very high class of sport, especially as the skins are never of any particular value, and in autumn, owing to the masses of yellow fat that are accumulated beneath them, are absolutely useless. In regard to the proper place to hit these animals, General Macintyre observes that "a bear, after being skinned and decapitated, looks very like a corpulent man with short muscular limbs, and its vitals lie in much the same region, with regard to its shoulders, as those of a human being. It is flat-chested, and its fore-quarters are straight and placed far forward, so it is necessary to plant your bullet a good span behind the shoulder, and pretty high up. This, of course, only applies when there is time for a deliberate aim and a good position for taking it from." Maize, fruits, nuts, and roots form the main rations of the black bear; acorns, walnuts, and chestnuts affording a large portion of its nutriment during autumn and winter; and while this species digs much less in the ground for roots and bulbs than its brown cousin, it is much more prone to climb in search of fruits. Honey is another favourite article of diet, in search of which it will sometimes not hesitate to enter villages; indeed, it not unfrequently displays a tendency to resort to the neighbourhood of human habitations. It has been mentioned that the brown bear occasionally makes a meal off a dead carcase, and the present species now and then displays a similar penchant for carrion. Nor is it by any means contented with dead animals, for it will not unfrequently attack and kill various domesticated species, including cattle and ponies; and it is stated to be the most carnivorously disposed of any Indian bear.

Since it inhabits, as a rule, a lower and warmer zone than its brown cousin, it would be natural to suppose that the black bear is a less thorough hibernator; and such seems to be the case, these bears undergoing only a partial sleep, safely ensconced in caves or hollow trees, and waking up in warmer intervals during the winter to refresh themselves by a walk and a feed. In the following account of bear-hunting in Burma, taken from the *Asian* of November 27, 1896, the writer regarded the animals of which he was in pursuit as sloth-bears, but as these do not occur in that country there is little doubt they belonged to the present species. Describing his first sight of the party, the narrator says: "It was indeed a fine sight. A family of bears were taking their constitutional; a huge fellow had gone on to a log which had fallen across the stream and was half-way across; two others were having a pleasant scramble for the right of precedence, but without the heart-burnings of a state function. It was too good a chance to lose, so, forgetting for the moment our main aim, I raised my rifle, and, taking a steady shot, rolled the old bear off the log, the ball going into the shoulders and coming out at the mouth. The remaining two bolted back whence they had come before the smoke rolled away. By this time the rear men had found out that a whole family of the dreaded 'mee-ay-woon' (ground-bear) had been run into, and there was a general dropping of pots and pans and a swarming up trees. One man only so lost his head that he tried to 'squirm,' up a smooth tree about fifteen feet in girth and was unable to get up; he then made similar attempts at other trees, and was yet running round and round, though imbecile with faintness, when we came back for them. In the meanwhile I loaded and went forward with the old man to see our prize; he stopped about ten yards off, and I went beyond the fallen tree and looked down; there was the bear, and he was not yet dead but trying to rise. I was weighing the propriety of finishing him, but the old man held up his hand and pointed away to the bison-valley. At this moment I heard horrible howls and growls behind me, and, turning round, saw the two bears which had bolted coming along at a gallop, now and then making grotesque jumps into the air. These animals had never heard a rifle-shot before, and had seen no living enemy. They were probably not charging me but returning to their friend. I was standing almost in their line, however, and a little covered by some young growth of bamboo. The wounded animal answered their calls and tried to climb out the ravine, but as I anxiously watched him, in a quandary as to my next move in this fix, which seemed turning into a tragedy, I saw him fall back again, and thus turned my whole attention to the real dangers. By this time the pair were about six paces from me; picking out the foremost and most savage one, I aimed for his breast and pulled triggers; he turned a somersault, and I reloaded in a flash, but before the smoke again lifted the pair had reached the 'kine' grass bordering the glade. One more glance at the huge fellow in the ravine and then I went forward to finish number two, heard moaning in the kine about thirty paces off. I followed their trail, along which the grass was bent down, till I was about six paces off, but could only see the grass waving. Another step and I saw both. The wounded one lay on his back whilst the other sat at his head and howled in sympathy, pawing him the while as if asking him to move on. I was full in view, but they failed to notice me. There were already two wounded, and I did not wish to have another on my hands." Eventually two members of the party were bagged.

Like other members of the genus, this bear is a good swimmer, crossing without hesitation rivers of considerable size. The cubs are born in spring, generally in a hollow tree-stem or among dense scrub-jungle. As the period of gestation in other bears is about six months, it is probably of the same approximate duration in this species. This would make the pairing season in the autumn; and since it is said that old males and females are only found together at the season in question, the fact that I have seen a family party of five in September or October, and that Mr. Darrah (*Sport in the Highlands of Kashmir*) records seeing four in company in November, serve to support this view.

Two cubs are generally produced at a time, which

remain with their mother till able to take care of themselves. When five individuals are found together, the party usually consists of the old male and female, one cub of the second year, and two of the first year. I have never heard of a party of six being seen in company.

In Japan the Himalayan black bear is represented by a closely allied species or race; and in the New World this group appears to be represented by the North American black bear (*Ursus americanus*).

THE BRUAN, OR MALAY BEAR

(*Ursus malayanus*)

NATIVE NAMES.—*Wek-won*, BURMESE; *Bruan* OR *Bruang*, MALAY

(PLATE ix, fig. 11)

At first sight there might seem to be some connection between the Malay *bruan* and the term *bruin*, so often applied to bears in Europe; but since Malay has no relationship with the Aryan languages, the resemblance between the two words must apparently be due to coincidence.

Although black, the Malay bear is very different from the preceding species; being not only of smaller dimensions, but also a lighter-built and longer-legged animal, with a shorter and broader head, a longer tongue, and a closer fur. Its gait, too, is different, being quicker and less deliberate than that of most other bears; and the animal, judging from menagerie specimens, appears to be of a more restless disposition, pacing up and down for hours at a time, when it jerks its head from side to side with a peculiar motion, and now and then uttering a kind of plaintive grunt.

In addition to its broad head, short muzzle, and

long tongue, the Malay bear is characterised by its small and rounded ears, on which the hair is uniformly short, instead of shaggy, as in the Himalayan black bear. The general colour of the short and close fur is black, but in places it passes into brownish, and the muzzle, to beyond the eyes, together with the chin, has frequently a whitish tinge. A crescentic light-coloured gorget is conspicuous on the chest, its two "horns" being broad, and sometimes uniting so as to form an oval or heart-shaped patch with a black centre; in other instances the lower part of the patch is prolonged into a white streak running between the fore-legs. In colour the light gorget or patch varies from white, through yellow, to deep orange. It was at one time supposed that all Bornean representatives of this bear have the patch orange, while in Malay examples it is lighter-coloured, and two species were accordingly made; but it does not appear that there is any constant difference in this respect. Unlike those of the Himalayan black species, the claws are generally pale horn-colour.

Usually the Malay bear does not measure more than 4 feet from the muzzle to the root of the tail, the tail itself being about 2 inches; but it has been suggested that in unusually large examples the length of the head and body may reach 4½ feet.

Compared with those of the two preceding species, the skull of this bear is distinguishable at a glance by the shortness of the nasal region, and the great breadth across the temples, the cheek-bones forming greatly expanded arches. The molars are also relatively shorter and broader than in other Indian bears.

The range of this bear extends from the islands of Java, Sumatra, and Borneo, into the Malay Peninsula, and so on through Burma and Pegu to the Tenasserim province, Arakan, Chittagong, and the Garo Hills. In a notice contributed to the *Proceedings of the Asiatic Society of Bengal for* 1899, Mr. G. C. Dudgeon gave reasons for believing that the species is found as far west as the Darjiling district; and it reappears in the form of a local race in Eastern Tibet. There is at present no sufficient evidence that the insular representatives of this bear can be distinguished either from one another or from the mainland form, so that local races cannot yet be established, although fuller materials may render this possible. The nearest relative of the species seems to be the spectacled bear (*Ursus ornatus*) of the Chilian Andes.

In 1905 the publisher of this volume received the skull of a bear reputed to come from either Eastern Tibet or the north-western provinces of China. It was clearly that of a bruan, but since I had some doubt whether it was really from the Tibetan area, I gave it no further consideration. I subsequently learnt that the skin of the same animal came with the skull; and that the entire specimen was mounted and sold to the Bergen Museum as *Ursus torquatus*. The skin, I am informed, has much longer black hair than the ordinary Malay bear, with long fringes to the ears, and the usual whitish gorget on the throat.

In 1907 the same firm received another bear-skull of similar type from the Tibetan area, which came with a skin of *Felis scripta*. As to its being Tibetan (in a wide sense) there seems no question. It belonged to a fully adult bear of the *Ursus malayanus* type, as is evident from its width and relative shortness. Its extreme basal length is 8.75, and its maximum width 8.5 inches; these dimensions comparing with 8.5 and 8.3 inches in an old and large skull of the typical *U. malayanus* measured by Dr. W. T. Blanford. So far as I can see, there are no characters by which this skull (in a limited series of specimens) can be distinguished from that of the typical *U. malayanus*; nevertheless, in a paper published in the Zoological Society's *Proceedings* for 1907 I assigned the Tibetan bruan to a distinct race, with the name of *Ursus malayanus wardi*.

The skin of the Bergen specimen is stated to be more like that of a Himalayan black bear than a Malay bruan.

THE ASWAL, OR SLOTH-BEAR

(*Melursus ursinus*)

NATIVE NAMES.—*Rinch* OR *Rich*, *Bhalu*, AND *Adamzad*, HINDUSTANI; *Bhaluk*, BENGALI; *Riksha*, SANSCRIT; *Aswal* OR *Aswail*, MAHRATHI; *Yerid*, *Yedjal*, AND *Asol* OF THE GONDS; *Bir-menai*, ORAN; *Bana* OF THE HO-KOL; *Elugu*, TELEGU; *Kaddi* OR *Karadi*, TAMIL AND CANARESE; *Panikaradi*, MALABARI; *Usa*, CINGALESE.

(PLATE ix, fig. 12)

With its long, shaggy, coarse black hair, mobile snout, long extensile tongue, and large and powerful claws, the aswal or sloth-bear, as it is commonly called by sportsmen, must be regarded as very distinct from more typical representatives of the family *Ursidæ*. Still more important points of distinction are revealed by its anatomy, which are regarded as sufficient to justify the separation of the animal from the genus *Ursus*, and its reference to a group (*Melursus*) by itself. One of these points of difference is a reduction in the number of the upper front, or incisor, teeth from three to two pairs; while another is the small proportional size of the cheek-teeth; and a third the excessive width, length, and concavity of the bony palate of the skull, and the great convexity of the profile of the latter. With the exception of the extremity of the snout (which is dirty grey), of a narrow white horseshoe-shaped gorget on the chest, and of the white claws, the sloth-bear is entirely black; the long and shaggy hair, which is more elongated over the shoulders than elsewhere, gives such a generally untidy appearance that not even its best friend could say that it was a comely or graceful creature.

This bear is somewhat smaller than the black Himalayan species, the length from the muzzle to the root of the tail varying from about 4½ feet to 5¾ feet. The tail is, however, longer than in other bears, measuring from 4 to 5 inches in length, exclusive of the long hair with which it is clothed. About 280 pounds appears to be the average weight of old males in good condition; but one enormous specimen, which was probably unusually fat, is stated to have scaled 320 pounds.

The sloth-bear is one of the comparatively few large mammals restricted to peninsular India and Ceylon,[1] its range in the former country extending from near the foot of the Himalaya to Cape Comorin, and as far west as Kutch and Kathiawar, although farther north its range is limited by the Indian desert. It is known to occur in Eastern and Northern Bengal, but whether it penetrates into Assam has yet to be demonstrated. Its fossilised remains have been discovered in a cave in the Karnul district of Madras, and the skull of a nearly allied extinct species has been obtained from the Siwalik Hills; no other representative of the genus *Melursus* being at present known.

Although in general somewhat timid and retiring, the sloth-bear occasionally makes ferocious and unprovoked attacks on man, when it inflicts terrible wounds with its long talons, usually on the head and face. Such wounds are, however, more frequently recovered from than those received from the tiger. When such unprovoked attacks are made they generally arise from the bear being suddenly surprised, and not knowing how to escape; and as these animals are

[1] In the absence of corroborative evidence, the capture of a young bear in Pegu, stated to have only four upper incisors, can scarcely be regarded as sufficient to prove the occurrence of this species to the east of the Bay of Bengal.

dull of sight and less quick-witted than either tigers or leopards, they find more difficulty in deciding on their line of flight, so that such encounters are more frequent than in the case of the two animals last mentioned. A female bear with her young ones is more prone to attack than is a solitary individual; and, of course, one brought to bay is at all times dangerous. Still there appear to be instances where these bears have attacked without any assignable reason. It is often stated that when at close quarters they rise on their hind-legs for the final rush; but this is denied by Mr. G. P. Sanderson (from whose account many of the following observations are taken), and it is quite certain that the sloth-bear does not "hug" its victim after the fashion popularly, but erroneously, attributed to other members of the bear tribe.

As an illustration of the power of these animals, it may be mentioned that during the winter of 1897-98 an encounter took place between a polar bear and an Indian sloth-bear at Sanger's Circus, in which the latter came off an easy victor. It seems at first sight remarkable that such a powerful animal as a polar bear should have been so easily vanquished, but it was doubtless the cruelly long claws of the Indian species that did the business, while the length and shagginess of its coat would protect it from the teeth and shorter talons of its northern antagonist.

It is commonly asserted by sportsmen that when one of two sloth-bears in company is struck by a bullet, it immediately institutes a savage assault on its companion. Mr. Sanderson, has, however, thrown doubt on the truth of this statement, although I can vouch for its correctness in the case of the Himalayan brown bear.

A novice in tracking may easily mistake the footprints of a sloth-bear for those of a man, but close inspection will show that there are four where there should be only two, while further examination will reveal the fact that bear-*spoor* is shorter and wider than that left by the human foot.

Jungly hill districts, where there are numerous small isolated outliers at the foot of main ranges, are the favourite haunts of the sloth-bear, the most favoured situations being those where numerous large boulders cover the surface of the ground, or where rocks are fissured by ravines and crevasses, or hollowed into caverns. In such cool retreats, protected from the fierce rays of the sun, and safe from the attacks of insect plagues, the bears pass the hottest hours of the day, issuing forth at evening to feed. When the ground is of such a nature as not to show their footprints, the presence of these animals may frequently be revealed by the curious humming sound proceeding from the depth of the rocks, produced, it is said, by the bears sucking their paws. Although the greater part of the day is usually passed idly in such subterranean retreats, in cloudy weather, and more especially at the commencement of the rainy season, when the hardness of the ground during the preceding hot weather has prevented them from obtaining a sufficient supply of insects by digging, they may be seen abroad at all hours in districts where they are little disturbed, busily engaged in searching for food. It should not, however, be imagined that rock-fissures and caverns are the only places where sloth-bears are to be found, for, in the absence of these, they are content to lie hidden in scrub-jungle, at the root of a clump of a tall bamboo, or even in the open beneath some shady tree.

Except when the female is suckling her cubs, both sexes may be seen in company, but when three bears are observed together, these generally comprise a female and a couple of cubs ; and if it be a fact that triplets are occasionally produced, a party of four might sometimes come under the same description. The females display great affection for their offspring, carrying them on their backs during their nocturnal prowls, until of such a size that there is only room for one, when the other has perforce to walk behind alone. After a time its fellow is discarded from the maternal back, and has likewise to trust to its own limbs for the means of locomotion, when the first cub remounts. During the time that both cubs are permitted to ride, they are carried by the mother to the feeding-grounds, on arrival at which they dismount, scrambling up again to the same seat on the approach of danger. At the time that the two sexes are in company, an equal degree of affection is displayed by the male towards his partner, and when one is wounded, a chorus of piercing shrieks is immediately raised by its companion. When commenting on the alleged statement that one wounded sloth-bear will attack its fellow, Mr. Sanderson observes that "a wounded bear's companions generally rush to him to ascertain the cause of his grief, joining the while in his cries, when he, not being in the best of humours, lays hold of them, and a fight ensues, brought about by the affectionate, but ill-timed solicitude of his friends."

The small size of the cheek-teeth of the sloth-bear indicates that its diet consists neither of flesh nor of vegetable substances that require much trituration. And although by no means averse to an occasional meal of carrion, these animals subsist to a great extent on ants and termites, or white ants, together with the grubs of beetles and other insects. For digging out such creatures from their subterranean haunts, as well as for opening the nests of wild bees, for the sake of the honey they love so well, their long curved claws are admirably adapted. Regardless of the stings of either ants or bees, these bears plunge their muzzles straight into the nests, licking up the smaller insects or the honey of the larger ones with their long extensile tongues. Although the bees must almost certainly make their presence felt in an unpleasant manner on the naked nose of the bear, the shaggy fur with which its hide is elsewhere protected must doubtless render those weapons of offence innocuous. Fruits of various kinds, as well as the fleshy flowers of trees like the mohwa, which at times fall in showers on the ground, form no inconsiderable portion of the food of sloth-bears. And being, like most of their kind, expert climbers, these animals ascend trees not only in search of fruits and honey, but also to levy toll on the contents of the pots hung by the natives on the trunks of the date-palm to receive the sweet juice from which a fermented liquor is manufactured. According to native reports, the bears, being clumsy creatures, not only drink the liquor, but smash a considerable number of the pots, and at times become helplessly intoxicated from the effects of the fermented palm-sap.

The presence of sloth-bears in a district where there are fruit-trees or date-palms is indicated by the marks of their claws as they ascend and descend the stems; their claw-marks being likewise visible where they have been digging for white ants. Many of the latter, as well as wood-boring grubs, are drawn out from their retreats by the sloth-bear's power of suction; the animal in this operation first giving a great expiratory puff from its nose, which is placed close to the nest or hole, in order to clear away the dust, and then taking an equally deep inspiration. The sound of these respiratory movements is audible at great distances.

The visual powers of these creatures are by no means strong, and since their hearing is but little better, it is not difficult to approach them within a short distance, when their strange antics and uncouth gambols may be watched. When feeding on a hill-side and suddenly disturbed by an intruder, they are said to show no hesitation in rolling headlong into the valley below.

Although exterminated or much reduced in numbers in many districts where they once abounded, sloth-bears are still common over a large portion of India. Three methods of hunting are in vogue. One plan is to discover the cave, or other lair of the bear, and to take up a position above or near its entrance during the night while the occupant is abroad, and await his return soon after dawn. This, however, is weary work, and many sportsmen prefer the plan of driving the bear from covert with a line of beaters ; although this is practicable only when the animal is in scrub-jungle or among sugar-cane or other cultivated crops. The third and most sportsmanlike method is by tracking, when the bear is followed up to its feeding-place (which it frequently does not leave till the morning is well advanced), or in some cases to its lair, when this is in the open. In the Mysore jungles tracking is most easy during the months of September and October, when a plain trail is left through the dewy grass, which at this season is about a couple of feet high, and therefore easy to traverse. In regard to this method, Mr. Sanderson observes that "bear-shooting conducted on proper principles, with two or three bears afoot together, lacks neither excitement nor amusement. It is not very dangerous sport, as the animal can be so easily seen, whilst he is not so active as a tiger or panther. Still he is very tough, and to any one who would value him for his demonstrations he would appear sufficiently formidable. If a bear charges, he can generally be killed without more ado by a shot in the head when within two paces."

The same sportsman also practised bear-tracking with the aid of dogs. According to his experience, a sloth-bear, despite its great muscular power and bodily activity, may be easily held by three bull-terriers, one being trained to seize by the tender muzzle, which affords a good grip and renders the animal almost helpless. It might have been thought that the bear's claws would inflict grievous harm on its canine assailants, but harmful as they are to the skin of man, to the tough and yielding hide of a dog they do little damage.

Sir Samuel Baker, who regarded it as one of the most vicious animals with which he was acquainted, records two occasions where a sloth-bear has attacked an elephant, one of these instances being altogether unprovoked.

MARMOTS

(*Arctomys caudatus, etc.*)

NATIVE NAME.—*Drun*, KASHMIRI

The traveller who for the first time crosses the range forming the north-eastern barrier of Kashmir—whether his route takes him into Maru-Wardwan *via* the Margan Pass, to Dras by the Zogi-la, or to Tilel and so on to Astor by the Bandipur and Tragbal road —will be startled as he nears the summit by loud whistling screams proceeding simultaneously from several points around. On looking about to discover the source of these cries, he will observe a number of little red and black animals standing up on their hind-quarters, and looking inquisitively round to ascertain the business of the intruder on their domain. On approaching one of these marmots the traveller will find that when within a certain distance, the little creatures will disappear suddenly, with a parting scream, into the recesses of its burrow, on the entrance-mound of which it had been sitting, to venture forth once again when the danger appears to be over.

Marmots are burrowing members of the squirrel family, recognisable by their comparatively large size, small ears, and moderately long bushy tails. The red marmot (*Arctomys caudatus*), the species now under discussion, may be compared in size to a cat, and is one of the largest and most brilliantly coloured of the Himalayan and Tibetan members of the group. It is characterised, among other features, by the length of its tail, which approximately equals half that of the head and body. The general colour of the moderately long and somewhat harsh fur varies from yellowish tawny to bright orange red, with more or less of black on the back, and the tip of the tail of the same sable hue. A blackish patch also surrounds the eye, the rest of the face being brown, while the under-parts and legs are reddish brown. A good-sized specimen will measure about 3 feet, or just over, in total length; 12 or 13 inches being taken up by the tail.

Marmots are unknown on the ranges south of the Kashmir valley, and belong to the Tibetan rather than to the proper Himalayan fauna. The red marmot is found on all the ranges to the north and north-east of the valley of Kashmir, at heights varying from about 8000 to 14,000 feet, and extends northwards through Astor to the bleak and inhospitable plateau known as Deosai, or Devil's Plains.

In Rupshu and Ladak, and thence northwards to the Kuen-Lun and eastwards to Lhasa, at elevations of from 13,000 to 18,000 feet or more, the place of this species is taken by the Tibetan marmot (*A. himalayanus*), distinguished by its relatively shorter tail and greyer colour. On the other hand, in Sikhim, Nepal, Bhutan, and the neighbouring districts of the Eastern Himalaya there is the smaller Hodgson's marmot (*A. hodgsoni*), in which the proportionate length of the tail is still less than in the last, not being quite one-third that of the head and body. Even these do not exhaust the list of species found in the area treated of in this volume, since there is one species (*A. dichrous*) in Northern Afghanistan, and another (*A. robustus*) in Eastern and North-Eastern Tibet.

It may be a question whether marmots should be included among "game animals." Their skins, although handsomely coloured, are too coarse and wiry to be satisfactory from the furrier's point of view; and although they are collected by some sportsmen, they are not regarded with favour by the majority.

Marmots feed chiefly on roots, and live in colonies, excavating their own burrows. In shooting them, it is essential that they should be killed outright at the first shot, as otherwise they drag themselves down their burrows out of reach of the sportsman's arm before he can get up to the burrow, to the entrance of which they resort when danger threatens. After being once fired at and missed they will generally reappear after a short interval ; but, in my own experience, after having been twice shot at, they consider discretion the better part of valour, and remain under ground. In the absence of a rook-rifle, I used to kill marmots by shooting them in the head with a charge from a shot-gun, but there is little doubt that the former weapon would be better for such sport.

HARES

(Genus *Lepus*)

NATIVE NAMES.—*Khargosh*, HINDUSTANI, PUSHTU, AND PERSIAN ; *Khara*, *Susra* OR *Sassa*, HINDUSTANI, BENGALI, AND MAHRATHI ; *Lambha* OR *Lambhana*, HINDUSTANI ; *Malol*, GOND ; *Kulkai*, KOLS AND SANTALS ; *Koarli*, KORKU ; *Manye*, HILL-TRIBES OF RAJMEHAL ; *Sassa*, *Saho*, OR *Seher*, SINDI ; *Yun* AND *Phu-goung*, BURMESE ; *Malla*, CANARESE ; *Musal*, TAMIL ; *Kundeli* AND *Chourapilli*, TELEGU ; *Moilu*, MALABARI ; *Hava*, CINGALESE ; *Rigong*, TIBETAN.

As hares clearly come under the designation of "small game," the more important species found in the area treated of in this volume receive brief mention.

In many parts of the world there is a tendency to compare long-eared animals with the despised but useful ass. Thus the Persian name for a hare (khargosh) means the donkey-eared animal, while in the United States other members of the group are designated "jackass rabbits." Similarly, in Argentina the name "mulita" (little mule) is applied to a long-eared armadillo.

Sportsmen accustomed to European hares will be somewhat surprised to see the Indian species, when hunted, not unfrequently take refuge in holes. Except in the case of the bristly rabbit (*Lepus hispidus*) of the Eastern Himalaya and Assam—which receives no further mention here—such holes are not, however, dug by the rodents themselves, but are the burrows of other animals —such as foxes—they may encounter in their flight. In default of holes, hares in the Nilgiris when coursed sometimes seek asylum in the hollow trunks of trees. The black-naped species (*Lepus nigricollis*), which is the hare of Southern India and Ceylon, may be distinguished at a glance by the presence of a large black patch on the back of the neck. It is found in the peninsula to the south of the Godaveri river, and is met with commonly on the Nilgiris, as it is on the plateau of Newera Ellia in Ceylon.

From other Indian members of the genus *Lepus* (apart from the black-naped species), the North Indian hare (*L. ruficaudatus*) is distinguished by its harsh fur and reddish-brown upper surface of the tail, the ears being nearly naked. The general colour of the upper-parts is light reddish brown, mingled with black on the face and back, the chest and legs being more decidedly red, and the chin, the upper portion of the throat, and the under-parts white. A narrow black line margins the tips of the outer surface of the ears. With the exception of Western Rajputana, Sind, and the south-western districts of the Punjab, where its place is taken by the next species, this hare is found throughout the greater part of Northern India, ranging from Hazara in the north-west to Assam in the east. It is known to occur at least as far south in the peninsula as the valley of the Godaveri, and it may extend into parts of the Deccan. Its favourite haunts are among grass and bushes in dry districts, whether cultivated or jungle. When coursed with greyhounds in districts where the ground is favourable it affords fair sport.

All hares have a groove in the upper front teeth, which, in some species, penetrates the interior of the tooth in a branching form, and in the present species the complexity of this branching reaches its highest development.

The Sind hare (*Lepus dayanus*), the common species of North-Western India, is distinguished from the preceding species by its soft, silky fur and the blackish-brown colour of the upper surface of the tail. It is also greyer, the general hue of the fur of the upper-parts being greyish brown with the usual mixture of black.

The range of this well-marked species includes the more or less sandy and arid tracts of Sind, Kutch, the Indian Desert, and probably a portion of the Punjab. It is a rather smaller animal than the last, the length of the head and body being about 17 inches, instead of between 18 and 20 inches.

In common with the Afghan hare, the Burmese hare (*Lepus peguensis*) differs from the two last noticed by having the upper surface of the tail black; its other special characteristics being the generally rufous tinge of the fur and the presence of a large black patch at the tip of the outer surface of the ear. The fur of the upper-parts is a mixture of rufous and black, while the under-parts are white, a sharp line marking the limits of the dark and light areas. This hare, which is absent from the coast region and dense forest tracts, inhabits a considerable portion of Burma, although its precise limits are not ascertained.

The generally greyer tone of the fur seems to be the best and most easily recognisable feature by which the Afghan hare (*Lepus tibetanus*) may be distinguished from the last, which it resembles in the black upper surface of the tail. The general colour of the soft fur of the upper-parts varies from light greyish to light reddish brown mingled with black, the rump of some examples exhibiting an ashy tinge, and the under-parts, with the exception of the light brown chest, being white. Externally the ears are brown at the sides and buff behind, but towards the tips they become gradually black; their entire margins being frequently buff. Nineteen inches is the usual length of the head and body, against 21 inches in the Sind hare.

The range of this hare includes a large portion of the Upper Indus valley, notably in Baltistan, or Little Tibet, and extends towards the west over the greater part of Afghanistan and Baluchistan, the species being met with in the neighbourhood of Quetta and in the Khirtar range of Sind. Although found at considerably higher levels in Baltistan, in Baluchistan (where it was first described under the name of *L. craspedotis* by Dr. Blanford), it descends as low as about 500 feet above the sea. It is stated to have been obtained from the Nubra valley, in Ladak.

The two common Tibetan hares (*Lepus oiostolus* and *hypsibius*) are nearly allied to the blue or mountain hare (*L. timidus*[1]) of Europe, of which they may be local races, and differ from all those noticed above in that the upper surface of the tail is almost or completely white. In accordance with the nature of the climate of the elevated region in which they dwell, the fur is soft, thick, and woolly, and in the species first named, at any rate, the ears are densely furred on their external surface. This species (*L. oiostolus*), often called the woolly hare, although the smaller of the two, has relatively longer ears, which considerably exceed the head in length. The general colour of the upper-parts is yellowish brown mixed with dark brown, the rump being ashy grey, the tail nearly white, the fore-part of the neck and chest pale fawn, and the rest of

[1] This name is often applied to the English hare, of which the proper title is *L. europæus.*

the under-parts white. This hare occurs typically in that part of Tibet lying immediately north of Nepal and Sikhim, whence skins were obtained and named by Brian Hodgson ; but in all probability it also extends farther towards the east, and specimens have been obtained from high valleys to the south of the great snowy range in the Sikhim district.

The Ladak, or upland hare (*L. hypsibius*), is probably nothing more than a local race of the last, from which it is stated to differ by its somewhat superior size and shorter ears. The tail is pure white throughout, and the blue-grey tint of the hind-quarters stands out in striking contrast to the brown of the rest of the back.

This hare is definitely known from the higher valleys of Ladak, such as Chang-chenmo, as well as from the plateau of Rupshu, where it is met with at elevations between 14,000 and 15,000 feet, or even more, above the sea. I have, however, shot hares in plantations a few miles higher up the Indus valley than the town of Leh, at considerably lower elevations, which I am inclined to believe belonged to the present form. A hare from North Tibet and Kansu, identified by Dr. E. Büchner, of St. Petersburg, with *L. oiostolus*, has been regarded by Dr. Blanford as probably representing either a variety of *L. hypsibius* or an undescribed species.

In the small patches of *Eleagnus* jungle growing along the water-courses in the neighbourhood of Chang-chenmo blue hares, as they are commonly called, are extraordinarily abundant, and sufficient to supply the traveller's camp with food for a week or more may often be shot in the course of a few minutes. In my own opinion their flesh is decidedly superior to that of the hares of the plains of India, although this favourable verdict may be partly owing to the keen appetite developed by camp-life in Ladak. Anyway, blue-hare soup is excellent.

INDEX OF SPECIES, ETC.

Index of Species, etc.

Index of Species, etc.

Index of Species, etc.

THE END